# CHICAGO STUDIES IN THE HISTORY OF AMERICAN RELIGION

*Editors*

JERALD C. BRAUER
AND MARTIN E. MARTY

A CARLSON PUBLISHING SERIES

For a complete listing of the titles in this series,
please see the back of this book.

# The Anglican Left

## RADICAL SOCIAL REFORMERS IN THE CHURCH OF ENGLAND AND THE PROTESTANT EPISCOPAL CHURCH, 1846-1954

Bernard Kent Markwell

PREFACE BY MARTIN E. MARTY

CARLSON
*Publishing Inc*

BROOKLYN, NEW YORK, 1991

Please see the end of this volume for a listing of all the titles in the Carlson Publishing Series *Chicago Studies in the History of American Religion*, edited by Jerald C. Brauer and Martin E. Marty, of which this is Volume 13.

**Library of Congress Cataloging-in-Publication Data**

Markwell, Bernard Kent.
  The Anglican left : radical social reformers in the Church of
England and the Protestant Episcopal Church, 1846-1954 / Bernard
Kent Markwell ; preface by Martin E. Marty.
        p.   cm. — (Chicago studies in the history of American
religion ; 13)
  Includes bibliographical references and index.
  ISBN 0-926019-26-0 (alk. paper)
  1. Church and social problems—United States. 2. Church and
social problems—Anglican Communion. 3. Radicalism—United States-
-History. 4. Social reformers—United States—Biography.
I. Title. II. Series.
HN64.M384 1991
261.8—dc20                                91-28031

Typographic design: Julian Waters

Typeface: Bitstream ITC Galliard

Case design: Alison Lew

Index prepared by Jonathan M. Butler.

Printed on acid-free, 250-year-life paper.

Manufactured in the United States of America.

# Contents

In memory of my grandfather
Albert H. Presseau
and of my mother, Virginia Lee Markwell

No work of men's hands but the weary years
 Besiege and take it, comes its evil day:
The written word alone flouts destiny,
 Revives the past and gives the lie to Death.
 ——Hrabanus Maurus

# An Introduction
# to the Series

The *Chicago Studies in the History of American Religion* is a series of books that deal with topics ranging from the time of Jonathan Edwards to the 1970s. Three or four deal with colonial topics and three or four treat the very recent past. About half of them focus on the decades just before and after 1900. One deals with blacks; two concentrate on women. Revivalists, fundamentalists, theologians, life in the suburbs and life in heaven and hell, the Beecher family of old and a monk of new times, Catholics adapting to America and Protestants fighting one another—all these subjects assure that the series has scope. People of every kind of taste and curiosity about American religion will find some books to suit them. Does anything serve to characterize the series as a whole? What does the stamp of "Chicago studies" mean?

Yale historian Sydney Ahlstrom in *A Religious History of the American People*, as influential as any twentieth-century work in its field, pays respect to the "Chicago School" of American religious historians. William Warren Sweet, the pioneer in such studies (beginning in 1927) at Chicago and, in many ways, in America at large represented the culmination of "the Protestant synthesis" in this field. Ahlstrom went on to name two later generations of Chicagoans, including the seminal Sidney E. Mead and major figures like Robert T. Handy and Winthrop Hudson and ending with the two editors of this series. He saw them as often "openly rebellious" in respect to Sweet and his synthesis.

If, as Ahlstrom says, "a disproportionate number" of historians have some connection with the Chicago School, it must be said that the new generation represented in these twenty-one books carries on both the lineage of Sweet and something of the "openly rebellious" character that scholars at Chicago are encouraged to pursue. This means, for one thing, that the "Protestant synthesis" does not characterize their work. These historians question the canon of historical writing produced in the Protestant era even as many of them continue to pursue themes shaped in a Protestant culture. Few of them concentrate on the old "frontier thesis" that marked the early years of the school. The shift for most has been toward the urban and pluralist scene. They call into question, not in devastating rage but in steady patterns of inquiry, the received wisdom about who matters, and why, in American religion.

So it is that this series of books focuses on blacks, women, dispensationalists, suburbanites, members of "marginal" denominations, "ethnics" and immigrants as readily as it does on white men of progressive urban bent in mainstream denominations and of long standing in America. The authors relish religious diversity and enjoy discovering the power of people once considered weak, the centrality to the American plot of those once regarded as peripheral, and the potency of losers who were once disdained by winners. Thus this series enhances an understanding of an America overlooked by the people of Sweet's era two-thirds of a century ago when it all, or most of it, began.

Rebellion for its own sake would not long hold interest; it might tell more about the psychology of rebels and revisers than about their subject matter. Revision, better than rebellion, characterizes the scholars. Re+vision: that's it. There was an original vision that characterized the Chicago School. This was the contention that in secular America and its universities religion mattered, as a theme in the national past and as a presence in the present. Second, it argued that the study of religious history belonged not only in the seminaries and archives of denominations, but also in the rough-and-tumble of the secular university, where no religious meanings were privileged and where each historian had to make a case for the value of his or her story.

Other assumptions from the earliest days pervade the books in this series. They are uncommonly alert to the environment in which expressions of faith occur. That is, they do not take for granted that religion comes protected in self-evidently important and hermetically sealed packages. Churches and denominations are porous, even when they would be sealed off; they cannot be understood apart from the ways the social environs effect them, but their power to effect change in the environment demands equal and truly unapologetic treatment. These writers do not shuffle and mumble and make excuses for their existence or for the choice of apparently arcane subject matter. They try to present their narrative in such ways that they compel attention.

A fourth characteristic that colors these works is a refusal in most cases to be typed in a fashionable slot labeled, variously, "intellectual" or "institutional" history, "cultural" or "social" history, or whatever. While those which concentrate on magisterial thinkers such as Jonathan Edwards are necessarily busy with and devoted to his intellectual achievement, most of the books deal with figures who cannot be understood only as exemplars in a sequence of studies of "the life of the mind." Instead, their biographies and circumstances come very much into play. On the other hand, none of these writers is a reductionist who sees religion as "nothing but" this or that—"nothing but" the working out of believers' Oedipal urges or expressing the economic and class interests of the subjects. Social history becomes in its way intellectual history, even if the intellects are focused on something other than the theologians in the traditions might like to see.

Some years ago *Look* magazine interviewed leaders in various denominations. One was asked if his fellow believers considered that theirs was the only true faith. Yes, he said, but they did not believe that they were the only ones who held it. The editors of this series of studies and the contributors to it do not believe that the "Chicago School," whenever and whatever it was, is the only true approach to American religious history. And, if they did, they would not hold that Chicagoans alone held it. To do so would imply a strange solipsistic or narcissistic impulse that would be the death of collegiality in the historical field. They have welcomed the chance to be in a climate where their inquiries are given such encouragement, where they find a company of fellow scholars in the Divinity School, the History Department, and the Committee on the History of Culture, whence these studies first emerged, and elsewhere in a university that provides a congenial home for massed and massive concentration of a special sort on American religious history.

While the undersigned have been consistently involved, most often together, in all twenty-one books, we want to single out a third person mentioned in so many acknowledgment sections, historian Arthur Mann. He has been a partner in two or three dozen religious history dissertation projects through the years and has been an influential and decisive contributor to the results. We stand in his debt.

Jerald C. Brauer
Martin E. Marty

# Editor's Preface

Although there were reformist movements in British Anglican evangelicalism, until 1846 the Anglican Church there and the Episcopal Church in the United States had the image of being established, upper class, aristocratic, and removed from the struggles of ordinary people.

Then, as Bernard Markwell dates the change in this pathbreaking book, Frederick Denison Maurice and a company of colleagues began to devise and patent a concept called "Christian Socialism." Some said it was too socialist to appeal to most Christians and too Christian to appeal to the rough and tumble socialists. Yet it was not without consequence in the church that was formally established in Britain and was the informal establishment in the United States.

The *Chicago Studies in the History of American Religion* series stresses the environmental context of various movements and events. As Markwell well shows, the American Anglican left is not comprehensible without a thorough understanding of the British context. He provides a narrative and an analysis of what went on east of the Atlantic before concentrating on the American version.

In the American instance, the author portrays three leaders, each of them interesting in his or her own right, but together illuminative of the whole movement. Father James Huntington lined up with the single tax movement of Henry George, but by linking it with Christian motifs found a religious base for transforming society from the raw individualism that he saw as destructive of faith and the lives of the industrial order's victims. The Reverend W. D. P. Bliss was another importer of British Christian Socialism who reworked it for the American context. He supported not single tax but Fabian forms of Christian Socialism.

The third character—and she was a character in more senses than one—was Vida Scudder. We follow her as dramatist, novelist, activist, teacher, who grew discontented with what she considered the too subtle, almost glacially paced Fabian approach to change. She turned toward blending Marxism and Christianity. The three played high-risk games, since they were projecting such drastic change in society that many thought it could come only through violence.

As Markwell observes them, these leaders were radicals, but they wanted to find alternatives to violence in class struggle. They found their motifs in the Christian faith, particularly in their peculiar interpretation of the Anglican witness. They may not have changed the world, but they changed the church, which never could go back in simple repose to support of the status quo.

In Markwell's telling, the Anglican left offered a social vision at a time when many Christians of the Anglican sort were settling into passivity, accepting the ills of the new social disorder or contenting themselves with isolated acts of mercy to help the victims. They combined creative naivete about faith and futures with realistic analyses. The leaders gave support to and were joined by "ritualist" slum priests who, as the phrase goes, "got their hands dirty" by engaging in direct action, thus assuring that the movement was not merely a parlor and vestry exercise. They helped disengage the Anglican Church and the Protestant Episcopal movement from automatic identification with one social outlook, and thus helped enlarge the range of options for their fellow believers.

There is still an Anglican left, perhaps a forlorn one in decades that find reaction dominant in many Christian circles. Yet the contributions of these pioneers was permanent, and their place is more assured thanks to this fine narrative by Bernard Markwell, who treats them with critical caution and loving care.

Martin E. Marty

# Preface/ Acknowledgments, 1990

Since this study was completed in 1977, new works in the area have been written. I mention the following for those interested in pursuing further the persons and movements I have discussed. For the English Church see E. R. Norman, *The Victorian Christian Socialists* and works by John Orens, particularly his unpublished Ph.D. dissertation from Columbia, *The Mass, the Masses and the Music Hall: Stuart Headlam's Radical Anglicanism*. A much shortened version appeared as a Jubilee Paper. As Orens remarks, "the neglect of Stuart Headlam by both churchmen and historians is nothing less than scandalous."

Equally scandalous, I believe, is the continuing obscurity of the American, W. D. P. Bliss. There is no biography of Bliss, but Peter J. Frederick's treatment of him in *Knights of the Golden Rule: The Intellectual as Christian Social Reformer in the 1890's* is sympathetic and perceptive.

Thankfully, Vida Dutton Scudder and her work have attracted the attention of Peter Frederick, Eileen Boris and Theresa Corcoran, S. C. Boris wrote Scudder's article in *The Dictionary of American Biography* and examines her from a unique perspective in *Art and Labor: Ruskin, Morris and the Craftsman Ideal in America*. Sister Theresa's full length study *Vida Dutton Scudder* and my work complement each other. I emphasize Scudder as Anglican reformer, she sees her as an American woman. Quite appropriately she wrote the article on Scudder for *Notable American Women*.

Father Huntington is now remembered by the Church Calendar in America on 25 November. Such remembrance is the closest act to the proclamation of sanctification in the Anglican Communion. It seems fitting that finally one of the Anglican Left is numbered among the "great crown of witnesses" that the church commemorates.

During the years I have been writing and not writing this study I have accumulated a large number of debts some of which it is now my pleasure to acknowledge publicly.

My most long standing obligations are to Ruth Dougherty and the late Francis Dixon Mardorf who introduced me to history and taught me to love books.

Three inspired teachers at Wesleyan University—Carl Schorske, Norman O. Brown and Willard M. Wallace—profoundly affected my intellectual development and led me to choose history as a career.

James Hastings Nichols introduced me to F. D. Maurice, and I discovered Vida Scudder, W. D. P. Bliss and J. O. S, Huntington in Martin E. Marty's seminar on nineteenth-century American Church History at the University of Chicago. He encouraged me to write this study, and guided its development during its first incarnation as a doctoral dissertation. John Coatsworth, an old and valued friend, generously read that entire manuscript. Each of his criticisms was pertinent, and on more than one occasion he save me from Anglican parochialism.

Fr. Kenneth Leech, who in his multiple roles as priest, author, speaker, and social reformer plays a leading role in the Anglican Left in Great Britain today, recently read the dissertation and made valuable suggestions for improvement. His works, particularly, *The Gospel, the Catholic Church and the World: the Social Theology of Michael Ramsey* carry the story of Anglican reformation into the twentieth century and should be noted by everyone interested in this subject.

Harvey Arnold and the staff at the old Divinity School Library at the University of Chicago went out of their way to help me. Mr. Arnold's encyclopedic knowledge of church history is matched only by his willingness to share it with others. His presence is sorely missed.

Arthur Mann, James Bowditch, Brother Ansgar, Mother Patti Ellis, Mildred Capron, Lucy Kent, Mrs. Landes Lewitin, and Mrs. Virginia Huntington kindly shared personal recollections of Vida Scudder with me. Ralph Carlson has been the kindest and most helpful of publishers.

I am grateful to Dale and Marilyn Fitschen and to Muriel Stange, who read, typed, advised and otherwise assisted the birth of this manuscript. *Pas sans vous.*

I am, finally, most deeply indebted to Albert Tannler, the late Richard Brumbaugh and my parents, Virginia Lee and Bernard Marlin Markwell. They have patiently and courteously suffered through endless versions and revisions of the *urtext*, and have made countless valuable suggestions. They know how much I owe them.

My mother was always a buttress of support, and my father is "the intelligent general reader" each author longs to reach. This work is addressed to him. It is for them and Christopher.

Bernard Markwell
Chicago, Illinois
Advent 1990

# The Anglican Left

# Introduction

In the United States during the last quarter of the nineteenth century the Episcopal Church began "leading the Protestant world in social reform."[1] Contemporaries, even those who were both sympathetic and well informed, were astonished to discover that "the Church of wealth, culture, and aristocratic lineage is leading the way."[2] This leadership was particularly astonishing since, as Walter Rauschenbush pointed out, "the Protestant Episcopal Church . . . failed to take any leading part in the older conflicts with alcohol and with slavery."[3]

American Anglicanism previously had not played a leading role in movements for social change. Very early in colonial times, according to William Manross, an official historian of the church, Anglicanism had "acquired something of that quality of 'upper-classishness' which has handicapped its work in his country ever since."[4] Up to the end of the Civil War during the first seventy-five years of its independent existence the Protestant Episcopal Church had done little to dispel its upper class image. Essentially, it remained a conservative institution that catered primarily to the needs and the interests of its own communicants.

Not all Anglicans were wealthy or even well off, but few of them came from the ranks of the urban poor or from that ever-increasing group that Karl Marx identified as the industrial proletariat. As the century progressed the numbers of this group were swollen by European immigrants, most of whom had no connections with Anglicanism. It is not surprising to discover, therefore, that respected Anglican spokesmen expressed opinions that, if not openly hostile to the lower classes, were at least insensitive to their conditions and to their needs.

One such spokesman was the Reverend Dr. Alonzo Potter. His small book *Principles of Political Economy* reflects the main current of opinion among pre-Civil War Anglicans. Written when he was professor of moral and intellectual philosophy and political economy at Union College in Schenectady, New York, it was specifically addressed to the "young mechanics

1

and apprentices" of that town who were suffering from the economic depression of the 1830s.[5] Potter's advice combined the unrestricted individualism of the Manchester School of Political Economy with the moral rigorism of popular Protestant piety. The professor of moral and intellectual philosophy offered positive suggestions: work hard; don't drink; don't waste free time, but read for self-improvement. Soon your own efforts will enable you to lift yourself out of economic misery. The professor of political economy issued a caveat: avoid trade unions. At best they are futile; at worst they are harmful, subverting the natural community of interests between owners and workers. Trade union organizers, he charged, were often foreign, atheistic demagogues, men whose poisoned principles inflamed popular passions.

Like other nineteenth-century economic liberals, Potter warmly championed the sanctity of private property. His regard for this principle was so high that Henry May observed that it "tended to deprecate democratic government itself." Of the disadvantages incident to a popular government, Dr. Potter warned, "perhaps the most serious is that untiring spirit of change which is apt to possess the people, and which involves in uncertainty all investments of capital, and almost every description of industry."[6]

Potter's language and opinions were no more extreme than those of numerous prominent divines in other denominations. His subsequent election to the episcopacy in Pennsylvania in 1845 demonstrates that a majority of the lay and clerical delegates did not mind that his statements made him unsuited for the church's highest office in a state yearly becoming more urban and industrialized. The delegates of the laity gave him a unanimous vote of confidence, and the lengthy chapter that his biographer devoted to this election makes no mention at all of social issues.[7]

Two generations later Bishop Potter's opinions would not have gone unopposed. In fact, his son Henry, who became bishop of neighboring New York, was a social reformer nicknamed "friend of the poor" because of his efforts on their behalf. Conservative fathers often beget liberal or even radical children, but the differences of opinion within the Potter family cannot be explained away on purely personal grounds. Neither man was an extremist in his own time; their differences reflect a change of attitude that took place in the Episcopal Church during the course of the nineteenth century. It was a remarkable transformation, and it is not difficult to understand why contemporaries were astonished.

When Walter Rauschenbush, an extremely well-informed contemporary, tried to explain the leading role of the Episcopal Church in American social reform, he mentioned at once the church's close connection with the "advanced social movement" in the Church of England.[8] Since Rauschenbush, all of the major studies that discuss the Anglican role in the social gospel make this same point, but most authors go on to discuss other causal factors, or they proceed directly to a consideration of the movement itself.[9] No one has offered a detailed examination of the connection between American social gospel Anglicanism and the "advanced social movement" in the Church of England. Even Spencer Miller and Joseph Fletcher, who devoted three chapters of their informative study *The Church and Industry* to the English movement, are content to generalize, "The Work begun in England by the leaders of the Christian Social Movement became the ferment which was presently to be reflected in an awakened interest in industrial problems in the United States."[10]

My study investigates the Anglican social reform movement on both sides of the Atlantic, showing how the examples of the earlier English movement influenced three leading American social gospel radicals: James O. S. Huntington, William Dwight Porter Bliss, and Vida Dutton Scudder. But before I discuss the English influence on the three Americans I must consider the growth of the English movement itself. The history of its development is complicated, and a respect for narrative clarity demands looking at the English movement primarily as a self-contained unit. Therefore, the first part of this work deals with events in England. Particular English influences on each of the Americans are detailed later, when the latter are considered individually.

The discussion of the English movement concentrates primarily on the period between 1846 and the mid-1890s, although I return to the 1830s briefly to pick up the Tractarian background for Anglo-Catholic radicalism. Also, certain aspects of the history of the Guild of St. Matthew and the Christian Social Union carry into the early twentieth century. The English movement did not come to an end in the 1890s, and its full story is not encompassed by the fifty-year period on which this study concentrates. But by the 1890s the American movement had become mature enough to be recognized as an equal to the English, and in subsequent years followed paths increasingly its own.

Moreover, by the 1890s the theological foundations of the mature Anglican social reform movement in both England and America had been completed and firmly laid. Subsequently, many reform organizations dedicated to specific social programs flourished in both national churches; and although the social superstructure changed with the issues and with the secular ideologies of the times, the theological foundations were not substantially altered.

Anglican social gospel theology evolved in England during the decades after 1846; this evolution and the movements it engendered are the primary focus of my study of the English scene. First I examine the incarnational theology of Frederick Denison Maurice and the early Christian Socialist movement of the late 1840s and early 1850s. Then I concentrate on the social implications of the Oxford Movement as they were developed in the 1860s and early 1870s by the revived Anglican religious orders and the ritualist slum priests. Finally I observe how elements of the two preceding movements came together from the late 1870s to the 1890s in the Guild of St. Matthew and the Christian Social Union to inspire the Anglican social gospel era.

This social gospel era flourished on both shores of the Atlantic. Industrialization had begun earlier in England than in the United States. But when urban and industrial problems became serious in the United States in the decades after the Civil War, Anglicans here looked for guidance to the reform movement in the mother church, which had become securely established during the several decades of its existence. Americans emulated their contemporaries in the Christian Social Union and set up a similar body in the United States, but they were also attracted to the work done by religious orders, to ritualist slum priests, and to the early Christian Socialist movement.

If American and English Anglicans shared a common religious heritage, there were also important differences between the two countries and between the roles played by the Anglican Church in each. The Church of England was the state church and was closely connected to the monarchical, aristocratic establishment. The Protestant Episcopal Church had a "quality of upper classishness," and its High Church Party believed that it was the only true church in America; but to most Americans it was only another religious denomination.

The state church in England was organized into a countrywide parish system and felt at least a theoretical responsibility for all the English. Its clergy were officers of the state; its hierarchy sat in Parliament and were great national figures. The Episcopal Church was a small, relatively affluent denomination with no official responsibility and almost no connection with the urban, immigrant proletariat, who frequently spoke little English and whose religious affiliation—if any—was continental Protestant, Roman Catholic, Eastern Orthodox, or Jewish.

Recognizing these important social and political distinctions between the two churches makes it easier to understand the differences between the two reform movements. The English movement had avenues both to the establishment and to the proletariat denied to the American movement. As a result the English movement was more significant in the political life of the nation, while the American Anglican social reformers, who lacked official status, were more important as individuals. The latter formed organizations, of course, but these organizations were frequently transitory and none was ever of serious national importance.

Thus the second part of this study, dealing with the movement in the American church, concentrates on the lives and works of three major individuals. There were of course many important American Anglican reformers, some of whom appear in these pages. But no one in the pioneering post-Civil War generation was more important, no one did more to put Anglicans in the forefront of the reform movement, than did James O. S. Huntington, William Dwight Porter Bliss, and Vida Dutton Scudder.

Moreover, each of them was a radical thinker; they defined the Anglican left. At this point it seems appropriate to say something specific about my title, *The Anglican Left*. What does the term mean? The modern political usage of *Left* developed during the French Revolution, when the followers of Philippe Égalité, formerly Duc d'Orléans, sat together on the left side of the National Assembly Chamber.[11] The word's genesis should indicate that it describes a direction, not a dogma.

Since the French Revolution *left* has been associated generally with radicalism. But *radical* is also a difficult word to define exactly; often in contemporary parlance *radicalism* signifies extremism: one can speak of a radical left and a radical right.

Even though *extreme* is a legitimate synonym for *radical*, this study is not concerned with extremism per se. Rather I focus on two other synonyms, *original* and *thoroughgoing*, qualities exhibited in varying degrees by all the major figures I discuss.

The Anglican radicals were original in the sense that they were among the first either to formulate or to hold advanced opinions, opinions that only later gained general acceptance. They broke new ground; they were innovators, pioneers. I have mentioned the pioneering social movements in the nineteenth-century English church. Here I should emphasize the significance of James Huntington, W. D. P. Bliss, and Vida Scudder as innovative thinkers in American Anglicanism. Their lives and works represent the most advanced

5

social attitudes in the Episcopal Church from the end of the nineteenth century to the end of the Second World War. During the 1880s and early 1890s Father Huntington's campaigns on behalf of Henry George and the single tax made him the leading American Anglican radical. Later in the 1890s that role passed to the Reverend W. D. P. Bliss, progressive reformer and champion of Fabian Christian Socialism. Early in this century Vida Dutton Scudder moved beyond Fabian gradualism to a synthesis of revolutionary Marxism and Christianity, and for the next forty years her work exemplified the concerns that motivated the Anglican left. In studying Huntington, Bliss, and Scudder we see the whole development of Anglican radicalism in America.

The thoroughgoing quality exhibited by Anglican radicals can be explained more readily since it refers less to their role in the historic development of ideas than to a specific opinion about society. Unlike the moderate social gospel liberals who fundamentally accepted capitalist society but wanted to mitigate its inequities and abuses through limited reforms, the radicals rejected the system at the root and looked forward to a new society. They wanted a thoroughgoing re-formation of the social order, even though on the whole they eschewed the extremist means of revolutionary violence.

Ideas can change dramatically over the course of a century—particularly in modern times—so we must not expect dogmatic unity from the Anglican left. Later members of the movement, people like Headlan, Huntington, and Scudder, for example, recognized the important, innovative, and original roles played by Maurice, Ludlow, Pusey, and the like, but they never felt constrained to reiterate the earlier opinions point by point. The ideology and practice of the Anglican left always remained open to experiment and innovation. My story follows the development of ideas as we trace the work of successive generations of pioneers, each one with its own vision of a new society.

The emphasis on transforming society, on changing the system, is the quality that distinguishes the modern movement for social reform in the Anglican communion from its immediate predecessors, particularly from the Evangelicals, who emphasized changing the individual. But the movement for a Christian reformation of society was not only a reaction to the evils of the industrial revolution. Rather it was the modern expression of a continuing religious tradition, and as I shall show, modern reformers derived insight and inspiration from the varied sources of that tradition. The Anglican left looked back to the Evangelicals, to Reformation Anabaptists, Diggers, and Quakers, to medieval Franciscans and Dominicans, to the early fathers, to the primitive church, and not least to the pre-eminent example of Jesus Christ.

Indeed, the Anglican communion's modern movement for social reform belongs to a tradition older than Christianity itself. Its origins go back at least to the eighth century B.C. when the prophet Amos outraged by the social conditions in the ancient Kingdom of Israel proclaimed the word of the Lord: "Let justice flow like a river, and righteousness like an ever flowing stream."[11]

# ONE

# Frederick Denison Maurice and Company: Early Christian Socialism

The story of the Anglican left begins in England during the 1840s when a small "band of brothers"[1] gathered around Frederick Denison Maurice, John Ludlow, and Charles Kingsley. This modest group of amateur social reformers organized the Council of Promoters of Working Class Associations and became England's first Christian Socialists. At the time the Christian Socialists were not the only group of churchmen interested in solving the complex social, political, and economic problems that Benjamin Disraeli called "the condition of England question." And in the eyes of their contemporaries they were certainly not the most famous.

On the right stood the young, Romantic Tory backbenchers who called themselves "Young England." Reacting against the materialistic spirit of the age—and the Whig Party's alliance with manufacturing interests—they spoke out against the exploitation of the working classes and proposed the program subsequently styled "Tory democracy." Largely as a result of the influence of Lord John Manners, a young man with the highest aristocratic connections and avid Tractarian leanings, Young England looked to the church for leadership in the cause of social reform. Young England believed that because the church was a venerable, traditional institution, it could awaken gentlemen throughout the country to a sense of their responsibility for the masses and save society from the brutality and unbridled acquisitiveness of contemporary industry.[2]

At the other end of the ecclesiastical party spectrum stood the great Evangelical reformer, Sir Anthony Ashley Cooper, seventh earl of Shaftesbury. Throughout the course of a long and distinguished career, Shaftesbury waged war upon social injustice and, both in Parliament and out, tirelessly worked to improve the conditions of the lower classes.[3]

Contemporaries might reasonably have considered Young England and the Evangelical earl the primary living exponents of Christian social reform. Both had greater prestige and far more direct parliamentary influence than the Christian Socialist band. But even though the Christian Socialists may have appeared insignificant in their own time, historians recognize in their movement "the first organized expression of the social conscience in the English Church."[4] Neither Young England nor the earl of Shaftesbury can fit that description.

Young England was primarily a parliamentary faction, not an organization of churchmen. Its hybrid mixture of Tractarianism and Toryism contained a genuine concern for the poor, but its members were in no position to implement their program. To do that, they had to achieve political power; gaining power meant that parliamentary politics came first, and the political realities of the time did not favor Tractarian-Toryism. The largest Tory faction was composed of country backbenchers who had broken with the Tory prime minister, Sir Robert Peel, over the issue of agricultural protection. These were deeply conservative men who were as opposed to the new High Church Party, which they derisively called Puseyism and feared for its "crypto-Romanism," as they were to the repeal of the Corn Laws. Disraeli, who was the brains behind, as well as the spokesman for, Young England, realized that Tractarian leanings stood in the way of political leadership and quietly dropped the subject. Only a few years later, during the Crimean War, he openly courted the rabidly anti-Tractarian Protestant Alliance as an ally in bringing down Lord Aberdeen's Coalition Government, which included several prominent Tractarian sympathizers, notably William E. Gladstone. After 1874 when Disraeli finally achieved a secure political tenure, his government passed a series of significant social reform measures, but by that time his Young England days were long past and the High Church enthusiasms of his younger years had been forgotten.

The earl of Shaftesbury was a great individualist—one might even say lone wolf—and his philanthropic reform labors were very much a one-man operation. He did on more than one occasion work with reform societies, but his extreme Evangelicalism often led him to associate with Non-Conformists. His social conscience, as magnificent as it was, cannot be considered part of the organized expression of the Church of England.

The early Christian Socialists deserve to be remembered for what they accomplished in their own time, but their influence on the subsequent history of Anglican social reform is, I think, even more important. As Maurice Reckitt, Peter Jones, and many others have emphasized, all of the significant Anglican social reform movements during the late nineteenth and twentieth centuries have derived much of "their inspiration from the earlier Christian Socialist movement . . . led by the pioneers J. M. Ludlow, F. D. Maurice, and Charles Kingsley."[5] Their influence has been profound and it has been lasting.

*Maurice and Ludlow, the First Meeting*

One day late in 1846 a painfully shy young barrister named John Ludlow called upon the chaplain of Lincoln's Inn, Frederick Denison Maurice. Ludlow had come to enlist the chaplain's aid in a scheme for "bringing to bear the leisure and good feeling of the Inns of Court upon the destitution and vice of the neighborhood."[6]

Maurice, who had been appointed chaplain only six months before, was in no condition to respond to his idealistic and enthusiastic twenty-five year old visitor. The chaplain, to quote his son's description, was "utterly unhinged, prostrated, and without spring to answer any appeal."[7] During the preceding two years, death had claimed both his wife and his best friend. Despite his deep anguish, a "Puritan temperament"[8] drove him to overwork, perhaps as a means of escaping personal grief. In addition to his other duties, he had taken on both the Warburton and the Boyle lectures and subsequently prepared them for publication.

Either of the lectures would have been taxing; the combination left him exhausted. In the Warburton lecture, published under the title *The Epistle to the Hebrews*, he had attacked John Henry Newman's theory of "development"; and although some have seen it as one of his most brilliant controversial works, arguing against an opponent with Newman's massive learning and brilliant mind had demanded the most painstaking intellectual effort. The Boyle lectures, which were called *The Religions of Mankind* when they came out the following year, did not demand the same close attention to argumentative skill, but the subject did require extensive background reading.

Today, it is easy for us to understand why the exhausted theologian would hesitate to embark on a new venture, any new venture, let alone one that involved a radical departure from his previous lines of work. With characteristic generosity, however, Maurice discussed the subject with Ludlow and then introduced him to a neighboring vicar whom Maurice believed would offer the young man some help. Ludlow, who knew nothing about Maurice's mental state, was let down by his initial meeting with the man he later called "Prophet" and revered as master. He told his mother that he had met a "good man but very impractical."[9]

On the surface it had been a pointless meeting. No one, least of all the participants themselves, would have thought that Christian Socialism and the Christian Social Movement in the Anglican communion would grow out of it. Yet there are several reasons for beginning my discussion of the movement with Ludlow's first visit to Maurice's house in Queen's Square.[10] A close look will help to clear up some long-standing confusions about the later movement and its members.

The first thing to note is that Charles Kingsley was absent and John Ludlow was present. This may seem perfectly obvious, but for a long time Ludlow's role as a leader and founder of the movement was obscured by the figure of Kingsley. Later Christian Socialists almost invariably give top billing to Maurice and Kingsley. In 1909 Stewart Headlam published a study called simply *Maurice and Kingsley*. In his *Socialism and Church History* another great Anglican radical and social reformer, Conrad Noel, notorious during the 1920s and 1930s as the "red" vicar of Thaxted hailed the two men with the title "the Catholic fathers of the nineteenth century."[11] These examples reflect the consensus and even today they are echoed by most textbooks and general studies.

To a large extent Ludlow himself was responsible for his obscurity. He was an extremely shy and diffident man who shunned the limelight and performed his most useful work behind the scenes. Kingsley, on the other hand, was a "muscular Christian" who never hesitated to charge into the thick of battle even when the charge led him to center stage. His work as the most able and popular propagandist for the cause naturally resulted in his being identified with it in the mind of the public. Subsequently, he went on to become the popular author of *Westward Ho!* and something of a national figure. His personal fame helped maintain the memory of Christian Socialism long after Ludlow had been forgotten.

It is not my purpose here to elevate Ludlow at Kingsley's expense. Kingsley fully deserves to be included in the triumvirate of Christian Socialist leaders, second in importance only to Maurice and Ludlow. Owen Chadwick's amusing nautical description of the three men is an accurate evaluation of their respective roles within the Christian Socialist Movement. "Ludlow proffered the social ideas, Kingsley the prophetic fire, Maurice the anchorage in Christian doctrine. In this unusual crew Ludlow stood at the helm, Kingsley flew the flags and sounded the horns, Maurice poked around the engine-room to see that the engines were of authentic Christian manufacture."[12] Peter Jones put it more directly; he calls Ludlow "the real founder of the Christian Socialist movement in the fifties."[13]

The second reason for looking closely at Ludlow's first visit to Maurice has already been suggested by Chadwick; but it is so important that I wish to make it explicit. In 1846 we can observe the two Christian Socialist leaders before they had a chance to influence each other, and we see two very different men. Later—when they had become close friends and shared a common devotion to their cause—these personal differences, which still lingered on under the surface, are more difficult to detect. Here they stand out in bold relief.

Ludlow came to Maurice seeking someone who would join him in initiating a program designed to help the poor. The young man was a budding social reformer. For the moment he had no definite general reform program in mind, but the experiences of his youth had given him an awareness of vocation and a vague sense of direction.

Ludlow had been brought up in Paris by a widowed mother who was an old-fashioned radical. The atmosphere at the Ludlow home was urbane, cosmopolitan, and tolerant; judicious reason was valued more than dogmatic certainty. At the age of nine he observed firsthand the revolution that replaced the would-be absolute monarch Charles X with the citizen-king Louis-Philippe. Caught up in an enthusiasm for change he took to remaking the map of the world, bending over his atlas and "carving out and modelling according to what seemed to be their natural boundaries states new and old."[14]

Life in July-monarchy Paris offered him a variety of experiences denied the ordinary Englishman. Of these the most important were educational and religious opportunities. Ludlow was a conscientious, hard-working young man who took full advantage of the rigorous education provided him at the Collège Bourbon. The curriculum, which had been reformed during the Napoleonic era, emphasized geography, history, and modern languages; it was far more advanced and modern than the curricula of the contemporary English public schools. Ludlow excelled at these subjects and won numerous prizes. More important, he developed a deep respect for logic and method that never left him. His mind always remained more French than English, and he never quite

13

adjusted to the amateurish, slapdash approach to problems he found across the Channel.

The Protestant religiosity he found in Paris was at once more modern and more old-fashioned than its English counterpart. The churches he attended in Paris had experienced no Evangelical awakening; they combined a spirit of moralistic rationalism, reminiscent of the nineteenth-century English latitudinarianism, with a modern concern for scientific, political, and social issues. Ludlow was too psychologically sensitive to be satisfied with moralistic rationalism, but he readily appropriated the concern for social and political issues.

When John finished school, the Ludlows moved to England, where he studied law with the distinguished Whig lawyer, Bellenden Ker. As always, he was an excellent student, but he was unhappy in the country of his fathers. For some years he could not make up his mind to stay there, and he traveled to Paris as often as time and finances would permit.

Not long after coming to England the news of an earthquake in Martinique gave him a violent shock. He imagined that his beloved older sister and her family had all been killed. In fact they were safe; but he was so moved by the experience that he underwent a religious conversion and became an Evangelical. But if Evangelicalism satisfied his personal religious needs more fully than had the intellectualized faith of his youth, its nearly exclusive concern with personal salvation offered him no answer to the social problems of the time. These, he increasingly came to feel, could be solved only by socialism.

During a visit to Paris in 1846 he met a Lutheran pastor, Ludwig Meyer, who combined a rich personal Evangelical faith with philanthropic social concerns. Meyer and a pastor of the Calvinist Reformed Church directed the Société des Amis des Pauvres, a "visiting society" of young men who devoted themselves to the relief of poverty and distress. Meyer suggested to Ludlow that he undertake the same kind of work in London. When he returned to England later that year, Ludlow presented this program to Maurice. Maurice, as we know, courteously listened to the plan and then sent the youth elsewhere.

But Maurice was a resilient man whose "puritan temperament" would not permit long periods of inactivity even for the justifiable purpose of recuperation. The letters published by his son reveal that by the spring of 1847 his "prostration" had passed and he had once again become actively involved in numerous outside causes in addition to his duties as chaplain at

Lincoln's Inn and professor of history and theology at King's College. These causes were almost invariably related to religious controversy, but they had wide political and educational implications.[15] Nowhere, however, is there evidence of a concern with the plight of the poor, much less an interest in social reform. Ludlow's visit seems to have made very little impression on Maurice. Ludlow's plans could find no room in a mind already crowded with a host of religious concerns.

One of the great ironies in the historical record of these men, second only to Ludlow's obscurity, is that, until recently, "in so far as he [Maurice] was remembered at all, he seemed to be remembered only for his part in the Christian Socialist Movement. . . . No one else of my acquaintance then," writes Alex Vidler of the period before World War II, "had any interest in Maurice as a theologian."[16] The rediscovery of Maurice as a theologian, begun by the last Archbishop of Canterbury in his book *The Gospel and the Catholic Church*, did not gain momentum until the late 1940s and the early 1950s.[17] The almost exclusive identification of Maurice with Christian Socialism is ironic; although this aspect of his life is significant in its way, it covers only a small segment of his interests and does not serve to identify him properly.

Maurice always considered theology his vocation; as he wrote to Ludlow at the height of the movement, "I am a theologian and have no vocation except theology."[18] "It will be evident to the reader of any part of these volumes that I have felt as a theologian, thought as a theologian, written as a theologian; that all other subjects in my mind are connected with theology, and subordinate to it."[19]

Yet Maurice, like Ludlow, was himself partially responsible for the confusions and misinterpretations that became attached to his memory after his death. If he was, as Maurice Reckitt calls him, "the greatest English theologian of the nineteenth century," he was also one of the most difficult to read and understand. There are two reasons for this difficulty.

The first is Maurice's writing style. It can be inspired and eloquent, but it is also "often extraordinarily tangled and obscure . . . his work repeats itself . . . and sprawls over chapters and pages."[20] It bears all the marks of the unsystematic and unusual method of composition described by his son:

> It was a very great relief to him to compose his books by dictation and avoid the labor of mechanical writing. His usual manner of dictation was to sit with a pillow on his knees hugged tightly in his arms or to walk up and down the room still clutching the pillow, or suddenly sitting down or standing before the

fire with the pillow still on his knees or under his left arm to seize a poker and violently attack the fire.[21]

The second difficulty was caused by his aversion to systems of thought and even to a systematic approach. Ludlow described his attitude as a "system phobia." "When once a man begins to build a system," Maurice wrote in his *Ecclesiastical History*, "the very gifts and qualities which might serve in the investigation of truth, become the greatest hindrances to it. He must make the different parts of the scheme fit into each other; his dexterity is shown, not in detecting facts, but in cutting them square."[22] Since Maurice believed that systems obscure rather than illuminate the truth, he produced no systematic statement of his beliefs. Nor did he attempt any all inclusive, if unsystematic basic work; rather he wrote in response to the demands of the occasion and with particular and limited issues and aims in mind.[23] Such a deliberately unsystematic and topical approach has brought upon him the criticisms of being misty, confusing, and fragmentary;[24] for many years people simply refused to read him. If his theology is more popular today, we must thank his commentators and biographers who, if they have not systematized, have at least ordered his thought.

It is doubly ironic that, even today, Maurice is most often remembered as a Christian Socialist because, as Torben Christensen has remarked, Maurice "was not really a radical in politics."[25] He favored an "organic Christian society" in which "Monarchy, Aristocracy, and Socialism . . . were recognized as necessary elements."[26] "A Churchman," Maurice wrote, would "say that he belonged to every party in the state and to none. He is a Loyalist, and so far an ancient Tory; he is a constitutionalist, and so far an ancient Whig; he feels for each man as a distinct living creature, having distinct wants and sorrow . . . and so far he is a radical."[27] The socialism that Maurice advocated was not a revolutionary political ideology, but rather "the acknowledgment of brotherhood of heart in fellowship and work."[28] Of course Maurice was no apologist for the status quo; even before he became involved in social problems he deplored its inadequacies in the most categorical terms and urged reform. But Maurice's theological perspective led him to conceive of reform in the literal sense of the word, which means the restoration of an original excellence by the elimination of the abuses that have come to mar it.

To reform signifies literally to form again or form anew. Instead of being equivalent with putting one thing away and putting another thing in its place it implies what is almost opposite to this, the putting into its proper and original shape that which has gotten out of shape . . . you ask a surgeon or physician to come in as a reformer . . . you do not ask him to give you some new functions.[29]

It is obvious that Maurice thought of reform in a profoundly conservative sense; his conception of it is much closer to that of his mentors Plato and Samuel Taylor Coleridge than it is to that of Ludlow, whose French experience had taught him that reform could signify a progress to something new and better.

These differences later led to disagreements about the nature of the movement, but they never undermined the deep and lasting affection that Maurice and Ludlow felt for each other. Both recognized that each brought something important to the other. Ludlow's concern for the poor made Maurice aware of the social implications of his theology. Maurice's teachings gave Ludlow a theological basis for his social concerns. Previously he had found it difficult to reconcile the communitarian aspect of socialism with the individual emphasis of Evangelical piety. Maurice "provided the theological speculative framework within which Ludlow's essentially executive mind could act."[30]

## The Brotherhood and Its Work

Two years after their unsatisfactory first meeting, the momentous events of 1848 brought them together again. This time their meeting was a success. Out of it grew the group of inspired pioneers who became England's first self-proclaimed Christian Socialists.

The year 1848 was the annus mirabilis of revolution. Metternich fled Vienna in a laundry cart, and all over Europe west of Russia the old order tottered. Even England was affected, Chartist agitation had inflamed the lower classes, and bloodshed, if not civil war, seemed imminent.

On February 24 revolution broke out in Paris, and Ludlow hurried across the channel to protect his sisters. When he arrived, much to his surprise, he found them safe and sound. He had feared riots and confusion, but discovered joy and enthusiasm. When a friend showed him around the city, he noticed a great spirit of community. Social, not political, issues dominated the discussions at the countless meetings being held almost constantly throughout the city.

The atmosphere in Paris convinced him that the principles of social revolution would spread and capture the imagination of the world. Enthusiastic as he was at what he had seen, the religious Ludlow believed that a purely secular socialism would ultimately prove to be a curse on mankind. Only if it were linked to the highest Christian principles of self-sacrifice and brotherhood could socialism become a blessing. Alone, both Christianity and socialism would fail; together they might redeem the world.

At this point he took a decisive step. "I returned to England," he tells us, "penetrated, overwhelmed by the gravity of the crisis. To whom should I address myself? I did a strange thing considering the absence of anything like intimacy between myself and Mr. Maurice, I unbosomed myself to him in a letter."[31]

Maurice was profoundly moved by the letter. Like Ludlow, he had been jolted by the revolutions of 1848. At the time he was giving a series of sermons on the Lord's Prayer, and unlike most Englishmen, he responded with approval to the social developments across the channel. He also became irritated by the exclusive, self-righteous, sectarian attitudes that prevented most Christians from recognizing the significance of what was going on. Immediately replying to Ludlow, he urged him to come and discuss the issue with him.[32] Some ten days later he wrote again to advocate "the necessity of an English theological reformation, as the means of averting an English political revolution and of bringing what is good in foreign revolutions to know itself."[33]

During the next weeks Chartist agitation reached its peak. A mass meeting was called for April 10; after the meeting the plans called for a march from Kennington Commons to the House of Commons, where a petition said to contain five million signatures would be presented. The incendiary language used by some Chartist leaders had so terrified the government and ruling classes that the Iron Duke, Wellington, was given command of the troops and special constables were enrolled. But violence never occurred. The mass meeting broke up in a pouring rain and Chartism ended in a fiasco.

The failure of the Chartist rally inspired Ludlow and Maurice, now joined by Maurice's friend Kingsley to take action. They put up posters addressed to the "WORKING MEN OF ENGLAND." The posters, which were written by Kingsley, expressed sympathy for the suffering of the lower classes, but counseled against violence. Also they proclaimed the friendship of the "working clergy" and concluded with the promise of a "nobler day."[34]

The same evening that the posters appeared, Maurice, Ludlow, and Kingsley agreed to publish a "penny journal." It was their first significant undertaking. The journal, which ran from May 6, 1848, to the end of July 1848, carried the name *Politics for the People*; Maurice and Ludlow were the editors. On the first page of the first number Maurice announced their intention to consider controversial contemporary issues like the relation of capitalist and worker, the extension of the franchise, and what government can and cannot do to find work for the poor. The paper was addressed to the workers and it was sympathetic to the problems of the poor. Its basic assumption was the belief that God, not man, rules the world.

*Politics for the People* never attracted many workingmen. Its analyses were too rationalistic, its tone too donnish to generate a mass appeal. Kingsley, under the pseudonym Parson Lot, produced some fiery propaganda and Ludlow wrote some excellent social criticism, but by the end of June 1848, it was clear that the paper had not lived up to its founders' expectations. It had not opened up avenues of communication with the poor. Most of them still considered Christianity to be, at best, irrelevant.

But the failure was not total. The paper had attracted some attention. It was denounced by the Chartist paper *Commonwealth* for being too clerical; the *Oxford Times* was appalled by its "democratic tendencies."[35] When the paper failed, it became obvious that a new approach for reaching the poor must be tried. The "band of brothers" realized that their inadequate knowledge of what passed through the workers' minds had caused their failure. Despite the sympathetic approach, *Politics for the People* talked *at* the working class. Some means must be found for talking *with* the people.

Ludlow took the initiative and contacted Walter Cooper, a strongly anti-Christian Chartist leader. At their meeting Cooper was persuaded to come and hear Maurice preach at Lincoln's Inn. Cooper was impressed by the obvious sincerity of the preacher and suggested that Maurice meet with the working-men. Maurice was at his best in direct personal conversation. His profound humility made him open to learning from anyone. Few of the workingmen had ever met a clergyman like him, and open discussion flowed. The men talked frankly and the band of brothers listened and responded. The meetings were not entirely harmonious; arguments flared and sometimes threatened to get out of hand, but communication had been opened. The great gap between the Victorian lower and middle classes had been bridged. Once the traffic of ideas flowed both ways across this bridge, the band of brothers and the workingmen discovered that they shared a common interest in social reform.

If Maurice's uniquely beautiful personality had brought the two divergent groups together, it was Ludlow's practical and observant mind that pointed out the next step. He returned from a trip to Paris with a proposal for establishing workers' cooperatives. These were a form of industrial organization in which producers owned the business and received the profits.[36] Cooperatives were not new to England; the Rochdale Pioneers had opened cooperative stores in 1844, and there were several cooperative societies in the north of England. But these were consumer cooperatives, owned by consumers who received the profits. The form of producer cooperatives that Ludlow advocated was new to England.

At first the workers favored founding "home colonies," experimental communities based on the theories of communal ownership of property advocated by Robert Owen. Maurice himself talked of founding such a community based on the example of the primitive church at Jerusalem and medieval monasticism.[37] Ludlow promised to join any colony that Maurice would lead, but, after some discussion, the plan for producers' cooperatives was accepted.[38] Ludlow's was potentially the more radical scheme. Communities founded on complete communal ownership, when they survive at all, have a tendency to become so ingrown, even sectarian and self-possessed that they allow the world to pass them by. Producers' cooperatives were a witness in the midst of the marketplace; they attempted to demonstrate that cooperative ideals could inform the entire economic system.

In December 1849 it was decided to set up a working tailors' association under the management of Walter Cooper. In 1850 Maurice, much to Ludlow's pleasure, suggested that they call themselves Christian Socialsts,[39] and asked Ludlow to plan a series of "Tracts on Christian Socialism." The title, he declared, was a true definition of the purpose, and it would commit him at once "to the conflict we must engage in sooner or later with the unsocial Christians and the un-Christian socialists."[40]

Maurice's statement reveals the goals of the Christian Socialist Movement, as I may at last refer to it without anachronism. Their task was twofold: to Christianize socialism and to socialize Christianity. Almost all of their subsequent actions can be seen as attempts to accomplish these goals.

Maurice and Kingsley were most active in attempting to socialize Christianity. Maurice worked through sermons, articles, and lectures. Kingsley turned to more popular media and produced the stirring pamphlet "Cheap Clothes and Nasty" and two famous novels, *Alton Locke* and *Yeast*. *Alton Locke*, published in 1850, was based on the life of the Chartist tailor-poet,

Thomas Cooper.[41] Its style and message made it something of a literary sensation. Each chapter denounced some aspect of contemporary life: Tractarians, Calvinists, Tory parsons, aristocrats, physical-force Chartists, and many others came under Kingsley's guns. But beyond all the specific abuses held up for castigation, Kingsley exposed an indifferent society that permitted the poverty, squalor, and brutality of the slums. Soon thereafter, he exposed the problems of the rural poor in *Yeast*.

Christianizing socialism, however, required more than literary talents, and although all the Christian Socialists were involved here, Ludlow stands out. He made the first contacts with the poor and he did the day-to-day spade-work necessary for setting up producers' cooperatives and giving them a legal basis. Assisted by Vansittart Neale, a wealthy philanthropist, and Thomas Hughes (now remembered as the author of *Tom Brown's School Days*), he helped draft an act of Parliament securing adequate legal protection for co-operative societies and their businesses.[42]

More than any other member of the brotherhood, Ludlow wished to get into the workers' world and find out and discuss their problems and difficulties. Only then, he felt, would a viable Christian Socialism be possible. In 1850 he decided to start his own journal, which he named *The Christian Socialist*. Unlike the "Tracts" and *Politics for the People* which were written by and appealed to the educated classes, the new journal contained articles written by the workingmen themselves.[43]

Some measure of Ludlow's success in establishing rapport with the lower classes is demonstrated by the fact that during "the first national conflict between labourer and employer in English history"[44] the leaders of the striking wire-workers looked for advice and sympathy to the Christian Socialists. Even the Chartists, who remained hostile, admitted that they were the leaders in the cooperative movement.[45]

If the Christian Socialists were at least partially successful in winning the confidence of the lower classes, they failed to make the producers' co-operatives work. Since these associations were the practical economic embodiment of their reform ideals, their failure is extremely important.

At first the scheme worked well. Middle-class capital launched workshops for tailors, builders, shoemakers, piano makers, printers, bakers, and blacksmiths. Vansittart Neale put nearly sixty thousand pounds into the venture and rapid expansion ensued. Lord Shaftesbury came into the movement to help set up an association of needlewomen, and Bishops Wilberforce and Wiseman—not yet cardinal archbishop of Westminster—ordered livery for their footmen from the tailors' association. There was no single cause of the failure. As in any business there were many day-to-day problems and the associations were without properly delegated authority for handling them. The personal weaknesses of all concerned contributed something to the problems. Maurice was too soft-hearted, inflexible, and impractical. Ludlow was too imperious and distant in his personal relations with others, and he had serious disagreements with everyone. The workers were bound by traditional attitudes and full of human frailties. Their wives refused to purchase their own husbands' products.

Ludlow felt the failures more deeply than anyone, and he attempted to initiate reforms. When these were opposed by Neale, Ludlow tried to force him out of the council for promoting the associations. He failed miserably. In an overwrought moment he resigned from the council and—as soon as a new editor could be found—from *The Christian Socialist*.

The process of finding a new editor brought him even more agony. First, Maurice wisely refused the position. Then, when Thomas Hughes agreed to take it, Maurice urged him to drop the name *Christian Socialist* from the masthead. Ludlow was horrified and called the action surrender; he accused Maurice of following the advice of men who were in every way his inferiors.[46]

The differences between Maurice and Ludlow that I have mentioned now grew into acrimonious disagreement. Both men were stubborn when they felt themselves to be in the right, and on this occasion each did. It would be a mistake to see this as an argument about abandoning Christian Socialism as a principle; the disagreement revolved rather around what Christian Socialism meant to each. For Ludlow it was a revolutionary principle that could transform all of society. For Maurice it was a moral means of production much to be preferred to the competitive factory system. Maurice was as devoted to the principle as Ludlow, but he imagined it operating within the framework of contemporary hierarchical society. Although he never described his beliefs in such terms, his vision had more than a little of the neo-medievalist attitude that later found expression in Ruskin's writings on social reform.

In a remarkably bitter letter, whose tone fully reveals deep distress, Ludlow accused Maurice of abandoning the name because he wished to keep his professorship at King's College. Maurice, who was prone to imputing selfish motives to himself, was too scrupulous to deny it. Ludlow acidly replied that Maurice had better keep to the college, because he was doing no good among the workingmen.[47]

Maurice was deeply hurt by Ludlow's criticisms and accusations, but he did not return criticism for criticism. Rather, in a remarkably beguiling series of letters, he admitted his personal limitations as a man, but stuck to his guns. Throughout these letters one can hear the theme, "God help me, I can do no other."[48] Ludlow was far too fond of Maurice to allow their argument, serious as it was, to ruin their friendship. When Maurice's position at King's College was seriously threatened, Ludlow stopped arguing and came to his friend's aid.

During June 1851 Kingsley had delivered a fiery sermon on social questions that resulted in a public denunciation and nationwide notoriety. Conservative journalists quickly used this event as an excuse to attack Christian Socialism and its clerical leaders Kingsley and Maurice. John Wilson Crocker, now remembered only as the prototype for the odious Mr. Rigby in Disraeli's *Conningsby*, but in his own time a famous Tory journalist, published a scathing denunciation in the ultrarespectable *Quarterly Review*.[49] "*Murder*," he wrote,

> is openly advocated—all property is declared to be robbery—the rules by which marriage is declared sacred and inviolate are treated as the dreams of dotage—obedience of every description is denounced as a criminal cowardice. . . . Incredible as it may appear, there is a clique of . . . men . . . who from, as it seems, a morbid craving for notoriety or a crazy straining after paradox, have taken up . . . the task of preaching, in the press and from the pulpit . . . under the name *Christian Socialism* the same doctrines in a form not the less dangerous for being less honest . . . Mr. Maurice, we understand, is considered the head and founder of the school and it certainly adds to our surprise to find the reputed editor of "Politics for the People" and the avowed author of other works . . . of a still more heterodox character, occupying the professorial chair of Divinity in *King's College, London*.[50]

Maurice's son describes the public reaction to the article as the "hailstorm of calumny with which at this time my father and his friends were assailed."[51] Naturally, respectable citizens who knew nothing about the doctrines espoused by Maurice and Kingsley were alarmed to discover that Church of England clergymen were advocating free love, financial anarchy, and murder—as well as unnamed opinions "still more heterdox!" Something of a nineteenth-century academic witchhunt developed and King's College felt threatened by the fact that Maurice was giving them a scandalous reputation. Wealthy trustees became alarmed and demanded that Maurice explain himself.

Crocker's charges were so obviously absurd that Maurice had no difficulty refuting them. The Council of King's College accepted Maurice's explanation and reaffirmed their confidence in him, but their resolution also suggested, in a veiled way, that Maurice stop advocating controversial doctrines that might produce an unpleasant "impression on the public mind."[52] He was, in effect, placed on probation with "good conduct" for a surety. Maurice, however, never allowed personal security and reputation to stand between him and the performance of his duty. He realized that sooner or later King's College would be forced to sever its connection with him and proceeded without fear of the consequences.[53]

In February 1853 he began a series of sermons in Lincoln's Inn Chapel on the main doctrines of Christianity. Subsequently each sermon was turned into an essay. The complete set of *Theological Essays* was published in June and almost immediately became the subject of controversy. Maurice had addressed the work to the Unitarians, hoping to clear up the theological differences that kept them out of the Church of England. The Unitarians rejected hell and the idea of everlasting punishment; Maurice agreed. St. John, he argued, talked about a quality of life, not an endless time, when he used the term eternal life.[54] The important point of the Gospel message, Maurice stated, was God's love for all men, not a theory about rewards and punishments.

Maurice's opinions ran against the strong current of nineteenth century popular theology. Many saw the doctrine of rewards and punishments as the greatest bulwark to social order. Now a man long identified with Christian Socialism declared that this important doctrine, which few had ever questioned, had no New Testament basis. The Evangelicals were especially outraged and their journal *The Record* leveled its oratorical guns at Maurice and King's College. A man who did not believe in everlasting punishment was not fit to train clergymen.[55]

It is not necessary here to trace the very complex theological and moral arguments that ensued. Dr. Jelf, the principal of King's College, personally believed Maurice's interpretation to be erroneous, and he begged him to resign for the good of the school. Maurice refused. He no longer wished to remain, but insisted that he be dismissed as incompatible with Dr. Jelf. Above all, Maurice wished to preserve the right of Anglican clergy to deny without retribution the doctrine of endless punishment. As he explained to Ludlow:

> I cannot and would not teach under a principal who objects to my teaching, but I must bear what testimony I can for the right of English divines to preach the gospel of God's love to mankind and to maintain that Lord Shaftesbury and the Bishop of London do not care more for the outcasts of the race than He does. If Humanity and Theology are not to be forever apart, the regeneration of the

working classes is not to be given up by Christians to infidels. This point must be settled somehow.[56]

This letter also reveals the close association in Maurice's mind between his theological opinions and his social concern.

Maurice's dismissal from King's College led the brotherhood to its last significant venture. On December 27, nearly a thousand workingmen assembled at Castle Street to present him with an address. The men, their chairman said, were grateful to Maurice for presenting a more liberal, genial, and merciful interpretation of Holy Scripture than that usually given to them.

The struggle over the years at King's College had directed Maurice's interests more and more toward educational problems. Now, responding to the workingmen's address, he suggested that education equal to that at King's College should be offered to them. They replied that since Maurice was barred from teaching at King's, he might become a professor in a college for them.

The Workingmen's College opened October 31, 1854, with 120 students.[57] As usual, Ludlow had handled the practical arrangements and had drawn up the organizational scheme. Maurice was principal. All the leading Christian Socialists helped with the teaching—Neale, Tom Hughes, Ludlow. Later John Ruskin and Dante Gabriel Rossetti joined the faculty and gave lectures. The college remains the most lasting contribution of the movement and the brotherhood.[58]

It is customary to regard England's first experiment in Christian Socialism as a failure, and it is true that producers' cooperatives never replaced finance-capitalism as England's basic mode of industrial production. The failure of several associations and the rising prosperity of England and its workers during the mid-1850s ended that facet of the brotherhood's work. At the time, some of the brothers were severely disillusioned. Thomas Hughes lost faith in the group because he believed that the members worked better as individuals.[59] Ludlow, who had put more of himself into the movement for producers' cooperatives than any of the others, was the most upset. He brooded over what he called Maurice's betrayal of the cause when he turned his interests to the education of workingmen. "Mr. Maurice," he wrote in his autobiography, "never understood the crushing nature of the blow he had given me."[60]

Yet it can be argued, I believe, that the failure of the producers' co-operatives did not mean that the movement itself had failed. No movement that has exerted such an influence on subsequent events can be counted a historical failure. Maurice's influence will become obvious when I discuss

Anglican radicals of later periods, but at this point I should at least mention Ludlow's role as mentor to the German socialists.

Ludlow had formed a warm friendship with Aimé Victor Huber, a German Lutheran who is sometimes called the father of German Christian Socialism. Huber greatly admired Ludlow's opinions and exerted his influence to have *The Progress of the Working Class* translated into German. Ludlow's book strongly affected a brilliant young Roman Catholic, Lujo Brentano, who came to England virtually as a disciple. It was Ludlow who directed Brentano to study the trade unions, and Brentano's *On the History and Development of Guilds and the Origin of Trade Unions* was gratefully dedicated to Ludlow. Through Brentano, Ludlow's concerns and ideas were directed to the "Socialists of the Chair." These men were the nonrevolutionary State Socialists who pioneered the development of the welfare state and helped draw up Bismarck's great insurance acts of the 1880s. Perhaps their most significant achievement was the founding of an institutionalist, not individualist, school of economics that broke with the assumptions of classical laissez-faire.[61] Their work was later picked up in England by the Fabians and was brought to the United States by Richard T. Ely, the Anglican economist who was probably the most famous and influential of the American social-reforming moderates.[62]

Also, the influence of Christian Socialism was larger than that of its individual members. The Workingmen's College lived on after the co-operatives failed. Its work as an educational institution can never be accurately quantified, but two direct results of its existence should be mentioned.

John Ruskin's experiences as a teacher at the college helped to turn him toward social reform. At first, he was primarily interested in simply communicating with the workingmen, but the communication led him to begin economic investigations of his own. Less than five years after he had begun teaching at the Workingmen's College, the apostle of beauty had become the social critic of *Unto This Last*. Ruskin's audience was very wise, and his influence was profound. J. A. Hobson, a social critic of high reputation himself, said that "he has done more than any other Englishman to compel people to realize the nature of the social problem in its wider context."[63]

The Workingmen's College with its spirit of human brotherhood beyond class and its program for improving the conditions of the poor through education can also be seen as a prototype for the modern settlement house movement. Toynbee Hall, England's initial venture for bringing together the poor and the privileged university youth in a settlement house in the slums was organized by men who were aware of the work of the early Christian Socialists.[64] During the 1890s settlement houses multiplied in England, while at the same time Toynbee Hall inspired a College Settlement Association on this side of the Atlantic.[65]

Maurice spoke with his usual prophetic insight when he wrote during the early days of the Christian Socialist Movement, "It is but a first start; perhaps we shall fail utterly; but the principle I think is sound, and will spread, and bear fruit hereafter."[66]

27

# The Seed Grows Secretly: Tractarians, Ritualist Slum Priests, and the Religious Revival

After the dissolution of the Council of Promoters of Working Class Associations no organized body with a specific concern for social Christianity existed in the Church of England until Steward Headlam founded the Guild of St. Matthew in Bethnal Green in 1877. On the surface this interim period of nearly twenty-five years might appear barren and without significance. But it is a mistake to see in this absence of formal organization a sign that the cause was dead. To use Maurice Reckitt's phrase, "the seed was growing secretly," and when an organized social Christian body reappeared in the late seventies, its character had been profoundly altered by the years of secret growth. Christian Socialism in the late forties and early fifties had been a Broad Church effort to establish producers' cooperatives; in the late seventies and eighties it became a High Church campaign in behalf of Henry George's single tax.

The most significant development of these decades of secret growth for Anglican social Christianity was the work performed by members of religious orders and ritualist slum priests. Leaving behind the comfort and security of university quadrangles and family homes they moved into the most squalid and sordid slums in Victorian England, where their presence was a living witness to the fact that the Church of England had not entirely forgotten the congregation of God's poor. These second generation Anglo-Catholic activists were the heirs of the Oxford movement and to understand them properly we must go back and examine the work of their Tractarian fathers.

There was nothing obviously radical about the social philosophy of the Oxford movement. John Keble's famous assize sermon, "National Apostasy," which John Henry Newman always considered "the start of the religious Movement of 1833,"[1] attacked a reform measure introduced by a Liberal government. As many studies of the Oxford Movement have pointed out, Tractarianism was a reactionary movement, in the sense that it derived its inspiration from looking backward—to the church fathers, to the Caroline divines, and, to a somewhat lesser extent, to medieval Catholicism. To find an acceptable model for a just English society, W. G. Peck tells us, "their minds travelled back to the Caroline Church and State as to a last point of departure from which the English Church had descended to degradation."[2] Hurrell Froude in his last sermon, "Riches a Temptation to the High Minded," urged rich and poor alike to "submit themselves to their spiritual rulers as the means to a better social order."[3] This was the Tractarian social ideal—a return to a golden age of the past where "spiritual rulers" guided secular rulers and justice was dealt to rich and poor alike.

The implications of such a conservative position, however, proved to be more revolutionary than they at first appeared. Froude's sermon proclaimed no gospel of wealth; he had little use for any variety of "whatever is, is right" conservatism. Although he had been raised in an old-fashioned High Church, High Tory home, he mocked what he called the "old Tory humbug."[4]

For the Tractarians, the most unacceptable tenet of "old Tory humbug" was its Erastian view of the church. In theory the Tories were the traditional church party, the zealous defenders of the exclusive privileges of what had been "by law Established." In practice, however, the Tories, like the Whigs, were practical politicians. They had come to regard the church as little more than another department of the state, a department whose better positions were an excellent source of that political patronage so necessary for the building of strong parliamentary alliances. The Tories were content to allow the church the privileges and protections of an established institution, but they expected that in return the church would support the secular policies of the establishment. In effect, Erastian establishment meant subservience to secular power.

The Tractarians regarded this type of Erastian attitude with horror; for them it was little better than blasphemy. Like the Tories, the Tractarians favored a protected and privileged church, but for very different reasons. They held that the church's privileges were a gift of God and part of its sacred character; these privileges were not dependent on the whim of the secular establishment. The church that the Tractarians proclaimed was no merely English institution; it was a universal divine society established by God.

The most eloquent exponent of the Tractarian viewpoint on this issue was John Henry Newman and a few brief excerpts from his *Parochial Sermons* reveal it clearly.

> Properly it [the church] is not on earth, except so far as heaven can be said to be on earth . . . except in such sense as Christ or His Spirit are on the earth.
> . . . The Church is not in time or place . . . it is in the Holy Ghost . . . the heavenly Jerusalem, the mother of our new birth, it is in all lands at once. . . that is wherever her outward instruments are found. . . . Such is the City of God, the Holy Church Catholic throughout the world, manifested in and acting through what is called in each country the Church visible; which visible Church really depends solely upon it, on the invisible—*not on civil power, not on princes or any child of man, not on endowments, not on its numbers, not* on anything that is seen. [emphasis mine][5]

It is difficult to imagine a more explicit declaration of ecclesiastical independence or a more radical reputation of the gentlemen's agreement between church and state that provided the basis for the Erastian status quo. But Newman went farther yet. Not only was the church independent of the civil power, it was also superior to it. In another sermon delivered from the pulpit at St. Mary the Virgin, Newman expounded the principle of apostolic succession in a manner calculated to appeal to the romantic historical associations that were an integral part of nineteenth-century conservative ideology, and used those very conservative arguments to establish the superior authority of the church.

> He set it on the foundations of His twelve apostles, and promised that the gates of hell should not prevail against it; and its presence among us is a proof of His power. He set it up to succeed to the four monster kingdoms of this world which then were; and it lived to see those kingdoms crumble into dust and come to naught. It lived to see society new formed upon the model of the governments which last to this day. *It lives still and it is older than them all. Much and rightly as we reverence old lineage, noble birth, and illustrious ancestry, yet the royal dynasty of the apostles is far older than all the kingly families which are now on earth. Every bishop of the Church whom we behold, is a lineal descendant of St. Peter and St. Paul after the order of a spiritual birth.* [emphasis mine][6]

Newman, of course, later lost faith in the independent authority of the Church of England, but his views on the independence of the church remained a vital part of the Tractarian message. The new breed of High Churchman who followed him were no longer content with the privileges of establishment. They saw the independent church functioning as the conscience of the nation and they were not afraid to criticize the crimes, both of commission and omission, committed by contemporary society. Newman himself was a social conservative, but within forty years men who viewed themselves as part of the movement he had begun were openly championing radical causes. In his history of the Arians, Newman wrote, "the Church was framed for the express purpose of interfering, or (as irreligious men will say) meddling with the world."[7] The second-generation Anglo-Catholic ritualists took him at his word and as churchmen began a vigorous meddling with the world against the establishment on behalf of the poor.

The Oxford movement's advocacy of a high doctrine of the church has long been recognized, but often it has been forgotten that Tractarian writings express an equally high doctrine of the poor. This attitude finds its fullest expression in the sermons of Edward Bouverie Pusey—the learned, mystical, melancholy man who reluctantly assumed the leadership of the movement at Oxford after Newman went to Rome. Even more than John Keble, who most often kept to his quiet country parish at Hurseley, Pusey was the man who transmitted the Tractarian message to devout young people in the Church of England, and it was Pusey who was recognized as adviser, protector, and Father in God by the new generation of religious and slum priests.[8] In statements such as the one that follows we can recognize the call that sent idealists into the slums and the doctrine that carried them through the years of discouraging hard work and persecution as they served the poor.

> But if we would see Him in His Sacraments we must also see Him wherever He has declared Himself to be, and especially in his poor. In them also He is "with us" still. And so our Church has united mercy to His poor with the Sacrament of His Body and Blood, and bade us, ere we approach to receive Him, to remember Him in His poor, that so, "loving much," we, who are otherwise un worthy, may be "much forgiven," we "considering" Him in His "poor and needy," may be permitted to behold Him; and for Him parting with our earthly substance, may be partakers of His Heavenly. . . . Casual almsgiving is not Christian charity. Rather, seeing Christ in the poor . . . we must . . . seek them out as we would seek Christ, looking for a blessing from it, far greater than any they can gain from our alms. It was promised of old time, as a blessing, "the poor shall never cease out of the land," and now we know the mercy of the

mysterious blessing, for they are the Presence of our Lord. "The poor," He saith, "ye have always with you, but Me ye have not always," not in bodily Presence, but in His poor whom we shall ever have.

The poor of Christ are the Church's special treasure, as the Gospel is their special property. . . . The poor are the wealth, the dowry of the Church; they have a sacred character about them; they bring a blessing with them; for they are what Christ for our sake made Himself.[9]

I have quoted Pusey at such length not only because the text is so intricately wrought that deletions are difficult, but also because I believe this statement to be the finest possible refutation of those who describe his social teachings as mere palliative charity. No nineteenth-century social reformer, to my knowledge, has ever equaled the mystical intensity of Pusey's description of the holiness of the poor. During an era when poverty was all too often equated with sin, Pusey proclaimed the poor as a means of grace, a manifestation of the incarnate God like unto the sacraments of the church. The boldness of his argument is astonishing. He cites the favorite text of those who claim that social injustice is ordained of God, but sees in it a mysterious mercy that confounds their argument more profoundly than any rationalistic *explication de texte*. We must help the poor, he says, not for their sake, but for ours. It is the poor who bless, not those with the means to help. His position undercuts any possibility of pride and self-satisfaction in the mind of the do-gooder. His insights are truly revolutionary on a psychological level.

But Pusey was not content to stop at a deepened subjective understanding. He urged his audience to become involved with the social problems of the day and at their own personal expense. Looking around at the condition of England during the 1840s he warned that "year by year there is more need; the poor are multiplying upon us, and distress on them."[10] To meet the needs of the time "we must . . . empty ourselves of our abundance . . . of our self conceit, our notions of station, our costliness of dress, our jewelry, our luxuries, our self love."[11] with the passion of a medieval friar, he called upon men to renounce the cherished vanities of that status-conscious age and devote their wealth to relieving want.

Pusey's private life equaled the standards set in his public preaching. Although he was a wealthy man, he allowed himself only an ascetic standard of living. In an age famous for its elaborate and enormous meals, his own fare was scant. "The Rev. W. Tuckwell describing Pusey's life in the early 'fifties says that his Friday dinner was one poached egg on spinach, with one glass of port wine."[12] The money saved by strict self-denial was generously given away, chiefly to causes offering relief to the poor. He contributed five thousand pounds to Bishop Blomfield's Metropolis Churches Fund[13] and responded to the vicar of Leeds's request for help to build churches in his city—at the time Leeds had five churches and a population of over 123,000—by paying for the construction of the church of St. Saviour's entirely out of his own pocket.[14] His concern was not exclusively expressed in financial terms; during the great cholera epidemic that swept London's East End in 1867, Pusey joined with the ritualist clergy and nursing sisters of the area in trying to offer some relief. At a time when the hospitals in the rest of London were almost empty, but refused to admit the cholera-contaminated poor, Pusey and Lord Halifax, later the head of the English Church Union, were seen carrying stricken children into the emergency hospitals in their arms.[15] Pusey not only gave generously to the poor, but he risked his life on their behalf.

No one, I think, would dispute the depth of Pusey's concern for the poor, his generosity or capacity for self-sacrifice; and yet, a modern man might ask, "Was not this concern and generosity misplaced? Is it not mere charity to give away all that money for church building? And why, if you want to help the poor, should you build churches?" These are sharp questions, but I think they can be answered. First, we must remember Pusey was interested in saving souls, in reaching individuals with the means of sacramental grace offered by the church. But we must also remember that the church dispensed more than the sacraments; however inadequate it may have been, it was often the only social-service-oriented institution in a slum neighborhood. A concerned priest was in a very good position to know the needs of the unfortunates in his parish, and if he had sufficient funds and staff, he could relieve those needs. He could feed the starving, clothe the naked, teach the illiterate; and if he did not, often no one would. Certainly the state-operated workhouses were not a decent alternative. Mere relief is inadequate, almost everyone would agree, but few would claim that starvation and neglect are superior. Both of the above reasons influenced Pusey, but the most significant consideration behind his church-building was a desire to change the system, to effect a peaceful social and spiritual revolution. The passing of the hungry forties with its threats of Christian rebellion did not diminish his passion for change. During a heyday of prosperity and Victorian equilibrium, he wrote:

> We need missions among the poor of our towns; organized bodies of clergy living among them . . . *to grapple with our manufacturing system as the Apostles did with the slave system of the ancient world* . . . if by God's help we would

wrest from the principalities and powers of evil those portions of his Kingdom, of which, while unregarded by the Church, they have been taking full possession. [emphasis mine][16]

Pusey proposed that "organized bodies of clergy" living among the poor would form the vanguard of this revolution, and St. Saviour's, was a kind of pilot project for the implementation of the plan. In fact, it became the first of the ritualist slum parishes.[17]

It appears that Hurrell Froude thought up the plan that Pusey attempted to put into practice. As early as 1833 he wrote,

It has lately come into my head that the present state of things in England makes an opening for reviving the monastic system.[18] I think of putting the view forward under the title of "Project for reviving Religion in great Towns." Certainly colleges of unmarried priests (who might, of course, retire to a living, when they could and liked) would be the cheapest possible way of providing effectively for the spiritual wants of a large population.[19]

It is not clear whether Pusey borrowed the idea from Froude or arrived at it independently, but by 1838 he had taken steps toward realizing it. Cannon Liddon, Pusey's faithful friend and disciple, referred at some length to plans for a college of clergy in a large town parish in his biography of Pusey, and describes them as "the inspiring ideal of the generous efforts connected with the establishment of the Church of St. Saviour's Leeds."[20]

Pusey's work prepared the ground for the revival of the religious life in England, but, contrary to his expectations, the true pioneers of the movement were women. On Trinity Sunday, 1841, Marion Hughes took vows of poverty, chastity, and obedience privately before Pusey, and then went to St. Mary the Virgin where she received communion from Newman. She was "the first Anglican Sister since the Reformation."[21] Although she was not able to commit herself fully to the religious life until the death of her ailing father eight years later, her profession marks the beginning of the revival of the religious life in the Church of England.[22]

The first functioning Anglican religious order, the Sisterhood of the Holy Cross, was established in 1845 as a memorial to the poet Robert Southy, who had long championed the idea of Protestant Sisters of Mercy.[23] Eighteen additional women's orders[24] were established before the first lasting Anglican religious order for men, The Society of St. John the Evangelist.[25] By this time there had been women's orders for twenty years. As A. M. Alchin observes, "the general development of Christian monasticism, from contemplation to activity, and from male to female was reversed in the case of the revival in the Church of England."[26]

The women who began the revival of the religious life in England during the middle of the nineteenth century shared two common concerns. The first was a desire to lead lives totally consecrated to God. The second was the desire to commit themselves to the service of humanity. They were vividly aware of the social problems surrounding them and they felt that something had to be done. The following passage from the writings of Mother Emily Ayckbown, founder of the Community of the Sisters of the Church, eloquently expresses the social concerns that were so intricately bound up in the religious revival.

> And what do you think is the special need of the present day? . . . Active orders of women. . . . Women who come forward with their lives in their hands, daring everything in the cause of suffering humanity. I feel as if I could pray God to raise up some prophet among us, to enter . . . warm and scented drawing rooms, crying Woe! Woe! to such as sit unconcerned there while the poor die in body and soul around them.[27]

The rules of the women's religious orders reflect the importance of their two concerns. The sisters' daily schedules provided time for communal religious observances—often at first held in a neighboring parish church—private meditation, and active works of charity. There is only one exception at this time to the general emphasis on the active life. In 1856 the Second Order of the Society of the Most Holy Trinity was formally constituted. This group, the so-called Englishe Nuns, devoted itself to acts of reparation and intercession, but their rule bade them to pray especially for "a blessing on the labours of their Sisters of the two other orders."[28] These labors were nursing the sick poor, teaching, and general "works of mercy and charity."[29]

Most of the early sisterhoods passed through two common stages of growth. At first they were small bodies—seldom over ten at the onset—closely associated with the work of a particular church. They functioned as a semiofficial part of the staff and engaged in various general works of mercy responding to the particular needs of the situation. In the second stage, as their numbers increased and the sisters became more experienced, the sisterhoods developed individual identities and increasingly became independent of the parish church. At this time the sisterhoods tended to specialize; they concentrated more on the alleviation of particular problems and less on works of general mercy. Greater specialization enabled the sisters to become more professional.

One should not overstress the aspect of professional specialization; most of the orders did various kinds of work, but four general kinds of activity seemed especially popular. These were teaching, especially younger children, particularly poor girls; nursing, particularly the poor and hopeless cases; the care of orphans and abandoned children, and managing "penitentiaries for fallen women." These last, despite the now ominous sound of the name, were early attempts at social rehabilitation centers. They were based on the recognition that poverty bred "vice," and attempted to provide outcast and ruined women with sufficient skills to enable them to earn a living by some other means than selling their bodies. This was an attempt to go beyond the inequities of a man-made, conventional morality, and, if it did not eliminate the causes, it at least mitigated the effects of a great social evil.

During the latter decades of the nineteenth century Anglican sisterhoods continued to prosper, individual orders expanded, and the numbers of orders increased. By 1870, twenty-five orders had been founded; in 1900 there were forty.[30] By the turn of the century, "almost every Protestant sect of any size had recognized sisterhoods as an essential part of its religious and social organization."[31]

The success of the sisterhoods was remarkable; doubly remarkable when it is contrasted with failure of so many attempts to revive the religious life for men; thrice remarkable when we remember that the conventions of the day prescribed that the place of the woman was in the home, in the "warm and scented drawing rooms" that Mother Emily Ackybown found so culpable.

Florence Nightingale, a contemporary woman with a similar desire for service, described the situation in the forties and early fifties.

> The Church of England has for men bishoprics, archbishoprics, and a little work. . . . For women she has what? I had no taste for theological discoveries. I would have given her my head, my hand, my heart. She would not have them. She did not know what to do with them. She told me to go back and do crochet in my mother's drawing room; or, if I were tired of that to marry and look well at the head of my husband's table.[32]

This description, of course, does not apply to the new High Church party fathered by the Oxford movement, but at the time High Churchmen had little influence in the hierarchy of the established church. Nightingale's description does fit the respectable Evangelical middle-class morality that strongly influenced the church's popular teachings and defined the social conventions of the time. There the sanctity of family life was venerated with almost superstitious reverence, and family life was strongly patriarchal. Women were put upon a pedestal and worshiped in theory, but in practice they were expected to subordinate themselves to their fathers and husbands.

It was, I think, the very limitation of independent opportunity for women during the mid-nineteenth century that helped promote the success of women's religious orders. Men who longed to lead a life consecrated to God and social service could find existing institutions that offered them an opportunity to work. But, as Florence Nightingale pointed out, women with the same aims had nowhere to go. Before they could accomplish anything, they had to create a new institution, or more precisely, breathe new life into an institution long presumed dead.

Also, religious orders were real communities that shared a common life and purpose. Associating with like-minded women, sharing common aims and difficulties must have helped sustain each individual's attempt to break out of the narrow confines of social convention. If women religious had to face strong opposition from society and, often, from their families, they also received encouragement and advice from sympathetic males who took a truly fatherly interest in their communities. This fatherly support was most important during the difficult early period of development.

Pusey probably supported more orders than any other man, but there were others whose influence was as deep if not as widespread. John Mason Neale, the founder of the Cambridge Camden Society, translator of ancient hymns, and historian of the Eastern church, devoted himself to the Sisters of St. Margaret, a nursing order he founded at East Grinstead. Indeed, his day-to-day care was so intense that he looks like an ecclesiastical variation of the Victorian paterfamilias.[33] But the women's orders outlived Pusey, Neale, and the other fathers of the early days. They went on to become remarkably independent organizations that resisted masculine attempts to assert authority, even when the male in question was their episcopal visitor.[34]

By the 1870s women's religious orders were becoming accepted as a normal part of Anglicanism.[35] Their work had proved that women were capable of confronting the serious affairs of the world on their own without the protection of the patriarchal family. The Anglican sisterhoods offered opportunities to a young woman wishing to engage in full-time welfare work, nursing, or teaching that were not easily found in the world at large. As such they represent an important first step in the emancipation of women and in the modern movement for greater sexual equality.

Women's orders succeeded because they were able to satisfy the personal needs of individual women in a manner that was also beneficial to society as a whole. They offered women an expanded area of purpose and meaning and their work helped alleviate some of the most pressing social problems of the day. The emphasis on a practical and socially useful active life is not found in the earliest attempts to establish male orders. Most often these communities had no specific aim other than the revival of the religious life itself.[36] Without questioning the sincerity of these early unsuccessful "monks," it should be pointed out that far too frequently they appear to be overly enamored with the trappings of medieval monasticism. It is as if they were fleeing the harsh realities of industrial England, hoping to find God in more suggestive, artistic surroundings. Without the demands of an active mission of service to balance the introspective tendencies of a life withdrawn from the world, they became preoccupied with minor details of organization and liturgy. The desire to restore the contemplative life may have been a noble one, but it was fraught with difficulties. There were no authoritative models to follow, and individual attempts often produced results that were eccentric, even bizarre. The women's orders were too busy with social service to have the time to engage in such ecclesiastical tomfoolery, and the women's orders survived.

It is interesting to note in this context that the first Anglican order for men that survived, the Society of St. John the Evangelist, was the result of intensive planning and study and was established as an active order in response to a specific need. The Cowley fathers—the name comes from the village of Cowley near Oxford where they began their work—were not specifically concerned with the problems of the poor. They addressed themselves to the upper classes, particularly to young men at the universities. Their task was to combat "infidelity," to present the Christian message in terms calculated to appeal to the intelligentsia.[37] This task remains a vital part of their work. The mother house in England is located near Oxford University and the mother house in the United States is located on the banks of the Charles River near Harvard. The next two successful Anglican communities for men were also active orders, but they were established decades later and played no role in the period I am discussing.

During the middle of the nineteenth century the real counterpart to the women's orders was not men's orders but the ritualist slum priests. As mentioned, the nuns and these priests often worked hand in glove in slum neighborhoods. If anything, the slum priests were even more active in outlook and direction. They began their work with the desire to preach the gospel to the poor and alleviate human suffering; but as time went on, many of them came to realize that before these tasks could be accomplished social conditions would have to change. They followed Pusey's directive and began "to grapple with [the] manufacturing system as the Apostles did with the slave system of the ancient world."[38]

As the German scholar Dieter Voll has pointed out, "A comprehensive description of work in the slums by the Ritualist clergy, one of the most absorbing chapters of English Church history of the last century, is still lacking."[39] The standard histories of the nineteenth-century church concentrate almost exclusively on their ritualism and the controversies it engendered. Little enough is said about their work as slum priests.[40] Such an attitude has some justification; squabbles over ceremonies became one of the standard issues of ecclesiastical party warfare during the last half of the nineteenth century, and the innovations of the ritualists have profoundly influenced the ceremonial style of subsequent Anglican worship. But the ritualist slum priests were more than ritualists. Ritualism was only part of their attempt to bring Christianity to the poor, and it is best understood when seen in the context of their wider program.

This wider program grew out of accumulated experience in slum parishes; it was never officially drawn up and each individual priest introduced variations that suited his conditions and personal temperament. This was a "grass roots movement,"[41] not a formal organization with stated principles. But most of the slum priests knew one another and they exchanged ideas concerning their common problems. Successful ideas were passed on and gradually most of the slum parishes came to adopt most of the characteristic practices of the wider program.

The slum priests saw themselves as home missionaries. Their idea of a home mission was, however, very different from one that was later to gain wide acceptance in the Church of England—preaching in a parish for a period of roughly ten days to two weeks. What they had in mind was rather the establishment of permanent missions where they could live among the poor, and share their lives and problems. They wanted both to bring the gospel to the poor and to demonstrate that the church was concerned about their welfare. Their inspiration came from the work done at St. Saviour's and from the careers of such diverse men as John Wesley and St. Vincent de Paul.

In order to bring the gospel of Christ to the poor they developed a strikingly new propagandistic technique that combined the most elaborate ceremonialism with Evangelical preaching. Tractarian theology with its emphasis on the real presence of Christ in the sacrament provided a theoretical justification for increased ceremonialism even though the Tractarians themselves were never ritualists and did not support the movement until it faced persecution.

The ritualists believed that the King of Heaven, who was truly present in the consecrated elements, deserved the deepest reverence that man could bestow. They saw the gorgeous rituals of the medieval church—and of nineteenth-century Roman Catholicism—as the proper expression of that reverence and they felt obliged to recover for the Church of England this important aspect of its Catholic heritage. As a group, however, they were far too busy with their day-to-day parochial duties to devote themselves to the niceties of liturgical scholarship. They freely borrowed Roman Catholic forms of religious worship, assuming that they were restoring ancient Catholic rites.

During the middle decades of the nineteenth century Roman Catholicism was extremely unpopular in England. Sectarian denominationalism was rampant and the recent restoration of the Roman hierarchy in England had infuriated both the prime minister, Lord John Russell, and the wide majority of Evangelical Protestants. Russell denounced the restoration of the Roman hierarchy as an act of "papal aggression," and the ritualists were seen as a kind of fifth-column movement who had infiltrated the English church on behalf of a foreign tyrant. If they were not out-and-out traitors, they were at least Catholic dupes and sympathizers. Sincere men felt it necessary to "put down ritualism" in order to save the Protestant heritage of the Church of England.

The outrage against ceremonial innovation expressed by the majority of the churchgoing public was not shared by the slum dwellers who attended the services in the mission churches. They weren't shocked by chasubles, the eastward position, or lighted candles on the altar because they had no traditional standards of comparison. They did not know how an ordinary Church of England service was conducted because previously no one had taken the trouble to get them into a church. Objections were voiced by older and wealthier members of the congregations who, for the most part, had moved out of the inner city into newly fashionable suburbs or by neighbors who never attended the services—except to cause a disturbance and make trouble for the "Romanizers."[42]

The use of ceremonial in divine worship "was essentially a means of bringing colour and vividness into the drab courts and alleyways of the slums—a technique which General Booth was later to use with corresponding success."[43] Solemn celebrations were an attempt to teach the soul by means of the senses and the lesson taught was that "the day Spring from on high" had visited His people in their slums. It was an effective demonstration of God's presence to largely illiterate audiences that would never have understood the subtleties of theological argument.

The fact that the congregations did respond to ceremonial worship is demonstrated by their support for their priests when these men were subjected to ecclesiastical censure or legal prosecution. After Alexander Mackonochie, the vicar of St. Alban's, Holborn, had been suspended for ritualistic offenses, a group of workingmen from the parish decided to take a stand. They formed a committee in support of their vicar and drew up a protest with more than five hundred signatures on it. When Archbishop Tait granted them an interview they expressed their viewpoint with a directness that his Grace was most unaccustomed to hearing—unless, of course, he was listening to the queen. The workingmen informed the archbishop that they wanted Holy Communion "as we have it at Saint Alban's" and when Tait tried to argue with them, their secretary bluntly told him,

> This is a working man's question; and when the working classes of this country become aware of the way in which their heritage in Church matters is being attacked, they will rise up, and the Church of England, as an established Church, will fall. The working men themselves could cause the whole fabric to fall about your ears.[44]

Tait smiled and replied, "Nonsense, nonsense," but he could not have mistaken their meaning. We are told that his Grace "did not take formal leave" of the deputation.

The reintroduction of magnificent ecclesiastical ceremonies was, however, only part of the ritualists' propagandistic technique for bringing the Gospel to the poor. Another part, and one equally important, was fervent, even "enthusiastic" Evangelical preaching. Since this style of preaching was not uncommon at the time, the ritualists' use of it has attracted comparatively little attention. The high mass at Saint Alban's on Sunday morning rapidly became infamous, but every Monday the same church had evening services with revivalist hymns, evangelistic services and extempore prayers.[45] The Protestant association never found good reason to complain about these services and they are almost never mentioned.

At high mass on Sunday morning the emphasis was communal; the people of God were gathered together in the presence of the Lord of Hosts. On Monday evenings the individual sinner was encouraged to develop in his heart a one-to-one relationship with his personal savior, Jesus Christ. These Monday evening services were often conducted by Father Arthur Stanton, an avid social reformer who remained in St. Alban's slum parish as an unpaid curate for fifty years. According to Dieter Voll, who has studied Stanton's sermons, he can stand comparison with any great Methodist preacher, a statement that sounds less surprising when we remember that Stanton used the sermons of the great Baptist revivalist, Spurgeon, as one of the models for his own.[46] His other model was Pusey's biographer and spiritual heir, Cannon Liddon.

Stanton's rhetorical style reflects the influence of the Evangelicals; he preached from the heart to the heart, eschewing the decent sobriety that had characterized so much previous High Church preaching. But the Evangelical influence went beyond rhetoric. Stanton's great themes were personal conversion and continuing sanctification through the redeeming merits of Jesus Christ. The forms of piety that he encouraged were "Catholic," but the basic message could have been delivered by John Wesley or, even, John Newton.[47]

If, today, an emphasis on personal sanctification sounds too much like a rehash of the old "petty Protestant moralism," remember that Stanton's audience, like Wesley's, often came out of a life-style that was demoralizing and semibarbarous. These were the oppressed "dregs of society" who lived in a world without meaning and often without hope. Theirs was a world where men fought in the streets with knives for the momentary favors of a prostitute, where parental drunkenness could mean starving, neglected children, where premarital intercourse might condemn to a "life of shame" a girl who lacked the skills necessary for survival. Stanton, like his fellow slum ritualists, knew these problems at first-hand. He loved these people—in his will he left money for the "undeserving poor"—and his sermons proclaimed, in the emotional terms that the people understood, the redemptive love of Jesus Christ. He preached salvation to the oppressed, a salvation that meant human civilization and personal self-respect.

The slum priests realized that if salvation was to mean more than "pie in the sky, bye and bye" the men and women that they served must break out of the social patterns that were destroying their lives. This concern helps to explain the emphasis on personal sanctification in their preaching. But it soon became obvious that preaching alone was not enough; a private, personal method of dealing with individual problems was also required. The method hit upon was regular sacramental confession to a priest.

The Church of England had never forbidden private confession, but the practice had fallen into disuse during the later decades of the seventeenth century. During the eighteenth century and early decades of the nineteenth century it had almost been forgotten. The Tractarians had regarded it with approval, and regular private confession was used by many High Church clergymen and religious. But the great majority of the laity were horrified by the idea; it summoned up fears of rampant clericalism and vague apprehension of immorality. Men feared for the sanctity of the home, and even sympathetic members of the hierarchy were convinced that confession should be used with the greatest discretion and then only in the most exceptional circumstances.

It was the Society of the Holy Cross, an organization of ritualists founded by the slum priest Charles Lowder of St. George's-in-the-East, that championed the idea of regular private confession as a useful pastoral device.[48] The Society of the Holy Cross argued with justification that in their parishes exceptional circumstances were the rule of the day. These priests were convinced that private confession was a useful instrument of discipline, a means of assisting their parishioners to overcome those "occasions of sin" that stood between them and their desire for a more meaningful life. By stressing divine forgiveness and personal reformation the clergy hoped to free their parishioners from a life-style that offered at best only a temporary relief from personal problems, a temporary relief that all too often resulted in ruin and early death.

But the problems of the poor were far too complex to be solved by personal reformation. Their problems were bigger than any individual, even though it was as individuals that they needed help. This help the slum priests attempted to offer. They developed programs that provided basic material necessities for the poor, demonstrating the church's concern for their welfare by giving them a way to survive and a reason for hope. Each individual parish developed its own program, but certain characteristic elements stand out. First, the slum parishes attempted to provide food, clothing, medicine, nursing—often done by sisters when they were available—and, even, alcohol. The last was distributed doubtless for medicinal—in the widest sense of the term—purposes. Beyond dispensing these basic material necessities, the slum parishes introduced innovations that anticipated the programs later developed by institutional churches and settlement houses. These innovations included educational opportunities of a wide variety: day care centers for working mothers, gymnasiums for children's play and physical development, workingmen's clubs, and homes for the elderly.

These programs helped to make life possible and even bearable, but they were essentially palliatives. The slum priests also tried to change the basic social environment by what would now be called community organization. They attempted to arouse the inhabitants of the slums to put down "vice" by joining in campaigns to close down notorious public houses and brothels, and they agitated for basic improvements in housing, transportation, and drainage. A statement attributed to Robert Dolling, the ritualist reformer who served in the slum parish of St. Agatha, Landport, in Portsmith, might be taken as the credo that inspired all these reformist activities: "I fight for the drainage of the district because I believe in the Incarnation."[49]

Such was the wider program of the men known as ritualists. To recapitulate briefly, it might be summed up as a combination of ceremonial worship, Evangelical preaching, personal direction in confession, regular social service, and community organization. It grew out of the experience of coming to grips with immediate problems more than from predetermined principle, but it became a comprehensive program that attempted to reclaim the "lost sheep of England" for church and society. In retrospect it appears to have been a noble, well-intentioned, and far-seeing movement, but at the time it aroused the fierce opposition of men of undoubted good will.

The opposition to their wider program of slum work, as well as their experiences in the slums, made the ritualist priests increasingly alienated and progressively more radical. The earliest slum ritualists, men like Charles Lowder and Alexander Mackonochie, had been Tories like the Tractarians before them. Gradually the whole High Church party moved to the left. This move was made easier by William Gladstone, who began his career on the Tory right but ended up a Liberal prime minister. Gladstone had always been extremely sympathetic to the High Church Party; many of its members were his friends, and friendship and personal respect for Gladstone had helped effect a political transition that broke up the old alliance between the Tories and High Churchmen. Younger slum ritualists, men like Arthur Stanton and Robert Dolling, who began their work in the sixties and seventies, started out as Liberals; their pointed attacks on the social abuses of the time led their opponents to suspect that they were dangerous radicals. Some even accused them of harboring socialist sympathies.[50]

Men like Stanton and Dolling were not unsympathetic to socialists, but the slum ritualists were not political radicals in the ordinary sense of the term. They were not strong "party men"; they had little interest in politics either as a theoretical discipline or as a method of gaining power and governing. Their devotion to social reform was the result of their practical experience in the

45

slums and their religious principles. For them, the church was paramount; the state was a secondary matter.

The great focus of their radicalism and alienation was the established church, not the state. Their greatest battles were with ecclesiastical conservatives. At first, the battle lines were drawn up on the question of ecclesiastical ceremonial. Opposition came from respectable hard-line Protestants and an ecclesiastical hierarchy, composed mainly of Evangelicals and Broad Churchmen, determined to prevent Romanizing innovations. In this struggle prelates and Protestants alike attempted to enforce their opinions through the exercise of the coercive power of the law. The ritualists, who were strong-minded, even stubborn men, refused to abandon their principles and openly resisted the hierarchy.

The ritualists' resistance marks a significant development in the history of High Church tradition. As far back as the early seventeenth century High Churchmen had been advocates of a high view of the episcopacy. This aspect of tradition had been strongly reinforced by the writings of the early Tractarians. In the late nineteenth century the ritualists defied the episcopacy with a vigor that would have done credit to the staunchest Puritan.

The extreme on the ritualist left went beyond disobedience; they openly advocated the disestablishment of the church. Men like Mackonochie took this position because they were concerned about religious liberty. The younger clergy added to the question of individual religious liberty wider social concerns. They envisioned a church that was both Catholic and democratic, with bishops chosen by the church, not appointed by the governing classes. Only when the church was free of Erastianism, they believed, could it take up its social mission to the downtrodden. They had taken the Tractarian tradition of anti-Erastianism, used by them against Liberalism, and converted it into a justification for social reform and a free and democratic church. During the nineteenth century when the church by law still maintained the closest connections with the secular state, ecclesiastical radicalism took the ritualist slum clergy to the very doorstep of political radicalism. In a short time, men who recognized these ritualist clergy as their progenitors crossed the threshold and advocated political change.

The twenty-five years between the dissolution of the Council of Promoters of Working Class Associations and the establishment of the Guild of Saint Matthew was not a barren period for the cause of Christian social reform. The religious and slum priests of the second period of the Catholic revival had taken the Tractarian high doctrines of the church and the poor and developed a social program of great significance. They brought the church to the industrial slums; they reached the dregs of society. Their work anticipated the social services of the welfare state and the institutional church. They provided an example of apostolic poverty and Christian communism to an age flush with material success and enamored of private gain. They proclaimed the mission of the church to all men, and they spoke for a freedom of the church beyond the narrow necessities of status quo.

# THREE

# The Social Gospel Era

On St. Peter's Day in 1877 (29 June) forty members of the Church of St. Matthew, Bethnal Green, formed a parish guild that they named after their patron. The guild's three basic precepts were explained in its constitution. Two professed aims, encouraging frequent reception of Holy Communion and combating secularist prejudices against the church, were common Anglo-Catholic objectives that this guild shared with other religious organizations in High Church parishes.

A third precept, however, set the Guild of St. Matthew apart from its predecessors and demonstrated its individual character. Members of the guild were pledged to "promote the study of social and political questions in the light of the Incarnation."[1] The third precept led the guild into the political arena, where its activities soon defined the front lines of the movement within the Church of England advocating social reform. The long-range effects of the guild were to prove so significant that the organization meeting held on St. Peter's Day, 1877 can be recognized as a turning point in the history of social Christianity in Great Britain. The years of "secret growth" were over; the era of the Social Gospel had begun.

My concern is with the English background of the Social Gospel movement in the American church. As mentioned, the American movement acquired an independent character in the late eighties and early nineties. Thus discussion of the English movement is limited to approximately the first fifteen years of its development. During these years the course of social Christianity in the Church of England was determined by two organizations, the Guild of St. Matthew and the Christian Social Union. They shared a common devotion to Christian social reform, but in most other respects exhibited dramatic differences.

The Guild of St. Matthew was a small radical band[2] with an extravagant, even flamboyant, style. It staged controversial activities calculated to attract attention and demonstrate to society at large that basic social change was an immediate necessity. Like their contemporaries in artistic Bohemia, guild members were pleased to *épater la bourgeoisie*, and they successfully outraged the conservative sensibilities of many solemn, satisfied Victorian churchmen. The guild identified itself with the then radical single tax program of Henry George, and championed George's program with an enthusiasm worthy of the most zealous sectarian. Functioning most successfully as a gadfly, the guild stung complacent churchmen into an often exasperated awareness of the pressing social problems of the time. The guild's warden, Steward Headlam, and his closest associates never found significant positions in the clerical establishment; they remained clerical outcasts who were unable to exert direct influence on the formation of official church policy.

The Christian Social Union, on the other hand, was led by liberal reformers who held high positions in the clerical hierarchy. The union's first president, the noted theologian Canon Westcott, was advanced to the see of Durham during his presidency; and its two most conspicuous leading lights, Charles Gore and Scott Holland, became respectively bishop of Oxford and canon of St. Paul's. The leaders of the Christian Social Union came out of what has been called the "aristocratic, privileged, well-travelled, classically educated, academic, and clerical-minded Eton, Harrow, and Oxford elite."[3] This group produced some fiery oratory and provocative journalism, but as a whole the organization eschewed both the radical platform and the flamboyant tactics of the Guild of St. Matthew, preferring instead to work for social reform within the existing system while adhering to acceptable standards of decorum and good taste. These tactics attracted members and at the height of its popularity in the early 1900s the Christian Social Union numbered over six thousand adherents,[4] most of them drawn from the liberal elements of the governing classes and intelligentsia.

If the Christian Social Union failed to exhibit the brio and sense of urgency that the guild brought to social issues, it did demonstrate that the cause of social reform could be socially respectable; it thereby became, more than any other organization, the medium by which the vital message of the Social Gospel reached the conscience of the governing classes of Great Britain. The Christian Social Union embodied the response of the most sensitive members of the Anglican establishment to the serious social problems of the time and the gadfly stings of the Guild of St. Matthew. Together these two organizations were instrumental in effecting that decisive change of consciousness which enabled the Church of England to recognize the social problems brought about by nineteenth-century industrialism. Also, and perhaps even more important, the guild and the union offered a theological perspective that emphasized the Church's duty to solve these problems.

## Stewart Headlam and the Guild of St. Matthew

Any discussion of the Social Gospel era in the Church of England should begin with Stewart Duckworth Headlam. Headlam was a rare being, one of the select company of great English eccentrics whose lives continually enlivened and ultimately improved the course of their country's history. A determined, cranky individuality and fearless, relentless iconoclasm cost him preferment and popularity during his lifetime; but neither quality should obscure his significance now that the passage of time permits us to appreciate the totality of his career.

Headlam was born in 1847 at Wavertree near Liverpool. The family was middle class, intense, independent, and Evangelical. Religion played an important part in the Headlam household. Stewart's father, Thomas Headlam, was a convinced, but by no means narrow-minded, Evangelical who delighted in religious controversy. His passionate discussions with a brother, who had been a High Church curate in Liverpool, exposed the family to the various religious opinions of the time. Certainly some of Stewart's own affection for ecclesiastical debate was inherited from the father who "used to waylay an old-fashioned High Church clergyman on the Common for the express purpose of arguing with him about Baptismal Regeneration."[5] The stimulating atmosphere of a pleasantly contentious home produced effects that soon became apparent. "Stewart talks and argues well," his father was reported to have said of the young boy, "but the worst of him in argument is that he is less keen on finding out the truth than in demolishing you as an opponent."[6] Thomas Headlam was not the last man to level such charges against his son, but in all fairness to Stewart it should be mentioned that most of his vociferous critics could not or would not stand up to him in debate. Headlam was a fierce but fair opponent who enjoyed a good intellectual fight for its own sake. His father's criticism was voiced before the young man had discovered his "truth."

Headlam's personal beliefs began to take shape when he went away to school at Eton. The years between 1860 and 1865 that he spent there were among the most pleasant in his life and as much as he criticized other established institutions, he always remained loyal to his old school. During these formative years both his religious devotion and social conscience began to develop. He started attending the early celebration at a local church, and a teacher, William Johnson, exposed him to the thought and work of Charles Kingsley and Frederick Denison Maurice. It was Maurice who most profoundly influenced his early development.

At Trinity College, Cambridge, from 1865 to 1869, Headlam read Maurice's books, listened to him lecture, and attended private at homes where the professor of moral theology read Aristotle's *Ethics* with interested students. "It was his theology," Headlam told his biographer, F. S. Bettany,

> which drew me to Maurice at first. . . . It is easy to imagine what good news his teaching as to eternal life and eternal punishment was to such of us as had been terrified by the reiteration of the doctrine that half the world or more was condemned to future torment. . . . Not that his teaching as to eternal life was the more important part of his teaching. That was the Fatherhood of God with, as its corollary, the eternal Sonship of Christ and consequently the Brotherhood of Man. It was from the doctrines of the Incarnation—God made Man—and the Atonement—Man reconciled to God, made at one with God by the sacrifice of the Son—that he derived what unifies his social teaching.[7]

Headlam was completely won over by Maurice's theological insights, and he adopted them as a standard for testing other men. After hearing Pusey preach at St. Clement's he confessed that he found him "awfully dreary" by contrast.

Thomas Headlam was upset when he discovered that his son had adopted a position at such variance with Evangelical opinion and attempted to convert him by sending him to study with two friends, Herbert James and C. J. Vaughn. Neither man had any success. Herbert James, who came to know the younger Headlam quite well, reported with sorrow to his father, "His thoughts still run in the same grooves of Maurice, and from what I know of his character I do not think that they will be lightly given up."[8]

In 1870 Headlam accepted a curacy at St. John's, Drury Lane. This first clerical position lasted three years and it was not a particularly happy time. The problems were mainly personal: Headlam was an intensely social person, but here he was frequently alone. Principle told him that a good clergyman should live among his flock and accordingly he took inexpensive rooms in the parish. St. John's parish wasn't the sort of place where a gentleman would live, and when he moved there Headlam cut himself off from his old Eton-Cambridge associates. Headlam was not a man to mope and he threw himself into parochial duties with characteristic energy and commitment. Ultimately, this period of lonely isolation proved beneficial, for it was during his curacy at Drury Lane that he discovered two interests that developed into lifelong passions. In the St. Martin's National School nearby—St. John's had been carved out of the venerable parish of St. Martin-in-the-Fields—the future independent member of the London School Board first became acquainted with the problems of popular education. Whatever disadvantages it may have had as a respectable residential area, the Drury Lane district offered easy access to culture and it was at this time that Headlam began to fill his lonely nights with visits to the theater, opera, and ballet. Ballet profoundly attracted him and he became a true devotee of the art. His affection for dancing put him in a difficult position. Most of his fellow clergy thought of dance as an occasion of sin; Headlam saw it as a means of grace. Several years later he organized the Church and Stage Guild "to break down the prejudice against theatres, actors, music hall artists, stage singers, and dancers . . . too common among Churchmen."[9] Father Stanton of St. Albans was a "bulwark" of the guild and served on its council, but he, of course, was another fiercely independent spirit who was persona non grata to the establishment.

The Church and Stage Guild gave Headlam his first strong taste of notoriety, and eventually his passionate concern for a just attitude to the stage was to bring about a crisis in his pastoral work. But at St. John's it was his devotion to Maurice that raised personal difficulties and delayed his ordination to the priesthood. He had spoken in his sermons of the wide possibility of pardon in the future state, a position that upset some members of the congregation, R. G. Maul (his vicar), and Bishop Jackson. Headlam declined to change his views and felt obligated to promote them, and soon after he was ordained to the priesthood the vicar reluctantly asked for his resignation. Headlam left Drury Lane for Bethnal Green, where for the next five years he served under Septimus Hansard, a tolerant man who in his youth had had ties with both the Broad and High Church movements.

The years at St. Matthew's were probably the happiest and certainly the most critical of his life. To this period can be traced the flowering of his sacramental social theology, his affection for ritualism, his quarrel with and defense of the Secularists, his agitation on behalf of the theater, and the foundation of the Guild of St. Matthew. Here too he met Frederick Verinder, then a pupil teacher at the National School, who became his strong right hand and closest associate. Headlam took an apartment at 135 Waterlow Buildings, where he held study evenings for schoolteachers and interested parishioners. Out of these local study groups emerged the parish guild of St. Matthew.

During the first year of its existence the guild remained a parish organization led by the local curate. Only after Headlam left Bethnal Green in 1878 did it spread its influence over a wide area and become "the red hot centre of Christian Socialism" in England"[10]

"The Guild was a society at once intensely religious and intensely political. It appealed primarily . . . to the conscience, and its theology led directly to its political action."[11] Since the guild's political actions were the outgrowth of its theology, it seems appropriate to consider that theology—which was Headlam's—before discussing the guild's activities.

Headlam was primarily an activist, not an intellectual; but paradoxically his most significant contribution to the development of social Christianity had more to do with his theology and basic intellectual outlook than to any of his specific social reforming activities. Many subsequent important Anglican reformers who found his theological outlook provocative and inspiring also felt obliged to differ with him strongly on specific points on his social reform program.

Headlam's theology found its clearest expression in three of his most important books: *The Laws of Eternal Life* (1887), *The Meaning of the Mass* (1905), and *The Socialist Church* (1908). The first was written when the Guild of St. Matthew was approaching the height of its fame; the last two were published after the guild had long passed the peak of its activity and was nearing its demise. It is both characteristic and a fitting comment on the quality of the man that the failure of his most dearly beloved project only stimulated him to a fresh affirmation of his basic principles.

Headlam's basic intellectual outlook derived from two sources: Frederick Denison Maurice and the ritualist slum priests. He was the first significant figure in the English church to combine within his own outlook insights offered by two of the most important innovative elements in nineteenth-century Anglicanism. After him almost every important Anglican social reformer drew on both traditions. From Maurice, Headlam acquired a basic theology; from the ritualist slum priests, his Eucharistic doctrine, his religious terminology and practices, and his ecclesiology.

Maurice's influence was the more important because the central insights of Headlam's theology were based on Maurice's incarnational teachings, and it was Maurice who taught him the necessary connection between theology and social concerns. Maurice's incarnational theology stressed the organic unity of all life. When the Word became flesh, "the head and king of our race," dualistic distinctions between sacred and secular and between the church and the world were abolished. As a result nothing was secular. For Headlam, dualistic secularism, whether advocated openly by atheistic propagandists or practiced secretly by Evangelicals and High Churchmen who denounced the world as evil, was a terrible mistake based on an incorrect apprehension of things as they clearly are.

Many traditional Evangelicals and High Churchmen who accepted the tenets of classical laissez-faire economics had attempted to compensate for the miserable standards of lower-class life by promising the righteous an eternal reward in heaven. Headlam found this doctrine heretical; its dualistic assumptions created divisions between the spiritual and physical aspects of man's life and separated him from common humanity. Christ, he believed, drew men together and saved individuals as members of a redeemed and common humanity. His salvation was not "mere immortality," but more abundant life both in the here and now and in any future state. Christians continued Christ's work of salvation by offering their fellow men this more abundant life. Therefore a Christian was by his very nature a social reformer: "It becomes impossible for a priest, who knows what the Lord's Supper means, not to take a part to the best of his power in every work of political or social emancipation; impossible for an earnest communicant not to be an earnest politician."[12]

Here we have the Mauricean core of Headlam's thought, the core that "harmonizes and unifies . . . [the] varieties of disconnected things" that interested him. But as Headlam himself explained to Bettany, "In certain directions I may have gone—have gone—further than Maurice went in his day—thus my devotion to the Sacrament of the Altar—though not further, perhaps than he would have gone had he been alive today."[13]

It is more difficult to describe Headlam's debt to the slum ritualists, whose influence was less profound, if more obvious on the surface. One might sum up the situation by saying that Headlam had basically a Mauricean mind combined with mainly Anglo-Catholic attitudes.

Headlam's Anglo-Catholic leanings developed after the Mauricean core of his thought had been firmly established,[14] and therefore the Anglo-Catholic attitudes were either mixed with the Mauricean core or were added around the surface periphery of his thought. The ascetic tone of most Tractarian theology never attracted Headlam; it was too much like the Evangelical "Puritanism" that he detested. But in one very important area he accepted Tractarian teaching into the vital center of this theological thought: like his ritualist friends Stanton and Dolling, Headlam went beyond Maurice and accepted a

Tractarian doctrine of the sacrament of the altar. As the preceding quotation shows, Headlam recognized that his sacramental theology was not strictly Mauricean; but he minimized the difference between Maurice's ideas and his own.

Whatever Headlam may have thought, however, this difference is too important to pass over; Maurice himself objected to the ritualist position in the strongest terms:

> The Ritualists say that, at all events, they are magnifying the Eucharist, and that for this merit we ought to overlook what appears to us, though not to them, trivialities. . . . They scandalize me by practically and habitually denying what I have always regarded as the glory of the Eucharist, that it testifies of a full, perfect, and sufficient sacrifice, oblation, and satisfaction, which has been once made for the sins of the whole world; that it testifies that there is an access by the Spirit through the ascended Christ to the Father. Their attempt to bring Christ back to the altar seems to me to be the most flagrant denial of the Ascension, and therefore of the whole faith of Christendom, that can be imagined. We give up everything to them if we charge them with an excess of belief: the complaint should be of their unbelief.[15]

A classic definition of the Tractarian-ritualist position on the sacrament was advanced by the High Church fellow of Oriel College, Archdeacon Denison. Denison taught a doctrine of the "Real Presence in the Eucharist," affirming that

> . . . the Body and Blood of Christ are supernaturally and invisibly present in the Holy Communion by virtue of the act of consecration, that both parts of the Sacrament, outward and inward, are received by all who communicate, and that worship is due to the Body and Blood of Christ present under the forms of bread and wine.[16]

One should note that Denison by no means taught the classic Roman Catholic doctrine of transubstantiation.

Maurice's doctrine of the Eucharist, as one might expect, is broader than Denison's. It is also much more difficult to summarize. According to Horton Davies, "he offers us a combination of the Patristic doctrine . . . with a Calvinist modification."[17] The Patristic doctrine was that the Eucharist is essentially a celebration of a sacrifice already made. As Maurice phrased it:

> I have maintained that because the sacrifice had once for all accomplished the object of bringing our race, constituted and redeemed in Christ, into a state of

acceptance and union with God, therefore it was most fitting that there should be an act whereby we are admitted into the blessings thus claimed and secured for us.[18]

In the celebration of the Eucharist the visible church militant joyfully joined the invisible church triumphant to claim the merits of the eternal sacrifice that gave them union with God. It is important to note here how central this Patristic doctrine of the Eucharist is to Maurice's whole wider theology of unity.

Like the Tractarians, Maurice believed in the "Real Presence" in the sacrament of Communion. The words of institution are to be taken literally; there is a real, objective presence of Christ that does not depend on the faith of the communicant—although faith is the means by which the real objective presence is perceived. But unlike the Tractarians, Maurice did not believe that Christ descended into the elements at the moment of consecration. Like Calvin[19] Maurice identified the body of Christ with the glorified body that ascended into heaven. The body did not come down into the elements, the elements were taken up into the body. Those who received the elements were taken "within the veil," where they were united with the risen Lord and experienced a communion with the living head of the church. Maurice stressed the importance of the glorified body of the risen Lord. "The words of institution were to get their life from events to which those who first heard them had not been witnesses."[20] It was not at the Last Supper, but after the ascension, that the apostles realized what those words meant, because it was only after the ascension that their full meaning became clear. We can sum up Maurice's position by saying that he taught a doctrine of the real and objective, but not the local presence of Christ in the Eucharist.

Headlam taught the real, objective, and local presence of Christ as the following line from a sermon aptly demonstrates, "In the worship of Jesus really present in the Sacrament of the Altar before you . . . you are worshipping the Saviour."[21]

At first glance, the differences between Maurice's and Headlam's doctrines of the Eucharist may appear to be of interest only to theological specialists. In fact, though, these Eucharistic doctrines point out that Headlam and Maurice had very different kinds of minds. Also, Headlam's acceptance of "local presence" decisively defined his religious practice and terminology.

Maurice's eucharistic doctrine was subtle and complex, sophisticated and profound. Once comprehended it is intellectually satisfying, but a mind not accustomed to intellectual speculations and theological distinctions would find comprehension difficult. It is the product of a learned mind and might be expected to appeal most immediately to other learned minds. Headlam's position is simple and straightforward. It appeals more to the heart than to the intellect. Jesus is here on the altar before you. It may be a difficult fact to believe, but once you accept it, the rest is easy. It does not take much intellectual sophistication to understand that you are communing with God directly when you can personally receive the bread and wine that are His body and blood. Maurice's subtlety went into his thought. Headlam was a man of relatively simple and direct ideas, which he expounded with Evangelical fervor. Maurice hoped to convince; Headlam wanted to convert.[22]

When Headlam accepted a Tractarian rather than Mauricean doctrine of the "Real Presence," he opened himself to the full influence of the ritualists. The ritualists, it will be remembered, justified their elaborate ceremonial innovations on the ground that they were simply paying all due reverence to the King of Heaven locally present on the altar. Headlam adopted the ritualists' ceremonial practices including their interpolations from the Roman missal into the prayer book service. He joined the "extreme" Guild of All Souls which offered masses for the "faithful departed" and like his friend Stanton, he became a chivalric champion of the cult of Our Lady. His private devotions were as Anglo-Catholic as his public practice, and his books are full of the distinctive terminology that marked him as a party man.

There is a very real sense, though, in which Headlam used Anglo-Catholic terminology to express essentially Mauricean points of view. For example, he preferred to call the service of the greatest sacrament "the Mass"; and he was among the first to say, "It is the Mass that matters."[23] But he used the term because it was an expression of unity and it reminded him that the Christian Church is international, that "the same unique Christian service is offered in St. Petersburg, Vienna, Rome, Berlin, Paris, London."[24] Headlam's use of Anglo-Catholic terminology to express Mauricean insights gave High Churchmen and Mauriceans a common language, and it greatly facilitated the acceptance of Maurice by subsequent Anglo-Catholic theologians.

Headlam's ecclesiology owes more to the Anglo-Catholic tradition than it does to Maurice, although here again Maurice made his influence felt. Anglo-Catholics since Keble's famous sermon on national apostasy had deplored the Erastian establishment of the Church of England. In order to restore the church to its original freedom they developed a high ecclesiology that emphasized that the church was older than, independent of, and more important than the secular state. Radical ritualists, like Mackonochie and Stanton, had flouted the authority of Erastian bishops and courts and even advocated disestablishment in the name of ecclesiastical freedom. Here Headlam was their disciple; he did the same. Indeed, he moved one step and advanced from ecclesiastical radicalism to political radicalism.

Maurice's theology had taught Headlam that a Christian was a social reformer, but Maurice never associated true social reform with either ecclesiastical or political radicalism. The thrust of Maurice's theology of unity, with its repudiation of the distinction between the sacred and the secular, was to deny the possibility, let alone the advisability, of separating church and state. Maurice was in the Anglican tradition running from Hooker through Coleridge that asserted church and state were two different aspects of a common community.[25] For Maurice the question was never one of separation between church and state, it was one of the unity between Christ and the human community.

Headlam's ideal church was coterminous with the human community but he lived and preached an independent church of militant reformation. His friend Canon Adderly once described his understanding of the mass as "the weekly meeting of a society of rebels against a Mammon-worshipping world order."[26] In the same sermon already quoted, the "Jesus really present in the Sacrament of the Altar before you" is described further as "the founder of the great socialistic society for the promotion of righteousness, the preacher of a revolution, the denouncer of kings."[27] This great socialistic society founded by Christ is, of course, the church; and it is the independent, militant, Anglo-Catholic conception of the church made politically relevant that Headlam is describing. Both Maurice and Headlam saw Christ as "the transformer of culture," to use the descriptive phrase of H. Richard Niebuhr. Maurice thought that Christ's rule over the spirits of men would transform culture by changing the "habits, thoughts, words, and acts" of men.[28] Headlam, like Ludlow before him, and like many other Christian radicals since, expected Christ to transform culture by changing external conditions. The instrument for proclaiming the necessity of change and for affecting it was the prophetic church, Christ's body.

Of course Headlam never convinced the established church of its duty to remake society, and he had to make do with his small radical band within it.

The history of the Guild of St. Matthew can be divided conveniently into four periods: 1877-1878, the year when it was a parish guild; 1878-1884, when debating the secularists and agitating for church reform were of paramount concern; 1884-1895, when social reform clearly emerged as the primary issue; and 1895-1910, the final years when no important new programs were proposed and the guild gradually disintegrated. It is the third period, 1884-1895, that chiefly concerns me here, but to understand this period it is necessary first to examine briefly the guild's activities from 1878 to 1884.

At the end of the seventies Headlam became associated with a group of radical curates who joined the guild and contributed greatly to the development of its program. These curates were George Sarson, Thomas Hancock, and John Elliotson Symes. All three were zealous High Churchmen who had come to ecclesiastical radicalism along the road laid out by rebellious ritualists like Dolling and Stanton. A common desire for church reform was the issue that brought these Young Turks together. The church's problems, they felt, were the result of its institutional ties to the state. They wanted a free church and freedom could come only with disestablishment. Disestablishment would enable the church to democratize itself and to destroy the patronage system that gave the wealthy power over most clerical appointments. The reformers wanted the clergy to be free from arbitrary episcopal power and they wanted the laity to exercise genuine rights and abilities as a group.[29]

A radical program led to radical action. Since a small number of insignificant curates possessed no power in the church, they made themselves conspicuous and publicized their position by causing rows at church conferences. They began with the Junior Clergy Society, which met in the vestry of St. Martin-in-the-Fields. At the opening session at King's College, Hancock turned to Headlam and said, "We'll take our places on the extreme left."[30]

Some years later they extended their audience by agitating at church congresses. At Croydon in 1877 they distributed pamphlets, and Headlam and Sarson produced a paper with the startling title, "The Church's Mission to the Upper Classes." At the Leicester Conference three years later, they openly debated "Existing forms of Unbelief" and admitted knowing Annie Besant and Charles Bradlaugh, the two most prominent secularist leaders of the day. Headlam told the congress, "It is because the Christian church has not got itself recognized as a society for the promotion of righteousness in this world that the secular society is so strong."[31] He was tired of the church's bleating about empty buildings when it deliberately closed its eyes to social evils. Next, the indefatigable debater went on to "address the astonished members" on "Church Patronage and the Position and Claims of Curates." He demanded that each diocese set up an elected council to select candidates for ail clerical positions. "It is monstrous that we should be in the arbitrary power of a few Bishops. It is absurd to say Convocation is the voice of the Church, it is hardly the squeak of the Church."[32]

Symes admitted that the guild deliberately tried to shock the audience, and they must have been successful. As the delegates left the hall, many probably still reeling from Headlam's radical rhetoric, they were met by other guild members who passed out leaflets on poverty, the moral dangers of workshop life, preferment, and the need to have trade union leaders at future church conferences. One can easily imagine a clerical conservative returning from Leicester pondering secularism, disestablishmentarianism, and trade unionism in his heart, wondering if these fellows would ever stop. If he returned to the next congress at Reading in 1883 he soon discovered that they would not. Headlam delivered an anti-Sabbatarian diatribe calculated to outrage the Evangelicals, and more important, the Guild of St. Matthew set up a bookstall where Frederick Verinder sold copies of Henry George's *Progress and Poverty*.

F. S. Bettany writes, "If Maurice was the first big inspiring influence of [Headlam's] life, Henry George was the second; if the one man fixed the colour of his religious beliefs, the other supplied him with the main plank of his socialistic platforms."[33]

Henry George's magnum opus, *Progress and Poverty*, appeared in England in 1880 and Headlam quickly developed an intense admiration for the author. He accompanied George during his barnstorming tours of England in the eighties, became a valued personal friend, and served as a leading member of the Georgist Land Reform Union from its inception in 1883. When Headlam joined the Fabian Society three years later, he quickly became identified with the Georgist "left wing." According to Sidney Webb, "it was his persistence and influence in the discussion that secured the insertion in the [society's basis or "creed"] of some of the declarations that were afterwards considered most 'extreme' or most in need of judicious interpretation."[34] Most important for this study, in 1884 at its annual meeting on St. Matthew's Day, the guild adopted Headlam's "Priests' Political Programme" and passed a resolution that "urges on all Churchmen the duty of supporting such measures as will tend to restore to the people the value which they give to the land."[35]

Henry George's single tax, a program that advocated "the confiscatory taxation of the increment of land values"[36] was to the Guild of St. Matthew what producers' cooperatives had been to the original Christian Socialists and what community organization for local improvements had been to the ritualist slum priests: namely, the sociopolitical expression of their religious beliefs. It is not necessary to develop a detailed discussion of George's economic theories here because it is unlikely that Headlam was attracted to George by his very personal economics. Peter Jones speculates that one of the sources of George's appeal to the majority of his audience was that his approach was entirely consistent with their Victorian religiosity. Certainly George's rhetoric was as Christian and ethical, if not so Catholic, as Headlam's. In a farewell banquet for George in 1884, Headlam denounced private property in land because it was in "ethical opposition both to the Ten Commandments and to the teaching and life of Jesus Christ."[37] Christ, not abstract economic principle, was always Headlam's guide to the better society.

Ultimately, the fact that the Guild of St. Matthew adopted Henry George's program for the single tax is of far greater significance than their reasons for its adoption. The previous program of the Christian Socialists and slum ritualists had been based on the principle of individual, voluntary association. After 1884 the guild's program announced that the community of the whole nation through its political arm, the state, should set up laws that would bring about a new and just society. The guild had made a decisive break with the previous reform tradition, a fact that Headlam himself seems to have recognized.

> While showing all respect for cooperative shirtmakers and cooperative decorators, and for the many little communistic societies of monks and nuns, and for all other little private experiments, we at the same time call upon churchmen to take a wider view, and advocate and support such legislation as will help to remedy private evils.[38]

The central position given to Henry George's single tax program distinguishes the Guild of St. Matthew from all other Anglican social reform organizations, but it was not the only plank in their party platform. The historic 1884 resolution cited above went on to urge support for measures designed

1.  to bring about a better distribution of the wealth created by labour;
2.  to give the whole body of the people a voice in their own government;
3.  to abolish false standards of worth and dignity.[39]

Point two obviously recommends full political democracy, and points one and three advocate greater social and economic equality. The guild's resolution must have seemed very radical at that tine. In 1885 Headlam made these rather general proposals more specific when he urged guild members to ask their candidates for Parliament to support, in addition to some strictly Georgist proposals, "free education an eight hours bill, a bill shortening the hours in shops, an increase power for municipalities to undertake industrial work."[40] On another occasion he came out in full support of a progressive income tax. These proposals were specific and concrete, and they also show how thoroughly the guild's warden was willing to bring about social reform through the intervention of the state.

The ideological shift from a program of social reform through voluntary association to an advocacy of social reform by state intervention increased the importance of public propaganda. The guild's outlook was democratic; the members imagined that the social reform measures introduced by the state would reflect the will of the majority and they would have repudiated social reform by the dictatorship of the proletariat or any revolutionary elite.[41] Since only a majority of the community at large could effect the all-important social changes, it became extremely important to reach the community at large with the guild's message. In fact, most of the guild's time and energy seems to have been devoted to getting its message across. No specific, single device was adopted; rather a shotgun approach developed and each individual member did what he could.

The most ready weapon available to a group of literate, well-educated reformers, many of whom were clergymen, was the pen. Headlam himself was a prolific writer, as were many of his associates. In addition to those radical curates already mentioned, some of the more important of these associates were Henry Carey Shuttleworth, W. E. Moll, Charles Marson, Percy Dearmer, and Conrad Noel. H. C. Shuttleworth alone produced seven major works in book form.[42] Books were supplemented with a tremendous variety of other forms of written expression: hymns, innumerable pamphlets and broadsides, poems, and letters to the editors of important newspapers. A magazine, *The Church Reformer*, edited by Headlam with the unflagging assistance of Frederick Verinder, kept members of the guild informed about its activities, reported news items of social importance, and tried to convert the working class to its position. George Bernard Shaw, a Fabian friend, thought the *Reformer* "one of the best socialist journals of the day"; and John Ruskin wrote, "I have never yet looked through a paper I thought so right or likely to be so useful," but it always operated at a loss and had little influence on the working classes. Bettany wrote, "If it went into more than one hundred East End homes I should be surprised."[43]

For most nineteenth-century clergymen the voice was even mightier than the pen; preaching was their métier. Social Gospel sermons were an important method of communicating the guild's message. But with the exception of Henry Shuttleworth, who was rector of St. Nicholas Cole Abbey in the heart of the city of London, and Charles William Stubbs, who became dean of Ely in 1894, most of the guild's clerical members either served obscure parishes lost in the depths of the country or, like Headlam, had no parish at all. This lack of preferment had a fortunate result. Because guild clergy were denied access to the church's prominent pulpits, they were forced to carry their message out of the church and into the country at large. Numerous speaking tours were arranged, and since many guild members shared Headlam's skills at lecturing and debating, they attracted a following which, while small, extended throughout England. Several provincial branches were founded, the most important being those at Bristol and one at Oxford, the old center of clerical conservatism.

The guild received valuable publicity and also enlivened its own gatherings by inviting distinguished men from all walks of life, whether Christian or not, to join in its meetings and partake of the friendly, high-spirited, no-holds-barred debate. Guild meetings were rarely, if ever, dull.

Both Headlam and Frederick Verinder, who like Ludlow was an expert at handling day-to-day administrative work, had a genius for publicity and brought attention to the guild at every opportunity. Probably the most successful means of attracting attention to the guild and its message was the public demonstration. Soon after the organization entered its period of social agitation (October 1884), an open-air demonstration was held in Trafalgar Square for the express purpose of affirming the four-point program of single tax, more democracy, and greater economic and social equality. Public demonstrations were really an extension of the old radical curates' policy of causing rows at church conferences, only this time the rows attracted national attention and effectively demonstrated that the guild appealed to the country at large. Here again the guild broke new ground for Anglican social radicalism. The early Christian socialists had put up placards designed to cool off worker enthusiasm and get them out of protest demonstrations; the guild led demonstrations designed to heat up the atmosphere and stir things up.

The year 1885 opened with a demonstration of the unemployed held in the open air outside the Royal Exchange in bitter January weather. In 1886

Headlam officiated at the funeral of the first socialist martyr, Linnell, and led the long procession of the coffin, attended by William Morris and W. T. Stead, through London. The guild organized a series of meetings on Christian Socialism and many clerics were seen participating in unemployment marches often headed by Headlam. At a demonstration in 1886 Thomas Hill put the famous motion of 1884, and it was enthusiastically passed a second time. With continuing unemployment, more protests were organized in 1887, and once again the motion was passed, this time unanimously, by a crowd in Trafalgar Square. Pleading the necessity of maintaining order, the home secretary banned all meetings in Trafalgar Square and refused to meet with a deputation from the guild. Headlam was outraged by this denial of free speech, and he openly defied the home secretary's ban in November.[44] Conservatives in church and state alike were angered, and Headlam was subjected to public affronts and private abuse.[45] Despite the personal pain it cost him, Headlam had won. He was notorious, but he was known. Men might denounce the guild, but they could not deny its existence. Some index of the success of the gadfly's stings be found in the guild's increasing membership. By 1890 it had five times the number of its original members; by 1895 it had nearly doubled again.[46]

Yet even as membership figures climbed and national recognition was achieved, several ominous events occurred in the late eighties and early nineties almost as portents of the guild's dissension and decline after the Oscar Wilde trial in 1895. In 1889 Scott Holland, Charles Gore, J. R. Illingworth, and others organized the Christian Social Union, and the Oxford branch of the Guild of St. Matthew almost immediately went over to the less dogmatic, more comprehensive, less radical union. Many London guild members followed suit (Percy Dearmer became head of the London branch of the union), although they continued to maintain their guild memberships. The aims of the guild and union were not mutually exclusive, but the union was a rival organization and its very existence meant that in the future there would be two groups competing for the allegiance of Anglicans interested in social Christianity. The union's immediate attractiveness to guild members, combined with the guild's inability to attract dedicated social Christians like Gore, Holland, Illingworth, and their circle, was an accurate indication of the union's greater potential drawing power in the country at large.

Even more serious was the sign of deep disagreement within the guild itself. The first crisis occurred in 1891 when Headlam issued an election manifesto called "The Duty of the Clergy towards Board Schools and Elementary Education." London School Board elections were being held that year and

Headlam was a candidate for reelection. Strictly speaking the issue had nothing to do with stated guild policy, but the question of state education touched the deepest beliefs of guild members. Most Anglo-Catholics, and the guild was almost exclusively Anglo-Catholic, opposed the idea of secular, state education. They were even more emphatically opposed to the idea that the state should inspect schools run by the church. This Anglo-Catholic policy followed directly from the ecclesiological doctrine of the founders of the Oxford movement: namely, that the church was a sacred institution ordained by God and that the secular state had no right to interfere in its administration or to limit its independence. Anglo-Catholic stalwarts like Archdeacon Denison had seen state control over religious education as a life and death issue. Forty years before he had vowed that "he would never permit an emissary of Lord John Russell or any other Turkish Bashaw to enter his school,"[47] and in 1891 feelings on the matter still ran strong.

As he had done so many times before, Headlam swam against the stream, and when he swam he made waves. As mentioned, Headlam's lifelong interest in public education began when he was a curate in Drury Lane. Like many reformers since his day, Headlam believed that education offered the dispossessed an excellent opportunity to get beyond the squalid limitations of their existence. As such, education was a national problem too important to be left to religious denominations. Here social concerns proved more important than Anglo-Catholic attitudes, although his position on state schools was consistent with his religious opinion that the church should be disestablished.

The real cause for discord, however, was not the difference of opinion, deep as that was, but rather that Headlam did not differentiate between the statements he made as a private individual and those he made as warden and spokesman for the guild. In this case it seems Headlam tried to impose his views on the guild, and many of the guild's old stalwarts, chief among them Shuttleworth, felt bound by conscience to oppose him. At the annual meeting held in September 1891, the guild adopted the manifesto, but not without a sharp fight. After the meeting Shuttleworth published a minority report which many guild members signed.[48] In time the disagreement was smoothed over, but the basic problem had not been resolved. Headlam and the guild had become so closely identified that it was virtually impossible to tell them apart. When Headlam spoke, nearly everyone (perhaps including Headlam himself) assumed that he spoke for the guild. When the same problem came up four years later, it virtually destroyed the guild's ability to function as an effective organization.

The Oscar Wilde case destroyed the Guild of St. Matthew; it limped along for another fifteen years of official life but never recovered from the events of 1895. Its influence waned and new organizations, the Christian Social Union and after 1906 the Church Socialist League, moved into the front lines of the battle for Christian social reform. Deep personal loyalties kept the guild officially alive, but the vitality and zest were gone. Even Headlam neglected the guild and turned his attention more and more to educational matters.

The Wilde trial revealed late-Victorian society at its very worst. From beginning to end it was a sordid affair, and Headlam's conduct at the time is one of the very few decent aspects of the whole business. After the collapse of his libel suit against the Marquess of Queensbury, Wilde was arrested on a charge of committing "acts of gross indecency." When his first trial resulted in a hung jury the judge was forced to grant bail, which he set at the exorbitant amount of five thousand pounds. Until bail was met Wilde remained in jail. Bail was extremely difficult to raise; the scandal had ruined Wilde financially. At the demand of his creditors, his house and all his possessions had been auctioned off at absurdly low rates. The few friends who stood by him could not raise the money on their own. Finally after a month in jail Wilde was released. His bail had been met by Lord Douglas of Harwick, Queensbury's heir, and Stewart Headlam. Each man had paid half.[49]

Headlam's was a totally disinterested act and it expresses his whole way of life. He admired Wilde as an artist[50] but he did not know the man personally. This is the explanation Headlam printed in *The Church Reformer*:

> I became bail for Mr. Oscar Wilde on public grounds. I felt that the action of a large section of the Press, of the theatrical managers, . . . and of his publishers, was calculated to prejudice his last case before his trial had even begun. I was a surety, not for his character, but for his appearance in court to stand his trial.[51]

Headlam was brought into the Wilde case by his friend Selwyn Image, the Slade professor of fine arts at Oxford. Image had been asked to give assistance, but he did not have the money and so passed the case on to Headlam with the warning that if he did go bail everyone would say that he did it for the sake of publicity.[52] Image's caveat made Headlam hesitate, but after he spent a day pondering the situation he decided to go ahead, even though he knew the probable consequences. "I knew quite well," Headlam wrote in an unfinished autobiography, "that this action of mine would with many people damage my already damaged reputation and that it would sadly try some of my best friends whom I had already tried a great deal."[53]

Headlam's courageous action did more than damage his reputation: the press denounced him, a mob milled about his house threatening to break the windows, a housemaid left his service, and two Liberal journalists, Sir Henry Norman and W. H. Massingham, broke off their friendship.[54] Despite this persecution Headlam called on Wilde every morning and courteously escorted him to the Old Bailey; in the evening he took him through the jeering mobs and saw him home to the house of Ernest and Ada Leverson. When Wilde was released from prison on 19 May 1897, Headlam and More Adey, one of Wilde's most faithful friends, were waiting for him in a brougham. They drove immediately to Headlam's home where Wilde remained six hours meeting friends and trying to find somewhere to go.[55]

Headlam knew he would embarrass his friends, but it is doubtful that he could have anticipated the effect that his action would have on the guild of St. Matthew. After all, the guild had stood with him many times before when he had championed equally unpopular causes. But the Wilde case had generated what Sir Compton Mackenzie described as "prevailing hysteria,"[56] and guild ranks did not hold firm. Canon J. G. Adderly, an old friend and an otherwise courageous and convinced Christian Socialist, submitted an immediate resignation.[57] Shuttleworth gave up the presidency of the reconstituted Oxford branch at this time, and twelve less famous members left the guild.

The greatest harm, however, was done not by those who left, but by one who stayed in the guild, Charles Marson. Mackenzie writes, "How a man of culture, wit and charm could behave with such mobster vulgarity is a mystery."[58] Marson was a master of invective and he turned it on the Warden, sneering at his "chivalrously rushing into police court to bail out Jane Cakebread or some other notorious criminal." The high point of Marson's tastelessness was reached when he parodied the motto of *The Church Reformer* and exclaimed grimly that he was all for building a new Jerusalem on earth, but not for "wading through a Gomorrah first."[59]

Marson tried to raise feeling against Headlam, who had been a personal friend, before a London School Board election meeting, and he carried on the fight at the guild's annual meeting in 1895. The crowd was even larger than the one that had gathered during the crisis of 1891. Four months had passed since Wilde had been sentenced and Marson's language had cooled considerably. He spoke no invective at the guild meeting, but his opposition to Headlam remained strong.

After Headlam's address, Marson moved a change in the by-laws: "That Rule 15, so far as it relates to the Warden, shall be amended by the insertion of the words 'who shall be ineligible for more than one year at a time.' "[60] Since Headlam had been warden continuously since the guild was established in 1877, the motion was obviously directed against him. Had it passed Headlam would have been forced to retire at the end of the year.

Marson's address in support of his motion helps explain the mystery that Mackenzie saw behind his "mobster vulgarity." In Marson's defense it must be emphasized that Wilde was probably the only man he ever kicked when he was down. Usually Marson was the first to assist a man to his feet, and even here Wilde was not the direct object of Marson's wrath.[61]

Marson spoke admiringly but ironically of Headlam's achievements: he had taught the guild to "look for Christian coincidences in movements that do not suspect themselves to be Christian, for example Theatrical Dancing"; and he "had taught them to look for the gold of Christian socialism in the heaps of quartz and rubble called the Liberal Party." This good-natured ragging was very much in the spirit of guild addresses, but the tone turned serious when Marson spoke of sexual morality. "They wanted a Warden who would make a strong, immediate, and persistent protest on the subject . . . , who would make it very clear that the Guild rejected doctrines subversive of Christian marriage." Above all, and here Marson got to the root of the problem (the old problem of 1891), the guild should be independent of Headlam's private activities: "It should be made clear *that the members of the Guild are not 'Headlamites' but Christian Socialists.*"[62] Not that Marson loved Headlam less, but that he loved the guild more. Seen in this light, Marson's behavior, if not his vulgar rhetoric, is understandable.

Once again most members remained loyal to Headlam; Marson's motion won only seven votes (only members of the executive council voted) and was defeated ignominiously. The vote was a resounding personal victory for Headlam, who took it as a vote of confidence on his behavior during the Wilde trial.[63] This second crisis, though, was a great defeat for the guild. The Shuttleworth resignation and the Marson attack represented the alienation of the two most important provincial branches; the Bristol branch had supported Marson to a man. The events of the last six months had exhausted Headlam and the animosity dispirited him. He was nearly fifty and he had neither the energy nor the money to fight the good fight on so many fronts as before. In

December 1895 *The Church Reformer* suspended publication, and the guild lost its official organ. Headlam complained that the paper did not support itself; he personally had put £1200 into it over the years, losing about £110 a year. "There is a limit to the amount which one individual can be expected to spend on the education of the Church," he wrote.[64] Perhaps a new campaign might have served to reunite and reinvigorate the guild after the crisis of the Wilde trial. No one can tell, because there were no new campaigns. If one had come, the warden could have been the only man to initiate it, but the warden was tired and retrenching his forces.

Moreover, Headlam's ideological position had become set, and increasingly during the next decade his continuing advocacy of the single tax and his close association with the left wing of the Liberal Party appeared outdated to younger avant-garde Anglican radicals. Conrad Noel, one of the younger firebrands whose socialism was redder than Headlam's, wrote of the guild in its later days: "The weakness of the Guild was that beyond a general support of the working class movement it confined itself to land reform, and was dominated by the teachings of Henry George."[65] Noel's comment is not altogether just, but it does reflect the attitude of the younger men who carried on the struggle for social reform. When the guild could no longer appeal to the younger generation, its useful life was at an end.

The disintegration of the Guild of St. Matthew following the Wilde trial presents a disheartening spectacle, for one cannot escape the conclusion that the guild destroyed itself. Furthermore, the same qualities—concern for the underdog and a sense of social justice—that gave the guild its life, helped bring it to destruction.

But we must not allow the melancholy circumstances surrounding the guild's dissolution to obscure the significance of nearly twenty years of vital life. The guild's gadfly stings did help awaken the church; its activities did demonstrate that some churchmen were concerned about the fate of the workingman; and its theology presented a worldview that integrated religious and social concerns. The Guild of St. Matthew inaugurated the era of the Social Gospel in the Church of England, and despite many vicissitudes that era is not ended yet.

## Scott Holland, Charles Gore, and the Christian Social Union

Stewart Headlam and his associates in the Guild of St. Matthew were the pioneers of the Social Gospel movement; they were the hardy souls who blazed new trails both in social theology and in social action. The Christian Social Union explored no virgin territory; instead it settled the new lands opened up by the guild, cultivated them, and made them blossom and bear fruit. The guild had a genius for innovation; the work of the union was consolidation. Historically the guild had greater dramatic impact, but ultimately the union made a deeper impression on the life of the church. The leaders of the union possessed a high social and intellectual standing, and their great prestige gave them a secure place in the corridors of power. Between 1889 and 1913, sixteen out of fifty-three episcopal appointments were given to members of the union.[66] Wilfred Knox and Alex Vidler caught the essential spirit of the union when they wrote: "They were neither flamboyant Ritualists nor extreme Socialists of the type of Stewart Headlam; but they were Christian Socialists as well as Catholics, deeply influenced by the teachings of Westcott and Maurice, and thoroughly alive to the social and political no less than to the intellectual needs of the age."[67]

The Christian Social Union was organized in 1889, the year when labor, aided by Cardinal Manning, won the London dock strike, the year when English evolutionary socialism was given classic formulation in the *Fabian Essays*.[68] Like the Guild of St. Matthew, it had three basic precepts:

1. To claim for the Christian Law the ultimate authority to rule social practice.
2. To study in common how to apply the moral truths and principles of Christianity to the social and economic difficulties of the present time.
3. To present Christ in practical life as the Living Master and King, the enemy of wrong and selfishness, the power of righteousness and love.[69]

Members were explicitly directed to remember the union at Holy Communion, especially on the Feasts of the Epiphany, Ascension, and St. Michael and All Angels. These days possessed a symbolic significance associated respectively with Our Lord's manifestation to the Gentiles (and hence to all men), His heavenly rule of all creation at the right hand of the Father (there was at the time no Anglican Feast of Christ the King), and with St. Michael's role as protector of the church militant in her struggle with the demonic forces of evil and spiritual darkness. As one might expect from the preceding injunction, membership was limited to Anglicans. As Scott Holland explained in a letter, "the difficulty of course is not your excellent Nonconformist, but your fervid socialistic Nothingarian. So we thought it right, without a positive exclusive rule, to say that we were men who had a bond of union in the Sacrament of Christ's Body."[70] Bishop Gore, continuing in the line of Holland's thought, wrote: "Only Church people could awaken the Church. Only Church people sharing the same Sacramental system could awaken their fellows to the real social meaning of their baptism, their confirmation and their Holy Communion."[71] These statements suggest that at its inception the union took a step backward from the guild's courageous policy of proclaiming the necessity of social transformation to the nation and reverted to that part of the Christian Socialist program of the 1850s which called for "socializing Christianity."

But this step backward in social policy was countered by a step forward in Anglican unity. The union was never so narrowly Anglo-Catholic in the party senses the Guild of St. Matthew; the union welcomed churchmen of all persuasions, High, Broad, and Low. There is no indication that many fervent Evangelicals took part in the union's activities, but the first elected president of the union was B. F. Westcott, a noted Broad Church theologian and biblical scholar who was a canon of Westminster and regius professor of divinity at Cambridge. The guild's two leading luminaries, Scott Holland, a canon of St. Paul's, and Charles Gore, principal of Pusey House at Oxford, were both strong High Churchmen, but neither was an extremist. If both were friends of Canon Liddon, each reflected something of the comprehensive moderation of Dean Church of St. Paul's. There is much truth in Maurice Reckitt's description of the Christian Social Union as "the last-born child of Tractarianism,"[72] but we should also remember S. C. Carpenter's comments about *Lux Mundi*, a collection of theological essays published by Gore, Holland, and others during the same year that they founded the Union: "it represented the union of two streams, that which came through Church from Newman, and that which came from Coleridge and Maurice through Westcott and Hart."[73]

As an organization the union grew out of the work already realized by the guild; guild members were among the first adherents of the union. I have already mentioned how the Oxford branch of the guild reconstituted itself as a part of the union. The London branch of the guild did not vote itself out of existence, but many members also joined the union—Shuttleworth, Moll, Dearmer, and Adderly, to mention only the most famous. The memberships were so intertwined that Peter Jones flatly states, "The London branch of the C.S.U. . . . was barely distinguishable from the G.S.M."[74]

In an article written in the twenties, Bishop Gore frankly admitted that the union "was not new" and generously acknowledged the union's debt to the guild. "But, while we felt very grateful to it, it did not in some ways suit our purposes."[75]

Although the guild was an inspiration for the union and furnished many of its earliest active members, it would be a serious oversimplification to assert that the union was a child of the guild. The roots of the union go back to Oxford in the middle seventies some years before the guild was formed; and the union could rightly claim an independent lineage.

The Christian Social Union, like *Lux Mundi* and the Community of the Resurrection, grew out of what was known familiarly as "The Holy Party" formed at Brightstone on the Isle of Wight during the summer of 1875.[76] The central members of the Holy Party were Scott Holland, Charles Gore, J. R. Illingworth, and Edward Stuart Talbot; all were Oxford men in holy orders (Talbot, the senior member, was warden of Keble College) who wanted to get together during the long vacation at a country parish where they would assume the parochial duties and devote free time to reading and discussion. These summer reading parties met with remarkable regularity for the next forty years (from 1890 to 1915 the parties were held in Longworth, Berkshire, where Dr. Illingworth was rector) and this small group of friends, who were on occasion joined by others, had ample opportunity to consider the problems facing the church. "*Lux Mundi* . . . was to arm the Church to meet the mental challenge of the day. The Christian Social Union was the response . . . to the social challenge."[77]

Both Scott Holland, whose attractive personality provided a nucleus for the Holy Party and the Christian Social Union, and Charles Gore, who was to become the chief theologian of the group, had long been concerned about social and intellectual problems. The two had been friends from youth, when they lived near each other at Wimbledon.[78]

Gore entered Harrow in 1866, the appropriate school for a scion of the Whig aristocracy, where he was an excellent student and avid debater, intensely interested in the subject of politics. At an early age he displayed his characteristic political radicalism by arguing for the "abolition of University Tests, asserted that a Hereditary Legislative Body was a mistake, and upheld that a Republic was the best form of government."[79] At Harrow Gore came under the influence of Brooke Foss Westcott, then a shy and retiring young master.[80] Dr. Prestige says that Westcott opened Gore's mind to "the moral value of exact scholarship; the insight to be gained from a religious study of history; the spiritual glories of simple living; love of the poor."[81] Westcott, even in his days as president of the union, was never a social radical, but his personal asceticism was deeply bound up with a genuine concern for the unfortunate. In later life he gave up the modest use of wine, lest his drinking tempt another and lead him to ruin.[82] Gore's asceticism, strong as it was, never went quite that far, perhaps because he also came under the influence of the non-Puritanical, if ascetic, Father Stanton of St. Alban's, who taught him to "make his confession, to love the Mass, and to fast on Fridays." Gore developed an abiding affection for the ceremonialism he observed at St. Alban's and at other "advanced churches." Giving evidence before the Royal Commission on church discipline in 1905, he said: "I love as I hardly love anything in the world physically, except the beauties of nature, that type of ceremonial worship which is called ritualistic by many people, and Catholic by its maintainers."[83] St. Alban's was of course more than a hot bed of ritualism; it was a center of ecclesiastical radicalism and a rallying point for community social reform. Stanton's affection for the poor was as deep as Westcott's—and he knew them from firsthand experience—so his influence can only have heightened the young Gore's social awareness.

In 1870, Gore went up to Oxford on a Balliol scholarship and he continued his brilliant academic career. In 1872 he took a first class in Classical Moderations and in his final schools three years later he gained a first class in Greats. Not long after he sat for and won a fellowship at Trinity College. As an undergraduate Gore immersed himself in the fathers, particularly St. Athanasius, but he also read the theology of F. D. Maurice and the neo-Hegelian philosophy of T. H. Green.[84] Green's influence dominated Oxford during the years Gore studied there. Scott Holland, who felt it more strongly than Gore, described its liberating influence: "He broke us from the sway of individualistic sensationalism. He released us from the fear of agnostic mechanism. He gave us back the language of self sacrifice, and taught us how we belonged to one another in the one life of high idealism."[85]

It is doubtful that Gore was ever held in thrall by either "individualistic sensationalism" or "agnostic mechanism" and certainly Stanton and Westcott had given Gore "the language" as well as the practice of "self sacrifice"; but James Carpenter, Gore's most lucid and comprehensive recent interpreter, asserts that "in certain epistemological and sociological emphases Green's influence was profound." Also, thinks Carpenter, Green "first implanted in his mind a belief that ethical idealism was a cardinal ally of faith."[86] Nonetheless, Gore cannot really be considered a full disciple of Green as Holland and even more so Illingworth were. As A. M. Ramsey points out, Gore "shared only a very little in . . . the tendency to link the Christian faith rather naively with Hegelian philosophy. . . . The Bible was the pasture ground of his mind; and with its themes of judgment and catastrophe, of a God who punishes, chastens and raises from death."[87] It is not merely coincidental that Gore was appointed first principal of Pusey House in 1883; his outlook was less rigid than that of the Tractarians, but among other things, he never abandoned their prophetic pessimism about the human condition or human nature. Gore became a social reformer because he despised injustice and oppression; again and again in his works he warned that if they were permitted to continue they would bring "judgment." His social conscience was the result of a deep sense of Christian responsibility; it did not grow out of any facile optimism about the possibility of a speedy renewal of the social order. "Though he was convinced that Christian influence properly directed, could remove mountainous social abuses, he never assumed that anything like a thoroughly Christianized society could be reached."[88] Understood in the background of his view of man, Gore's long and active career as a social reformer is all the more remarkable.

Henry Scott Holland provided a counterbalance to Gore's ascetic, prophetic pessimism. His was a genial, affectionate nature that never completely lost its boyish high spirits and sense of fun. Family and friends, colleagues and students—all found him endearing. Who but Scott Holland would ever call the aristocratic, reserved Bishop Gore, "old dear"?

Holland's family did not have the aristocratic lineage of the Gores, but they had such "sufficient means" that George Henry Holland, Scott's father, was "independent of any business or profession." The elder Holland was something of a recluse who spent his life traveling, hunting, and driving a four-in-hand.[89] He sent his son to Eton, where Scott and Stewart Headlam were contemporaries. Significantly, although both men were devoted old Etonians, they never became friends then or later in life.[90] Holland displayed none of Gore's intellectual precocity; in fact, were he alive today, he probably would be labeled an underachiever. On more than one occasion his family considered taking him out of school and finding him a place in business or at the Foreign Office! But he was an excellent, if unconventional, athlete and his personality gained him the deep affection of a wide circle of friends, both among his fellow students and the masters. William Johnson, Stewart Headlam's mentor, was Holland's tutor, and although he was quite fond of Holland, Paget makes no reference to Johnson's ever introducing Holland to the works of Maurice and Kingsley.[91] Perhaps the tutor did not think his student would be interested.

After Holland left Eton, he spent some time with a private tutor preparing for the Balliol entrance examination. It was a difficult examination and when he tried it in October 1865, he failed so badly that the master advised him not to try again. But the failure did something to Holland, and when he tried again in January, he came in first, much to the astonishment and pleasure of all concerned. After this brief burst of intellectual energy, he settled into Balliol where there were old Eton friends, sports, and no particular inspiration to work hard. Paget calls these two years "a time of uneventful waiting,"[92] and Holland gained only a third class in moderations.

Three years later, in 1870, the perennial underachiever took a first class in Literae Humaniores and "was reported to have done the most brilliant set of papers that had been seen in the Schools for some time."[93] To round off the success of his undergraduate career, he was elected to a five-year senior studentship at Christ Church.

After an at best mediocre intellectual record as a youth—broken only by his first the second time around on his Balliol examination—Scott Holland had at last come into his own. Such late bloomings are always difficult to explain, but in Holland's case one must give primary credit to the influence of T. H. Green. After his triumph, Holland wrote to Green, "The real anxiety of the Schools was the dread of disappointing you. . . . For you have taught me everything of importance that I have learnt at Oxford. . . . And if I am grateful for the teaching, I am far more grateful for the great kindness you have shown me the last three years."[94]

Scott Holland was an affectionate, high-minded young man who had never felt the need for intellectual achievement. Why should he? He had money and family; his athletic skills won him admiration and popularity; and his personality attracted devoted friends. Then he fell under the influence of the remarkable T. H. Green, who appealed to Holland's affection and high-mindedness and directed their essential energy to the development of the life of the mind. In a very real sense Green brought Holland together as a whole man, uniting intellectual powers with the positive forces of his personality. Green and Holland had a Platonic relationship in the best and deepest sense, for their mutual personal affection derived from and contributed to the pursuit of the good, the true, and the beautiful.

Green also made more specific contributions to the development of Holland's thought. Like Gore's, Holland's epistemology was basically idealistic, very definitely antimaterialistic, although he won his Balliol first on the basis of his explanation of the tenets of the classic English utilitarian philosophers.[95] More important from the standpoint of his later career, Green awakened Holland's interest in social questions. Holland prepared a tutorial paper for Green, "Culture and the International," which Green admired but did not totally agree with. He commended Holland's interest in the "suffering classes" and half seriously predicted that when he began working among them he would "despise my life."[96] Green's letter indicates that even as an undergraduate Holland planned to combine intellectual pursuits with positive social action.

Perhaps most important for the development of the Anglican reform movement and social thought, Holland accepted Green's doctrine of the positive state. He was not afraid of passing laws to remedy social abuses: "the higher the spirit of citizenship, or the feeling for the commonwealth, in any community," he thought, "the more and the more elaborate were the laws in which it would rejoice—spirit and law corresponding to soul and body."[97] Holland wanted to Christianize the state because it was the major tool for social change. "We must have all we can get of State order, of State machinery," he wrote in the *Progressive Review*.[98] Holland's advocacy of the positive state was extremely important because he had the ability to influence the union to adopt his positions. Bishop Westcott would have never dreamed of anything as specific as passing laws, and radicals like Dearmer could never have won over the more traditional, conservative members. The guild had first championed the idea of the positive state, but the more influential and respectable union was the means by which the idea entered the mainstream of progressive Anglican social thought.

The decades preceding the First World War were full of significant social legislation enacted by the Liberal government. The union's activities were significant in preparing public opinion, especially in the church, most particularly among the hierarchy, to accept the changes brought about by the legislation. If its role in securing the legislation was not decisive, at the very least the union kept the church abreast of contemporary events.

Great as Green's influence on Holland was, though, it had its limits. Holland owed an enormous amount to Green, but he was always his own man. Their most serious difference was on the subject of religion. Green was a philosopher, not a theologian. The neo-Hegelian Green appreciated the church as a transmitter of world historical ideas (the church has a "higher and truer Gospel for the individual . . . in virtue of the ideas which it retains from the New Testaments"), but he believed that it rested "on doctrines that seem untrue." He certainly had no concept of the church as the body of Christ. The "High Church revival," he felt, "was due to the . . . disease of modern life."[99]

Holland was a sound churchman, and a High Churchman like his father. Writing in his early years at Oxford to his brother to prepare him for his confirmation and first Holy Communion, he expressed opinions on the real presence and apostolic succession that could have come from the pen of Archdeacon Denison:

> It is the body and blood of your Saviour which are given to you, the same which really hung on the cross, given spiritually. . . . It is given in the bread.
> . . . the body which walked the earth and died on Calvary is there, in the bread, mysteriously, ineffably, but most certainly. No religion which doubted those words had ever influenced mankind to purity and humility. . . . The Bishop stands before you as Jesus Christ on earth; he received the full stream of the Holy Spirit from Bethlehem; St. Peter's hand, our Lord's hand have touched that head and consecrated those hands.[100]

Green's teachings helped make that young Tractarian stalwart into a contributor to *Lux Mundi*, but the "professed heretic" (Green's own term) didn't undermine Holland's Catholic faith, nor did he attempt to dissuade him from becoming a priest. When it became certain that Holland would get priested, Green wrote an affectionate letter of encouragement, giving his approval: "nor am I so weak as to desire that you should sail in my boat."[101] Holland spent a summer studying to take orders, and it is interesting to note that Green's High Church student went for study neither to Liddon nor to Pusey, who were there at Oxford, but to Westcott, who was not. After his ordination to the diaconate he wrote his mentor, "I owe as much as ever to you."[102]

Holland began his work as a social reformer even before he was ordained to the priesthood. In 1872 during the last two weeks in Lent, he inaugurated a series of evening addresses at St. Savior's, Hoxton. In these services he and others attempted to refute "current objections against religion"; but his real purpose was to introduce young Oxford dons to "what was really happening in London slums" and have them "touch the new spirit of irregulated democracy."[103] The services failed to attract many outsiders, but Holland continued the project.

Holland stayed on as a teacher and administrator at Oxford for the next thirteen years and throughout this period he attempted to break down the ivory-tower isolation of both students and faculty by confronting them with the social realities of the age. He planned an attack on the Society for the Promotion of Christian Knowledge (S.P.C.K.) "for its one sided Political Economy publications—condemning so strongly all Trade Unions, and giving nothing but the master's view";[104] and he was instrumental in setting up the Christ Church Mission in the slum of Poplar. In 1879, several years before the guild was established at Oxford, he and Wilfred Richmond, another member of the Holy Party, founded PESEK, a discussion group that considered questions relating to "politics, economics, socialism, ethics, and Christianity." Although PESEK was only a discussion group, it was a unique organization and it "helped to prepare the way for the Christian Social Union.[105]

Meanwhile, Charles Gore had reached "the turning point in his life." He and Joseph Arch had toured the villages of Oxfordshire and the misery of the population convinced Gore that society was based on selfishness and the unrestricted love of wealth. The strict young moralist became convinced that the system was "rotten" to the core and could make no pretence of being Christian.[106] He looked for a decent alternative to competitive capitalism and, like Holland, found it in the cooperative movement.[107] The cooperative principle was ethical and it carried the blessing of the Christian Socialists of the fifties but it never seriously challenged capitalism as a means of production or distribution. Gore was too realistic not to recognize the limitations of the cooperative movement, and though he lent it his support, his own social awareness led him to look for a wider context of expression. Soon after he was appointed principal of Pusey House, he invited Stewart Headlam, then at the height of his notoriety, to address the Oxford undergraduates, much to the consternation of old-line Tractarians who were unaware of the social implications of the Oxford movement.[108] But, as has been mentioned, Headlam and the guild "did not suit [his] purposes," and he remained aloof and apocalyptic. Something of Gore's profound alienation from the acquisitive ethos of the society of his time can be detected in his response to the news of the Bloody Sunday labor demonstrations of 1887. "It's a pity they didn't loot the West End," he exclaimed at a luncheon at Pusey House.[109] That response reflects the momentary excessive radicalism of the helpless perceiver of events, and does not represent the true spirit of Gore's positive aspirations for a society based on Christian principles. Gore often made violent statements, but he never championed the cause of violent revolution.

In 1884 the prime minister, William Gladstone, appointed Holland a canon of St. Paul's Cathedral in London. Writing to Mrs. T. H. Green to inform her of the honor, Holland invoked the spirit of her late husband and announced that he had accepted the position because it would "take me nearer to the work that he would hold dear, among the working men of that great city. I pray to God that I may always carry to such work the hope and the spirit that I learned from him."[110] At St. Paul's Holland continued the work of awakening the church to social problems that he had begun at Oxford. The climate of opinion in the metropolis filled him with dismay. In 1888 he wrote Wilfred Richmond, his friend from PESEK days: "We live in economic blindness down here of the bleakest kind. The world seems to have reacted into the mind of 40 years ago. You would think that it had never talked democratic language. We are in a mad backwater, eddying furiously."[111]

Holland was writing to a sympathetic audience; his friend Richmond had just brought out *Christian Economics*, a collection of sixteen sermons designed "to enforce the principle that economic conduct is a matter of duty." Richmond rejected the classical school of economics and appealed instead to the authority of Arnold Toynbee and John Ruskin. Like them, he tried to make "Political Economy . . . a branch of morals" where justice and love would be the "Law of Exchange" and the "Law of Distribution." "The law of saintliness," Richmond wrote, "says at least subordinate competition to co-operation."[112]

Richmond's book appealed strongly to Holland and he attempted to dispel the "economic blackness" by getting Richmond to promote his opinions. Accordingly, during Lent in 1889, Richmond gave four lectures at Sion College on "Economic Morals." The lectures were well attended and attracted much attention in the press. Richmond was too cautious to advocate the nationalization of the means of distribution and production, but his bias was genuinely socialist. The lectures started many churchmen thinking; and as Peter Jones remarks "Scott Holland turned them into a movement: the C.S.U."[113]

Certainly the positions taken by Richmond in his lectures and in *Christian Economics* were far more advanced and concrete than the social teachings enunciated that year by other union spokesmen in *Lux Mundi*. Gore and Holland did not even treat the social question in their essays; Holland wrote on "Faith" and Gore on "The Holy Spirit and Inspiration." Perhaps the clearest statement of the social principles of *Lux Mundi* is found in some conclusions expressed by W. H. Champion in his essay, "Christianity and Politics":

> Christianity is certainly not pledged to uphold any particular form of property as such. Whether property had better be held by individuals or by small groups . . . or again by the State, as is the proposal of Socialists, is a matter for experience and common sense to decide. But where Christian ethics steps in is, firstly, to show that property is secondary, not primary, a means not an end.

The moral regeneration of society, he goes on, comes about through a "change of heart and the will," not by "mechanical alteration of distribution of the products of industry or of the mode of holding property. On the other hand it cannot be too often asserted that the accumulation of riches is not in itself a good at all." Christianity asserts that if there is private property, that property is a trust and "its attendant duties [must be] performed." Champion then holds up as "object lesson" the examples of monastic communities with their vow of voluntary poverty and the early church in Jerusalem, "in which those who had property sold it, and brought the proceeds and laid them at the Apostles' feet and distribution was made unto every man according to his needs."[114]

Champion's position could hardly be more moderate. Even the most conservative Evangelical would not take exception to his statement that social regeneration is the result of a change of hearts, not social systems, although one can imagine that same conservative upset to read that Christianity is not committed to the preservation of private properly. To be sure Champion rejects any gospel of wealth, but his nostalgic admiration for monastic poverty and apostolic communism hardly takes us beyond the positions held by Hurrell Froude and John Henry Newman in the 1830s. *Lux Mundi* became a controversial book, but it was theological radicalism, not social radicalism that gave offense.

Gore's essay, "Holy Spirit and Inspiration," caused most of the row. He argued that while the New Testament was "final and Catholic," the Old was "imperfect because it represented a gradual process of education by which man was lifted out of sin and ignorance." The point was simply that revelation came in and through the historical process, hardly a heterodox opinion. But Gore's attitude toward Daniel and Jonah raised problems. Gore thought they were dramatic, not historical, works. What then can be said about Christ's references to Jonah and to Psalm 110? Jesus thought David wrote the psalm

81

and that Jonah was swallowed by a great fish; does that not by definition make it true? Gore thought not. The clue to the problem could be found in the kenosis doctrine of the Incarnation. Kenosis means "self-emptying" and was used by Gore to safeguard the full doctrine of the Incarnation, namely that Christ was both very God and very man. Certainly it is obvious that the incarnate Lord was not omnipresent and that Jesus of Nazareth was not omnipotent. In the Incarnation God had emptied himself of these attributes. What about omniscience? Gore's argument here is quite subtle; his solution to the problem was to draw a distinction between (1) the revelation Christ gave of the mind, nature and character of God, the meaning of life, the divine purpose of redemption and (2) other matters that are merely matters of human information. As true God, Christ knew the former; as true man, he could be in error about the latter. The gospel tells us our Lord "increased in wisdom and stature"; does that not mean a self-assumed limitation of ordinary knowledge?

> He made His Godhead gradually manifest by His attitude towards men and things about Him, by His moral and spiritual claims, by His expressed relation to His Father, not by any miraculous exemptions of Himself from the conditions of natural knowledge in its own proper province. Thus the utterances of Christ about the Old Testament do not seem to be nearly definite or clear enough to allow of our supposing that in this case He is departing from the general method of the Incarnation, by bringing to bear the unveiled omniscience of the Godhead, to anticipate or foreclose a development of natural knowledge.[115]

Gore's conclusions disturbed many theological conservatives. Canon Liddon was particularly upset because he had been instrumental in getting Gore the position of principal at Pusey House; he had expected Gore to uphold the pure Tractarian faith, and the *Lux Mundi* article convinced him that Gore was letting down the barriers to intellectual disbelief. The book became a succès de scandale and went through ten editions in one year. Prestige tells us, "Old ladies spoke of Gore as that awful Mr. Gore who doesn't believe the Bible."[116] So great was the furor over Jesus' interpretations of Jonah that almost everyone failed to recognize Gore's patristic interpretation of the nature of the activity of the Holy Spirit. The spirit, he wrote, nourishes individuality, but also in its life-giving work "treats man as a social being who cannot realize himself in isolation."[117] This doctrine was, of course, full of vital implications for social reform.

*Lux Mundi* occupies an important place in the history of nineteenth century British theology; it brought Tractarian teaching up to date by abandoning the fortress mentality of the Liddon school and accepting the insights offered by history and biblical criticism. In adapting Tractarianism to the mental attitudes of Westcott and Maurice, the *Lux Mundi* writers created a liberal Catholic theology. In the future the Anglo-Catholic tradition could not be equated with theological conservatism.

In social theology, though, the *Lux Mundi* school did not advance significantly beyond the work of Headlam, Hancock, and other guild writers; the general social implications of *Lux Mundi* incarnational theology were very much like the guild's. Both groups agreed that the fact of the Incarnation abolished dualistic distinctions between spirit and matter and committed the Christian Church to the improvement of man's life in this world. They disagreed about the details of how man's life could be improved, but they recognized the same social obligation as Christians.

If Gore, Holland, and their circle offered nothing essentially new in social theology, their works made the subject intellectually respectable. Headlam was not really a theologian; Gore was probably the most important Anglican theologian since Maurice and he could not be dismissed as an eccentric crank. Bishop Gore was taken seriously even by his opponents. Without the work of Holland and Gore, Headlam's union of the High and Broad Church schools might have been forgotten. The *Lux Mundi*-Christian Social Union group established incarnational theology with its explicit social concerns as the major innovative religious movement of the day.

The social program of the union was hardly more radical than its social theology. The union was organized "to study in common how to apply the moral truths and principles of Christianity to the social and economic difficulties of the present time"[118] and especially during its early years it was principally concerned with studying and publicizing social and economic problems. It never proclaimed any platform as the guild had done in 1884. A defining platform would have narrowed the membership and the founders wanted the union to be as comprehensive as possible. It was decided, Bishop Gore tells us,

> that the Christian Social Union should be a union of Church people . . . who were agreed upon the necessity of awakening the Church to the social implications of its Creed and Bible and Sacraments and were agreed further upon the need of fundamental social reconstruction . . . whether they called

themselves Conservatives or Liberals or Radicals, whether they accepted or refused the name of Socialist.[119]

The union's message was a call to repentance. "For the first time in all history, the poor old Church is trying to show the personal sin of corporate and social sinning,"[120] wrote Scott Holland. To publicize this message the union adopted a wide variety of propagandistic methods that included lectures and sermons, group discussions, the issue of numerous leaflets and special studies, and the publication of three journals. First came the scholarly *Economic Review*, published at Oxford between 1891 and 1914; it was a serious quarterly whose main purpose was to encourage Christian discussion of economic moralists. In 1894 James Adderly launched *Goodwill*, a more popular paper designed to be sold with parish magazines. *Goodwill* had no official connection with the union but Scott Holland helped with the editing, and many of its leading contributors were union members. Some of its articles were based on union pamphlets, and its editorial notes advertised the union's activities. Within two years Adderly was able to claim a circulation of twenty-eight thousand.[121] Part of this popularity, no doubt, was due to the fact that the editor was the author of *Stephen Remarx*, a novel about a socially conscious clergyman which enjoyed a tremendous vogue during the middle nineties. The success of *Goodwill* convinced Holland that the union should sponsor a more popular publication, and in 1896 he began to publish *Commonwealth*, a monthly magazine dealing with social questions at large. Holland was an excellent editor and his magazine outlived both him and the Christian Social Union.

Much of the union's energy went into education and the attempt to convert the church to social reform, but it also became involved in specific attempts to initiate practical reform. Its first venture can be described only as a noble failure. Holland, Adderly, and other members of the London branch of the union recognized the significance of the London dock strike and tried their best to get the church to alleviate the suffering of the strikers' families and to give support to the workers. Bishop Temple of London (father of William Temple, the great social reformer who became archbishop of Canterbury in the 1940s) was on vacation in Wales, and union members rushed down to urge him to return to London and offer to mediate the strike. Rather reluctantly, Temple broke off his vacation and met with the strike leaders and then with "the Mayor, [Cardinal] Manning, and Sir John Lubbock." Holland described Temple's attitude as "rather stiffly economical in the older fashion of economy," but maintained that he was "working hard now in the cause."[122] Evidently the bishop's old-fashioned economic views were too strong to be altered by the arguments either of the strikers or his clergy. He issued a statement criticizing the dockers' position and returned to Wales where he resumed his vacation. Finally, the dispute was resolved by an elderly man who had been a Tractarian archdeacon before he became a prince of the Roman Church. Cardinal Manning, the rigid ultramontane supporter of Pius IX, helped the workers win a victory and became the hero of the hour. Episcopal intransigence had defeated the union's first attempt to initiate social improvement. Three years later this stain on the church's record was partially wiped out when the union's president, Bishop Westcott, successfully mediated the great Durham coal strike.[123]

The union didn't allow an initial failure to dampen its enterprise. Educational efforts were continued and then in 1892 Scott Holland, acting in his capacity as president of the London branch, issued a manifesto on the London County Council elections.

1. Wholesome and sanitary dwellings; pure and cheap water; open spaces; public baths.
2. Equalization of rates.
3. Fairer taxation, especially concerning rent.
4. Municipal licensing power to control the drink trade and gambling.
5. Fair wages and protection of child and "sweated labour."
6. Women county councillors.[124]

The manifesto represented an important step forward for the union and for the entire social Christian movement. It was a sign that education alone was not enough, a sign that an organization of respectable churchmen felt obliged to take a stand on issues that were explicitly political. The union's position was not socialist, but it was clearly Radical-Liberal reformist. The union had moved beyond Champion's *Lux Mundi* statement of Christian social responsibility; the manifesto was based on the assumption that the state could improve social conditions. The union did not stop trying to change men's hearts, but it also attempted to remedy social abuses by passing laws to improve the social structure.

The movement toward political realism also infected the hitherto more theoretical, conservative Oxford branch of the union. In 1893 they became an economic pressure group. A white paper was issued, listing twenty local firms that had adopted acceptable trade union wage rates, and the union encouraged its members and the public to buy only from these firms. The evils of sweatshops were to be combated by discriminatory purchasing. Acceptable firms alone should be patronized; others could be brought around by means of a buyers' boycott. Different branches of the union adopted the Oxford plan and Christian buying principles were urged on churchmen throughout the country.

Holland's leadership on this issue had been decisive. As early as 1890 he had assumed the presidency of the Consumer's League, an organization devoted to the principle of selective buying; Suttleworth and other union leaders were active members. "Christian shopping" was bitterly opposed by manufacturing and retailing interests "as unfair" and "un-English"; the vehemence of their attacks suggests that the union's program had some effect on the public.[125]

The union also attempted to use selective buying as a means of improving working conditions. Pottery workers were subject to a tragically high incidence of lead poisoning, but the manufacturers refused to adopt a new leadless glaze technique because it involved higher costs. When the union ran a national campaign on behalf of pottery made by the improved method, midland industrialists decided that if the old process was penny wise, its continued use would be pound foolish.

The union discovered that economic and political pressure could be effectively used to secure social reforms. During the later nineties and the first decades of the twentieth century these techniques were used with increasing frequency on behalf of the rights of workers and women. Political pressure was particularly useful since the union gained a parliamentary block when clerical members were appointed to the Episcopal bench in Lords and lay members were elected to the House of Commons. The high position and prestige of union members gave it an influence on the formulation of national policy enjoyed by no other group of Christian social reformers. The union's program may have been moderate, but its effect cannot be denied.

Critics of the Guild of St. Matthew and the Christian Social Union are correct when they assert that neither organization ever really appealed to the great body of workingmen. The church had lost the poor during the early days of the Industrial Revolution in the late eighteenth and early nineteenth centuries and neither the guild nor the union could win them back. Yet at the beginning of the twentieth century, most churchmen recognized that social improvement, however vague and indefinite their conception of the term might be, was part of the church's mission. The Christian Socialists of mid-century had attempted to Christianize socialism and socialize Christianity. By

1900 Christianity in the Church of England was well on the way to being socialized.

# FOUR

# James O. S. Huntington: Ritualist Slum Priest, Religious Founder, and Single Tax Radical

In 1886, New York City residents experienced one of the most exciting, hotly contested municipal election campaigns since the end of the Civil War. That year, three important candidates vied for the mayoral office: the Democrats nominated Abram S. Hewitt, a respected Congressman and millionaire iron manufacturer; the Republicans chose a colorful, Harvard educated, gentleman-cowboy named Theodore Roosevelt; and the newly formed United Labor Party selected Henry George, a social reformer whose book, *Progress and Poverty*, had gained him an international reputation as the father of the single tax. George represented the forces of change; Hewitt who, thanks to the Tammany machine, emerged as George's primary antagonist, claimed that he was fighting to "save society."[1] The candidates offered the voters a clear-cut ideological choice, and partisan political feelings ran high. On election day, Henry George polled more votes than Theodore Roosevelt, but Tammany Hall elected Abram Hewitt. Once again the machine had triumphed, but the reformers had fought a good fight.

Looking back on the controversial election of 1886, George's close political associate, Louis F. Post, recalled

One of the sensations I experienced in that campaign was caused by the sight as I approached a large street meeting near Cooper Union of a speaker in priestly robes addressing the crowd from a truck and raising it [*sic*] to a high pitch of enthusiasm by his advocacy of Henry George's election. He was the Reverend J. O. S. Huntington.[2]

The sensational behavior exhibited by this rabble-rousing priest during Henry George's first campaign for mayor of New York City marked the emergence of the Anglican left into the arena of American politics. Today, Father Huntington enjoys a modest reputation in his own communion—especially in High Church circles—for the role he played in establishing the religious life for men in the Protestant Episcopal Church. Only a few Social Gospel historians recall that he was also a radical social reformer. And yet, the father founder of the Order of the Holy Cross was the first important representative of the Anglican left in America. When Huntington entered the political arena as a radical champion in 1886, William Dwight Porter Bliss had not yet received priestly orders from an Episcopal bishop, and Vida Dutton Scudder still was searching for her proper calling. Huntington, who was slightly older than either Bliss or Scudder, was the true pioneer; by the time he entered the George campaign, Huntington had been working with the poor for more than six years.[3]

During those six years, Huntington recapitulated in his own career, the primary stages of the developing movement for social reform in the Church of England during the preceding three or four decades. Huntington has no single counterpart in the English Church, but three parallel figures come to mind. Like Alexander Mackonochie, he was one of the first ritualist slum priests; like Richard Meux Benson, he founded an enduring religious order for men; and like Stewart Headlam, he was a social radical who championed the cause of the single tax.

It is only fitting that James Huntington is chiefly remembered as the father founder of the Order of the Holy Cross because his labors to establish an American religious order for men were to be crowned by enduring success. Even today, when religious vocations are few, this order flourishes.[4] For reasons that I will detail later, his activities as a ritualist slum priest and radical social reformer were cut short when the Order of the Holy Cross left New York City for Westminster, Maryland, in 1892. After the move, he never again held a slum parish or campaigned as a radical activist; his later years were completely devoted to his duties as a member of a religious order.

It is unfortunate, however, that the success of his religious foundation has obscured his role as the pioneering figure of the Anglican left, for any picture that ignores his social concerns does not do full justice to Father Huntington.

Also, any account of the Anglican social reform movement that fails to mention his contributions to it, would be, quite simply, inadequate. His career as a social reformer was brief, but it was significant.

## The Early Years

On Sunday morning, July 23, 1854, Hannah Dane (Sargent) Huntington gave birth to her third son. During the delivery, the father, Frederick Dan Huntington, was performing his ecclesiastical duties as a Unitarian minister at Boston's historic South Congregational Church.[5] When he returned home, he was delighted with the good news, but this delight was tempered by a deep sense of religious responsibility for the infant. "We ought to feel the Father nearer, and Heaven more natural. To the glory of the one, and a wise preparation for the other, may this child live, so long as he is permitted to stay in the world."[6] The parents named the boy James Otis Sargent. They were old family names.

Both the Huntingtons and the Sargents descended from sound Puritan stock, and they were proud of their heritage. None of their ancestors had been particularly famous, but many of them could boast of a modest local reputation in the towns of Massachusetts and Connecticut. Although neither family was wealthy, both were moderately well off. They stood a cut above the common people, not so much by reason of wealth, but because of their superior manners and education. The Huntingtons in particular produced a long line of clergymen, in the days when a cleric was one of the most important figures in New England village life.[7]

For generations they had been Calvinists, but James's grandfather, Dan Huntington, broke with family traditions and joined the rising Unitarian movement that challenged New England orthodoxy in the decades after the Revolution. When they became Unitarians, the Reverend Mr. Huntington and his wife, Elizabeth Phelps, were excommunicated by the family church in Hadley, Massachusetts. The excommunication process dragged on for some time; it was an unpleasant business and Mrs. Huntington was deeply grieved by it. Her son, Frederick Dan Huntington, who was a boy of nine at the time, was profoundly affected by his mother's grief and he developed lifelong aversion to "stern, forbidding, unrelenting Calvinism."[8]

Frederick Dan Huntington went to Harvard and then followed his father into the Unitarian ministry. His success was rapid; a year after the birth of his second son, James, he received a call from his alma mater to become a preacher in the college and Plummer professor of Christian morals. The family moved to Cambridge and James spent his early years in what was then a pleasant, semirural university town. When he was six, however, his father resigned his positions at Harvard in order to join the Protestant Episcopal Church.

It was not a hasty decision. Huntington Unitarianism developed out of an aversion to "stern, forbidding, unrelenting Calvinism" with its "black doctrine of reprobation." His Unitarianism was a liberal religion that owed more to Arminianism than to eighteenth-century Socinianism or Arianism, and it by no means involved a direct and total repudiation of the divinity of Jesus Christ whom it recognized as redeemer. In 1851 while he was still a Unitarian divine, F. D. Huntington wrote:

> We are as unable as we are undesirous to doubt that in regard to that deep wide line that distinguishes the infinite from the finite, and the Divine from the human, Christ the Redeemer does not stand by His nature on the human side. We discover no way by which an estranged, lost family on earth could be raised, restored and justified, but by one who should bring the Deity to earth, while he lifts man up toward Deity. The Redeemer must make God manifest in the flesh.[9]

Over the years he had become increasingly troubled by the disparity between his own beliefs and those espoused by other leaders in his denomination. By 1856, hardly a year after he had assumed his duties at Harvard, he had begun to give serious consideration to leaving the Unitarian ministry.

> Our own aversion to the Unitarian name, and our desire to be independent of it, arises partly from a belief that the term is not a description of our religious convictions on important points, and partly from a settled distrust of the general influence of the sectarian measures it covers, rather than from any want of friendship for its men, or of appreciation of its freedom.[10]

Dissatisfied as he was with Unitarianism, though, his aversion to Calvinism prevented him from returning to the religion of his forebears. Nor was the theologically sophisticated Plummer professor of Christian morals at Harvard attracted by the revivalistic techniques practiced by rising denominations like the Methodists and Baptists. Family loyalties, affection for his old university, and the absence of an acceptable denominational alternative kept him in the Unitarian fold for the next four years.

Huntington's intellectual world, however, was not limited by his immediate environment. He was a well-read man and his reading introduced him to a school of orthodox, yet liberal, theology developing in the Church of England. Its leader—although he would have denied the term—was Frederick Denison Maurice, himself a convert from Unitarianism. Huntington studied this new theology, accepted it, and made it his own. As his son's biographer, Vida Dutton Scudder, has phrased it—and with only slight exaggeration— "Maurice above all has been the master of his mind."[11]

When James was seven years old, his father was ordained to the priesthood and became rector of the newly formed Emmanuel parish in Boston. The family lived on Boylston Street opposite the Boston Public Gardens until 1869, when Frederick Dan Huntington was elected bishop of central New York. James grew up happily in almost idyllic surroundings: the family assiduously cultivated wide intellectual and artistic interests, and they had ample means to live a simple but refined, good life. Young Huntington was a rather ordinary, if sensitive, boy who understandably evidenced a very deep interest in religion. His sister, Mrs. Ruth Huntington Sessions, later recalled: "It was he who in childhood when his parents were absent would read the service from the Prayer Book to his little sisters, he who learned the catechism most easily and understandingly, he who placed the Prayerbooks at home services and made the responses most promptly."[12]

Nature was his second love. During his youth the Huntington family spent their summers at Forty Acres, the ancestral home at Hadley where they had been established since 1753.[13] Here James was most happy, wandering about the New England countryside with a book in his pocket; when he entered his teens, solitary walking trips, which sometimes lasted weeks, were his favorite form of recreation.

Much of his early education was supervised by his father, but he also attended the Roxbury Latin School where he prepared for college. At seventeen, he followed his father's example and entered Harvard. A sound, but not particularly brilliant scholar, he participated in numerous collegiate activities, helped found the *Harvard Magenta*—later renamed the *Crimson*, when the college's true color became known—and served as one of its first editors. His own religious impulses, as well as family tradition, destined him for the ministry, and at Harvard he spent much of his time working with the St. Paul Society, an organization for Episcopalian undergraduates.[14] Even as a young man he had already begun to move toward Anglo-Catholicism, and in the spring of his junior year we find him writing to tell his mother, "I have asked the Bishop to let me use the De Profundis instead of the Canticles in the (Ash Wednesday) service."[15]

While he was studying at Harvard, James happened to read a pamphlet by an English clergyman named Pullen called "Modern Christianity a Civilized Heathenism." Many of his friends were deeply disturbed by it, but James went farther; it brought him to a spiritual crisis characterized by "disastrous doubts and fears." In this crisis he turned for help not to any local cleric or teacher, but rather to his father in central New York. "He saved my life," the son said afterward.[16]

Immediately after he graduated from Harvard, Huntington began his theological studies with his father at St. Andrew's Divinity School in Syracuse, New York; while still a seminarian he was ordained deacon, and in 1880 he became a priest.[17] By this time we can already notice a developing inclination toward social reform. His first attempt at altering the status quo, however, was a dismal failure. In a revolt against class distinction, he insisted on boycotting family meals in the dining room and eating in the kitchen. Presently the cook gave notice: "Mrs. Huntington, if Master James doesn't know his place, I know mine."[18]

Recognizing his son's interest in helping the poor, Bishop Huntington had put him in charge of the Calvary Mission, a small church on the outskirts of Syracuse whose communicants were recruited from among the German and English immigrants who worked in nearby clothing mills. Here, the newly ordained Father Huntington was more successful than he had been in the Episcopal kitchen. His enthusiasm and devotion attracted the working classes who had been accustomed to clerical neglect, and since many of them had no strong religious tradition, they took no offense when he introduced ritualistic practices into the public worship.

> There were no conservatives in Calvary Parish; in fact, the people themselves were deeply interested. The church achieved its first altar cloth, green with handsome gold embroidery; friends sent beautiful altar linen. Candles were not introduced until later, however; they still represented a ritual somewhat more extreme than the Diocese of Central New York had embraced. But we had bookmarks to mark the seasons in varied colors, and the candles went to sick-beds with a smaller Cross, the Bishop's own, the chronicler thinks. And then came the training of a boy choir; a great pleasure.[19]

But despite his success at Calvary Mission, James Huntington felt dissatisfied with himself. His work in Syracuse—valuable as it might be—seemed like a serious and elaborate children's game played by him and his younger sisters. As long as he remained at home he would be forced to take his meals in the dining room. A bishop's son must know his place in a place where he is well known.

Father Huntington's development at this stage in his life becomes easier to comprehend when we compare him to his older English contemporary, Stewart Headlam. Both Headlam and Huntington later became clerical champions of Henry George's single tax, but even more important, they shared a remarkably similar theological outlook. This is not to say that Headlam directly influenced Huntington; there is no evidence to substantiate such a claim. Rather, Huntington and Headlam were both influenced by common theological movements: the Broad Church tradition of Maurice and the High Church Party, which descended from the Oxford movement via the slum ritualists.

For Huntington as for Headlam, Maurice's incarnational theology was at the very center of his religious thought. Huntington, of course, unlike Headlam, never had a chance to study under Maurice personally, but the single most important teacher in Huntington's life was his father, the bishop. James studied with him as a child, as an adolescent, and as a seminarian. It is a sign of the bishop's profound influence that when troubled by doubt his son turned to him for aid. Bishop Huntington was one of the earliest and most prominent exponents of Maurice's theology in the United States. In his own time he was second only to Phillips Brooks, who was a more famous preacher.

The Mauricean core of Father Huntington's thought clearly stands out in his article "Philanthropy: Its Success and Failures." By far the most extensive and important statement he printed about Christian social reform, it was published as part of a collection entitled *Philanthropy and Social Reform* in 1893, thirteen years after his ordination and one year after the Order of the Holy Cross withdrew from New York City to Westminster, Maryland. It might even be considered his swan song as an Anglican social activist. Several brief selections from the essay will demonstrate the Mauricean influence: "We are all one in Humanity's Head and Lord; we are members of one another; we are fellow-heirs of the gifts of God, . . . We are made for unity, . . . my true self is a social self and cannot be achieved in isolation . . . others are a part of myself."[20] Some pages later he continues: "I acknowledge that the unseen righteousness and love are manifested in a word of God made flesh in Jesus Christ, the Head of Humanity, the ruler of a visible and enduring Kingdom in which love and law are one."[21] Elsewhere in the article he points to Maurice's Working Men's College as the forerunner and source of the whole settlement house movement, a cause he warmly championed because it started out "with the conviction that we are all of one piece."[22]

As a theologian and a reformer, Huntington was Maurice's heir, but like Headlam, Huntington combined this inheritance with ideas and practices that derived from a High Church position. I have noted that, as far back as 1874, during his junior year at Harvard, he began to enrich the ceremonial; by the time he reached Calvary Mission, his innovations clearly marked him as a ritualist, although not an extreme party man. We have no way of knowing definitely who first attracted Father Huntington to the High Church movement; perhaps his personal religious development, like his father's, owed much to private reading. We do know, however, that as a little boy he became acquainted with the Church of the Advent, one of the most important Anglo-Catholic parishes in America.[23] During the years Huntington was at Harvard, the parish was directed by members of the Society of St. John the Evangelist.[24] One of the order's chief purposes was to combat skepticism among the educated classes, particularly young men at universities.[25] It is certain that Father Huntington was well acquainted with the order before 1880; he says so himself.[26] It is probable that the example of the Cowley fathers was instrumental in shaping the character of his churchmanship; it is certain that they furnished the occasion for his decision to join the religious life.

### Religious and Ritualist Slum Priest

In 1880, the year of his ordination, James Huntington attended a retreat given by Canon Knox-Little at the Cowley Fathers' Church in Philadelphia. Here he decided he had a vocation for the religious life.[27] Returning by train to New York, he discovered that the same call had reached another young priest, Robert W. Dod. Soon thereafter they were joined by a third, James G. Cameron, who had been working among the Indians on the Onondaga Reservation in the diocese of central New York.[28]

Although Father Huntington is recognized as father founder of the Order of the Holy Cross, in his own account of the formation of the order he modestly affirmed that "Father Dod was the leader in the enterprise."[29]

Both he and Father Cameron had spent some time with the Cowley Fathers at Oxford, and, in addition, Father Dod had discussed the idea of founding an

American Community for men with Canon T. T. Carter, who was warden of the Community of St. John the Baptist and one of the greater leaders of the religious revival in Victorian England.[30] When Dod returned from England he became curate at the mission of the Holy Cross run by the sisters of Saint John the Baptist in New York. Here he was joined by Huntington and Cameron.

As a first step in the organizing of the new community on All Saints Day, 1881, in the Chapel of St. John the Baptist Church (then at 233 East 17th St., New York), Fr. Dod became a novice, and his two companions kneeling beside him were accepted as postulants. This was their initiation into the nascent Community. These two postulants became novices six months later, on the Feast of the Invention of the Holy Cross, May 3, 1882, after a week's retreat at St. Mary's Convent, Peekskill, New York.[31]

The three young men took their religious profession very seriously and were determined to deport themselves like religious brothers. One of Huntington's cousins, who stopped in New York on his way to Harvard, has left a vivid description of the monastic clergy house at Holy Cross Mission.

I found James at the station waiting for me. He took me to the Brunswick . . . and insisted upon my ordering a regular dinner, even asking me to take wine! I however ordered as simple and inexpensive things as I could. Then we went to the Clergy House. They . . . see about the wretchedest and wickedest side of life in New York. Several times they have had paving stones thrown at them, "not very hard," James said, by roughs but have had no serious trouble.

They rise at half-past five, work and have services till half-past eight, when they take breakfast. They have a great many services, nine a day, I think. He seems thoroughly happy in his work, and books, and says he is well.

Silence is always kept in the entries, stairways and chapel. On going down in the morning, no one speaks until Father Dod says something; then at breakfast all stand while one of the Fathers reads a chapter from the Bible, then bow while grace is said.

The house is very old and quaint, with wooden dadoes and small squares of glass in the windows. The inner wall of my room had settled a foot or more, making quite a hill from one side to the other. The first thing I noticed in the room was a kind of shrine or altar at one side. It was made of wood, shaped something like a small bookcase, and had a large crucifix painted on the back.

Indeed, all that evening, as I sat by the fire in the library filled with musty leather-bound books, old engravings of saints, and a cross over the mantle, the two priests in their long black gowns and the dim light which made the old room look large and hid all the modern incongruities . . . I could hardly realize that I was not in some old monastery. . . . I forgot to say that they had almost sixty boys there the night before, playing checkers and other simple games.[32]

The scene belongs to Victorian romance, but one suspects Huntington's young cousin was so enraptured with the ambiance of the Holy Cross Mission that he failed to catch the true purpose of the community. Only as an afterthought does he remember to mention the sixty neighborhood boys who had been entertained there the night before. Those neighborhood boys and not the suggestive religious decor were the raison d'être for the Order of the Holy Cross.

In his brief essay, "Beginnings of the Religious Life for Men in the American Church," Huntington lists both the Cowley fathers and Canon Clerver as inspiration for the Order of the Holy Cross. Written when the author was seventy-nine, the essay is extremely polite; no controversial issues are raised and humility dictates the tone. Nonetheless, the following line is suggestive: "Yet it was not a mere copy of its predecessor (the Society of St. John the Evangelist); *it had from the start a different ideal and ethos*" (emphasis mine).[33]

The Society of St. John the Evangelist was organized in Victorian England; its ethos was what might be called British aristocratic. Its founder, Richard Meux Benson, was a figure of authority; doubtless, he was a truly saintly man, but while he was superior he ruled his order like a lord. For many years the order did not even have a constitution,[34] and the American branch did not become self-governing until 1920.[35]

This concentration of authority in the hands of one man caused numerous difficulties between the superior and some of the most illustrious American Cowley fathers. It led Father Grafton, one of the original founding members of the society, who later became bishop of Fond du Lac, to submit his resignation.[36]

All the original members of the Order of the Holy Cross were well acquainted with the Cowley fathers and they did not want an order with a British-aristocratic ethos. By contrast, their spirit was American-democratic. Authority was vested in the community as a whole. The superior is elected for a limited term and by universal member suffrage. His authority is limited by the Rule, Constitution, and Customal, which themselves receive their sanction from the group and may be amended by it; appeal may be made from his rulings to a governing council also elected by the whole group, or, ultimately, to the chapter itself. The superior may be deposed at any time by a two-thirds vote, and another elected in his stead.[37]

The Society of St. John the Evangelist was an active order, but social service was never a primary ideal. Cowley fathers were intellectuals and propagandists and most resemble the Dominican and Jesuit Orders in the Roman Church. In the beginning, the primary ideal of the Order of the Holy Cross was social service. Its mission was with the Community of St. John the Baptist, an order devoted to works of mercy: reforming prostitutes, tending the sick and elderly, and caring for orphans. The Holy Cross fathers continued and expanded the work of the sisters. The sisters' primary concern was with women and children; the fathers took on the men and the boys.

Three young idealistic priests had succeeded in creating something new in the history of the church: a democratic religious order devoted to the ideal of social service. It was an impressive accomplishment, but they had no time to enjoy their success. The order had hardly been formed when it began to disintegrate. Father Cameron discovered that he and his colleagues did not agree about the nature of vows, and since the differences were irreconcilable, he resumed the life of a secular parish priest. Father Dod developed a very bad case of asthma and was forced to retire to a sheep ranch in Texas.[38] When he was professed on November 25, 1884, James Otis Sargent Huntington was the only father of the Order of the Holy Cross. And so he remained until Father Sturges Allen joined the order two years later.

The profession of a priest in an Anglican religious order was most unusual in 1884, and, like many bizarre happenings and curiosities, received wide publicity. A furor soon broke out in religious circles, and the one member of the Order of the Holy Cross was deluged with criticism. A Roman Catholic spokesman, Monsignor Capel, observed that "the monastic system is wholly alien to Protestantism." Protestant Episcopal laymen feared that the church might return to the pre-Reformation dark ages. *The Church*, a well-established Anglican journal, denounced the vow of chastity as a reflection on the sacred mystery of marriage, and ultimately as an indirect insult to the womanhood of all mothers.[39] Most important, Bishop Lee of Delaware, the presiding bishop of the Protestant Episcopal Church, denounced Bishop Potter of New York for receiving Huntington's vows.

Bishop Potter's reply to the head of his church is still worth reading:

Do you know, my dear and honored Presiding Bishop, what a tenement house in New York is? Do you know the profound and widespread apathy of the

Christian community concerning the schools of poverty, misery, and almost inevitable vice? . . . All this these young men came to see and know. . . . And then they said, "If we are to reach these people, we must first of all live among them." . . . And then, too, they said, "If we are to do this work we must strip like the gladiators for the fight. We must be disencumbered of every tie and interest that can hinder or embarrass us. We must be willing to be poor, to live alone, to obey a fixed rule (or regimen) of life so that we may give ourselves wholly to this work "[40]

Bishop Potter's remarks might be summarized: "I have accepted James Huntington's vows as a religious, so that he can serve to the best of his ability as a slum priest."

We must not forget that during the years of his postulancy and novitiate—during those years when the Order of the Holy Cross was being created—Huntington was serving as a slum priest. After Father Dod left for Texas, Huntington assumed the duties of curate at the Holy Cross Mission. When he entered his postulancy, he viewed his social service at least partly as a form of self-sacrifice, an ascetic discipline, an *imitatio Christi*. This traditional monastic outlook was combined in his mind with a typical nineteenth century attitude regarding personal charity as a form of noblesse oblige.[41] Later, after working among and with the poor, his ideas changed radically as the full social import of Mauricean incarnational theology became clear to him. He denounced the common view of charity for being entirely "hypocritical and deceitful." It was wrong to assume a "relationship of higher to lower. Man is your fellow . . . [we are] brothers and sisters under a common father."[42]

Almost from the very beginning, Huntington worked to improve the quality of his parishioners' lives. At first he attempted to reform individuals by inculcating them with a sense of Catholic piety and self-discipline. Like his ritualist brethren in England, he used the Sacrament of Penance as a ministerial tool for restoring self-respect and a sense of personal worth. He also favored a modified form of a technique learned from the temperance movement, "the pledge." "I promise by the help of God that I will not enter into any place where liquor is sold between the time I have my pay and at my supper."[43]

Soon, however, he came to realize that in many cases the individual, even armed with piety and self-discipline, could not triumph over adverse social conditions.[44] Then like the second generation ritualists, Father Dolling of St. Agatha's, Landport, and Father Stanton of St. Alban's Holborn, Huntington joined or initiated campaigns to remedy specific abuses. He denounced child labor, agitated for more parks in poor neighborhoods, helped initiate a

Consumers' League, advocated prison reforms, and agitated for the abolition of tenement houses.[45]

Gradually, Huntington became more radical. This growing radicalism first appeared in his sermons. Since a monk was something of an exotic object capable of attracting a sizable congregation, Huntington frequently received invitations to preach outside his own parish. On these occasions he often spoke freely and gave vent to stored-up radical feelings. "If Jesus Christ had lived in these days, He would have been called an anarchist or some other kind of ist," he once declared with proper affirmative fervor.

Father Schleuter, who was a choirboy at the Holy Cross mission during Father Huntington's tenure there, recalled a particularly impressive example of his radical sermonizing:

> I shall never forget that Sunday service. It was a very "swell" congregation. We began our service with hymns out of the Iron Cross hymn book.[46] I think the first hymn before the service was "Our Lord He was a Carpenter." The hymn before the sermon was, "I Ask Not for His Lineage, I Ask not for His Name." Then Father Huntington stood quite still in the pulpit. I can almost feel the silence now and the attention that as a boy I felt. I shall never forget it as his voice rang out: "Let him that stole steal no more, but rather let him labor, working with his hand, the thing that is good." The Church was packed, but during the service there were a number of ladies who left the Church. I am afraid it was too much for them when he began to quote Lady Macbeth's "damned spot" and pictured her as a lady of best society, who drew her income from slums and sweat shops. He never beat the air.[47]

By 1886 Huntington's growing radicalism burst into social action when he joined the campaign to elect Henry George mayor of New York City. More and more, Huntington had become convinced that sermons and specific reforms were not enough; society would have to change. The mayoral campaign gave him the opportunity to act.

## The Radical Pioneer

James Huntington's active career as a social radical was brief: it began with Henry George's mayoral campaign in 1886 and ended when the Order of the Holy Cross moved to Westminster, Maryland, in 1892—a period of only six years, and during the last two his pace started to slacken. Lifelong devotion to social causes will guarantee William Dwight Porter Bliss and Vida Dutton Scudder a place in the pantheon of Anglican social radicals, but obviously Huntington does not merit recognition on those grounds. He deserves to be remembered as the first of the nineteenth-century American Anglican radicals, but the most remarkable thing about his career is that he ever became a radical at all. When Stewart Headlam championed Henry George's single tax campaign in England he followed in the footsteps of two generations of Anglican ritualists who had gradually been moving toward political and social radicalism. James Huntington had no similar tradition to follow in the American church; he traveled the whole road from self-sacrifice and noblesse oblige through the advocacy of specific reforms to political radicalism by himself, and he accomplished this journey in only five years. Naturally, his career did not spring ex nihilo; he had guides in the Mauricean and Anglo-Catholic tradition. Nonetheless, his transformation was remarkable.

Today he may not seem very radical to us at all, for unlike many latter-day reformers, he never expressed any sympathy for socialism, either Fabian or Marxist. (He might have approved of Guild Socialism, but that movement appeared on the scene long after he had abandoned radical politics.) His intense feeling for personal liberty—embodied in the ethos of the Order of the Holy Cross—prevented him from making any alliance with a movement that emphasized a theoretically omnicompetent state. Such a state reminded him of the benevolent elephant that inadvertently crushed a little brood of partridges that he had tried to protect.[48]

Instead, he preferred the single tax proposals of George, which offered him a social vision and the labor movement. It is difficult to believe that Huntington was attracted solely by Henry George's highly individual form of economics. There were also personal qualities in George that drew Huntington to him and made them fast friends. George had been raised in the Episcopal Church and, if in later life, he abandoned organized religion, he still remained a nondenominational prophet of the road crying out with Old Testament fervor for social justice. Huntington must have recognized a kindred spirit. Also, as his perceptive biographer, Vida Dutton Scudder, has suggested:

It is easy to see how [the Single Tax movement] met his needs. He knew at its best a rural life where land monopoly had not reared its ugly head. He loved the wide freedom, the wholesome life, of the farmer; as we have seen, he has shared the delights of a countryside as yet unspoiled. . . . From such surroundings he had come to take up his dwelling among the congested horrors, the smells, noises and miseries of the city tenements. . . . The Housing Problem vexed him as much as it does us in 1940; his agitation for Tenement House Reform had brought him in sharp impact against exploitation by landlords and had been the subject of some of his most powerful addresses. The Single Tax doctrine, the necessity that the land must be returned to the people, must have brought his mind intense relief.[49]

Like George, Huntington had broken with classical economic liberalism because he recognized that man could not be changed unless his economic background was altered; both agreed that society working through its instrument, the government, had a responsibility to effect that change. In the single tax he saw a way to change the economic background without introducing the—to him—equally oppressive system of state socialism. Therefore, Huntington threw himself into George's mayoral campaign and took to the streets to rouse the masses on its behalf. Rabble-rousing was shocking, unheard-of behavior for an Anglican clergyman of his time and his old critic, *The Churchman*, took him sharply to task for it."[50] When Tammany Hall handed Abram Hewitt the election victory, Huntington joined the Anti-Poverty Society, an organizational embodiment of the single tax movement, and continued to champion the cause.[51] Several old friends maintain that he remained loyal to the single tax until the end.[52]

If the single tax program offered Huntington a social vision, the labor movement offered him a method for social change. The reforming monk desired a radical transformation of society, but without a violent social revolution. In the labor unions he found a movement that advocated united action for social change through the application of economic—and sometimes political—pressure. Organized violence was not part of the union program. He campaigned for Henry George as the candidate of the United Labor Party, but he went farther and personally identified himself with the union cause by joining the Knights of Labor.[53] It was a radical action; he was doing something unprecedented, something new. At approximately the same time, William Dwight Porter Bliss joined the Knights of Labor in New England, but it is highly unlikely that either man knew of the other's action. Each acted for himself on his own.

He often spoke at Knights of Labor meetings, and since he was a popular platform speaker, he lectured throughout the East, Midwest, and Canada on behalf of union labor and the single tax. In 1888, he investigated the bitter struggle between miners and owners in Spring Valley, Illinois, and reported findings harshly critical of the owners' behavior in the *Chicago News*.[54] In 1890, he unfortunately caused a disruption in the ranks of the People's Municipal League, an anti-Tammany coalition attempting to unite behind a reform candidate for mayor, when he demanded that any candidate for mayor must be endorsed by the labor unions.[55] At the very end of his radical career, when the Order of the Holy Cross was preparing to migrate to Maryland, Huntington let off a final salvo against Henry Clay Frick and the Carnegie Steel Corporation for their behavior during the famous lock-out and labor war of 1892. Once again *The Churchman* denounced the firebrand son of a famous bishop,[56] but his actions on behalf of labor prompted W. B. Prescott, the president of the International Topo-Graphers Society to declare that Huntington's name is "enshrined in the hearts of the struggling wage earner."[57] Prescott thought little of the clergy in general.

Perhaps the most interesting and unusual incident in the entire history of his relations with labor occurred during the summer of 1889 when he put away his cassock and gained firsthand knowledge about the life of the poor by hiring himself out as a farm laborer. At first the continuous physical exertion nearly broke him, but by the end of the summer he had become acclimated to the life. More important, since he had kept his identity hidden he could speak to the poor not as a prominent sympathizer but as one of them, and in the evenings he did speak. His subjects were Christianity, labor unions, and the single tax.[58]

Huntington's reputation as a radical derives from his activities as a champion of labor and the single tax, but the most lasting social contributions of this zealous churchman were made within the church. Labor unions were grateful for his assistance, but they would have survived without it, and nothing that he did prevented the single tax program from becoming another of the noble lost causes in American history. But as a churchman he made his influence felt.

The church, he believed, had forgotten her mission: "I want to point out to the Church why the people have lost faith in her. I want to see her again take up her mission as the leader, the hope, the salvation of mankind."[59] First, he went to work to restore this sense of mission in his own parish. When the Church of the Holy Cross moved into a new building in 1885, he converted the old structure into a parish house where the local inhabitants could escape from the crowded tenements and find relaxation, recreation, and useful education. St. Andrew's Cottage, a summer camp for boys at Farmingdale, Long Island, carried the parish house project one step farther. At St. Andrew's boys were offered a changed environment—even if it was only temporary—and a chance to experience life anew. Expanded opportunities were offered through education.[60] Holy Cross Mission deserves mention as one of the first institutional churches, and its parish house prefigures the American settlement house movement.

Although he continued to develop these parish projects as long as he remained at the mission, Huntington realized that parish work alone was not enough. The church at large must be activated to fulfill her mission. In 1887, the year after George's defeat, the radical activist set up the Church Association for the Advancement of the Interests of Labor (C.A.I.L.). The first meeting took place in the Holy Cross Clergy House and the New England radical, William Dwight Porter Bliss, soon to emerge as Huntington's more famous successor, drew up the plan of organization. Even though he never became a social gospel radical, Bishop Frederick Dan Huntington bestowed a paternal and episcopal blessing by serving as president of the newly formed organization.

C.A.I.L. had three preeminent objectives: (1) to work closely with labor unions for the elimination of social abuses; (2) to propagate social reform projects within the Protestant Episcopal Church; and (3) to offer church mediation in strikes and other areas of labor-management conflict. At first its mediatorial role was most prominent; in one year alone, Huntington helped resolve six strikes.[61] Later it championed the municipalization of public utilities and the purification of politics.[62]

C.A.I.L.'s founders were radical, but the organization itself was not. It pursued moderate aims and thereby was able to help move many churchmen to the left. By the end of the century, it was spreading throughout the country[63] and "almost every bishop in the American Church and several in the British Provinces became . . . Honorary Vice-Presidents."[64] Howard Quint observes that it "represented the first organized attempt by a church denominational group to counter the accusations that religious groups were laggard in meeting their common responsibilities."[65] One might say that C.A.I.L. enabled the Episcopal Church, and not some groups of radicals within it, to begin "leading the Protestant world in reform," and it is certainly Huntington's single greatest legacy to the cause of Anglican social reform.

C.A.I.L. flourished for fifty years, but Huntington was actively associated with it only a brief five years, for in 1891 he and Father Allen left the mission at the Holy Cross in the hands of a young German priest who had graduated from General Theological Seminary, and moved to a house in the upper part of the city at 120 Pleasant Avenue.[66] A year later they established the order at Westminster, Maryland, in a house given to the order by Lucretia Van Bibber of Baltimore.[67]

One may wonder why Huntington abandoned the city mission for a pleasant country town. Certainly the health of the order was a significant causal factor. At the end of ten years, the order had only two members and it was felt that the order must have a fresh start if it were to survive. Scudder suggests that Huntington may have been uneasy over the fact that part of the money supporting the mission came from rent on East Side property.[68] That would surely upset such an avid single taxer. The most significant reason, however, was put forth by Huntington himself:

> A question will occur in some minds as to why the work in the tenement district of the East Side was abandoned by the men who had apparently dedicated themselves to it. A suspicion might arise that use had been made of the work in the slums to foist upon the American church a form of life alien and unwelcome to its spirit. In all fairness to those who commended the enterprise—most of whom have passed away—it should be said with as much emphasis as possible, that any such notion is entirely contrary to the facts.
>
> The men who gave themselves to the work of the Holy Cross Mission did so in all sincerity. They had no thought of a future change of place. But their experience of years on the East Side showed them that "the tenement house problem" was far more difficult and intricate than it appeared at first sight. One factor in the problem was the instability of the population. Families were constantly moving—some every few months, others every few weeks. They migrated to the Bronx or across the river to Long Island. The possibility of building up a permanent congregation became more and more remote. The work was like preaching to a procession. To outward appearance the district remained the same, but the human element was in flux and flow.[69]

Father Huntington, unlike many of his contemporaries, understood that man was not an absolutely free, independent individual, but was strongly influenced by the environment in which he found himself. That understanding made him a radical; it also led him to the realization that one could not be an effective slum priest unless the community provided an environment stable enough to support a program for change. The polyglot East Side offered no such environment to an Anglican priest. Slum ritualism had worked with the

English poor; it did not work on the East Side. One might suggest that it was Huntington's superior sense of social understanding that convinced him that the Holy Cross fathers could not accomplish their purpose at the mission. The problems were too vast for two men.

So in 1892 the Order of the Holy Cross moved to Westminster, Maryland, and began a new life. They flourished there and in 1904 moved to their present quarters in West Park, New York, where they continued to expand. Today the Order of the Holy Cross constitutes a living memorial to their father founder. But let us not forget that James Otis Sargent Huntington was also a father founder of the American Anglican left.

# FIVE

# William Dwight Porter Bliss: American Christian Socialist

W illiam Dwight Porter Bliss is the most famous Anglican social reformer in the history of the American church. No major historian of the social gospel movement has failed to review his life and work appreciatively. Yet Bliss never became father founder to any organization whose continuing life preserved his name, nor did his numerous publications capture for him an enduring audience. No specific cause he put his life into has lasted, but he is well remembered.

Why has history been so kind to his reputation, while other reformers like Huntington and Scudder have remained in comparative obscurity? It can be argued that Bliss's fame is the result of the significant impact he made on the American church in his own time. Here was a man who proclaimed the cause of social reform with dauntless energy and unflagging zeal. Time and time again he crossed the country preaching and organizing—carrying his message to the people at the grass roots. And always—almost morning, noon, and night, it seems—he was writing; pamphlets, newspapers, books, Sunday school lessons, and encyclopedia came flooding out of his active pen. When one project failed, he adopted another; his dreams might fade, but he kept on trying. So tireless were his labors that Howard Quint, in his classic study of the development of American socialism, was moved to compare Bliss with St. Paul the Apostle.[1]

Yet energy and zeal alone cannot guarantee a significant impact. Admitting that these splendid personal qualities played their part, we must look elsewhere for deeper causes. The hypothesis I advance to help explain both his impact and reputation is this: Bliss was part of the mainstream movement of middle-class liberal American Protestant social reform; Huntington and Scudder were not. All three were American middleclass social reformers, but there were important differences.

When Scudder and Huntington became Anglo-Catholics they joined a recent movement whose doctrines and ceremonies had been developed in England. It was a foreign import, not only alien to the indigenous American religious tradition, but a foreign import that self-consciously rejected that tradition. Anglo-Catholics repudiated the name Protestant with sectarian party zeal. Most Americans during the late nineteenth century were not concerned about *jure divino* episcopacy, the theology of Caroline divines and church fathers, or the revival of medieval and baroque ceremonialism. Most of them are not today; they regard such preoccupations as merely quaint or eccentric and find it difficult to take the proponents of these opinions seriously. The Anglo-Catholic movement did considerably influence the subsequent development of the Protestant Episcopal Church, but outside of that church its direct impact on the mainstream movement of American religious life has been small.

Bliss was born and bred a Protestant; he became an Episcopal priest, not an Anglo-Catholic. He was a Broad Churchman, indifferent to the sectarian trappings of Anglo-Catholicism, with a liberal theology and comprehensive ecumenical outlook. He even welcomed Unitarians into the Church of the Carpenter.[2] In the 1880s the Anglo-Catholics were an extreme party; in order to join them one had to repudiate the Protestant tradition. That repudiation is a radical act and it is significant that Bliss never joined this minority on the fringe. Bliss changed churches, but he did not abandon his basic religion. He remained a man of the majority in the moderate American mainstream.

Essentially the same moderation characterized his political outlook. He believed in reform, believed in it so passionately that he gave his life to the cause, but his approach was that of a majoritarian gradualist who favored working through traditional institutions. As we have seen, Huntington's concern for reform ultimately led him to withdraw into the country and devote himself to the religious life. Later I shall show how Vida Scudder's concern for reform led her to adopt an apocalyptic variety of revolutionary Christian Marxism. Neither Scudder's nor Huntington's solutions have appealed to the majority of America's reform-minded Protestants. Like Bliss, they have preferred overwhelmingly to work within the system.

Because Bliss accepted the Protestant tradition and because he espoused moderate methods—even if his rhetoric often was fiery—his impact as an apostle for change was significant. He is an example of the liberal, middle-class, Protestant reformer at its best—passionately concerned about the necessity for change, yet deeply attached to the values of the American tradition.

Why, then, include him in this study? Does he belong to the American left? Yes, he belongs: even though his churchmanship was moderate and his political methods were gradualist, his social vision was revolutionary. The moderates wanted to remedy the system's abuses and make it work better; Bliss wanted to abolish the capitalist order and replace it with another. Bliss believed in Christian Socialism, and this belief involved him in more radical activities than most clergymen of his own or any subsequent generation. Most of his contemporaries saw only his radicalism: Bishop Potter, a reformer known as the "People's Friend," felt obliged to warn the clergymen of his diocese against his influence.[3]

Men are more complicated than the labels we affix to them, and Bliss was more complex than most. But to understand his complexity and to appreciate his career we must examine his life in more detail.

## Background and Beginnings

On August 20, 1856, William Dwight Porter Bliss was born in Constantinople, the ancient center of Orthodox Christianity.[4] His parents, Isabella Holmes (Porter) Bliss and Edwin Elisha Bliss, recently had moved to the cosmopolitan capital of the Turkish Empire from the provincial town of Marsovan where they had spent five years in the Congregational Church's mission to the Armenians. Both at Marsovan and at Trebizond, the scene of their labors from 1843 to 1851, their evangelical work had "suffered severe persecution at the hands of the orthodox Armenians."[5] The Reverend Edwin Bliss had contracted malaria at Marsovan and thereafter he was never completely free of the disease. Realizing that the illness rendered him unfit for the arduous work in the field, but hoping to retain the fruits of his vast learning and experience, the Congregational Board of Foreign Missions transferred the elder Bliss to more comfortable surroundings in Constantinople, where he embarked on an editorial career that lasted until his death, thirty-six years later. Like his more famous son, Edwin Bliss simultaneously edited several newspapers and produced numerous tracts and pamphlets. Also, he wrote a *Bible Handbook* in Armenian and contributed frequent articles to the *Missionary Herald*. Porter Bliss's penchant for journalism and his incredible energy and capacity for hard work were traits he obviously inherited from his much beloved missionary father.[6]

Young Bliss spent his early years in the exotic and venerable cosmopolis, and he received the beginnings of a modern, Western education at Robert College, a Congregational school located in that city. Returning to the United States he prepared to enter college, at Phillip's Academy. After he was graduated by his father's alma mater, Amherst, he entered the Hartford Theological Seminary with the intention of following his father, an uncle, and an aunt into the foreign missions, but when he finished seminary in 1882 he did not return to the Middle East. Instead, he accepted a call to a parish in Denver and headed west.[7] Poor health, however, soon forced him to relinquish his position in frontier Colorado and come back to Massachusetts. Settling in the town of South Natick, he resumed his career and served the local Congregationalists as their minister. On June 30, 1884, he and Mary Pangalo, another native of Constantinople, were married.[8] Theirs was a happy union and through the years Mary Bliss loyally supported her husband even when his devotion to the cause of social reform entailed great personal sacrifice on her part.[9]

Bliss's concern for social issues probably developed in South Natick; there he confronted the horrors of life in a New England mill town, an experience that one of his biographers has described as spiritually sickening.[10] His outrage at what he beheld was strengthened by reading Henry George and a series of articles on social problems featured in the *Christian Union*. The year of decision for Bliss was 1885: he joined the Knights of Labor and became a confirmed Anglican; these acts mark the beginning of his active career.

While reading for Anglican orders Bliss spent the next three years as a licensed lay reader at St. George's Church in Lee, Massachusetts, another industrial town.[11] His friend and disciple, W. J. Ghent, writes that during the mid-eighties he read the works of F. D. Maurice and Charles Kingsley, developed a strong personal admiration for the men, and became deeply influenced by their thought and Christian Socialist activities.[12] By 1887 Bliss was also well aware of the Guild of St. Matthew, which figures prominently in "Socialism in the Church of England," written at this time. Not content with reading, writing, and ministering to a congregation, he also took an active and serious interest in his duties as Knight of Labor, and quickly rose to become master workman of the local assembly. Bliss's direct participation in the labor movement was extraordinary for a clergyman in his time, and it won him the respect and trust of the workers. They sent him as a delegate to the

Union Labor Convention held in Cincinnati in 1887, and he received the short-lived Massachusetts Labor Party's nomination for lieutenant governor.[13] This honor he declined.

In 1887, after receiving his priestly orders, Bliss left St. George's and became rector of Grace Church Mission, an organization supported by the Episcopal City Mission for the poor of Boston's south end. The same year while visiting in New York City he proposed the organizational plan for C.A.I.L. He continued to read omnivorously and like many Americans of his era fell under the spell of the utopian vision of a socialist state presented by Edward Bellamy in his novel *Looking Backward*. Ever anxious to convert thought into action, Bliss became a charter member of the first Nationalist Club, an organization formed to promote and realize Bellamy's ideals. But both the atmosphere of the club and its goals were too secular for Bliss, and early in 1889 he and a few like-minded friends organized the Society of Christian Socialists.

### Christian Socialism and the Church

In 1885 when the horrors of industrial life in South Natick convinced Bliss of the necessity for basic social reform, he made two significant decisions: he joined the Knights of Labor and converted to the Anglican Church. Today, we can easily understand why a social reformer might be attracted to the labor movement, but it is difficult to imagine why such interests might impel a man to change his denominational allegiance. As Christopher L. Webber, himself an Anglican priest, has observed, "In 1885, when he entered the Church, no such interest in industrial and social problems was evident."[14]

Yet Bliss did not act out of ignorance. The article that the *Andover Review* generously published for their erstwhile Congregational brother in 1887 reveals his thoughts during this crucial period of his life. For an American, especially a recent convert to Anglicanism, Bliss was remarkably well informed about the social reform movement in the Church of England. The historic tradition is mentioned with respect—Maurice and Kingsley get their just due, along with Wycliffe, Cranmer, Latimer, and other great figures—but specific current information is so plenteous that "Socialism in the Church of England" reads more like a news article than a scholarly study. It is clearly written by the pen of an interested activist, not an intellectual. As I have mentioned, the Guild of St. Matthew is given particular attention. Bliss knows who the leading members are—he singles out Headlam, Moll, Shuttleworth, and Hancock—and he is obviously very familiar with their literature, especially Headlam's paper, *The Church Reformer*.[15] But he does not limit himself to a discussion of the guild's activities. Growing socialistic interest among the episcopacy receives its modest due, and the work of the Broad Church Canon Barnet, who was instrumental in founding Toynbee Hall, is singled out for special notice.

A concluding passage is most significant because here Bliss stops reporting and reflects on "why the Church of England is peculiarly open to such influences."

> It is the Church of the rich and the poor, not of the middle class, not of the manufacturing centers where *laissez faire* has taken its deepest root. . . . A state church, again, is in itself naturally a religious socialist institution. If a socialistic government is to be religious, its most natural outcome is a state church. Once more, the independent position, practically freeholds, of at least the beneficed clergy, makes it much more possible for them to maintain radical positions than it can be for men dependent upon the support of their congregations. But above all, what Stanley called the fortunate "secularity" of the Church of England must be the main cause for socialism taking a deeper hold of this church than of any other. The beneficed English clergyman is . . . a civil officer. This . . . must make him magnify the power of the state and so magnify his own office. At the same time his intimate relation and acquaintance with the poor and the underprivileged must tend to make him a democrat and often a radical, the union of state rule and democratic feeling ending naturally enough in belief in socialism.[16]

"Socialism in the Church of England" is the only existing contemporaneous document that exposes the reasons behind Bliss's Anglican conversion. What can it tell us? First, it suggests that the example of the English church and not the American was the primary factor in his decision. Second, there is the absence of any strictly ecclesiastical motivations; he does not mention Anglican theology, polity or worship—no bishops, no prayer book. (When discussing the guild he notes that it is High Church, but erroneously concludes that it is more socialist than High Church.)[17] Instead, Bliss seems most drawn to the Church of England by its "fortunate secularity," by its involvement in the political and social life of the nation. Bliss's personal "intimate relation and acquaintance with the poor [of South Natick] . . . made him a radical." In the English church he saw an institution free of deadly laissez faire, whose clerics were "civil officers" who could maintain radical positions because they were not dependent on the support of their congregations. An Anglican cleric, he thought, could help the poor and lead the way to the future. How much he must have envied their happy position!

Of course, Bliss tremendously overestimated both the freedom and the radicalism of the English clergy; he was attracted by an idealized vision of *Ecclesia Anglicana*. Nonetheless, the fortunate secularity that he so much admired was based on historical fact. When Bliss converted he adopted the classic English ecclesiology—formulated by Hooker, emphasized by Coleridge and Maurice—that viewed church and state as two different aspects of a common community. English radicals in the Guild of St. Matthew wanted to separate church and state; Bliss's conversion is a sign that he wished to bring them together again.

For the rest of his life Bliss pursued the dream that had inspired his conversion, but his activities during the first decade of his Anglicanism must form the chief concern of this study. This is the period when Bliss attempted to make his dream come true by planting a Christian Socialist organization on his own native soil. If longevity were the only standard of judgment, the first organization that Bliss played a part in, C.A.I.L., would have to be deemed the most successful. Its useful and vigorous life lasted almost four decades, and when it disbanded in 1926 its work was continued by the church's Department of Social Service.[18] But though oriented toward labor and social reform, C.A.I.L. was by no means a Christian Socialist organization. Also, it was based in New York and Boston was the center of Bliss's mission.

A year after C.A.I.L. was founded, Bliss tried again and became a charter member of the first Nationalist Club. Nationalism, however, proved far more unsatisfactory than C.A.I.L. Later, Bliss gave voice to his specific objections to nationalism in *The Dawn*. Bellamy's utopian state was static in character; therefore, its doctrine contradicted the laws of evolutionary development to which Bliss was deeply attached.[19] Nationalism's methods—its military regimentation and coercive centralized authority—were even more distasteful.[20] Perhaps most important, Bliss disdained nationalism because it refused to acknowledge that it was socialist.[21] Probably these specific objections manifested themselves to Bliss only after he had broken with the nationalists; at the time, it is likely that he simply found it impossible to work with the retired military officers and Theosophical journalists who dominated Boston's Nationalist Club.[22] Ecumenical as he was, Bliss hardly could have felt at home with the disciples of Madame Blavatsky, excepting of course, Annie Besant.

115

The nationalist movement had hardly gotten off the ground when in February 1889 Bliss and other nationalists whose Christian allegiance was paramount began planning an organization of their own. "Following a Nationalist meeting on May 7, 1889, Bliss, together with several other club members, including the Reverend Francis Bellamy, a cousin of the author, met at the Tremont Temple in Boston and organized the Society of Christian Socialists."[23] The interdenominational character of the society would have horrified High Church English radicals, but Bliss did not share their sectarian spirit. Both the Reverend Francis Bellamy and the society's president, the Reverend O. P. Gifford, were Baptists; Mary A. Livermore, a vice president, was a universalist laywoman; the Reverend Philo W. Sprague, another vice president, however, was an Episcopal priest.[24] It is typical of Bliss that he accepted for himself the society's most arduous, least glamorous office, that of secretary, and that he assumed the burdens of editing its journal, *The Dawn*, whose first number appeared only eight days later, May 15, 1889.[25]

This issue and many subsequent to it, carried the society's Declaration of Principles, which had been adopted exactly one month before.[26] The practical objects of the society were:

1.  To show that the aim of socialism is embraced in the aim of Christianity.
2.  To awaken members of Christian churches to the fact that the teachings of Jesus Christ lead directly to some specific form or forms of Socialism; and that therefore the church has a definite duty upon this matter and must, in simple obedience to Christ, apply itself to the realization of the social principles of Christianity.[27]

These practical objects may appear general and vague, but the sense of outrage that prompted their adoption is thoroughly detailed in a prefatory jeremiad directed against "the present commercial and industrial system." The system, *The Dawn* complained, was not based on Jesus' teachings of the Fatherhood of God and the Brotherhood of Man; its foundation was selfish individualism, and dire indeed were the results. Natural resources and human inventiveness were gathered into the hands of a few who, enriched on gains God meant for all, had become a "dangerous plutocracy." This plutocracy increasingly controlled the destinies of the wage-earning majority, while commercial and industrial crises were precipitated by plutocratic refusal to allow general economic planning. ". . . large occasion is thus given for the moral evils of mammonism, recklessness, overcrowding, intemperance, prostitution, and crime."[28]

From the beginning the Society of Christian Socialists manifested an enthusiastic missionary spirit: all who could subscribe to the Declaration of Principles were invited to establish like-minded fellowships. In order to generate interest the society offered to send out lecturers to speak before any organization.[29] In reality, Bliss was most often *the* lecturer: "He spoke in Episcopal churches and clubs, at the Cambridge Theological School, and sat on the platform of Tremont Temple when Father McGlynn appeared there in behalf of the single tax."[30] *The Dawn* carried reports and letters suggesting that the formation of the society had been greeted enthusiastically by like-minded readers, but none of them seemed able, even if they were willing, to establish another branch of the society. Local conditions away from the hub city seldom appeared propitious. In the heartland, Christian radicals felt it necessary to be more discreet. From Chicago, for example, *The Dawn*'s correspondent, the Reverend William E. Sillence, reported that it was not desirable to form a chapter because anarchism and socialism were too often confused in the mind of a public still outraged by the Haymarket bombing.[31]

When the new decade began in January 1890, the society's missionary zeal was rewarded; the Reverend R. Herber Newton, an Episcopal clergyman long identified with the cause of social reform, became president of a New York chapter of Christian Socialists.[32] Other Anglicans in the circle around C.A.I.L. became identified with the Christian Socialists, but Father Huntington remained aloof. Later, however, when *The Dawn* was faltering, he lent his personal support to Bliss by becoming an associate editor of the paper. In the East the new movement never did grow much beyond the confines of Boston and New York, so in the spring of 1890 Bliss embarked on a proselytizing tour of the Midwest. Quickened by his enthusiasm, reform-minded Christians in Cincinnati and Chicago, where the Haymarket tempest must have blown itself out, established societies for Ohio and Illinois.[33] In the autumn, a Kansas society became the fifth branch and the Christian Socialists reached their zenith.

The success of Christian Socialism as an institutional movement soon proved to be ephemeral; dissolution set in almost at once. Only the New York branch possessed an independent life of its own. Elsewhere, groups that had sprung up in response to Bliss's magnetic proselytizing withered away once his inspiring presence was removed. Even the Boston branch had begun to weaken. By November 1890, the situation had become so critical that Bliss was forced to assume the full financial burden of publishing *The Dawn* on his own. Since the paper was the society's only important, long-range project, abandoning the paper, in effect, was tantamount to giving up the ghost. Bliss printed no definite obituary so we do not know if the society ever formally disbanded, but after the beginning of 1891 *The Dawn* carries no mention of further activities. The Society of Christian Socialists lasted less than two years, a brief lifespan even for a radical organization. Reflecting on the society's early death, Quint concludes: "That Christian Socialism failed to take hold as in England was hardly the fault of the indefatigable Bliss. He had played his role of organizer to the very hilt. The trouble was that there were too few Christian Socialists who chose to be organized."[34]

The Society of Christian Socialists had a short life, but it lasted just long enough to cost its secretary his position with the Episcopal City Mission. Early in 1890 he was informed that he must either abandon *The Dawn* or relinquish his position at Grace Church. The mission felt that he could not do justice to both. Rudely, Bliss was awakened to the realities of the clerical position in the Protestant Episcopal Church: there were no independent freeholds here; a radical clergyman was dependent on the tolerance of his congregation—or in this case on the sympathy of a Board of Directors. It must have been a painful decision—the congregation at Grace Church was the first Bliss had served as a priest—but he promptly submitted his resignation and withdrew from the mission. The Socialist Labor Party's *Workingman's Advocate*, a paper frequently critical of Christian Socialism, abandoned sectarian animosity and firmly supported their brother, "an honest man and scientific socialist . . . driven from his pulpit for daring to preach the doctrines of the Carpenter of Nazareth."[35] The Episcopal City Mission may have driven Bliss from his pulpit, but their action did not alter his abiding affection for the church. "We think of the Church," wrote Bliss some years later, "as a lover who sees wrong in one he loves."[36] Disappointed though he must have been, Bliss chose to be guided by the highest example of all: "Jesus Christ stayed in the Church; clung to it though it killed Him—so partly he helped it to become what it is today."[37]

Bliss remained in the church, but losing his position at the Grace City Mission seems to have induced him to reexamine the whole issue of the church and its role in society; *The Dawn* alludes to this subject frequently during the years 1890-91. In June he announced:

The Church needs an earthquake shock. She is waking from her sleep; no one can doubt this, but will it be simply to rub her eyes, to discover at last that others have done her work before her? . . . The Church today, sometimes, seems dying of fine talk. What it needs is *action*. It needs to lead. It does not particularly need better preachers. It does very particularly need better guides.[38]

First on the agenda, Bliss hoped, would be a new reformation in theology that would strip away excess credal baggage to expose Christianity's central message.

We believe that her theology needs simplifying. Various systems, orthodox and unorthodox have overgrown the simple religion of Jesus Christ. Christianity, as popularly conceived, as ordinarily practiced, and often as thought today, has come to have little in common with the faith and love, and life, inculcated by the Master. Christianity is a life, not a creed; a way, not a philosophy; a "battle not a dream."[39]

Once "the simple message of Jesus Christ" was revealed, the widest possible Church union was the necessary second step. "Denominationalism is sin. Church unity is a crying need. It cannot be reached by compromise, by contract, by human scheming. It must evolve. The Christ must bring it in, if it is to be His church. It must be democratic, federated, catholic—'one body with many members.' "[40]

One notes here the absence of any Anglo-Catholic principle or polemic; both in theology and ecclesiology Bliss was the broadest and most ecumenical of Broad Churchmen. Indeed, as is often the case with Bliss, he is so broad and inclusive in intention that his expression is vague and misty.

Elsewhere, though, in *The Handbook of Christian Socialism*, Bliss revealed the theological perception on which he based his social and religious thought. As one might expect from an admirer of Frederick Denison Maurice, the doctrine of the Incarnation is central. "In Christ God became man *on earth*. He took all Humanity into Himself. Christ was not only a man but MAN—man in his entirety, man in art, in science, in letters, in politics, in society, in commerce, and in industry. In the Incarnation all life entered into God. There is the breath of the Incarnation."[41]

The Incarnation, Bliss realized, gave all human existence its meaning; also it was the ground on which all men were united. Since all men were in fact united in God, why could they not embody this unity in the way they lived? Bliss dreamed of expressing this ideal existence and described the details of his vision in *The Dawn*. "Seven years ago the writer dreamed of a church different from any church he knew." It would be a brotherhood whose members would live in separate homes near the church. Every morning they would gather for prayer and sing a hymn, then work for eight hours in cooperative industry for the good of all. Meals would be taken communally in a common hall, and children would be educated by members of the brotherhood. Work done, the evenings would be spent in the church house, where there would be "dances, laughter, music and instruction." Early Sunday morning the community would celebrate the Eucharist; later in the morning there would be a sermon and prayer; in the afternoon all would sing vespers; in the evening came "popular lectures on Christ in Art, Christ in Industry, Christ in All. The little church was to be called the 'Church of the Carpenter.' We dreamed the dream by day. For seven years we have been living in its light. We have established a 'Mission of the Carpenter preparatory to the Church.' "[42]

Bliss was a great dreamer, and he continually attempted to make his dreams come true. Losing his position at Grace Church freed him to create a mission-church of his own that would demonstrate the true character of social Christianity. The first service of the Mission of the Carpenter was held on April 13, 1890. Over three hundred people crowded into the hall Bliss had rented for a church.[43] *The Churchman*, a popular Episcopal publication, commented on the auspicious beginning of the new enterprise: "Mr. Bliss is a young clergyman of marked ability. . . . He has gained the confidence of people both within and without our communion. No one can tell what his enterprise may lead to, but it has certainly begun well, and an unexpected number of people are interested in it."[44]

Finally, Bliss had been able to establish an organization that reflected his own ideals. Probably the Mission of the Carpenter with its attendant organizations was his most original contribution to the cause of Social Christianity; it lasted for six years. Bliss set several important goals for the mission. First it was to cut across economic lines and class distinctions by appealing to all, rich and poor alike. Unlike Grace Church and countless other missions run by the major Protestant denominations, the Mission of the Carpenter was not set up by the wealthy for the poor. "Bliss took pride in the Mission's progress, especially since it was almost entirely dependent financially on contributions."[45] Second, Bliss hoped to witness against the sin of denominationalism by attracting a congregation from many churches. But it would have been contrary to the evolutionary principles of Christian Socialism to begin a new church; such action would have only further divided Christ's body.

The Mission itself is connected with the Protestant Episcopal Church, and its services are the services of that church, because as Socialists we believe in Union and not in Disunion. . . . We therefore start no new sect in the already divided body of the church, but in connection with a branch of the church, strive to reform the church on the lines of Christina Socialism. . . . The Mission is connected with and subject to the laws of the Protestant Episcopal Church, so far as this church is catholic with its creeds . . . but it declines to be considered an Episcopal Church in any sectarian sense for it strives to be absolutely catholic or universal.[46]

The Mission of the Carpenter gave expression to Bliss's dream of social and ecclesiastical unity; it was an example of what the visible church should and could become. But Bliss, the indefatigable activist, felt equally concerned about what the church could do to improve present conditions and aid the cause of social reform. The Mission of the Carpenter needed a strong secular arm to fulfill its witness, and when Bliss sensed a need, he was not a man to hold back. After the mission's first religious service had been concluded, Bliss met with about twenty of the three hundred men and women who had been present for worship; this group of stalwarts, which included George McNeil, a prominent trade union leader and personal friend whom Bliss had converted to Anglicanism, agreed to form the Brotherhood of the Carpenter. The aims of this organization, printed in *The Dawn* for all to see, were frankly practical and political.

The Brotherhood of the Carpenter, which . . . is not restricted to adherents of the Episcopal Church, is a Brotherhood of Work, and proposes to work at present, by spreading the literature and ideas of Christian Socialism, by ascertaining what firms best treat their employees, with a view to concentrating patronage upon them, and by helping to find employment for any member of the Brotherhood out of work.[47]

Originally, Bliss had hoped that the brotherhood would remain closely tied to the mission, operating more or less like a parish guild. (The mission was incorporated as an Episcopal parish with Bliss as rector in 1892; George McNeil served as senior warden.) Its meetings were scheduled to follow the mission's service of evening prayer and sermon. After seventeen months had passed, however, it became obvious that a brotherhood with nearly one hundred members could not realistically be considered an adjunct guild of a parish that never listed more than seventeen communicants in any one year.[48]

Bliss accepted numerical reality and dissolved the relationship between the brotherhood and the mission, explaining his motivation in *The Dawn*.

> We believe as deeply as ever in the strength and comfort of the Sacramental Life . . . but many of our Brotherhood not believing in, or perhaps misunderstanding, the church, we would not, even in appearance force . . . upon any, the to us dear and helpful forms of the church. . . . The effort will be to emphasize those points on which we can all agree, and to come together in the name of the unity, of the Father, and all mankind. To us, the Episcopal Church stands for that unity, but if others think not so, time will best show who is right. Those who have the most confidence in truth are least anxious to be always pressing their views as such truth.[49]

Ever since his conversion to Anglicanism Bliss had dreamed of a church whose existence would testify to the organic unity of life as a whole, and when he established the Church and Brotherhood of the Carpenter he had reason to hope that his conception had become a living reality at last. Then the brotherhood left the church and his living reality once again faded into a dream. And, grand though it was, it was a dream Bliss could share fully only with those few persons who maintained membership in both the Brotherhood and the Church of the Carpenter.

In the summer of 1891 two priestly reformers, W. D. P. Bliss and J. O. S. Huntington, faced the same problem: neither man could effectively realize his most cherished dream of creating a viable socially active Christian community. Pondering this dilemma Huntington decided that his primary responsibility was to insure the continuing existence of his religious community. The Order of the Holy Cross left New York City and moved into a cottage in the country near Westminster, Maryland, in the summer of 1892. The order survived, but it was no longer corporally active in the cause of reform.

Discouraged by the Church of the Carpenter's apparent failure to attract even a moderately sizable congregation, Bliss also contemplated withdrawing to the country to establish a social-religious community. When he discussed the idea with some sympathetic friends, he felt sufficiently encouraged to run the following advertisement in *The Dawn*: "Wanted—to buy and carry on, near Boston, a Union Farm, or the beginning of a Neighborhood or Fellowship of Christian Socialists."[50]

The Holy Cross fathers had come into possession of a country retreat through the generosity of a devout woman with strong Anglo-Catholic sympathies, but it appears that no one in the neighborhood of Boston with

Christian Socialist sympathies had a farm to sell, much less to donate. This project never went beyond the discussion stage, which was probably just as well, since it seems to have been the result of a momentary enthusiasm born out of a sense of desperation. Some years later Bliss criticized the idea that co-operative communities could significantly influence the transformation of society as a whole in an article that the radical Christian newspaper, *The Kingdom*, printed under the title "Self-saving Colonies Condemned."[51] Even when he contemplated establishing just such a community himself he was careful to distinguish its aims from those of its predecessors, most notably the famous Brook Farm Colony.[52] It is very difficult to imagine that the eternally peripatetic Bliss ever could have settled into the routine existence of life on a farm.

Unlike Huntington, Bliss did not retreat into the country; instead he enlarged the scope of his activities in the city by organizing the Wendell Phillips Union. The union, named for one of the few prominent clergymen of the preceding generation who had espoused the interests of labor, was essentially what we now call a community center. The Brotherhood of the Carpenter made its headquarters there, and rooms were rented out as meeting places to the Central Labor Union, the Knights of Labor, the Amalgamated Building Trade Council, and the Bricklayers Union.[53] Other social reform groups were encouraged to make full use of the facilities, and a series of lectures on religious, economic, and social issues was organized to attract the public at large. Bliss seemed determined to prove that if he could not unite Christians and social reformers into one body, he could at least bring them together under one roof. Expanding on work already begun by the brotherhood, the union organized a Purchaser's League, a variety of consumer cooperative designed to force employers to improve working conditions.[54] Following in the steps of England's original Christian Socialists, the union then established a producers' cooperative for the manufacture of children's clothing, but like its predecessor across the ocean the cooperative received few orders.[55] This venture ended in disaster when it was discovered that working conditions at the cooperative did not meet the standards regarded as minimal by the Purchaser's League.[56]

Naturally, Bliss was tremendously embarrassed and upset by the revelation that the Wendell Phillips Union had inadvertently spawned a sweatshop, but even if he had wanted to supervise the union's activities, his other pressing duties allowed him no leisure to do so. In addition to the time consumed working for the parish, the brotherhood, and the union, many of his hours were spend editing and providing copy for *The Dawn*, which he continued to bring out despite constant financial pressure. Then in the summer of 1892, Bliss accepted another exciting but arduous responsibility when he agreed to become the organizing secretary for the Church Social Union and undertake a three-month lecture tour on their behalf.

Bliss was uniquely qualified for the job: not only was he a superb organizer, but he was intimately acquainted with the developing social gospel movement in the English church. And the Church Social Union was certainly the most important example of the direct influence exerted by the Social Gospel movement in the Church of England on that in the Protestant Episcopal Church. In 1890, the Reverend Robert T. Holland, a priest from St. Louis, became acquainted with the English Christian Social Union while on a visit to that country. He returned to the United States convinced that a similar body should be formed in the American church. He turned for assistance to Bishop Huntington, the president of C.A.I.L., and Richard T. Ely of Johns Hopkins University. A Provisional Executive Committee organized the union on April 3, 1891; Bishop Huntington was elected president and Professor Ely became secretary. The Reverend Mr. Holland subsequently became president of the St. Louis branch and a union vice president.

From its English parent the American union adopted its name, its organizational structure, and its principles.[57] Most important, it adopted the English union's moderate stance on social issues. As Ely phrased it, the union "seeks progress, but progress with safety. Its watchword is—progressive conservatism."[58] At a general meeting held in Baltimore in October 1892 the union decided to avoid controversy by eschewing any definite economic philosophy. Churchmen of every economic persuasion were welcomed into membership, but few stand-pat conservatives were attracted by its principles.[59]

Most of the union's leaders—men like Bishop Huntington, Professor Ely, and Dean George Hodges of the Episcopal Theological School in Cambridge, Massachusetts—reflected its moderate stance on social issues, yet the radical Bliss was made organizing secretary and was elected to the Executive Committee. It is significant that the spirit of rivalry and competition that characterized the relationship between the English Christian Social Union and the radical Stewart Headlam was absent in the relationship between the American Christian Social Union and the radical William Dwight Porter Bliss. One can explain this absence fairly simply by pointing out that the Guild of St. Matthew was very much a going concern when the English union was organized, whereas the Society of Christian Socialists was already in the grave

124

when Bliss became organizing secretary for the American union. Such an explanation should not be disregarded, but neither should it be accepted as sufficient; one must also remember that the two men had very different personalities.

Stewart Headlam's opinions were fixed and definite; he was a vigorous critic, an avid controversialist, and tireless champion of unpopular causes. Because he believed so passionately in Anglo-Catholicism and the single tax, other forms of churchmanship and reform seemed to him to represent less than the whole truth. He recognized few adiaphora, and there was always a sectarian edge to his enthusiasm. Bliss also was an enthusiast, but he was resolutely opposed to all forms of religious and political sectarianism. He dreaded divisive conflict and longed for the cooperation of all men of good will; his passion for unity both political and religious equaled that of his admired mentor, F. D. Maurice. Therefore when the American union was organized Bliss feared no rival, but rather welcomed an ally whose aims were complementary to, if not exactly the same as, his own.

The union's moderate leaders, who were personally acquainted with Bliss through their common work in C.A.I.L., knew that his opinions were more radical than theirs, but they also knew that he was one of the most tireless and successful organizers in the church. His performance on behalf of the union did not disappoint them. During the organizing tour of 1892, which lasted only three months, Bliss delivered sixty-five addresses. On the average he spoke two days out of every three, even while traveling. It was a grueling campaign, but he had every reason to regard it as a success. As a direct result of his efforts five new branches were organized, and he prepared the way for five or six others.[60]

Thus far I have emphasized Bliss's role as an organizer, but he recognized that before men can be organized to solve a problem, they must first be made aware of its existence; and while he actively organized the few, he also attempted to educate the many. Throughout an active career as a social reformer, which lasted just over thirty years, Bliss labored almost without ceasing, it would seem, to reach the public and awaken them to the cause of reform. Of course, he was an active preacher and lecturer, but in his day the written word was the most effective means of mass communication, and Bliss was also a prolific writer. During the early nineties, for example, in addition to *The Dawn* he edited two collections of the selected social writings of Ruskin and Mill, *The Communism of John Ruskin* and *The Socialism of John Stewart Mill*, as well as an abridgment of Thorald Roger's *Six Centuries of*

*Work and Wages*. In 1895 he prepared a popular explication of the principles and historical development of socialism, which he published as *A Handbook of Socialism*, and began editing *The American Fabian*, another periodical. His most significant work, *The Encyclopedia of Social Reform*, "the real pioneer among sociological reference books, which blazed the trail for *The Encyclopedia of the Social Sciences* twenty years later,"[61] appeared in 1897. From 1904 to 1906 he collaborated with A. H. Tolman in compiling and publishing *Social Progress, A Year Book*. In 1908 he began his last important educational project, a series of Social Gospel Sunday school lessons called *The Gospel of the Kingdom*. Published under the aegis of the American Institute for Social Service, it "attained widest circulation of any material published in the interest of social Christianity during its first half century, reaching more than 40,000 readers in churches, Y.M.C.A.s, colleges, universities, and theological schools."[62] Bliss relinquished this project—his last major contribution to the cause of social reform in the United States—in 1916 when at the age of sixty he left for Switzerland to work with French and Belgian soldiers interred there during the First World War.[63]

Bliss's literary output was prodigious, but most of his writing was either strictly topical or an editorial compilation from other sources. Arthur Mann's critical judgment of his oeuvre is perceptive and fair: "At his best in presenting the ideas of other men, W. D. P. Bliss's own thought, however, was often vague, obscure, superficial and imitative."[64] His works are most important as historical sources for his own life and thought; they have had little enduring significance. To pass over them quickly is to do Bliss no injustice; he wrote not for history, but for his own time. He wanted to educate his contemporaries and convince them that social reform was a necessity; the sizable circulation of *The Gospel of the Kingdom* is a sign that his labors were not entirely in vain.

Bliss was able to work so effectively and happily within the Church Social Union because its members shared his enthusiasm for social education. "Professor Ely suggested that the Church Social Union be a social university—an educational institution in the broadest sense"[65]—and the union's educational program was conceived on a broad scale. It sponsored numerous conferences; circulated lists to its members of suggested readings, which included *The Dawn*, and, most important of all, financed the publication of a series of original pamphlets on current social, religious, and economic subjects.[66] By 1900 the union had circulated nearly seventy publications.[67]

Christian Social radicals like Bliss and Vida Scudder contributed essays to this series and thereby gained the ear of the union's substantial membership.

Bliss could only applaud the union's extensive educational program, but for him education was a first step toward social reformation. Particularly during its first seven years, however, the union seemed to regard its educational program as its total raison d'être. Bliss did not believe that pamphlets and conferences alone could effect a social reformation, and he criticized the union in *The Dawn* for its failure to emphasize action.[68] Gradually the union responded to the criticisms of its radical members and in 1898 the Executive Committee decided that "study should bear some fruit." Members were urged to support the campaign for the Saturday half-holiday and to join consumers' leagues.[69]

In 1892 when Bliss undertook his first organizing tour for the Church Social Union he had high hopes that the new People's Party, formed only two years before, would become the rallying ground for all those forces desiring social transformation. While he was lecturing in the West, Bliss had occasion to meet with populist leaders and he returned to Boston exhausted and disillusioned. He was impressed with the sincerity of the populist stalwarts, but he recognized that the various reformers were too far apart to permit hopes for any immediate political reformation.[70] In *The Dawn* he announced his intention to appeal "more and more to the religious sense. The need is great, the political outlook doubtful, the religious outlook one of hope."[71] For the next three years (1892-95), "with the exception of participating in a local tenement-house reform agitation, he devoted himself almost completely to religious affairs at the Mission of the Carpenter."[72]

Here too he was to experience disillusionment. Despite his strenuous efforts the congregation at the Church of the Carpenter never grew beyond seventeen communicants, and the brotherhood remained fixed at about one hundred members. Finally in 1896, when its rector decided to devote himself to full-time organizing for the numerically successful Christian Social Union, the little congregation voted itself out of existence.

The Church of the Carpenter lasted only six years, but it should not be written off as a failure. Its companion organizations, the Brotherhood of the Carpenter and the Wendell Phillips Union, provided useful and necessary services for the labor unions and the poor of Boston. Also, the church served to bring together a stimulating company of like-minded persons who were in the forefront of the emerging movement for social reform. The valiant labor union leader George E. McNeil served as its senior warden; Vida Scudder attended the services,[73] and such diverse figures as the prominent Anglican cleric W. S. Rainsford, the novelists Hamlin Garland and William Dean Howells, and the socialist theoretician Daniel De Leon made appearances.[74] Moss significant, however, was the Church's prophetic witness: by rejecting the economic and credal barriers so significant in its own time, the Church of the Carpenter prefigured the more comprehensive, ecumenical outlook of Christianity in the twentieth century.

During the remaining twenty-eight years of his life, Porter Bliss served as priest in four more Episcopal parishes, but none of these was a full-time occupation. Never again did he attempt to establish a Christian Socialist church or brotherhood. Instead, most of his energy was devoted to lecturing, writing, and political action.

### Christian Socialism and Social Reform

In 1885 the horrors of industrial life in South Natick, Massachusetts, convinced Bliss that basic social transformation was necessary. He devoted the rest of his life to effecting that transformation through social reform. I have shown how Bliss's decision to become a social reformer shaped his career as an Anglican clergyman; I now turn to the social reforms he sought to realize. What did Bliss mean by Christian Socialism? What was its goal?

Not long after the Society of Christian Socialists was organized, Bliss answered that question in the summer 1890 issue of *The Dawn*. The object of Christian Socialism, he said, was "an earth located spirit state, where there shall be the highest individuality for every member realized in the most highly developed social organism."[75] This statement—one characteristic of his rhetorical style—reminds us of Mann's observation that Bliss's thought was often "vague and obscure." Contemporaries also noted this characteristic indefiniteness. Richard T. Ely, a sympathetic fellow Anglican, reflected that Bliss's Christian Socialists seemed to be motivated by "a certain Spirit rather than a fixed creed;[76] Nicholas Paine Gilman, an unsympathetic Unitarian critic of the Christian Socialists, grumbled that they were "something like a society for the propagation of virtue in general."[77]

The vagueness and obscurity of Bliss's thoughts and expression have contributed to a disagreement among historians of the Social Gospel movement. Both James Dombrowski and Charles Howard Hopkins, who wrote their pioneering studies of the social gospel movement during the red-tinted 1930s, had questions about "the genuineness of Christian Socialist socialism."

> On the whole Mr. Bliss and his followers had more in common with Henry George and Edward Bellamy than with Karl Marx. Like most of the Christian Socialists of his day, Bliss thought of Socialism often in vague and sentimental terms, appropriating those elements of socialist philosophy congenial to general notions of brotherhood and ignoring the remainder. Bliss and his followers were too much the children of the nineteenth century fully to apprehend the significance of socialist theory, or to accept its radical notions when they were freely exhibited. These nineteenth century Christian Socialists seemed unaware of *the basic socialist doctrines of "surplus value," the class struggle and economic determinism. Their socialism was built on the ideas of French Revolutionary Democracy more than on scientific socialism.*[78] [emphasis mine]

Although Charles Hopkins's tone was less openly critical of Christian Socialism than was Dombrowski's, Hopkins also expressed reservations about the socialism of the Christian Socialists.

> The Christianized fabianism of Bliss and his followers was a compound of religion, evolution and socialism. Accepting uncritically the "ruling ideas" of the day—an immanent God, the organic view of society, and the present reality of the kingdom of heaven—these crusaders developed an *evolutionary reform philosophy* that included the spiritual values of socialism and many of its critical and constructive elements, but that rejected its materialistic and atheistic aspects. *The Boston Christian Socialists were first of all Christians, and socialists secondly* and only insofar as socialistic goals could be embraced in the arms of Christianity.[79] [emphasis mine]

Historians whose work has appeared since the Second World War have been more willing than their confreres in the thirties to accept the socialism of Christian Socialists as genuine. Howard Quint discussed Bliss at length in *The Forging of American Socialism*, and Henry F. May flatly stated "Bliss was an appropriate spearhead for the left of the social movement. His Christian Socialism was actually socialism."[80] Webber championed May's opinion and criticized Dombrowski and Hopkins for "missing the point" by reading "latter-day news of Russian Marxism into a socialism as yet unsullied by such associations."[81]

Although I am in essential agreement with Webber's criticism of Dombrowski and Hopkins—Dombrowski in particular seems to assume that socialism equals scientific socialism, i.e., Marxism—I take exception to

Webber's assertion that class-consciousness, economic determinism, etc., constitute a latter-day view of Russian Marxism. These positions are, of course, part of classical Marxist analysis and have been held by many who would never sympathize with Soviet totalitarianism.[82] Furthermore, it should be emphasized, even though Dombrowski and Hopkins tend to equate socialism with Marxism, their critical insights remain useful. It is true, for example, that the Christian Socialists were Christians first and socialists second and that they were far closer to Henry George and Edward Bellamy than to Karl Marx.

My task, though, is to disclose Bliss's personal position. It is easier to discern this position if I briefly recapitulate its intellectual sources; then I examine his attitude toward the labor movement and his Christian Socialist program. Finally, I shall consider the method he proposed for realizing that program.[83]

There is no evidence that Karl Marx played any part in Bliss's decision to become a reformer. His desire for a social transformation grew out of personal experience in South Natick and was strengthened by Henry George and articles in *The Christian Union*.[84] During the mid-eighties he became acquainted with the work of Maurice, Kingsley, and the early English Christian Socialist band; their ideas stimulated his vision at the time of his conversion to Anglicanism. In the May 1892 issue of *The Dawn*[85] Bliss described a religious community whose members lived together and worked in cooperative industry for the good of all. The cooperative industry principle, or producers' cooperatives, was central to early English Christian Socialism and Bliss wanted to make it the basis of the Church of the Carpenter.

After his conversion he continued to pursue his interest in the reform movement in the English church; "Socialism and the Church of England" shows that his interest expanded beyond the early Christian Socialism and included all the contemporary reform currents in the church. It is significant that in this article these various reform currents are described under the general heading, "Socialism." Socialism itself is not defined, but is used as a catchall phrase for social reform in general. This vague and general use of the word, it will be recalled, was also employed by English clerical social reformers at the end of the century.

W. J. Ghent, Bliss's younger friend and Christian Socialist disciple, writes that all his life Bliss was an omniverous reader[86]—a fact confirmed by the great mass of miscellaneous material on social issues that appeared in *The Dawn*—so it should not be surprising to discover that this interest in English reform was by no means confined to its ecclesiastical exponents. He knew the works of William Morris, John Ruskin, John Stewart Mill, and Thorald Rogers, among others, and when he set out to educate the public at large during the 1890s he chose to prepare the works of secular social critics for mass distribution.[87] If he neglected to edit the works of ecclesiastical reformers,[88] he also ignored the Marxists.

The last significant formative intellectual influence to affect Bliss before he embarked on his own active career as a Christian Socialist was the nationalist doctrine set forth in Edward Bellamy's utopian novel, *Looking Backward*. Although Bellamy never used the word *socialism* to describe his program, his nationalism advocated state ownership of all forms of production and distribution.[89] Bellamy's state socialism was not unlike the society favored by the Marxists, but the middle-class novelist rejected their emphasis on class struggle as a law of history and as a means of introducing the socialist state. Bellamy insisted that the "transition from a competitive, capitalistic society to a co-operative nationalist order would be slow, orderly, and in accord with the innate workings of economic evolution under capitalism." The nationalists, he wrote,

> propose no revolutionary methods, no hasty or ill considered measures provocative of reaction, no letting go of the old before securing a hold on the new; but an orderly progress of which each step shall logically follow the last, and shall be justified to the most short-sighted by its immediate motives and results without involving any considerations of ultimate ends. Those who wish to go only a step at a time we welcome as allies, and we pledge them a cooperation which is not the less cordial and considerate because of the fact that results which they regard as ends seem to us but means to ends.[90]

Even though Bliss found Bellamy's nationalism very attractive, he could not long remain active in an organization dominated by Theosophists who refused to acknowledge that they were socialists. Nor should we forget that during the period when Bliss was responding to the intellectual influence of Mauricean Christian Socialism, English social criticism, Bellamy's nationalism, et al., he was also an active Knight of Labor. Associating with the labor movement certainly helped shape his views: Bliss himself wrote that he had learned more—both in spirit and in economic wisdom—from his friend George E. McNeil, the labor union leader—than from any other man.[91] Not long after he left the nationalists, Bliss criticized them for failing to work more closely with organized labor. It was a fatal mistake, he believed, to see labor unions as a class movement. Christian Socialists, he was sure, would give a "hearty Godspeed to their brothers of the factory and plow."[92]

*The Dawn* gave them more than Godspeed; during the bitter industrial conflict of the early 1890s some of Bliss's most radical rhetoric was expended on their behalf. When miners lost their lives in the sporadic industrial warfare that erupted in the Pennsylvania coal fields, *The Dawn* printed a four inch box framed in heavy black borders. Inside, the message read:

SHOT
By hired tools of the capitalists
CHILDREN OF GOD
For such *The Dawn* mourns
"In as much as ye have done it unto one of the least
of these my brethren, ye have done it unto me."
Matthew XXV. 40[93]

Divine retribution is suggested here, but Bliss did not believe that the workers should sit passively by and wait for God's ultimate justice to right their wrongs. Unlike most middle-class reformers, Bliss believed that labor should fight back. When railroad switchmen went out on strike against the New York Central, he championed their right to protect themselves against the assaults of company strikebreakers. *The Dawn* asked: "If corporations have the right to arm private detectives and fire upon almost any pretext, why has not organized labor an equal right to form, arm, and drill a similar body to defend themselves?"[94]

*The Dawn* also championed labor's cause in situations where laws were broken to achieve humane ends. When rebellious miners in Tracy City, Tennessee, released three hundred prisoners by burning down the stockades that imprisoned them, Bliss reviewed their actions affirmatively.

[They] broke the laws of men, to obey the laws of justice . . . we honor them for it. We welcome this sign of returning manhood. They committed no violence to life. But where will it end, when workingmen begin to appeal to the propaganda of the deed?—where their brave deeds ended who poured tea into Boston Harbor?—In a revolution?[95]

Statements like these help explain why moderates like Bishop Potter denounced Bliss as a dangerous man. He did not attempt to soothe the workers' wounds with promises of a socialist future; rather he congratulated them when they fought to achieve justice now. In his refusal to subordinate social justice to bourgeois law and order Bliss showed himself to be as radical as any revolutionary Marxist. Yet he did not espouse the cause of violence and he remained resolutely opposed to the Marxist doctrine of class conflict. For a Christian clergyman his position on violence was remarkably unmoralistic; he opposed it because he did not think it would work. After the failure of the often violent Brooklyn trolley strike in 1895 Bliss wrote

> Workingmen are learning fast that American justice and American laws exist mainly to keep workingmen down and protect property, while capitalists can disobey the laws *ad infinitum*. It is well. Workingmen must learn that they can gain nothing by appeal either to violence or to legal proceedings. Their only way is to strike through the ballot and overcome the capitalistic ownership of the country.[96]

Writing in *The New Encyclopedia of Social Reform* Bliss defined socialism in the following terms: "Socialism may be said to be: the collective ownership of the means of production by the community democratically organized and their operation cooperatively for the equitable good of all."[97] Note that this definition excluded Marx's dictatorship of the proletariat and ignored Bellamy's equal distribution of all income.[98] The political-social-economic system here described was radical: it envisioned a new order and not merely the elimination of contemporary society's most notorious abuses. This new order was to be introduced through democratic methods—the "strike through the ballot" that would overcome capitalism. Bliss realized, however, that at the moment the democratic majority did not favor socialism; they would have to be won over to the socialist cause through education. As we have seen, Bliss devoted an enormous amount of energy throughout his life to the cause of social education.

Educating the public does, though, take time, and Bliss understood that the collective ownership of the means of production was a goal and not an immediate prospect. While he pursued his goal, he was constantly pre-occupied—as his articles attest—with the question "What to do now?" Education was not enough; it had to be complemented by immediate action. "Socialism does not claim to reach the ideal at a bound," he wrote in *The Dawn*, "only to improve gradually upon the present."[99] During his career he championed myriad movements that he thought would both improve the present and hasten the dawn of socialism. He lent his support to labor unions and settlement houses, and he was a leader in the agitation to improve living conditions in tenements. He favored the Australian secret ballot, women's suffrage, the eight-hour day, compulsory education, prohibition, and public works to relieve unemployment. As a necessary step toward collective ownership of the means of production, he advocated the nationalization of railroads, public utilities, and natural resources. Local transit, light, and heat, he believed, should be municipally managed.[100]

Bliss was particularly anxious to distinguish the gradualistic methods of Christian Socialism from the piecemeal philanthropy greatly acclaimed by moderate religious reformers:

> . . . we are not to work to establish a Christian cooperative colony, no system of profit-sharing, no individualistic scheme, no *ignis fatuus* of associated charities and model houses and aristocratic patronage. We are to work for the development of the Christian State, and so for the conversion of people to our ideas.[101]

Unlike the moderates, Bliss did not conceive of gradualistic reform as an end in itself; for him it was merely the most effective way to reach the goal. He never hesitated to acknowledge that Christian Socialists were state socialists.[102]

Christian Socialists were state socialists, but they were first and foremost Christians. As socialists they rejected reform as an end in itself, and as Christians they rejected state socialism as an end in itself. For them state socialism was only one aspect—though a necessary aspect—of the Christian state, the Kingdom of God.

> We are not to be in haste to turn everything over to Uncle Sam, trusting to Uncle Sam to realize God's Kingdom in the United States. With every respect for Uncle Sam we still believe in the necessity of the development of the individual. We are to be eternally democratic. . . . Christian Socialists are to make their main stand for the divine conception of the State, and the necessity of a true environment as one of the elements though by no means the only element, in the development of perfect character.[103]

Christian Socialists looked beyond state socialism to the Kingdom of God where God alone was king and all men were united in loving brotherhood.

Bliss's approach to realizing socialism was inherently peaceful, democratic, and gradualistic; it was also pragmatic and political. The Christian Socialists were a very small group whose efforts—however heroic they may have been—had little chance to win over the majority of Americans to their cause. Only by working with other like-minded reformers could they hope to make an impression on society at large. Political necessity dictated that they find allies.

Fortunately, Bliss's temperament and outlook coincided with the demands of necessity. He was an enthusiastic joiner who could work with others for the accomplishment of a common purpose—even if their ideas did not agree exactly with his own. Ultimately his political realism was founded on a Mauricean passion for unity, a unity that Bliss knew theologically to be more real than the surface diversity among men. All his life Bliss sought to transcend divisions through cooperative fellowship. The Church of the Carpenter ignored contemporary social and denominational boundaries, and Bliss's campaigns on behalf of the Church Social Union demonstrated his willingness to give himself wholeheartedly to an organization whose views were not identical with his own.

After his resignation from the Church of the Carpenter Bliss spent nearly twenty years trying to organize an umbrella organization that would unite various reform groups. The American Fabian League, the Union Reform League, and the Social Reform Union were all the results of his efforts, but like the Society of Christian Socialists before them, none of them experienced long-lived success.[104] As always, Bliss expended himself freely, but the reformers disagreed too much among themselves to unite in a common organization. Finally, Bliss found a home in the American Institute for Social Service, where he devoted himself to preparing *The Gospel of the Kingdom.*

In the early years of his Christian Socialism, before the election of 1892, Bliss had urged reformers of all persuasions to unite under the banner of the People's Party to achieve common ends. He became disillusioned with his own campaign for a popular front in politics, however, when firsthand experience convinced him that the populists goals'—whose sincerity he did not question—were too narrow. Thereafter he withheld his support from third-party movements, attempting instead to work for reform within the traditional two-party system. In 1896 and 1900 he supported the Democratic standard-bearer, William Jennings Bryan, whose reform platform Bliss believed would advance the cause of socialism in the United States.[105] When Bryan lost, Bliss was not disheartened; instead he rejoiced that a reformer could elicit such wide support.[106] His optimism was truly remarkable; after each defeat, he returned to the fray confident of victory in the future.

Bliss's decision to support the reform candidate of a major party rather than an avowed socialist spokesman from either Daniel De Leon's Socialist Labor Party or the rising Social Democratic Party has provoked the unsympathetic criticism of recent historians. Even Quint, whose treatment of Bliss is ordinarily characterized by sympathetic understanding, openly questions his motives. "The unwillingness of Bliss in particular . . . to work with and through a promising and essentially revisionist socialist political party, indicated a lack of political courage characteristic of the whole middle-class socialist movement.[107]

My purpose is not to justify the wisdom of Bliss's political decisions in bygone elections, but rather to uncover his motivation. The middle-class socialist movement as a whole may have lacked the political courage to support the Social Democrats—each reader must decide for himself the wisdom of Quint's generalization—but Bliss's long career as a champion of unpopular causes hardly suggests that he was a coward. Bliss was not afraid to support socialist parties; he objected to them for the same reason he became disillusioned with the populists—they were too narrow. Daniel De Leon's obsession with ideological purity, which finally reduced the Socialist Labor Party to a small, ineffective, personal sect,[108] was as repugnant to Bliss as was the party's "gospel of class hatred."[109] The Social Democrats, of course, were not nearly as dogmatic as the De Leonites, but in the first years of the twentieth century, the party was plagued by numerous factional disputes.[110] Bliss attributed this factionalism to the "evils attendant on the party system in general and on a class party in particular."[111]

Bliss's position on class-based party socialism as the natural outgrowth of his lifelong passion for comprehensive unity, a unity that his incarnational theology believed to be the underlying reality of all life. His career reveals a consistent opposition to sectarianism, both religious and secular. He was a Christian Socialist who eschewed both denominational Anglicanism and class-party socialism. In Anglicanism he saw an imperfect representation aspiring to be the Body of Christ; in socialism he recognized a movement working for the Brotherhood of Man. Like Maurice before him, Bliss has justly been accused of being misty, vague, and confusing. Perhaps in both cases, however, the fault lies not entirely with the men but with a fallen world whose language has no words capable of precisely describing Jerusalem, the vision of peace, our happy home. All we have, as Maurice would say, are suggestions and hints.

Most historians who review the events of Bliss's career sympathetically conclude that he was a noble failure. None of the projects that he so diligently pursued was a success. His disciple W. J. Ghent concludes the earliest biographical sketch of the reformer:

He is best remembered for his moral force, his passion for justice, his crystalline sincerity and perfect disinterestedness. He believed what he professed; he was a missionary who carried his religion into the workaday world. Unaggressive yet persistent, he preached his gospel of social salvation to all who would listen and read, and did it with sheer disregard of personal consequences. He died a poor man.[112]

Yet we must conclude that Bliss was no failure. Had he adopted the dogmatic stance of De Leon, Headlam, or many another well-intentioned, sincere reformer, one might equate the collapse of his projects with personal failure. But Bliss, involved though he was with his own dreams, looked beyond them to a vision he shared with other men.

Bliss's passion for comprehensive unity involved him in the wider mainstream of American political life. He realized that one could not reach the ideal in any one bound, but only gradually improve upon the present through common consent. Many of the specific causes Bliss advocated have been realized by reformers working through the system of democratic, majoritarian politics. Bliss would be the first to recognize that the social reforms enacted during the twentieth century have not produced the Kingdom of God. But he would be pleased by the current concern of both church and state to improve upon the present. This attitude was one he helped shape.

# SIX

# Vida Dutton Scudder:
# A Socialist Churchwoman

## Early Life

Vida Dutton Scudder was born in Madura, India, where her father, David Coit Scudder, ministered to a native flock under the auspices of the Congregational Board of Foreign Missions. David Scudder was a remarkably dedicated young man. As a boy he had been so captivated by the reminiscences of the Indian missionaries who were frequent and welcome guests in his family home that he resolved to follow their example and take the gospel to the East. Many young people dream of a high idealistic calling only to abandon it in later life for more mundane pursuits, but David was not one of these. On the surface he lived the life of an ordinary boy, rambling through the fields of rural New England, getting into minor mischief, and generally enjoying himself. Underneath the surface, though, there was a deep sense of religious location and the pursuit of a definite goal. He worked hard to prepare himself for the future.

Since the Congregationalists were committed by tradition to an educated clergy, young Scudder went off to college and seminary, but, loyal to his own particular calling, he added to the usual training extensive research in Oriental languages and philosophy. He undertook these studies so that he might preach the Christ in the language and intellectual framework understood by the people, but confronting the Indian religious classics at firsthand filled him with a deep respect for the Indian people and their culture. When he began his ministry, not long before the birth of his daughter, he was not burdened by provincial bigotry and his first contacts with the local population suggested that the future would be marked by success.

Unfortunately, the career so ardently prepared for was cut short. When Vida was scarcely a year old, her father went swimming in a local river; a dam broke in the hills and he was washed away in the flood and drowned. The tragic death of a promising man not yet twenty-eight deeply affected his family. His daughter reports that the news of David's death killed his father. His grieving wife quickly left the country of her affliction and returned with her infant daughter to the Dutton family home in Auburndale, Massachusetts. The child retained no memories of India, but throughout her life Vida Scudder was haunted by the image of her idealistic father whose life was cut off before its promise could be fulfilled.[1]

Young Vida grew up in a large Victorian family circle that was energetic, affectionate, and decidedly Brahmin. She could trace her descent from John Winthrop, among others.[2] If neither the Duttons nor the Scudders were wealthy, even by the more modest financial standards of the 1860s, both families were secure and comfortable. Brahmins moved in circles too established to be impressed by mere money; like the aristocrats who inhabited Proust's Faubourg Saint-Germain, Vida's relatives discriminated "among [their] neighbors on grounds not of their possessions but of their enunciation."[3] This disdainful attitude may appear narrow and snobbish today, but at least it avoided the more typical American vice of making money the measure of the person. Vida soon outgrew her family's narrow standards of discrimination, but she always retained the true aristocrat's disdain for mere money.

The family was an interesting and cultivated group. Her mother's brother, E. P. Dutton, founded the publishing company that bears his name; a paternal uncle, Horace Scudder, edited *The Atlantic Monthly*, authored numerous books popular in his time, and served as a literary adviser for Houghton Mifflin. Uncle Samuel, known as "the butterfly man," was a brilliant student of Louis Agassiz, and made important contributions to science; Aunt Jenny was a talented artist.

They were independent people who possessed a strong strain of humanitarian idealism. In the days when the timid and the time-serving persecuted the abolitionists and defended slavery, these high-minded Brahmins sympathized with the unpopular cause because it was righteous. Sometimes, though, family loyalties were strained when a relative's independent spirit seemed to pass beyond the limits established by sound common sense. For example, consider "Aunt" Eliza Scudder, a fiery, outspoken opponent of slavery, who rejected her Congregational heritage at first for Unitarianism, but finally for Anglo-Catholicism. Polite New England radicalism could understand Unitarianism—even if it disputed the Christological doctrine—but it recoiled from the excesses of Puseyism, although it was theologically orthodox.

"Retreats! Early Communion! Even, it was incredibly whispered, auricular confession!"[4]

Another relative who strained family loyalties was the black sheep, Uncle Horace Dutton. This younger brother of the famous publisher became a Christian social reformer devoted to the service of the poor. He worked in city missions, brought criminals and vagrants home to supper, and followed Christ's injunction to the rich young ruler by giving away every cent that he possessed. Eliza Scudder and Horace Dutton may have upset their more cautious and conventional relatives, but they were accepted because they were good people and, for all their eccentricities, they were members of the family. They must have been warm and genial souls because they captured the affections of shy, young Vida; she cherished them almost as much as the memory of her missionary father who had gone halfway around the world to save his fellow man by preaching the gospel. The family's characteristic independence and humanitarian idealism were passed on to Vida, and when she reached maturity she never hesitated to defy convention in the service of humanity.

Almost half of her early life was spent in Europe where the widowed Mrs. Scudder, often with another female relative or friend, led a quiet life devoted to the appreciation of the arts. These serious ladies filled their many leisure hours with travel, pictures, and books. Romantic authors had taught them to respond to the most subtle nuances of nature, and they cultivated exquisite sensibilities with the Puritan sense of duty that they had learned from serious New England forebears. This style of life was refined, gracious, and pleasant, but Vida found that it lacked substance. Much of the time she had little contact with children her own age, and this isolation made her feel cut off from common humanity and the life of the world about her. "From childhood the evasiveness of all I loved and touched and saw had tormented me. . . . I always felt as if in a dream, with the substantial world just around the corner."[5]

As a young girl she often expressed her frustration by throwing tantrums—which were quietly ignored—but she deeply loved her quiet, gentle mother and, growing older, emulated her by seeking solace in a world of books and dreams. Her life, full of stimulation but without challenge, gave her a vague feeling of perpetual yearning; while quite young she had fallen prey to the romantic *mal de siècle* that had tormented sensitive, high-strung intellectuals since Chateaubriand. In adolescence, she tried to confront life directly by becoming an artist. Life classes in a Parisian art school taught her "to look fixedly at a person or an apple and really to see them,"[6] but when she grew older she realized that her artistic standards were too high for her mediocre talents and she abandoned her artistic attempts.

If the isolation and rarified atmosphere of grand-tour living were frustrating, European cultural life was liberating, and these years left positive influences that remained with her after the frustrations had passed away. One winter when Vida was about fifteen, the Scudders moved to Paris and lived with a French family; it was hoped that Vida would take advantage of the opportunity and learn French. She studied "assiduously" and "read with avidity all the French books on which I could lay my hands."[7] The book that left the deepest impression was a life of Lacordaire. The self-described "young Protestant" was fascinated by the spiritual life of that group of liberal Catholic social reformers who gathered about La Mennais, Lacordaire, and the Vicomte de Montalembert. It is not likely that she would have gotten to know them in Yankee Boston where the Roman Church was identified with the superstitious practices of ignorant immigrants. This encounter with social Catholicism had no immediate results, but it affected the direction of her spiritual life and helped prepare her for her Oxford awakening.

The most significant influence made by the years in Europe was a heightened sense of the past. Vida longed for reality, and in Europe the past was real; it had a physical presence she could touch in ancient buildings and monuments, hear in the chants of cathedral choirs, and see in church frescoes and museum easel paintings. A childhood in Europe made her an emotional conservative tied to the masterworks of the past. This conservatism was revealed in her religious and literary tastes, and in later years it balanced her intellectual and social radicalism. Even when she championed the revolutionary ideals of Marxist socialism, she retained a profound Burkean respect for the traditional heritage. "Cathedrals, sacred art, liturgies, biographies, bore a witness I could not repudiate."[8]

When the family returned from Europe, Vida was enrolled at the Boston Girls' Latin School. Her European experience set her apart from the other girls, who knew little philosophy or poetry. Their public school educations had taught them nothing about Gothic cathedrals and Florentine primitives, but, much to her chagrin, she discovered that they always took home better grade reports. She continued to lead an isolated life, but the academic rigors of traditional classical education offered her intellectual challenge. Getting into the world was doubtless good for her, even if the Boston Latin School left no important enduring impression on her mind and personality.

Her years at Smith College were more significant. Finally, she broke out of her youthful isolation and began forming close friendships. These friendships made it possible for her to feel that she was participating in the life of common humanity, an experience more important to her than the intellectual stimulation of college academic life. She was a superior student, but standards were genteel rather than rigorous, and she did not work very hard. The pace was less frantic in those days; Smith was not preparing future scholars but educating young ladies. Nonetheless, she continued reading widely, and she became deeply interested in the new field of scientific sociology taught by J. B. Clark. Here, if only in the abstract, she first confronted some of the social realities of her time.[9]

Unlike many of her classmates—and famous contemporary women social reformers—Vida Scudder did not lose her religious faith in college. During the last decades of the nineteenth century, agnosticism and skepticism attracted many educated people who could no longer accept the bibliolatry and narrow dogmatism of an evangelical orthodoxy severely questioned by recent scientific and historical speculations. When Vida was a young girl, however, her mother was one of the many Boston Congregationalists who were converted to Anglicanism by the great rector of Trinity Church, Phillips Brooks. Brooks was the leading exponent of the theology of Frederick Denison Maurice in the United States, and he introduced Mrs. Scudder to the thought of the English theologian.[10] At first Vida resisted Anglicanism. "My childish loyalty clung long to the old traditions. . . . I was always naughtily indisposed to follow a popular cry, cause, or person. Moreover I was in a state of rueful befuddlement about religion."[11] But at fourteen, guided by the "gracious teaching of Phillips Brooks and the thought of F. D. Maurice, so dear to my mother,"[12] she decided to accept Episcopal confirmation.

Maurice's thought, which I have discussed, was more intellectually sophisticated than ordinary, New England popular Protestantism, much of which was at that time still tied to revivalism with its mechanistic interpretation of the doctrine of atonement. The revivalists, sincere as they may have been, alienated numerous sensitive, educated young people by loudly proclaiming the assurance of damnation and by overemphasizing personal conversion as the exclusive means of salvation. Unable to accept the tenets of revivalism, many of Vida's friends abandoned Christianity altogether.[13] But Maurice spared her "any crudities such as bothered many of my generation"[14] and she credits him with having saved her from religious disbelief.

When Vida was graduated from Smith in 1881, the Scudders returned to Europe, where she continued her education. They spent the second half of their trip at Oxford, and here Vida experienced a double awakening: she embraced Anglo-Catholicism, and John Ruskin made her a radical. It was one of the most momentous events of her life because it laid the foundations for her future development.

At Oxford she discovered that the religious conservatism revived nearly half a century before by Keble, Pusey, Newman, Froude, and their circle was still very much in the air; and the home of the Oxford movement reawakened in her that reverence for the spiritual traditions of the past that had previously been stimulated by the biography of Lacordaire, medieval cathedrals, and Gregorian chant. "Religious tastes were defined."[15] The word *taste* is significant. She did not adopt Oxford movement theology, only its founders' deep respect for the past. Her emotional nature responded to the aesthetic appeal of Gothic Revival buildings and splendid liturgy, an attitude more indebted to John Mason Neale's Cambridge Ecclesiological Society and to the second generation Anglo-Catholic ritualist slum priests than to the original Oxford reformers, who, it will be remembered, took little interest in the revival of ceremonialism. It took years for her tastes to develop into firm convictions. The process was not completed until she began studying St. Catherine of Siena twenty years later. Even then, when her convictions became firm, they never hardened into inflexible dogmas.

Vida Scudder had been brought up on Ruskin's evocative and imaginative art criticism, and it was the author of the *Stones of Venice* that attracted her to his lectures. But the lecturer that she heard speak was now the Ruskin of *Unto This Last*. His agonized social criticism forced her to wake up to "the realities of modern civilization," and, she writes, "[I] decided I did not like them."[16] A sense of "chivalric sympathy" drove her toward the poor. She hated her own privileges and joined the Salvation Army to register her protest against injustice.[17] Joining the army was only a gesture, though; its religious outlook differed widely from her own. Ruskin had only awakened her to social injustice; she was not yet aware of how to go about righting wrongs. She had no positive reform program in mind, and at the end of the year returned to the United States with only a "nebulous sense of social radicalism."[18] Why, one might wonder, was her radicalism so nebulous? Surely she might have found an answer to her problems in the Guild of St. Matthew, an organization that seems almost cut out to suit her. The explanation here is twofold. First, the Scudders lived a very retiring life at Oxford and were quite cut off from the affairs of the university and the world at large. As a result Vida knew nothing about the radical social reform movement in the English church. She never even mentions Headlam or the guild in *On Journey*, and no reference is made to them in her discussion of the development of English socialism in *Social Ideas in English Letters*. Second, and more important, Vida's conversions to Anglo-Catholicism and to the cause of social reform were two entirely separate events. At Oxford she became an Anglo-Catholic and a social reformer, not an Anglo-Catholic social reformer. At first she did not connect her two new enthusiasms. "That there was living connection between the two orders of truth and that for me there was no certitude on either line until they were fused, I did not as yet surmise."[19]

In retrospect the Oxford experience appears to have been one of the decisive turning points in her life, but at the time Vida Scudder had no way of knowing this; she understood only that her religious and social opinions were in a state of flux. But the Oxford term did give her one immediate, positive accomplishment. Her tutor, York Powell, inspired her to write a paper on the Gothic grotesque, which was published when she returned to the United States. Unlike Smith, Oxford had challenged her intellect and taught her the values of scholarship. Study became "an end in itself. . . I found it its own excuse for being."[20]

After the emotional intensity of her Oxford term, Vida Scudder felt let down when she returned to the United States. Day-to-day life in her genteel environment seemed to be an unending anticlimax. In her autobiography she perceptively characterized the girl she had been at twenty-three as a "Lady in Waiting. . . . I was restless during those two years at home,—and more unhappy, I think than ever before or since."[21] Her problem at this time was not a new one, but rather the old problem of her early adolescence, returning in a more acute and painful form. In a sense it is not fair to label this spiritual malaise "her problem," since the most important factor causing her restlessness and unhappiness was her environment, not some defect in her psychological makeup. To be sure, her environment was pleasant—a comfortable Back Bay home that she shared with her mother and a doctor aunt—and stimulating—all of the advantages of cultural Boston lay almost literally within easy walking distance—but again it was without challenge. One is reminded of the "warm, scented drawing rooms" denounced by Mother Emily Ayckbown. The social and intellectual challenges of higher education had rescued Vida Scudder from her adolescent difficulties by taking her out of herself and bringing her into contact with common humanity. The culmination of this process had been reached at Oxford, but when she returned home she had been educated. Challenge gone, the old difficulties returned. She felt that her life had no purpose and she became bored and disillusioned once again. Marriage was the conventional solution to her problem, but she was not conventional. What could an unmarried, financially secure woman with a "nebulous sense of social radicalism" do? Of course there was always the family and the church, Boston's women's clubs claimed some time, but none of these resources satisfied her longing for reality. A line from a dialogue she wrote in collaboration with her friend Sophia Kirk a few years later sums up her disappointment with her life. "We lead sham lives in our youth, and the sham knowledge deadens for us the reality."[22]

"For lack of anything better to do,"[23] she began working on "The Effect of the Scientific Temper in Modern Poetry," a thesis that qualified her to receive the master of arts degree from Smith College.[24] She was justly proud of her academic accomplishment (only a very few women in her generation ever became a master of arts), but writing literary criticism did not satisfy her creative impulses. Years before she had abandoned the visual arts when she realized that she did not have the talent to become an accomplished artist; now she began to hope that "authorship was to be my lot." She experimented with a wide variety of literary forms, producing a play, essays, travel sketches, poems, and stories; several of these early works were published. Buoyed by her success she contemplated writing a major work (probably a novel), but when she took up her pen she found that she had nothing to say. When that project collapsed, she felt at sea once again.

One wonders what subject or project left Vida Scudder speechless, because she produced books and articles on a wide variety of subjects during a literary career that lasted for nearly fifty years. Three works in particular written during this period show that she did indeed have important questions on her mind and that when she had something to say she could say it. These works, "The Moral Dangers of Musical Devotees," *Mitsu-Yu Nissi, or a Japanese Wedding*, and "The Educated Woman as a Social Factor" deal with significant questions related to art, social reform, and the role of women in society. All of them are related to her own problem: What can an educated, financially secure woman do with her life?

"The Moral Dangers of Musical Devotees" is, as the title suggests, a critical, almost polemical, work. Firmly grounded in their teachings of John Ruskin, the article directly repudiates the doctrine of art for art's sake fashionable at the time in some circles, and assumes that there is a connection between art and morality. Music is dangerous because its beauty does not inspire us to contemplate the good and the true. "In music . . . [we] find pure art, untainted by any intrusion on her sphere. The province of music is to present to us, in the only unmodified form that the world has yet discovered, abstract and perfect beauty." The function of beauty, she argues, is to arouse emotion, and therefore the "object and result" of music is emotion; it is music's ideal expression. She poses a question: "Is a purely emotional force apart from a suggestive cause, or an object to which it may be directed, a desirable or a moral influence?" The answer, delivered at some length, is quite obviously no.[25]

"The end of life," the author argues, is "purposeful activity and the function of emotion [is] simply to stimulate to action." Experiencing emotion for its own sake produces a dangerous subjectivity that tends to exclude common humanity and the real world. Consciously pursuing such a course leads to an "epicurean ideal," which has "usually been most in vogue among nations such as Rome under the later Empire . . . exhausted in luxurious indifference. . . . The evils incident on an unlimited indulgence in musical luxury" will produce a species of "unhappy nervous invalids" whose enervated nature, "too sensitive to desire or endure a genuinely earnest activity, will gain at second hand, itself remaining quiescent, the subtle self-consciousness which is its greatest pleasure. . . ."[26]

Thus far the argument has been moral and aesthetic, but Ruskin's disciple could not ignore the social implications of the issue. The emotional release offered by listening to music, she admits, would be beneficial to "whole classes . . . absorbed in mechanical routine and domestic cares," the factory-workers and their families. But only "the class which has leisure and money" has the opportunity "to profit extensively [from] the musical advantages of our great cities." Chief among these are "girls and women of the upper classes, not engaged in any engrossing occupation." These will be "rather demoralized than uplifted by these advantages." The author offers no antidote to music's insidious, immoral influence on the upper classes, but she concludes, "One can at least . . . point out a danger."[27]

The play, *Mitsu-Yu-Nissi, or the Japanese Wedding*, published the same year as the article on music, is a more positive and less polemical work. It is not a particularly impressive drama, but the situation described does have a definite biographical interest.

The heroine, a sensitive young Japanese girl, has been educated abroad, in the United States. When she returns to her homeland after a ten-year absence she discovers that the ideas she has acquired in the course of her education have cut her off from her native culture. Alienated by customs that she considers backward and barbarous, she cannot face the prospect of spending the rest of her life fulfilling the traditional role of a Japanese female. Only one person, Tasaku, understands her problem; he too has been educated in the West. Unfortunately, he is the son of her betrothed. The drama develops out of a critical choice they must make: shall they defy all social custom and responsibility and flee together to the freedom of the West, or shall they deny themselves and remain in Japan to devote their lives to the education of their countrymen? Each decides independently to remain, and in the last scene, through the offices of a deus ex machina in the person of an understanding Buddhist priest, they are united in marriage.[28]

The first thing to note is the semiautobiographical character of the play: like her heroine, Vida Scudder returned from an educational experience abroad to find herself alienated from the social traditions of her own country. For the first time she responded to a crisis situation in her own life by converting her personal problem into fiction. Later critical turning points in her life became the stimulus for her three semiautobiographical novels.

The second point of importance here is, of course, the solution to the dramatic problem: the decision of the principal characters to remain in their native land and work for change. The method of securing social change may not be radical—Tasaku is to assume the direction of education in Tokyo—but the conclusion to the play is far more positive than the caveat cry that ends "The Moral Dangers of Musical Devotees."

"The Educated Woman as a Social Factor," also published in 1887, is both critical and positive. The object of criticism is the feminist movement. Once again Vida Scudder levels her guns at "the girls and women of the upper classes not engaged in any engrossing occupation." This time, though, she does not decry the moral decadence behind their self-indulgent relaxation; instead she denounces the ridiculous futility of their active involvements. Suffrage bazaars filled with second-rate handicraft exhibitions are ludicrous or worse. "Did it not occur to the feminists, she asks, that the 'dreary futile, and petty array' of doilies, sachet-bags, crocheted mats and hand painted screens proved to the masculine world that women were solely interested in homemaking."[29]

Once again Ruskin's American disciple turned to the "realities of modern civilization" and brought up the social issue. "Here is a world of suffering needing to be healed, of ignorance longing to be enlightened; and here are women, the heaven appointed powers to illumine and to heal, devoting their energies to the embroidery of doilies, while they mourn the narrowness of their lives." Do not worry about the suffrage, she advised; study the new economics and support movements for greater economic "equality and fairness in the social order." Vida Scudder had not yet settled on any specific reform project or proposal as an outlet for her radical idealism, but she knew her direction and she was moving.

## The Scholarly Life: Teaching

The problems that had been troubling Vida Scudder since her return from England abruptly ceased when an old friend of her mother's, George Herbert Palmer, suggested that she teach. Oddly enough she had never considered the idea, but in the summer of 1887 she accepted a job at Wellesley College. Teaching not only gave her something specific to do, but also proved to be her true metier. Never again in her long life was she troubled by feelings of aimlessness and boredom. Her teaching and her interest in social reform, which began to manifest itself in definite, positive action at this time, kept her constantly busy.

For the next forty years she taught English literature at Wellesley, and although she became involved in many causes and movements, teaching gave unity and purpose to her life. The shy young girl who feared that she had nothing to say discovered that in front of a class she frequently had too much to say. Widely read, and gifted with an infectious ability to communicate enthusiasm, she was an inspiring teacher. Above all she tried to make her teaching relevant to her students by relating literature to the wider concerns of life. Although she never neglected the technical aspects of her discipline, she remained vividly aware that a liberal education is a humanizing process whose primary concern is the personal development of the student. She championed a "conscientious scholarship concerned with the quickening of life, rather than the accumulation of knowledge" for its own sake. Teaching for her meant "establishing vital contacts between one's students and racial experience at its most intense."[30] One can measure her success by the large number of students who followed in her footsteps and became teachers and social reformers.

One of these students who studied at Wellesley during the nineties and went on to become both an inspiring teacher and an important influence on behalf of social reform, Mary Barnett Gilson, left a vivid portrait of Vida Scudder as a teacher in her own autobiography, *What's Past is Prologue.*

> A rich gift of the gods was the indomitable, inspiring, never to be forgotten Vida Scudder. She had the rare capacity to make masterpieces of the past live not only in their own times, but as part of a social heritage. How we reveled in Spencer's [*sic*] *Faery Queen*, not only in its intrinsic beauty but in its roots nourished in the soil of the rich and colorful sixteenth century, and in its branches touching the present and reaching out toward the future. It was a real, living work, related to current life. And what an incomparable joy it was to study the nineteenth century novels and essays under the inspiring guidance of Vida Scudder! Somehow David Copperfield add Oliver Twist and Haity Poysu and Casaubon took on new import. You recognized them as persons of their place and time and as illustrations of the universal capacity of man to enjoy and to suffer. As for Ruskin, he might just as well have been protesting against the ruthless and inexorable despoiling of western Pennsylvania [the scene of Gilson's own childhood] by oil and coal and iron as against the transformation of England's beautiful countryside into that desolately ugly Black Country. *Vida Scudder made life more real and a sense of responsibility greater.* Her transitions were frequently breathtaking, and sometimes a bit of a strain on a dull imagination. Never does my memory grow dim of that birdlike creature in a mystical flight of poignant sorrow as she suddenly sped from Giotto's tower to the sufferings of the poor. [emphasis mine][31]

Wellesley had hired Vida Scudder to teach modern—that is, nineteenth-century—literature, and she gave classes in both poetry and prose. Her approach was novel and stimulating; as we learn from Gilson and other sources, she was not content to provide a mere explication de texte but attempted to relate literature to its intellectual context and to the general historical development of ideas.[32] The scholarly works that grew out of the material she presented in class reveal her approach. She edited Macaulay's essay on Lord Clive, Shelley's poetic drama, *Prometheus Unbound*, and (like William Dwight Porter Bliss) a selection from her beloved mentor John Ruskin. An article on Matthew Arnold prepared for *The Andover Review* is particularly stimulating, but the most significant works to come from her concentration on the nineteenth century are three volumes of literary and cultural criticism that appeared in the middle nineties: *The Witness of Denial, The Life of the Spirit in the Modern English Poets*, and *Social Ideals in English Letters*. This last book expands on the ideas presented in a class that she inaugurated in the academic year 1895-96.

All of these books attempt to come to terms with the challenge of life in the nineteenth century, but each work approaches the issue from a different perspective. *The Witness of Denial* is an unpretentious attempt at apologetic theology; *The Life of the Spirit in the Modern English Poets* focuses most directly on problems of intellectual history; and *Social Ideas in English Letters*, according to Arthur Mann, is "the outstanding example in the 1890s of literary criticism as social reform."[33] Although these books are not formally a trilogy, they share common concerns and should be taken all of a piece. The task assumed by Vida Scudder in this series reminds one of the work attempted by the *Lux Mundi*-Christian Social Union school in England several years before. *The Witness of Denial* and *The Life of the Spirit in the Modern English Poets* confront the intellectual problems of the time; *Social Ideas in English Letters* responds to the social question.

*The Witness of Denial* is a piece of Christian propaganda written "for those who seek, not those at rest. . . . Should it give one helpful hint to three, or two, or one of that number, its existence will be justified."[34] Its tone, the author announces in the Preface, is "candidly Christian and Catholic"; more important, it is distinctly Mauricean. The influence of Frederick Denison Maurice is far more obvious here than in any other of her published writings. One can see reflections of his apologetic style, his doctrines of Christ and the church, and his passion for unity.

Maurice's apologetic style and his method of approaching a subject shine through the very title of the book, *The Witness of Denial*. In traditional Christian usage, *witness* generally designates someone who can testify to the truth of the faith and thereby inspire others. The use of the word here is paradoxical, for it implies that denial has something to tell us about the truth of the faith. Maurice's controversial style was grounded in precisely that kind of paradoxical perception. He assumed that every opponent possessed some aspect of the truth and when writing he emphasized the positive side of his opponent's position before he subjected it to criticism. When he criticized he did not repudiate another position because it was wrong; his concern was to show how the truth was greater and more complex than his opponent had imagined.[35]

The following quotation shows how thoroughly Vida Scudder had appropriated Maurice's attitude. He might have written these words himself.

> Yet absolute tolerance is the only temper in which helpful thought about
> these matters is possible . . . the passionate and noble tolerance of the seeker

which springs from the love of truth. *If we trust God we must believe that he gives some of his truth to every seeking soul*; that the light coming into the world lighteth every man; and that the Spirit moves and guides in all differing attempts to solve life's mystery. [emphasis mine][36]

A few words about the specific content of the book are in order here. It begins with "The Movement of Doubt," a brief chapter discussing those movements which, in the pursuit of "Truth," destroyed forever the simple verities of the old order. These movements are, on the political level, democracy and the French Revolution; on the intellectual level, utilitarianism and Darwinian evolution; and on the religious level, what we now call biblical criticism. The movement of doubt was, the author thinks, necessary: its motives were well intentioned, if not absolutely pure, and many of its results, particularly on the political level, have been beneficial. But, she argues, the evidence of history confirms that this movement was inadequate, that spirit was too negative: "In the midst of that which they may investigate men sought that which they may adore."[37]

Beginning about the middle of the nineteenth century, even before the movement of doubt had run its course, there arose a "Renascence of Faith," not a specifically Christian revival but a faith that logically followed from the assumptions at the basis of the movement of doubt. This took three major forms: a religion of mystery, seen best in the writings of Herbert Spencer; a religion of humanity, advocated by the English positivist, Frederick Harrison; and a religion of morality, whose most "finished exponent" was Matthew Arnold. These religions were rivals to Christianity and the author urged the seekers for whom the book is written to examine Christianity and its rivals, "impartially looking for that faith which answers most fully the needs of the human soul [and which is] most competent to set man free and make him noble."[38]

Notice the assumptions Vida Scudder chooses as a basis for her Christian apologetic. She does not urge the seeker to accept Christianity out of concern for his life after death or because it is something man owes to God. She begins with man here and now and asks her reader to consider Christianity in light of its potential to make him a better, more complete, and human personality. For all of her assertions about the Catholic tone of this book, there is no Tractarian teaching here; the emphasis is not on an a priori argument that Christianity is true because the church has preserved for us intact the means of grace transmitted by Our Lord to His apostles. Much as she admired Newman, he would have recoiled from such "liberalism." Her assumptions reveal that although her tastes were Anglo-Catholic, her theological perspective owed more at this time to Maurice and the "liberal Catholicism" of Bishop Gore than to Pusey, Canon Liddon, and the conservative heirs of Tractarianism.

Spencer's religion of mystery is a "Religion of the Unknowable" lost in awe before "the presence of an Infinite and Eternal Energy from which all things proceed." Thus far it is good; it recognizes the essential truth that religion is based on man's sense of his own finitude and his wonder at the sense of powers greater than himself. But is it new? No; quotations from both the Old and New Testaments demonstrate that Christianity is also a religion based on mystery, the mysterious abyss of godhead that is the Creator. Is Spencer's religion of mystery somehow better suited to man? Again, no; it "offers neither stimulus to effort, standard for conduct nor strength it failure."[39] The Christian God is as equally beyond description as Spenger's Infinite and Eternal Energy, but faith teaches us that the alpha and omega is a loving father. This knowledge is psychologically satisfying; it offers man a reason for existence and aspiration.

One would expect that a social reformer like Vida Scudder would be sympathetic to a religion of humanity dedicated to acts of benevolence and charity and this is indeed the case. She even singles out the Society of Ethical Culture's "practical ritual in settlements and guilds among the poor" as examples of a kind of activity that the "Christian church may well be glad to join." But the gospel of service offers nothing new "as a matter of social morality." Christ revealed the social gospel and, "however falteringly, His Church has followed Him. No height can be reached by the followers of a modern social morality which has not been trodden before by Christian feet."[40]

If the religion of humanity offers nothing new in the realm of ethics, can it perhaps suggest some finer spiritual ideal? Once again the answer is no. How can one worship humanity? Both the common majority and the select few offer grounds for sympathy, compassion, and service, but where is "scope for adoration," "an object of worship." In all history only one man is worthy of worship. That man is Jesus Christ. He alone is a fit subject for adoration and worship because he alone has given the world "a perfect standard of conduct."

In Him humanity loses its confusion, variableness, and failings, and is uplifted into perfect unity, holiness, and strength. Gathering up into Himself the fullness of all men, He is the Race-ideal, the perfect archetype. *Not as the Catholic faith has always held, a man—one unit in the multitudinous throngs of human lives—but Man essential, Man eternal, He appears as the Master of the race,* the Vine of which all are the branches, the Lord who draws to Himself with irresistible power . . . the very being of man. [emphasis mine][41]

I mentioned that *The Witness of Denial* reflects a Christological attitude that is profoundly indebted to Maurice. The above quotation is almost a perfectly encapsulated statement of Maurice's view of Christ as head and king of our race. Particularly noteworthy is the fact that Vida Scudder, in the passage, specifically repudiated a tenet of the Catholic faith in favor of a Mauricean position.[42] The same strong Mauricean tone is evident in Vida Scudder's description of the church.

And in the Church, the mystical body of Christ, we have a yet further extension of the idea for which the lover of humanity cries. *For the Church, both normally and ideally, includes the entire human race; . . . it is the representative of all, the earnest of the society to be.* . . . Made up as it is of faulty and distorted people, *it yet reaches up into a higher region, and witnesses to perfection, through its organic and sacramental union with a Head in whom are centered holiness, wisdom, and authority.* [emphasis mine][43]

In discussing the positive aspects of the religions of mystery and humanity Vida Scudder focused on general principles of value that they demonstrated: respectively, a sense of human finitude and benevolent gospel of service. Herbert Spencer and Frederick Harrison, the men, are quickly passed over. But Matthew Arnold, the man and his mind, come to the forefront of the description of the religion of morality. Indeed, it appears that the witness of this religion had less to do with any principle it embodied than the fact that Matthew Arnold was its advocate. Vida Scudder was deeply interested in Matthew Arnold; she wrote "The Poetry of Matthew Arnold" for *The Andover Review* and he appears again both in *The Life of the Spirit in the Modern English Poets* as a "Poet of Doubt" and in *Social Ideals in English Letters* as a social critic and prophet. Clearly he spoke to her in a way that Spencer and Harrison could never do; his agnosticism tempted her because she could deny neither his "exquisite culture" not his "Christian sentiment."

As a result her argument is fiercer in this chapter than heretofore. Obviously, she admired Arnold's conception of religion as "morality touched by emotion"; it is the work of a painfully honest, sophisticated, and sensitive man. She described the religion of morality as the "most subtly vital of all phases of agnostic thought" and readily admitted its influence even on many who remained in the church. "Many people . . . fail to see the distinction between this attitude and the attitude of the Church. Yet," she affirms "the distinction is absolute. The Church is the guardian of what her foes call dogma and she calls truth; that is of belief in central definite and objective facts. Only secondarily and as result is she the guardian of morals or the inspirer of feeling."[44]

Here we can detect the militant tone and stance of an Anglo-Catholic controversialist. The Mauricean emphasis on the positive aspects of an opponent's position is muted because the positive aspects of that position are all too obvious and attractive. She moves to the attack and her language is more polemical than previously. "Arnold would keep the aroma, but he ruthlessly flings the flower away."[45]

Above all she objects to his "method" and protests in the name of "intellectual honesty."

> Is it not, then, unwise . . . to take words which have already gained a vital and definite meaning through long use . . . and to insist on using them in a quite new sense, retaining what they adumbrate, but rejecting what they signify? . . . To mean an abstraction when one says "God" is neither fair nor honest. Words are flesh as well as Spirit. Try to strip away the flesh—historical implication, intellectual conviction—and the spirit, the emotional and moral power, becomes not only invisible, but unknowable. Let us at least keep the rough accuracy that comes from meaning by words what our fathers meant, what simple people mean, what the words themselves, taken at their face-value, seem to say. If we are to have a new religion, let us have a language for a new religion. . . . To borrow is evidence of weakness.[46]

Despite his errors in method, though, Arnold was a "rare spirit" and his search cannot be an illusion. What was there in his religion that can support the soul? Vida Scudder calls it "that tendency to righteousness which operates, mighty but unseen through all the course of human history."[47] and this tendency she equates with the Holy Spirit. Again we discover that secular religion has produced nothing new. Is Arnold's "tendency to righteousness" a concept superior to the Christian doctrine of the Holy Spirit?

> . . . believe in Spirit who proceeds from no Father and no Son, who has no source in absolute and loving being, no relation to a Humanity manifest, once for all as holy, and what certainty has life left? Where is a standard of conduct, where salvation from sin? Gone is the assurance of absolute right, gone the quiet certainty that a Spirit proceeding from such right . . . is guiding us into all truth.[48]

The answer is quite clearly no.

The final chapter, "The Religion of Christ," summarizes the discussion of the three previous chapters on the religions of denial and then goes on to advance a final point in favor of Christianity. This final point had been an implicit assumption in her previous argumentation, but here it is made explicit. This final point is the basic Mauricean passion for unity, for catholicity of vision, for wholeness.

The author had urged the seeker to find a faith that would "most fully answer the needs of the human soul." Previously, she had argued that the religions of denial had offered nothing new, nothing superior to Christianity. Each one had been rejected on its own terms. At this point she stands back and takes a wider view. Seen from a fuller perspective the fundamental difficulty of the religions of denial becomes apparent: each failed because its vision was too narrow and limited; each focused on one thing—human finitude, benevolence to one's fellow man, moral force in history. Christianity most fully answers human needs, has greater potential for ennobling and freeing man because the doctrine of the Trinity offers a unified and more truly comprehensive formulation of reality. Mankind can be truly satisfied only by a vision of the whole. "Here and here alone, the complex search of the century finds answer; here 'all strife is reconciled, all pain beguiled.' 'Turn us again, O God of hosts, show the light of Thy countenance; and we shall be whole.' "[49]

Scudder began her book with a brief history of those influences which produced the movement of doubt; she concludes by returning to history, this time to the history of the church in the nineteenth century. Her view is essentially optimistic. The movements of doubt and the religions of denial have not destroyed the church—far from it. Their challenge has caused her to shake aside "the torpor of assurance" and rise into new life. She can no longer command but, more important, she can convince. Coleridge gave her a "sharp intellectual stimulus"; the Oxford movement brought her "a sudden and mighty spiritual renewal." Finally, the movement inaugurated by Frederick Denison Maurice "reinforced the spiritual emphasis by the social." "Since the time of Maurice that social renascence, which is also essentially a Christian renascence, has steadily gained momentum. It has become the dominant spiritual fact in the closing century-decade, and bids fair to be the great and living interest leading us into the world of the future."[50]

The church must take up the challenge, and the signs are propitious. The century of intellectual struggle was a century of life. The struggle purified and strengthened the church, freeing her from the bonds of privilege and power:

"The Church Catholic may in the future command allegiance, not by the claims she asserts, but by the power she reveals; not by authority imposed from without, but by a life manifest from within."[51]

*The Witness of Denial* never became a popular success; it may have given some helpful hints to a few seekers, but it has remained one of her most obscure works. Scarcely anyone knows it today. Yet in many ways it is one of her most important books, especially to a student of her life and thought. It contains a comprehensive and often eloquent expression of her own religious faith during the 1890s, a faith that combined Anglo-Catholic tastes and language with a theological perspective deeply indebted to Frederick Denison Maurice. This faith was the basis both of her intellectual pursuits and her social concerns. *The Witness of Denial* is the first major work where she expresses herself as a Christian social reformer; it reveals that the two awakenings that she had experienced at Oxford had become fused into one vision. Both *The Life of the Spirit in the Modern English Poets* and *Social Ideals in English Letters*, far more popular books, expand upon basic concepts set forth here. *The Witness of Denial* is her seminal work.

*The Life of the Spirit in the Modern English Poets* was a much more comprehensive and ambitious project than its predecessor. In her second major critical work Vida Scudder attempted an interpretive study of English poetry from Wordsworth and Shelley to Morris and Swinburne. She examines in detail Wordsworth, Shelley, Keats, Clough, Arnold, Rossetti, Morris, Swinburne, Browning, and Tennyson. Byron and Coleridge are the only important poets of the period who are neglected.[52]

Naturally, she did not confine herself to a purely textual analysis of this poetry, although the volume abounds in closely read explications de textes. The passion for wholeness, for a comprehensive outlook expressed with vivid explicitness in the concluding chapter of *The Witness of Denial* is reiterated implicitly in her design for this book. Vida Scudder proposed to examine English poetry as it developed in a dialectical relationship with its social and intellectual context. She was really using poetry as a vantage point from which she could survey and plot the whole course of ideas in nineteenth-century England. *The Life of the Spirit* is literary criticism as intellectual history.[53]

In the preparation of this major work Vida Scudder drew upon both her classroom lecture notes and her previous publications. Her master's thesis at Smith College, "The Effect of the Scientific Temper in Modern Poetry," previously published in *The Andover Review*, was turned into her new book's first chapter, "Science and the Modern Poet."[54] An introduction to Shelley's

*Prometheus Unbound* written in 1892 became the basis for her treatment of that author throughout the book, but most especially in Chapter III, "Ideals of Redemption Medieval and Modern."[55] Insights into the character and poetry of Matthew Arnold, which had appeared earlier in *The Witness of Denial* and her *Andover Review* article, "The Poetry of Matthew Arnold" were distilled into her concise and moving discussion of that poet's plight in Chapter VI, "The Poetry of Search."[56]

This study is full of novel and stimulating insights into the nature of nineteenth-century England, the personalities of its poets and thinkers, and the quality and significance of their work. The product of an original and erudite mind, a mind striving after bold and comprehensive visions, the work carries the reader through to the end by communicating the author's enthusiasm for her subject. But in the end, the attempt outstrips the accomplishment, the sum of the parts appears greater than the whole, and for all its undoubted virtues *The Life of the Spirit* is not a flawed masterpiece but, unfortunately, a noble and, sometimes brilliant, failure.

As a collection of independent essays the book would have succeeded, for its major deficiency is the absence of a comprehensive organizational scheme capable of forging the work into a unified entity. One of Vida Scudder's greatest intellectual virtues was her ability to perceive society—and all life—as an organic and spiritual whole. This philosophical monism, which she inherited from Maurice, was central to her entire outlook; one sees it in both her life and work. As a result, when writing a major study she refused to compartmentalize; she could not be only a Christian, a literary critic, a social reformer, or an intellectual historian. Instead, she expressed all of these aspects of her mind and personality in her major works, although the demands of a specific occasion could bring one aspect to the forefront.

In this instance her greatest intellectual virtue proved to be the cause of her undoing. She simply attempts too much and cannot integrate all the facets of her work into an organic whole. Concluding her introduction, she writes, "we shall come to feel that the poetry of our age has a vital unity, and witness to an advance of the spirit, straight as the logic of experience from doubt to faith and cheer."[57] This vital unity is exactly what we do not come to feel.

We do not feel this unity because the author herself seems to have been of a divided mind when she wrote it. A crucial sentence reveals the problem: "Science, democracy, and the past are the guides of modern poetry; but the knowledge of truth is its goal."[58] In her exposition she fails to demonstrate how these guides directed modern poetry to its goal; how science, democracy, and the past led modern poetry to the truth.

Vida Scudder was doing two things in this book: first, she was writing an intellectual history showing how nineteenth-century English poetry develops in a dialectical relationship with its social and intellectual context (this is her method); second, she was attempting to demonstrate an "advance of the spirit . . . from doubt to faith and cheer" (this is her theme).

The goal of poetry is the knowledge of truth. As a believing Christian Vida Scudder equated truth with God, stating her belief with characteristic frankness: "the impulse which dominates it [poetry] has been . . . the search for truth. Or since poetry abhors an abstraction more than nature a vacuum may we not change the phrase? Shall we be far wrong in saying that the desire which controls the Victorian poets of England is the desire for God?"[59] The goal of poetry is then the knowledge of God. The theme of the book, slightly restated, is the advance of the spirit from doubt to the knowledge of God. This she affirms was the course of nineteenth-century poetry. In the concluding chapter the final lines read: "After long searchings, the Witness of the Spirit was to the Father and the Son. From pantheism towards Christianity: this was the spiritual pilgrimage of our modern English poets."[60] In the theme of this book we can detect its close relation to *The Witness of Denial*; both works attempt to confront what she believed to be the chief intellectual problem of the day—religious disbelief—and argue for the superior vision of Christianity.

I have pointed out that her method involved pursuing the development of ideas by focusing on the dialectical relation between poetry and its three guides, science, democracy, and the past, or, as she calls it elsewhere, history. Strictly speaking, the word *guides* is not correct. It suggests that poetry was a passive agent that was acted on and shaped by outside influences. Such a relationship could not be considered dialectical. Despite the use of the terms *guided* and *guiding powers* poetry is not described as a purely passive agent. It is also an active force influencing those very forces which are guiding its own development. "Science and poetry are friends not foes; the nature of one passes into the very being of the other . . . if science opens the road to the poet, it is no less true that the poet opens the road to science."[61]

As an example of poetry's positive contribution to the development of nineteenth-century thought she turns to the theory of evolution, widely considered the most significant scientific discovery of the century. It was not the scientists, she affirms, but the poets who discovered this principle. One can find evolutionary theory in Shelley's *Prometheus Unbound*, Browning's *Paracelsus*, and Tennyson's *In Memoriam*, each of which antedates Darwin's *Origin of the Species* by some years.[62] Similar advances were made by the poets in the areas of political and social thought, areas she subsumes under the heading, democracy. Shelley was a great prophet of democracy whose poems helped popularize the subject and Wordsworth in his writings opened up the path that led to socialism long before Karl Marx ever took pen in hand.[63]

How does Vida Scudder attempt to bring her theme and method together? A brief outline of the book's content will demonstrate. At the beginning of the nineteenth century English poetry takes its character from the interaction of science and democracy; this is a period of youthful high spirits inspired by a profound appreciation of nature and a strong confidence in the future of free men. Shelley and Wordsworth are the most representative voices of this time. The power of the past also made itself felt, particularly on the poetry of Keats, but history is definitely a secondary power during this period.

Science and history are paramount during the Victorian era, when the youthful good spirits fade and poetry either becomes obsessed with doubt or flees from harsh realities of the world into the dream world of art. Scientific skepticism destroys the faith of Clough and Arnold; the Pre-Raphaelites, "the spiritual sons of Keats," retreat into imaginative recreations of time past. Swinburne, going farther than his friends, boldly proclaims a neopaganism that openly flouts morality and Christian doctrine. Yet there are two poets, Tennyson and Browning, who—though also influenced by the forces of science and history—repudiate escape, confront doubt, and struggle into a more complete awareness of truth (God) than the poets of the early years of the century possessed.

Theme and method integrated until Tennyson and Browning enter the discussion, then the theme takes over completely and the method is dropped. The problem is that the method was unable to explain the point vitally necessary to the theme: one cannot describe the triumph of faith over doubt within the individual soul in terms of science, democracy, and history. The terms are too general; they are useful only for defining broad outlines.[64]

As a result the chapters on Browning and Tennyson become independent essays and the keystone is never put into the arch of her argument. Consider the following paragraph on Tennyson, a typical example of her treatment of the poet.

It is through air dim with shadows that Tennyson like his own Sir Perceval, rides after the Holy Grail. Agnostic of temperament, of hesitating and critical spirit, he sojourns with his younger brothers for a long time in the land of doubt. Only under the stress of personal loss and after long gropings and tarryings, does he attain to faith. And when he wins, it is by no triumphant conclusion of the force of the whole nature, mind, heart, and soul, but rather by a desperate superb venture of Faith. Yet that the poet has a right to venture who can doubt?[65]

This statement is a perceptive analysis of Tennyson's personal struggle, but it says nothing about the great powers—science, democracy and history—that Vida Scudder assured us "have guided the movement of modern song."

We must not, however, become so preoccupied with the imperfections of this work that we lose sight of its significance in the development of her thought. *The Witness of Denial* was a seminal work, but its scope was limited. It was a small success. *The Life of the Spirit* reaches out to encompass the major issues in nineteenth century English intellectual history, to relate them to one another, and to make them a coherent whole. Not surprisingly, such an ambitious, even grandiose, project failed, but what remains important is the expanded scope of the attempt; for this expanded scope points toward the future. Previously Vida Scudder had written small topical essays—even *The Witness of Denial* is hardly more than an extended essay; in the future she was also to produce comprehensive studies on the grand scale. Seen in the context of her personal development as a writer, *The Life of the Spirit* becomes a milestone marking that point in her "journey" when Vida Scudder reached full intellectual maturity and began to plan works on a scale commensurate with the scope of her vision. When this book was published in 1895 she was thirty-four years old.

Three years later, in 1898, "her speculations and scholarship came to ripe fulfillment in *Social Ideas in English Letters*"[66] probably her single most successful and influential critical work. Twenty-five years after its initial publication Vida Scudder was asked to prepare a revised edition to bring the book up to date, and in 1969 the original version was reprinted. In his introduction to the reprint Martin Tucker compares her work to that of Hippolyte Taine and assures us that "her insights and understanding of literature and its social value remain undated and of crucial relevance."[67]

In this volume the strong points of her earlier books are combined; we find both the argumentative skill and sustained thematic development of *Witness* and the comprehensive scope of *The Life of the Spirit*. Indeed, *Social Ideals in English Letters* is in some respects an even more ambitious undertaking than its predecessor since it moves beyond the nineteenth century and discusses representative medieval, Renaissance, and eighteenth-century writers. Beginning with the Venerable Bede and concluding with Robert Blatchford's *Merrie England* and the *Fabian Essays*, Vida Scudder surveys approximately twelve hundred years of English literature.

These years are divided into three major periods: The England of Our Forefathers, The England of Our Fathers, and Contemporary England. The England of Our Forefathers, covering roughly the first eleven centuries, is examined in a series of three interrelated essays on four authors, the Venerable Bede, William Langland, St. Thomas More, and Dean Swift. Bede and Langland represent the Middle Ages; More, the Renaissance; and Swift, the Age of Reason. The work of each author is carefully set within the social and intellectual context of his time.

> Literature [the author boldly announces in her foreword] is a series of social documents. . . . The epic, the drama and later the novel, reveal the collective experience of the nation from age to age. . . . As we follow from one generation to another the dreamers who are the truest prophets, we shall trace the gradual awakening of a social consciousness bringing with it the perception of social problems and the creation of social ideals.[68]

Bede reveals the spiritual and social revolution Christianity wrought upon the aristocratic and warlike society of early Anglo-Saxon England; Langland is significant because he expresses "the voice of the people, articulate at last" at the time when the "Middle Ages were dying."[69] More, the "representative scholar of the New Learning of the sixteenth century" shows that a "new revelation" had dawned on men. No longer content with Langland's age-old wisdom that "existing conditions are immutable facts," More envisioned a "social reconstruction" based on his own conception of the perfect state.[70] The cynical, pessimistic satires of Dean Swift mark no advance in social idealism, but they mercilessly expose the barbarities of a self-satisfied age. "The paradox of Swift was the paradox of his age. Augustan literature had lost the social with the spiritual outlook."[71]

The age of Swift was deeply imbued with the conviction that its institutions were immutable, but scarcely fifty years after the death of the brilliant satirist, the French and Industrial Revolutions had prepared the way for a new age. This new age Scudder calls "The England of Our Fathers"; it lasted roughly ninety years. It was a dynamic era, a period of rapid change:

Thus unguided, unrelated, helpless, with foundations slipping away in all directions, the thought of the century began. No one man could express such a period. We can select one writer to be a fair representative of the Middle Ages, of the Renascence [sic], of the eighteenth century: to gain even hints of the social moods, desires, and sorrows of modern times, we must know not one author only, but many. Each author expresses not a stable state of things, but one which, whether he knows it or not, is in constant flux under his very eyes.[72]

During the first forty years of the new era poetry was more progressive than prose. "During the revolutionary period, great passions stirred the poets, small fancies the writers of prose; and Wordsworth and Shelley were larger men than Lamb, Hazlitt, or De Quincey."[73] This period was an "age of vision" and the poets proclaimed the vision and became the "heirs of the revolution."[74] In the decade following 1830, however, poetry was replaced by prose, "the art-form of democracy," as the age of vision gave way to the "age of criticism," and novelists and essayists came to the fore. These essayists and novelists confronted the social realities of their time and the prospect was not pleasing. "To analyze the modern order was to indict it; to describe was to condemn."[75]

Three essayists—Thomas Carlyle, John Ruskin, and Matthew Arnold—stand out as the most perceptive social critics in the fifty years between 1830 and 1880. Their analyses of contemporary society read like indictments of laissez-faire capitalism. Carlyle denounced society because it was immoral; Ruskin, because it was ugly; Arnold, because it was absurd. Contemporary novelists only substantiated the positions taken by the essayists. Dickens and Thackeray, who were not primarily social critics but rather acute observers of the social scene, condemn society by describing it. Thackeray's upper-class gentlefolk are incurable dilettantes whose motto might read *amusons-nous*, and if the lower middle classes portrayed by Dickens are warmer and more humane, they are nonetheless as a group vulgar mammon-worshipers. Lesser novelists like Disraeli, Kingsley, and Mrs. Gaskell, who concentrated more specifically on social problems, portray a society based on a vicious exploitation of the poor, a society so enamored of materialism that it ignored its intellectual and spiritual poverty. "The great social literature before 1880 reveals the gathering of the forces. To discover the issue was the work of that period. To face it is the work of our own."[76]

The analyses and descriptions of the great writers of the age of criticism had discovered the issue. Their indictment of laissez-faire capitalism, which was based on moral, aesthetic, and intellectual grounds, was their greatest legacy; subsequent research by economists and social scientists had only confirmed, not superseded, their judgments. But what of their specific recommendations for social improvement? "What help is offered by our social guides?" After considering at some length the "ways out" proffered by Carlyle, Ruskin, and Arnold, she concludes, "at best not very much. . . . [They were] better at diagnosis than at prescription."[77] Vida Scudder found their spirit, their devotion, and their good intentions highly admirable, but she disagreed with Carlyle's bent toward authoritarianism, with Ruskin's neo-medievalist infatuation with preindustrial social and economic structures, and with Arnold's excessive fear of democracy.

Three general characteristics of the period, though, did strike her as particularly hopeful signs of a better world to come. The first she styled the "new intuition," and she noted its appearance early in the 1860s in the novels of George Eliot. Characters like Dorothea in *Middlemarch* and Daniel Deronda reflect the "new intuition" of the younger generation; they represent the "children of a new age." They demonstrate that the "social conscience is fully awake."[78] Deeper than the noblese oblige portrayed by Disraeli or Kingsley, the new social conscience combines an "impulse to compassion and service" with the readiness to suffer "with atoning pain for the sins of the world."[79] "By active ministry, and yet more by prayer, fast, and vigil, they seek to prepare the way for the spiritual democracy on which their souls are set."[80]

The two remaining signs of promise were general tendencies that she detected growing in strength and favor during the period as a whole. Looking back over the literature of the past ninety years, Scudder notices two great movements afoot, one toward greater democracy, the other toward greater authority. The movement toward democracy was obvious enough: the history of nineteenth-century England is one of the progressive enfranchisement of the people. But she had more than political democracy in mind; she also meant social equality and she saw it being championed not only by social reformers but also by Matthew Arnold, the apostle of high culture. "He wished for equality—a real solid material equality, let us repeat no mere figment such as is offered by the ballot—because he believed—that only in such a soil could the graces of life and the noblest joys of life flourish."[81] The movement toward authority, which appeared in Carlyle, Ruskin, Arnold, and a host of other writers, was essentially a reaction against the excesses of bourgeois liberalism. It stressed the social rather than the individual impulse and could be discovered in labor organizations and cooperatives, but above all in the "positive state," although she did not use T. H. Green's term. ". . . the converging lines of nearly all modern social speculation move towards a new insistence on the opportunity, the duty, the responsibility, of the state."[82] In the synthesis of democracy and authority, principles which, she averred, most Victorians would have found irreconcilable, she caught "faint glimpses" of a better future—social democracy and the socialist state.

The England of Our Fathers came to an end around 1880, and "again the social passion shifted; it passed over from literature to life . . . the age of experiment, in which we live, belongs to the men of action."[83] Contemporary England's idealists are no longer writing books; they have gone to county councils, boards of arbitration, to organized charities, or settlement houses. In the widest variety of ways they have begun to practice social righteousness.

From among the manifold varieties of reform activity flourishing in the newly nascent age of experiment three were selected as particularly relevant. As the author herself admits, the tentative nature of the data made the process of selection highly subjective, and for that reason her choices are of special interest. The three chief forms of collective expression that she finds especially arresting are the socialist movement, the "surprising spread of practical fellowship and intercourse between members of the alienated classes and the rise of the working man into self-expression,"[84] and the change in the spirit of the Christian church.

Her selection of modern movements was even more subjective than the text would lead one to believe, for her choices are nothing less than those aspects of social reform that occupied her own private extracurricular life. As such they form a quasi-autobiographical epilogue in which she speaks directly about projects and dreams close to her own heart. Essentially she says nothing new about the change in the spirit of the church, but only expands upon material presented in *The Witness of Denial*.

Reading the *Fabian Essays* in 1889 had completed a process begun by Maurice and Ruskin and converted her to socialism; therefore it is Fabian socialism that she describes and secretly expounds here. Throughout, her position is resolutely non-Marxist, almost anti-Marxist. The internationals are never mentioned, and socialism is presented as the logical culmination of nineteenth-century British social thought. She takes pains to emphasize that English socialism is by no means founded on a Marxist, materialistic theory of social evolution,[85] and also that English socialists believe the social forms of the future will be an organic growth from those of the present, not a mechanically invented substitution for them. In other words, English socialism is evolutionary, not revolutionary.

Her section on "the surprising spread of practical fellowship and intercourse between members of the alienated classes and the rise of working men into self expression" is nearly as misty and verbose as the title itself. It stands out as the only weak section in the book, and yet she considered that phenomenon more important than the socialist movement. Her analysis at this point is so general and without concrete example that it begins to make sense only when one remembers that during the decade of the nineties, the professor of English at Wellesley was also an active settlement house worker. Her experiences there, which also brought her into contact with the labor movement, had deep importance for her development; and her discussion of communication between the classes is not so much a historical record of its successes, as a statement of its value and a plea for more of it. "To hear one speech by a labor leader," she writes with a conviction born out of experience, "is more instructive than to read any number of brilliant studies of labor leaders made from the outside. . . . There is need of every social settlement, every labor conference, every association of professional men with manual workers to make the distance [between classes] less."[86]

*Social Ideals in English Letters* shows Vida Scudder at the height of her powers as a literary critic and also at the point when her idealism and optimism about society reached their first full bloom. Accordingly this book written in the age of experimentation looks forward to an age of fulfillment, a time when socialism, practical fellowship, and Christianity will be reunited, and "the love of God and man find in their sacramental union, freedom for more perfect collective expression than has ever yet been seen on earth."[87]

Taken as a whole the three volumes that grew out of Vida Scudder's classroom experience at Wellesley College during the 1890s stand as the most important single intellectual achievement of the Anglican left in the United States. Neither Huntington nor Bliss produced anything as significant. In attempting to come to terms with the social and intellectual problems of her age she created an enduring apologia for Christian social reform. Her erudition is deep, her argument skillful and fair, her idealism inspiring, and her vitality and enthusiasm truly infectious.

*Social Ideals in English Letters* reveals that her scholarly interests had begun to move beyond the nineteenth century. In 1905 she began teaching a seminar on Arthurian romance, which focused on the High and Late Middle Ages. Religious tastes and childhood associations made her feel particularly at home in that era. Her most lasting contribution to academic literary scholarship, *La Morte d'Arthur, An Introduction to Sir Thomas Malory*, grew out of her

Arthurian romance class. Even though it was published in 1921, it is still one of the standard works in the field.

## The Active Life: Social Reform

In 1887, the same year that she accepted a teaching position at Wellesley, the seeds planted by Ruskin began to sprout. Early that fall Vida Scudder returned to her alma mater, where she was reunited with her college friends Jean Fine and Helen Rand. The latter had also recently returned from England where she, like Scudder, had become acquainted with the idea of university settlements. During the course of a walk through the meadows that border the Connecticut River near Northhampton they decided to establish an American settlement house modeled on England's Toynbee Hall.[88] Toynbee Hall, which had been inspired in part by Maurice's Working Men's College, brought social reformers and university men together with the poor for purposes of education and fellowship. Settlement houses were located in the slums, and the volunteers living in the houses tried to make the day-to-day existence of the poor less dreary by sponsoring healthy recreation and entertainment, and also to help these slum-dwellers by widening their horizons and teaching them new skills.

Soon other women joined the original band of Smith alumnae. Katherine Lee Bates, the Wellesley poet who wrote "America the Beautiful," offered helpful advice and introduced the project to her colleague Katherine Coman, who in turn interested her wealthy friend Cornelia Warren. Adeline Thompson from Wellesley also joined, and then the circle widened to include Bertha Hazard from Vassar and Helena Dudley from Bryn Mawr. Together they began organizing the College Settlements Association, with chapters in all of these respective schools plus Harvard Annex (Radcliffe), Michigan, and Cornell. But the task proved to be more difficult than the young alumnae had imagined, and it was not until October 1, 1889, that the women were able to open their first settlement house at 95 Rivington Street in New York City.[89] As it was, though, the Rivington Street Settlement anticipated Chicago's more famous Hull House by two weeks. By May of the following year the College Settlements Association was formally constituted and in 1892 it was able to extend its activities by opening the College Settlement in Philadelphia and then Denison House in Boston.[90]

The College Settlements Association departed from its English model in one important aspect: it was staffed and managed entirely by women.[91] Indeed, the movement reflects what Arthur Mann has called "the self-consciousness of that generation." Vida Scudder and her friends knew that they represented the "first generation of college women. . . . We stand here as a new Fact—new, to all intents and purposes, within the last quarter of a century. Our lives are in our hands. . . . What is the relation which these lives should bear to the needs and demands of the time?" she asked in a paper presented to the Association of Collegiate Alumnae.[92] For herself and for her fellow settlement house volunteers the answer was clear: ". . . we are all agreed that the regeneration of the world is to be obtained not chiefly by speculation by practical brotherhood. . . . Educated women may, if they will, be a potent instrument in that purification of evils, that ministry to individual degradation, for which the modern would profoundly longs."[93] These college women had proven that they were capable of the same level of academic achievement as men; now they would justify their newly enhanced status by making use of their education in the service of the unfortunate for the benefit of society as a whole.

Realistic political considerations also prompted Vida Scudder to become involved in the settlement house movement and social reform. "Miss Scudder spoke for her kind when she remarked in her usual succinct style that reformation ought to come from above and not from below."[94] At the beginning of her career as a social reformer, Ruskin's disciple believed that "higher life must draw joyfully close to the lower before the lower can be uplifted."[95] There was more than a little upper-class snobbery behind her "chivalric sympathy for the poor." When the Rivington Street Settlement opened, the prospectus made it clear that the college women who went to live among the poor were not required to live like the poor. As the product of an earlier age, the building was well lit, well ventilated, and spacious enough to accommodate "a little maid," and a manservant. In *On Journey* Scudder looked back with pleasure to "that stately Rivington Street mansion with its silver-hinged mahogany doors."[96] Certainly one did not have to sacrifice gentility while "uplifting" the lower classes.

Both realistic political considerations and the desire to justify the enhanced status of women were important elements in Vida Scudder's involvement in the settlement house movement; but the most significant consideration was more deeply personal. Even as a child she had experienced an incredible longing for reality. In England she had joined the Salvation Army to get closer to this reality, but when she returned home the conventions of her age and class had condemned her to a seemingly purposeless existence. "We lead sham lives," she had written, "and sham knowledge deadens for us the reality."

> Ever since my Oxford days, I had been beating my wings against the bars—the customs, the assumptions of my own class. I moved in . . . an enclosure of gracious manners, regular meals, comfort, security, and good taste. . . . Yet sometimes it suffocated me. I wanted to escape, where winds buffeted, blowing free. . . . [I was] filled with a biting curiosity about the way the Other Half lived, and a strange hunger for fellowship with them. Were not the workers, the poor, nearer perhaps than we to the reality I was always seeking?[97]

In her a wish to share was complemented by a sense of need.

With the exception of her profession, the settlement movement became the single most engrossing interest in Vida Scudder's early years of active life. School vacations were spent in New York and Philadelphia at settlements located there, and when Denison House opened in Boston it became the center of her social life. She went to the South End on evenings, weekends, and on vacations; in 1893 a leave of absence from Wellesley enabled her to devote herself full time to work in the settlement. Of course she could never be a full-time professional worker, but she served on organizational committees, spoke with the neighbors when open houses were offered, and taught classes in literature, both English and Italian.

Contact with a wide variety of people, reformers as well as workers, brought her out of her shell and helped assuage her ache for reality by providing fellowship. Soon the snobbish noblesse oblige behind her "chivalric" sympathy began to wane as her estimation of the poor rose. Direct human contact taught her that the poor were in many ways more virtuous, more deeply Christian than would-be uplifting reformers. By 1892 she had expressed her confidence in the poor in terms that would have done credit to any Russian populist. In a friendly exchange with Robert Woods of Andover House published in *The Andover Review* she lauded settlement houses not so much for any utilitarian function they might perform but rather for offering an occasion for the expression of "pure and voluntary socialism." Settlements offered rich opportunities for those like her with "the deep conviction that only in return to the people can salvation be found."[98]

A return to the people produced new "adventures in fellowship." At Denison House she established "living contact" with labor leaders, and during the panic of 1893, when she was on academic leave, the settlement moved beyond its educational and recreational objectives and opened its doors to strikers who needed the building to hold meetings. Soon upper-class volunteers were actively assisting the strikers: collecting funds, addressing meetings, and marching in picket lines. Vida Scudder, together with her settlement companions Mary Kenny O'Sullivan and Helena Dudley, went so far as to help organize the National Women's Trade Union League.[99] "Chivalric sympathy" had become solidarity; in a brief six years Ruskin's disciple helped organize a movement devoted to bringing social reformation from below. Yet her own participation as well as that of other middle- and upper-class reformers insured that the movement for social reformation would not be limited to one class alone. It would be based on a solidarity born out of fellowship, an ideal to which she gave eloquent expression in *Social Ideals in English Letters*, written a decade after the settlement house project was begun.

> Children of privilege and children of toil will be united . . . thinkers and laborers; women and men of delicate traditions and fine culture, mingled in close spiritual fellowship with those whose wisdom has been gained not through opportunity, but through deprivation. They will have found a deep union in a common experience and common desire, underlying all intellectual and social difference. They will realize in a measure the old dream of Langland—fellow-pilgrims of Truth, while they share life and labor in joyous comradeship. And they will aim, like More, at a reshaping and regenerating of all society, shutting themselves up in no small or isolated experiment; for they will realize that the fellowship they love can never be perfected except under conditions of a literally universal freedom.[100]

This ideal, which Vida Scudder learned through her settlement house experience, was for her even more important than the development of a political socialist movement.

Even though the settlement movement was, for Vida Scudder, the most engrossing of her social-reform interests, it could not command her exclusive allegiance. Wisely, the members of the College Settlements Association had deliberately avoided giving their houses any definite religious character; they realized that the predominantly Protestant or Anglican beliefs of the volunteers would only constitute another barrier between them and their predominantly Jewish and Roman Catholic neighbors if there was any suggestion of active proselytizing.[101] Their decision was a happy one for the success of the movement, but for Vida Scudder social vision was rooted in religious belief.

The religious dimension of her social vision led her to establish contact with other like-minded Anglican radicals. She joined the Society of Christian

Socialists recently organized by William Dwight Porter Bliss; she contributed articles to *The Dawn*; and she read papers at the society's meetings. One paper, "Socialism and Spiritual Progress," which she presented on March 9, 1891, became something of a social-gospel classic and was printed three times—first in *The Andover Review*, then as a Christian Social Union pamphlet, and finally in an abbreviated form in *The Dawn*. Bliss called it "truly remarkable" and described it as "the shortest and best" of "four things we wish that every reader of *The Dawn* would read this summer."[102] Later, this article grew into *Socialism and Character*, her most venturesome, if not her most popular, book.

With Bliss and other Anglican reformers she helped organize The Church Social Union, the American child of England's Christian Social Union, and in 1894 she was elected to its governing council.[103] Also she took an active interest in two churches, devoted in different ways to the cause of social reform—St. Stephen's Church and Bliss's Church of the Carpenter. It is unusual for an Anglican to belong to two parishes, but the Church of the Carpenter was no ordinary parish. Meeting not in a church building but in an upper room on Boylston Place, the congregation would sing "with special zeal the Magnificat" and then have "wonderful suppers, true agape, when the altar at the back of the little room was curtained off and we feasted on ham and pickles and the hope of an imminent revolution."[104] Notices in *The Dawn* suggest that sacramental celebrations were irregular; the rector frequently was elsewhere serving the cause of social reform.

St. Stephen's Church and House was a more typically representative Anglo-Catholic slum parish. Located in "the most blighted area in the whole city," its establishment had been the first project undertaken by Phillips Brooks on becoming bishop of Massachusetts. Designed to serve as a city mission, it was staffed by two former members of the Society of St. John the Evangelist, Henry Martyn Torbert and Charles Henry Brent. These men, unlike Bliss, directed their social zeal into the parish ministry; they were more concerned about neighborhood improvement than about basic social change. Although they conducted many kinds of services and did not restrict themselves to the prayer book—here following the tradition begun at St. Albans, Holborne—celebrations of the "Sacred Mysteries" were accompanied by "color, light and pageantry."[105] At the Church of the Carpenter Vida Scudder found a place of worship, but the true spirit of the church reached its fullest expression in those agape suppers where one could feast on the "hope of an imminent revolution." At St. Stephen's she found a congenial interest in social reform and neighborhood improvement, but she also experienced that full participation in the sacramental life of the church that is a necessity for a devout Anglo-Catholic. The two churches complemented each other and allowed her to express in her religious practice her passion for unity, her desire for the whole.[106] It is interesting to note that although Vida Scudder was a fervent Anglo-Catholic, she was never associated with either of Boston's most famous Anglo-Catholic parishes, the Church of the Advent, or the Church of St. John the Evangelist. Neither of them, of course, could be described as a slum parish.

Of all the organizations and activities that attracted Vida Scudder in those incredibly active years at the end of the 1880s and beginning of the 1890s, the Society of the Companions of the Holy Cross proved to hold the most long-lasting interest. Like the College Settlements Association, the Society of the Companions of the Holy Cross was a women's organization. I have mentioned the role played by the revival of religious communities in the emancipation of women during the nineteenth century in England. The Society of the Companions of the Holy Cross was an outgrowth of that movement, but it also reflected how far that emancipation had progressed, especially among women of the middle and upper classes. In the 1840s, 1850s, and 1860s women who sought to combine devotion to God with the active service of their fellow man discovered that they were able to accomplish their aim most easily when they banded together behind the walls of a cloister. In order to minister to the world they had to withdraw from it. Fifty or so years later the college-educated women of Vida Scudder's generation desired a fellowship that would both allow them to maintain their varied active lives in the world and afford them an opportunity to withdraw for a time from their consuming activities in order to pursue the spiritual life. Therefore these women, quite without the assistance of any father figure such as E. B. Pusey or J. M. Neale, developed their own variation of the religious life, which combined the unity of corporate community with the personal freedom demanded by "modern woman." Not only did they draw up their own rule, they also designed and built their own retreat house, Adelynrood, in South Byfield, Massachusetts, and laid out and arranged their own gardens. Organized into a community that most closely resembled the Third Orders of the Middle Ages, they demonstrated convincingly that modern women need not be dependent on men.

The Society of the Companions of the Holy Cross, which numbered between four and five hundred women during the late thirties—far exceeding in size any Anglican religious order in the United States at the time—grew out of very modest and private beginnings. In 1884 Emily Malbone Morgan, the wealthy daughter of Dr. George Brinley Morgan, rector of the important Anglo-Catholic parish, Christ Church, New Haven, gathered a small company of women round the bedside of her dying friend, Adelyn Howard. Howard was a remarkable woman; even though she was in great pain and cut off by her illness from performing any active service in the world, she was determined to consecrate what remained of her life to suffering humanity. Since she could not minister to physical distress, she devoted herself to intercessory prayer on behalf of lonely and suffering people and for all the needs of the world.[107] After her death, the companions, inspired by her heroic example, remained together and continued to offer prayers of intercession. Vida Scudder, who had known Adelyn Howard and Emily Morgan, was attracted to the society after the death of her own beloved friend, Clara French, in 1888. French's death had left Scudder heartbroken, and the society helped to sustain her through her grief.[108]

The society could never have prospered had it not been based on the outgoing spirit of Adelyn Howard. The companions recognized a brotherhood of pain in which all humanity shared. Emily Morgan was well-to-do; Vida Scudder was comfortable; both suffered personal, emotional agony, but neither had experienced physical want. Rather than dwell on their own misfortunes, they followed Adelyn Howard and used their personal unhappiness as an occasion for increasing their sensitivity toward the suffering of others, particularly those suffering from physical want. When Vida Scudder became a companion she was deeply engrossed in the project for setting up a College Settlement; a year later she had read the *Fabian Essays* and was attracted to Bliss's Society of Christian Socialists.

Emily Morgan also took a personal interest in social reform, especially in improving the conditions of working women. Drawing on her own private income, she financed the construction of several vacation houses where working women could escape the horrors of slum life and find rest and refreshment. Later she generously provided the money for Adelynrood. Described by Vida Scudder as "halfway between a summer camp and a cloister,"[109] Adelynrood was used as a summer retreat by the companions, as a conference center for religious and reformist groups, and as the central gathering spot where the society met during the last two weeks in August to hold their "chapter."

Among the more prominent women concerned about social problems and involved in reform work who were attracted to the society were Margaret Lawrence and Harriette Keyser, both active in that pioneer American Anglican organization for social reform, the Church Association for the Advancement of the Interests of Labor. But one need not have been a social activist of any variety to join the society; it advanced no particular social doctrine and admitted women whose opinions could encompass the extremes of the political spectrum. All that was formally required was a personal commitment to the principle of social justice and a desire for the reunion of the church.

Likewise, the society welcomed all Anglican women; no shade or variety of churchmanship was excluded. It is only fair to add, however, that the society has strong High Church tendencies, and it is unlikely that any extreme Protestant would feel at home there. The companions live by a rule and their manual draws heavily on the monastic tradition. When they are gathered together prime and compline are recited in community. Also, most of the clergymen who were closely associated with them during their early days belonged to the Anglo-Catholic wing of the church. Bishop Arthur Hall, their first general advisor, and Bishop Charles Brent had been members of the Society of St. John the Evangelist, while Father Huntington, of course, founded the Order of the Holy Cross. These were broad-minded men, but they were all active proponents of Catholic doctrine and practice.

The Society of the Companions of the Holy Cross is unlike any other organization for Anglican churchwomen. They follow a rule that emphasizes both intercessory prayer and simplicity of life. Simplicity is an ideal with an old and honored lineage in Christian history. Doubtless, the economic standing of most Christians of apostolic times made it a matter of necessity; but when Christians became more affluent the ideal was not lost. Sts. Jerome and Augustine practiced it, and the monastic movement inculcated its values. During the later Middle Ages it was taken up by the laity, particularly those involved in the third orders. Newman and especially Pusey gave it the blessing of nineteenth-century Anglo-Catholicism; their blessing was reinforced by the aesthetic and social teachings of John Ruskin. The companions responded to the full range of these historic progenitors.

Simplicity of life is rooted in a conviction common to Christians of many denominations: namely, that the possession of private property is only a form of stewardship and not an absolute right.[110] But as practiced by the companions it is an idea with real teeth in it. Knowing that all they possess is held in trust for God, the companions attempt to limit their consumption to

174

a decent minimum. Of course, this is a moderate form of ascetic discipline and as such may have spiritual benefit for the practitioner, but its social purpose is even stronger. By limiting consumption a companion has a larger monetary surplus to devote to the relief of want and the pursuit of social justice. Also, she more nearly approximates the experience of the common lot of the underprivileged majority of mankind. Each companion follows her own conscience, but all attempt to live according to their ideals day after day.

The practice of intercessory prayer grew out of the society's earliest experiences about the bedside of Adelyn Howard, but as the concern for social justice developed among the companions it became the spiritual concomitant to simplicity of life. Its theological raison d'être was explained by Vida Scudder.

> The secret forces of thought and desire are creative. They vibrate through some common spiritual ether in which we all have our being. This science recognizes more and more. . . . To put the matter simply, "God" not only demands but, I dare say, needs, our co-operation on the spiritual as well as on the material plane. "God needs me as much as I need him," says Eckhardt. "The Cross-bearer of the universe as He passes in our midst, does not act for us, but in us." . . .
>
> Intercessory prayer is not easy to believe in or to practice. . . . But intercession unites most perfectly our love for God and for our neighbor; it is here that the last danger of spiritual self-culture is overcome, and that the Self is merged in oneness with redeeming love. Social intercession is in a peculiar sense the prerogative, duty, and self-expression of a Catholic democracy.[111]

Maurice would most certainly have approved of a desire to unite "our love for God and for our neighbor" and his theological perception that Christ was head and king of our race is at the basis of Vida Scudder's belief that man and God share a common work. But in this passage Scudder has clearly gone beyond Maurice. He would not have understood what she meant by "Catholic democracy" and the intensely mystical tone owes more to the Catholic than to the Mauricean tradition. Of course these words express her mature thought as it was formulated in the 1930s. They show that she was striving for and had only imperfectly apprehended in the 1890s when settlement houses, social reform, Christian socialism, and academic concerns were in the foreground of her thought and life.

## A Listener in Babel

Five years after the publication of *Social Ideals in English Letters* Vida Scudder produced her next important book, the novel, *A Listener in Babel*. Like her subsequent novels, *The Disciple of a Saint* and *Brother John*, *A Listener in Babel* is semi-autobiographical; a fictional re-creation of the first thirty-odd years of her life. Because they are autobiographical, the novels add considerably to our knowledge of their author's personality. Most of her publications were either scholarly or propagandistic, written in response to some social or academic stimulus, but the novel form enabled her to express herself more freely and directly. When used carefully, her novels are in some ways more revealing than her two autobiographies, which were written long after many of the events recorded had taken place. Also, the mask of fiction often made it easier for her to express what might have otherwise gone unspoken.

The novels were written in response to a personal need. They document her quest for a personal faith that would sustain her in the taxing, never-ending pursuit of social justice. They record her struggle with despair; and because they were written in the heat of battle, they have a vitality and immediacy that transcends stylistic conventions and that has survived the years. Christopher Lasch points out that the radical impulse was closely tied to the process of introspection: "It was for that reason the new radicals wrote most freely and convincingly in the autobiographical vein. What they had to say about American society was inseparable from their own re-education or 'disillusionment.' The problem of society was a problem preeminently of consciousness."[112] His description is as relevant to Vida Scudder as to more secular new radicals. The autobiographical novels mirror her consciousness and are therefore valuable aids in understanding her personality.

*A Listener in Babel* was set in a settlement house during the early years of the 1890s and reflects many of Vida Scudder's experiences at Denison House. In the first years of our country's pressing social problems, reform novels became a popular genre. *A Listener in Babel* was not, however, as Walter Fuller Taylor would have it, merely a variation of the typical plot that "turns on the revolt of a socially minded youth against the acquisitive life of his social group, and his discovery of spiritual peace in some effort toward improvement of the tenements." Hilda Lathrope, the novel's listener-heroine, revolts against refined aestheticism, not acquisitive capitalism; and her efforts toward the improvement of the lower classes lead her to disillusionment, not to spiritual peace. These differences are too important to be dismissed as "variations."[113]

Walter B. Rideout, accepting too uncritically the novel's subtitle—*Being a series of imaginary conversations held at the close of the last century and reported by Vida Dutton Scudder*—asserts that the work is "admittedly less a novel than a series of conversations on ideas and social movements current at the turn of the century."[114] In her autobiography the author explains that Plato and Thomas More influenced her to adopt the imaginary conversation form because "I had felt that form to be peculiarly adapted to rendering the drama not of action, but of thought."[115] Despite the critic's qualification, the story of Hilda Lathrope has the necessary dramatic unity and plot development to fit easily within the traditional novel form. It strongly resembles the Bildungsroman: Hilda Lathrope can be compared to Herman Hesse's Demian, Thomas Mann's Hans Castorp, and also, as Arthur Mann suggests, to Bunyan's Pilgrim. We must not be led astray by the novel's subtitle and miss the developing "drama of thought" that runs through the conversations—for above all else this novel deals with Hilda's consciousness. We should not lose sight of Christopher Lasch's acute observation that for the new radicals, "The problem of society was a problem preeminently of consciousness." That is certainly true for Hilda.

*A Listener in Babel* is not only semiautobiographical, it is also something of a roman à clef. Among the characters drawn from life are Father Phillips, Henrietta Morse, and Cousin Howard. Father Phillips is James Huntington, Henrietta Morse has many of the characteristics of Emily Green Balch, an economics instructor at Wellesley later prominent in the Women's International League for Peace and Freedom, and Cousin Howard expresses the opinions—at least once word for word—of E. P. Dutton, Vida's publisher uncle.[116] Hilda Lathrope is a fictional Vida Scudder, sharing her creator's background, concerns, opinions, and personality; but there are important differences that distinguish the author from her fictional creation. Hilda embodies personal possibilities that Vida Scudder had already abandoned. The heroine of the novel is an artist of some accomplishment who rejects an offer to teach at her alma mater so that she can devote all of her energies to settlement house work.

Why settlement house work? Like her creator, Hilda felt stifled by her too comfortable existence. She was smothered by the hothouse atmosphere of *fin de siècle* aesthetic gentility that pervaded her mother's world. College life in

America seemed like a breath of fresh air; she learned that "individuals can be as exciting as cathedrals"[117] and she longed for "reality."

Reality took the form of a young English socialist, Lawrence Ferguson, who awakened her social conscience and unknowingly became the object of her love. Unfortunately Hilda's best friend, Dorothy, and Ferguson were attracted to each other, and Hilda made the beau geste and kept her feelings hidden. One evening in Paris, suffering acutely from the pangs of unrequited love, Hilda looked out of the window and suddenly became aware of all the enormous agony and suffering hidden away behind the glittering facade of the modern industrial city. She realized that her private grief made her part of a great brotherhood of pain and, determined to renounce her own romantic suffering, which seems like a luxury when compared to starvation, sickness, poverty, and other social agonies, she made a pilgrimage to Assisi. In that town, made sacred by the memory of St. Francis, she wrote to America and applied for a position in a settlement house.[118]

Hilda's mother, her friends, and her old intellectual mentors all disapproved of her choice, and the ensuing discussions gave the author ample opportunity to compare and contrast the respective merits of art, education, and social service as a life's work. Social service does not score all the points. Nevertheless, despite the protests of her friends, Hilda remained determined to devote her life to serving the poor. She came down from the heights of Fiesole into the industrial metropolis where at Langley House in Brenton the sound of many immigrant tongues produced a veritable babel. She had made a decision and had taken a first step; but she was far from sure just what she should do. So she listened to the many voices around her and waited for her calling.

*A Listener in Babel* is, as the author remarked, a drama of ideas, not action. We do not learn much about what settlement houses did to improve the actual life of the poor, but we do get to know the types of people who were attracted by the venture, and we discover the issues, problems, and enthusiasms that motivated them.[119] Unlike many radical novels, this book has no scenes describing strikes, riots, and mass meetings; there are no waving banners, no marching feet. Of its characters only a few working girls, a labor union leader, and perhaps a Russian anarchist would feel out of place in a villa in Fiesole or on Thomas Mann's magic mountain.

But the discussions reflect the slum background even if most of the speakers do not. The Langley House circle was passionately concerned with the problems of immigrants, the agonies suffered by the poor during financial depressions, and the destructive effect of miserable working conditions. Each member of the circle has his own ideas and when they gathered around the dinner table all vigorously debated the relative merits of trade unions, socialism, and even revolutionary anarchism. They questioned the value of private philanthropy and attempted to do something about the dependence of higher education on the financial support of immoral mammon.[120]

During her stay at Langley House, Hilda participated in many exciting conversations, but seldom contributed much to them. Walter Ferguson had already converted her to socialism, but she sensed that her theories were as beautiful and unreal as the Burne-Jones reproductions she had hung in her room. How could she justify teaching art to people living on the verge of poverty and starvation? Day by day the agonies engendered by the panic of 1893 grew more intense. Hilda decided that talking and teaching were not enough; she must act.

Her action was hardly revolutionary. Hilda decided to visit a prominent clergyman of her acquaintance who sat on the mayor's poverty committee and to attempt to convince this man of God that public relief must be given to the unemployed. Dr. Wilkinson, pastor of the First Church, would not be convinced. Although he was privately generous and genuinely kind, he was concerned only with "winning souls to Christ." This noble aim kept him endlessly busy attending important meetings; there was the library committee, the Christian Endeavor committee, and, most taxing of all, a committee to discuss the new window in the east transept. He hardly had the time to drop in on his daughter's formal tea or to visit a "poor fellow in the hospital with a broken leg." Social action, he believed, sprang straight from the agnostic movement; it was an attempt to avoid "the vital thing . . . the personal religion of our fathers." Poverty, he informed Hilda, was the result of moral inferiority.

I shall say nothing at the meeting tonight—Dr. Wilkinson spoke almost solemnly—unless it were proposed that the city should extend charitable aid, whether or not disguised in the form of work, to the so called unemployed. In that case I should fervidly enter my protest. . . . It is impossible for any human being to starve in our country. It never has happened. It never can happen. . . . Take courage my dear young lady; we live in a Christian civilization.[121]

Unable to argue with such invincible ignorance, Hilda retreated in defeat. Walking back through the city toward Langley House, she felt consumed by frustration and rage. Too well bred to express her feelings directly to another person, she took some small relief by denouncing a pampered poodle she met on the way.

The failure of her visit to Dr. Wilkinson left Hilda disillusioned, and it had enduring consequences. Her concern for alleviating suffering turned into radicalism and she developed "an intolerant distaste for playing any part whatsoever in existing social machinery,"[122] but hers was the negative, critical radicalism that grows out of frustration, impotence, and alienation. The news that Lawrence Ferguson had accepted a governmental position further depressed her. She felt that he had betrayed his ideals, and this knowledge about someone she still loved and respected set in motion one of those cycles of morbid self-criticism to which the morally sensitive are particularly prone.

The value of her whole life was called into question. She realized that her work in the settlement house had only a minimal use. Indeed, if one judged settlement houses solely on the grounds of results, ignoring good intentions and strenuous effort, how could one justify them? They were merely a palliative, almost as worthless as charity; they had the good will, but they lacked the power to change society for the better. This realization led her to the edge of despair. The acid psychology of Nietzsche ate into her spirit and laid her open to total self-doubt. "Her Christian sentiment, strong and deep as it was, deserted her utterly at times, having no basis in Christian conviction."[123] She asked herself, what if pity were really cruelty in disguise?

A nightmare vividly manifested her doubts. Fleeing from a demon across the lurid, barren landscape of hell, she sought protection at the foot of the cross. "And as she knelt, clinging, sobbing, secure though tremulous, the figure on the cross released an arm, bent over her, and dealt her a blow that seemed to pierce between her soul and her body. Stung, dazed, aghast, she gazed upward; the thorn-crowned face of a devil leered with fierce malignity into her eyes."[124] A second dream brought her the vision of consoling faces, but she awoke on the verge of hysteria. She had reached a point of internal crisis.

Three influences helped Hilda survive and move beyond her despair. During a picnic outing with a trio of working girls, she found consolation in personal fellowship. The girls acknowledged that their hard lives had been easier to bear since they had realized that the settlement house workers cared about them. Hilda discovered that her work had not been useless; the beauties of art helped relieve the endless drabness forced on the girls by their surroundings. But the relationship went deeper. The ignorant working girls sympathized with Hilda; they were as concerned about her spiritual agony as she was about their material privation. "Fellowship with the humble" erased Nietzschean doubts.

This "new revelation of love" restored her faith in humanity, and therefore helped her believe once again in herself.[125]

Personal reassurance, however, could be only a beginning. Even if Hilda felt less despondent, the world's problems remained and she had not yet decided how to deal with them. Another journey outside the slums proved helpful. This time Hilda accompanied her friend Mildred Ellis to a retreat at an Anglican religious house. Here she encountered Father Phillips, "a man much at odds with his generation, yet modern in every fiber; a man of battles, leader of reforms, doggedly devoted to the interests of labor, an abrupt paradoxical figure scouted of newspapers."[126] Even though Hilda considered Christianity the most noble and beautiful form of human mythology, she sought his counsel, asking for something to lean on, an "answer to the eternal problem of the race." The priest gave her a fervid explication of the social gospel of Anglo-Catholicism, proclaiming the great church invisible, protector of the poor, mother of all men. He explained to Hilda the social significance of immortality as the strong consolation for the race. In the Easter experience he saw the essence of all meaning. "Turn your negations into affirmations," he advised.

> Eternity may reveal life as a blessing, and not curse to all the burdened millions. Or it may be that to us it is given to reclaim the earth, at least for the generations yet unborn, till it becomes the free and fair heritage of all men. Watch then; desire; work; and face the East. Live in the strength of hope. If you do not believe in Christ, you can follow Him; that is more important.[127]

Strengthened and refreshed, but not totally convinced, Hilda returned to Langley House, where once again she met Walter Ferguson.

The young socialist firebrand had cooled down during the passing years. Walter Ferguson had become a Fabian civil servant and, like Leonard Woolf, had entered the colonial service. Still a confirmed socialist full of faith in the future, he had decided to direct his energy toward building that future by influencing administrative planning. Mere criticism, he realized, was often self-defeating; it isolated the critic and alienated his potential audience. American political democracy filled Ferguson with hope, and he expected that labor unions and social planning would bring the blessings of true liberty and plenty to the masses. Society, he was sure, was evolving toward happier times: "for my part I've done with spinning theories, and with criticism and speculation. I throw myself into the world as it is, and try to push it along toward the world I want it to be." You are a "child of the future," he told Hilda, "your task is to live the life of the future in the present."[128] Hilda realized that Ferguson's advice echoed the counsel of Father Phillips, and she resolved to take up the fight again.

After their experiences at Langley House, many of the volunteers realized that for them a settlement was only a halfway house that had taken them out of the prison of class and prepared them to assume vocations. Now they had to go on. The concluding chapter announces "New Departures." Janet Frothingham, an intrepid radical, set off for the West to edit a Denver anarchist newspaper. Mildred Ellis decided to move to a neighboring street and open a house where Christian women from all classes could live in community, practicing the simple life witnessing to the true spirit of Christianity.[129] Hilda too, at last, had heard her call. Her plans owed an obvious debt to Tolstoy, Ruskin, and William Morris. For her, living in the future meant a return to her old profession, but this time she did not intend to pursue abstract beauty or art for art's sake. During the next decade she planned to work in factories and shops where she could master the techniques of weaving, dyeing and printing. Then she would know how to integrate handicraft work with modern industrial skills. Two of the working girls were going with her; they would set up housekeeping together and share their knowledge as well as a common life. In ten years Hilda felt that she might be able to make a positive contribution to society by producing work that was as useful as it was beautiful. "The beautiful only exists as found in use, as it springs from the common life of all and ministers to the common life of all. That is the kind of beauty for the lack of which America perishes."[130]

Not without hesitation, and with only a minimum of conviction Hilda Lathrope began a new life. The future was uncertain and she had not found peace, but her restless soul had not succumbed to despair. She could continue.[131]

## A Socialist Churchwoman

As I mentioned, Vida Scudder became a socialist convert when she read the *Fabian Essays* in 1889. *Social Ideals in English Letters* and *A Listener in Babel* testify to her continuing interest in the subject; but neither work is primarily concerned with socialism per se. In order to discover the fullest early expression of her socialist faith we must turn back to the paper she read before the Society of Christian Socialists one rainy evening in March 1891, first published in the July 1891 issue of *The Andover Review* under the title "Socialism and Spiritual Progress." Ordinarily one might be reluctant to rely heavily on an early work as an indication of an author's developed position, but in this case such reliance appears to be justified. Scudder herself allowed the work to be republished twice during the middle nineties, and nothing that she says about socialism either in *Social Ideals in English Letters* or in *A Listener in Babel* contradicts any position taken in that article. Also, *Socialism and Character*, the author's most fully developed exposition of her socialist principles (published in 1912), grew out of the speculations first advanced in "Socialism and Spiritual Progress."[132] Since during the period I am discussing "Socialism and Spiritual Progress" was neither contradicted nor superseded by any further statement, I assume that it is a reasonably accurate expression of the author's point of view. The article is, in addition, one of the most significant expositions of the Christian Socialist viewpoint published during the 1890s.[133]

When Vida Scudder wrote "Socialism and Spiritual Progress" the Christian Socialist movement in the United States was still newborn.[134] Most of the churchgoing public remained serenely unaware of its existence; but in those circles familiar with advanced thought the fledgling already had aroused immediate and sometimes passionate opposition. On the surface Christians and socialists seemed so far apart that Christian Socialism was considered a veritable contradiction in terms—a hybrid concept that could never become a living reality.

During the first two decades after the Civil War most self-acknowledged socialists were urban lower class, recent immigrants—primarily Germans[135]—who espoused the doctrines of Ferdinand Lassalle, Karl Marx, or Mikhail Bakunin. The Lassalleans, Marxists, and revolutionary anarchists, as the followers of Bakunin came to be called, were divided into three mutually exclusive rival sectarian camps; and, although their ideological and tactical disagreements were legion, all agreed on one point: they opposed organized religion. No impartial observer could confuse these radical foreigners with the native born, middle-class, respectable citizens who constituted the great majority of America's Protestant and Anglican Christians. The economic, social, and cultural gulf that separated Christians and socialists seemed equally great as that fixed between Dives and Lazarus where he lay on the bosom of Abraham.

The most serious differences between Christians and socialists, however, were intellectual. Clerical critics of socialism, firmly committed to a theology whose primary focus on the individual, simply could not accept socialism's collectivist assumptions—even when they agreed that society needed reformation. Henry Ward Beecher's successor at Plymouth Church, Lyman Abbott, makes an excellent case in point. Abbott was a moderate reformer and theological liberal, but he found the socialist approach to solving social problems erroneous and contrary to the methods of Christ. His article "Christianity versus Socialism," published in the prestigious forum of New England's intelligentsia, *The North American Review*, concludes:

> We rejoice in legal, social, sanitary reform, and give Godspeed to all such reformers; but in our work as churches and ministers, *we propose to work for the rebuilding of men rather than for the reforming of social organizations; for the change of character rather than of environment*; and by appeals to men in the order of moral supremacy, appealing first to the dominant sentiments of reverence, hope, faith, and love; second, to the intellectual and social considerations of prudence and present well-being; last of all to the metaphysical and animal nature and its needs. [emphasis mine][136]

Abbott sincerely believed that his method had the sanction of Christ.

Abbott was one of America's most prominent and successful progressive clergymen. In 1889, the same year that he published *The North American Review* article, *The Andover Review*, a journal with liberal social and theological leanings, opened its pages to one of his less illustrious clerical brethren, Edward S. Parsons. Although Parsons was sympathetic to the aims and intentions of socialism, if not to some of its methods, on the whole his article, "A Christian Critique of Socialism," was nearly as negative as Abbott's. Parsons did not appeal to the example of Christ to buttress his doctrine of individualism, but he was, nonetheless, concerned about its preservation. Implicitly, at least, his concern for individualism ran deeper than his desire for social improvement, for he feared that a society dedicated to equality might have such a leveling effect that it would reduce the opportunity for the practice of personal virtue. This leveling could have only tragic results. The essence of his critique is contained in a significant sentence: "The ideal of socialism, stripped of its Messianic drapery, is bodily comfort; the ideal of Christianity is, first and foremost, personal character."[137]

If Christian Socialism ever were to succeed in the United States, it would have to win over men like Lyman Abbott and Edward Parsons; they represented the progressive wing of dominant middle-class American Protestantism. This group was intellectually open to change and saw, if only through a glass darkly, the need for social reform. It was to this audience that Vida Scudder addressed herself in "Socialism and Spiritual Progress."

She was well suited for the task. Since she had grown up in a similar social and intellectual milieu, she shared important common assumptions with the progressives. Both considered an individual's personal moral character of primary importance and both accepted the social implications of Charles Darwin's theory of evolutionary progress through a process of natural selection.[138] Ralph Henry Gabriel writes that a "philosophy of individualism, supported by Protestant theology or Darwinian naturalism, became the ruling intellectual pattern of the period . . . which lay between 1865 and 1917."[139] In "Socialism and Spiritual Progress" Vida Scudder attempted to demonstrate that socialism and not individualism would most fully satisfy the aspirations of both Protestant theology and Darwinian naturalism.

Self-consciously disregarding all merely political considerations, Vida Scudder announces in the very first paragraph of her "speculation" that she is concerned about "What sort of men and women will we be when we get to socialism?"[140] The battles of the world are fought and won on great moral issues, and the issue between socialism and individualism, which is the leading issue of the day—indeed the greatest issue since the Reformation—is essentially a moral issue. Moral issues have great social consequences, but above all they are concerned with personal development. "It is not sufficient to show that the socialist state will rest on a truer basis than the present order: we must also show that it will develop a nobler personality . . . [since] the end of life is not comfort, but character."[141] Having stated the fundamental premise of her discourse she goes on to define her concept of socialism:

> I do not hold that it will imply of necessity the abolition of private property. I do hold it to imply collective ownership of the means of production. Material wealth will be distributed on the basis, not of service, but of need. This physical support will be insured to all. Absolute equality will not perhaps prevail, but outward conditions will be far more equal than at present. There will be no more violent extremes of riches and poverty, luxury and degradation. . . . At both ends disproportion will be cut away; no amount of cleverness, snap, effort, will enable a man to get much ahead of his neighbor in the race for wealth, and society will tend toward a dead level of external equality.[142]

Dismissing at once any question about whether such a condition could ever become a reality she turns directly to her ideal society's intellectual critics. Scorning dispute with lesser figures she confronts the "shining light of evolution and individualism," Herbert Spencer, the man Richard Hofstadter described as "to most of his educated American contemporaries, a great man, a grand intellect, a giant figure in the history of thought."[143] Spencer had declared that all forms of socialism were forms of slavery. Assuming that the value of life is in struggle, Social Darwinists asserted that "all individuality springs from the conflict with destiny." Without struggle life would be dull, without contrast, and there would be no possibility of improvement. To anyone concerned about the quality of life and the fate of the individual, the indictment is as serious as it is stern, and—Scudder admits—modern utopias tend to confirm the criticism. She found Edward Bellamy's *Looking Backward*, with its smug materialism and philistine preoccupation with personal comfort, "dismal"; and although the values of art, appreciation of nature, and human love described by William Morris in his *News from Nowhere* raised socialism to a higher plane, still she lamented that there was no scope or incentive for the development of character. She reiterates her initial premise in stronger terms: ". . . if socialism be not adapted to produce a higher character than the present order, of socialism we will have nothing. No, not if it bring never so much material comfort in its train; not though it bestow on humanity complete exemption from the grosser forms of vice."[144]

Yet, she suggests, perhaps this is not the whole story. Let us look around and see what conditions in our present society prove most conducive to the development of character; where do we find our great men, men "great in moral heroism, in intellectual and imaginative reach, in active power?" Not from among the ranks of the very rich or the very poor; these two classes of society are bored or tired. "They spring, I call all history to witness, from the ranks of the great middle class. . . . The long role of statesmen, saints, poets, and philanthropists is made up principally, though of course not entirely, of men and women who were nurtured in conditions of simple competence and peace."[145] This life-style has produced the highest type of character, but more important, it is the "life which Jesus Christ commanded." Christ denounced the rich with unfaltering revolutionary scorn. When he spoke the beatitude "Blessed are the poor," though, He was not talking about the worn-out poor destroyed by the fierce competition of modern industry; He was not describing Marx's proletariat. Rather, the author affirms in a burst of Jeffersonian agrarianism, He spoke of an agricultural poor that included small traders and craftsmen, "men free, in the healthful simplicity of their lives . . . to receive . . . the message of the Kingdom of God. From such men Christ chose those disciples who remodeled the world; *of such men He himself was one.*"[146]

Spencer had proclaimed that socialism was slavery. Scudder rejoins, in an argument deftly calculated to appeal to the prejudices and assumptions of middle-class Christian Social Darwinists—an argument all the more convincing because she accepted it herself—that the conditions that have produced the greatest men, the conditions inculcated by the teaching and example of Jesus Christ, are the very conditions that socialism aims to make universal.

Accepting as given the value of the Protestant work ethic, she hastens to assure her reader that work will not be abolished in the socialist state. Men do not want to work when they are tired, or diseased, or undernourished; social conditions produce this wretched state. Improved social conditions will change it. "Already, today, the work-impulse is strong in the normal man."[147] In the socialist state man will continue to possess incentives to spur on his natural impulse. The best work, even in our materialistic and acquisitive culture, has never been done merely for money. Man is stimulated by desires for praise, honor, fame, achievement, or by a concern for serving the common humanity. These incentives will not be destroyed by the collective ownership of the means of production.

In the first nine pages of her article the author attempted to refute the negative criticisms of her Christian and/or Social Darwinist opponents. In the remaining nine pages she stressed the possibilities inherent in socialism, showing how it is thoroughly consistent with the highest aspiration of evolutionary thought and Christianity.

> It remains for us . . . to show . . . that socialism is the next . . . logically inevitable phase in that grand and gradual sequence of energy which . . . by the operation of divinely natural law, is lifting man from the brute to the god. . . . [Socialism] must be shown not to deny, but to fulfill the past. It will eliminate none of those . . . powers which have so far governed evolution in its progress from body to soul . . . the study of the progressive action of such principles revealed by history, rightly apprehended, carries us straight, by purely scientific induction, to the threshold of the socialistic state.[148]

To support her claim she turns to "the latest work of the Science of the human mind," the *Psychology* of William James, applying to society at large his principle of the automatic life. James had argued that we must attempt to make necessary and useful functions as automatic and habitual as we can, so that our "higher powers of mind" will be set free for their own proper work.

Socialism, Scudder asserts, will do just this for the body politic, entrusting the "anxious supervision of physical needs to the State," freeing the individual for more creative pursuits. The history of civilization is a record of progress made in this direction: the savage was a self-contained unit who had to take care of himself; the medieval knight had greater freedom; the modern scholar and poet is free to work because society has freed him from an obsessive concern with threats of violence and need. But scholars and poets are exceptions; most men remain enthralled by worry, living in a state of insecurity because they have no assurance that their physical needs will be met.

Socialism, she insists, will not abolish work, but worry. "Work is holy, but worry is sinful." By freeing man from worry

> socialism would render possible, for the first time for centuries, literal obedience to the commands of the Master; it would enable men "to take no thought for the morrow," for it would remove from them the necessity of constant thought for what they shall eat, what they shall drink, and wherewithal they shall be clothed.[149]

Socialism will then fulfill the moral law of Christ as well as the natural law of psychology and history.

When worry is gone and man is free will life lose its meaning? What will the socialist state be like? Three things it will not be: it will not be a utopia; it will not be a dead level of characterless monotony; it will not be a sinless world. "A radical change in human nature socialism does not promise nor require. What it does promise is this: the uplift of the struggle of humanity to a higher plane, the removal of certain spiritual clogs that bind down to the earth the free spirit of man."[150]

Present society is held in bondage to the flesh by material cares. When this bondage is lifted by socialism man will be free to develop higher, more spiritual values. What would these be? Although they are not specifically labeled as such, they are the triune values of Plato and his disciples throughout the ages: the good, the true, and the beautiful. Scudder refers to art, the advance of knowledge through science and philosophy, and the improvement of character through moral struggle. The last is for her, of course, the most important.

Socialism would permit a transference of moral struggle from the outer life to the inner, from the physical to the spiritual. The struggle of right with wrong would not cease, but it would be transferred from the plain of battle to the depths of the soul. It is reasonable to assume that life in the future, in delicacy, in fire, in sensitiveness to fine moral issues, will bear to our own life the relation which ours bears to the fierce and crude morality of the elder world. . . . Our Lord Jesus transferred the external commands of the Mosaic law to the mind and the heart. This more secret and subtle wisdom, incomprehensible to the Hebrews of old, we, too, fail fully to apprehend; yet into its high mystery we are bound to penetrate more and more.[151]

Addressing herself once again pointedly to socialism's Christian critics she assures them that socialism does not propose to achieve through outward reform what can be only achieved through a purification of the heart. "Socialism makes no claim to achieve redemption through machinery."[152] It does, though, assert that it would translate the struggle of man to a higher and more spiritual sphere, and that in so doing it is in line with the whole process of evolution; and—more important—it is consistent with the method of Christ himself. One cannot make man good only by changing his environment; but by changing his environment at least we may not be leading him into temptation.

Finally, in a concluding paragraph, Vida Scudder makes yet another significant point. Socialism is not the end of history, not the Last Judgment, but merely the next stage in human development. Speaking of man's future history she writes,

Stage by stage he must leave behind him the false dreams of physical strife, the antagonism to his fellows, the sharp pursuit of his individual needs. He will not leave sorrow, he will not leave temptation. At every step will appear new evils to be conquered. This his curse is also his blessing, for only in battle can the soul of man be strengthened for immortality. But these evils will become ever more subtle, more mysterious, more inward; and the soul that treads them underfoot shall mount by them to ever new regions of holiness and power. For this struggle—ceaseless, eternal, glorious; the struggle upward by means of the perfect law of liberty, into celestial light—I believe that socialism will, in wonderful and unforseen measure, set free the soul of man.[153]

I have mentioned that Vida Scudder was particularly well qualified to serve as a socialist apostle to the progressive wing of middle-class American Protestantism because she shared its basic assumptions about evolutionary change and the importance of an individual's personal moral character. Her concluding speculations about the human future reveal that she also shared with them a similar—if not necessarily identical—philosophy of history. David

F. Bowers draws an illuminating distinction between the socialist and the traditional American progressive reformist attitudes toward the end of history. "In place of believing as does the socialist, that history will come to a neat climax or conclusion, the democratic humanist tends to envisage the drama of history as continuing endlessly and as ever moving from higher to still higher climaxes."[154] One might argue that Bowers's dichotomy tends to oversimplify the socialist position: not all socialists necessarily commit themselves to a doctrine that envisions a climactic end of history, and among those who do, only the unsophisticated dogmatists believe that "history will come to a *neat climax*." But even if Bowers's distinction is overdrawn, as a historical generalization it has the ring of truth. Socialism in both its utopian and Marxist varieties—although not in its Fabian variety—possesses an almost eschatological sense of urgency and offers a this-worldly fullness of promise not found in the historical speculations of traditional American Protestant progressive reform. Although the reformers were often severely critical of the status quo, their perception of the present was not ultimately bleak. Because they saw the present as a qualified good, a good better than the past—when for example there was no religious or political liberty—they were able to speculate about and work for a better future, a future that would continue to improve on the present, just as the present had improved on the past. Since the present was good, even if flawed, it did not need to be redeemed by some cataclysmic event; no fundamental transvaluation of values was required; history did not have to end so that man could begin to live.

In "Socialism and Spiritual Progress" Vida Scudder clearly speaks with the voice of Bowers's American democratic humanist. There is no eschatological urgency in her tone when she concludes that socialism will set man free to move "from higher to still higher climaxes," "into celestial light." No fundamental transvaluation of values will be required. It is not a serious oversimplification of her position to say that she advocates socialism with its collective control of the means of production so that the greatest possible number of people might become middle class and practice the higher bourgeois virtues. Finally, a this-worldly fullness of promise tends to be obscured by her concern with spiritual progress. She is less concerned that the land of promise run with milk and honey than that once man is there he will be able to journey beyond it into the interior recesses of the soul and into the celestial lights of the highest heavens.

There was nothing fundamentally revolutionary about the socialist doctrine that Vida Scudder proclaimed to the small group of reformers gathered together on that night in March 1891. Based on the idealistic and optimistic assumptions of late-nineteenth-century middle-class liberal reform, it proposed socialism as the logical and historically inevitable culmination of all that was best in that movement. Her statement reflects the moderate tone of the *Fabian Essays*, the work that had converted her to socialism two years before. Socialism will mean a more equitable distribution of wealth and the collective ownership of the means of production, but beyond these economic changes she envisions no sharp break with the past and present. There is certainly no suggestion that violence will be required to effect the necessary changes.

The socialist theory behind "Socialism and Spiritual Progress" was Fabian, but as she later remarked, "I was a Fabian with a difference, for the ultimate source of my socialism was and is Christianity. Unless I were a socialist, I could not honestly be a Christian."[155] It is clear that for Vida Scudder socialism is the handmaiden of Christianity. In fact, her intentions would have been more explicit had she named her work "Socialism *for* Spiritual Progress." The ultimate justifications for socialism are that it will enable human beings to give literal obedience to the command of Christ to take no thought for the morrow and that it will set free the soul of man to pursue immortality and the vision of God. Taken purely as a thing in itself and without its possibilities for enhancing an individual's religious growth, socialism would have been a "thing indifferent" to Vida Scudder.

"Unless I were a socialist, I could not honestly be a Christian." In one sentence Vida Scudder reveals the basis of her lifelong interest in social reform. It is true that John Ruskin and not the Broad Church Anglicanism of her youth awakened her to "the realities of the modern world," but it is significant that she turned to a religious organization, the Salvation Army, to register her protest against injustice. A Christian conscience drove her to hate her own privileges and formed the "sense of chivalric sympathy" that led her to right wrongs and champion the cause of God's poor. Wisely, the Women's College Settlement Association eschewed sectarian religious denominationalism in the pursuit of its work, and although it was personally the most significant, it was not the only non-Christian social reform organization to claim her allegiance. Vida Scudder was not limited by the ecclesiastical structures of her time, but her memberships in the Society of Christian Socialists, the Church Social Union, the Society of the Companions of the Holy Cross, and St. Stephen's parish bear witness to the fact that the cause of social reform was intimately bound up with her allegiance to the Anglican Church. Her books, especially the major works of the nineties, *The Witness of Denial*, *The Life of the Spirit in the Modern English Poets*, and *Social Ideals in English Letters*, proclaim the same message. Even her conversion to economic socialism was a direct outgrowth of her Christianity. The desire to be an honest Christian made Vida Scudder a social reformer and a socialist; she became a "socialist churchwoman." If we would truly understand her, though, we must not lose sight of the relative importance of the words in that term. *Socialist* is an adjective—a significant one because it serves to distinguish her from the majority of her Christian contemporaries—but only an adjective. It merely modifies, describes the noun *churchwoman*. First and foremost Vida Scudder was a churchwoman.

# SEVEN

# Vida Dutton Scudder: Beyond the Social Gospel

When Vida Scudder became a socialist in 1889, she joined a minority left-wing movement on the fringes of Social Gospel Christianity. Her Fabian doctrines were Christian, moderate, reformist, nonviolent, and seemingly almost apolitical; she accepted most of the presuppositions, aims, and methods of progressive, middle-class, democratic reforms but, nonetheless, she left almost all of her fellow reformers behind by advocating the equalization of income and the collective ownership of the means of production.

Gradually, over the next twenty-five years, however, as organized institutional Christianity increasingly became identified with the Social Gospel movement,[1] moderate socialist ideas were more readily accepted by Christian reformers. The early years of the twentieth century saw the dawn of a progressive era characterized by humanitarianism, social reform, and social service; with a few exceptions, such as the Republican old guard, the whole country appeared to be moving to the left. Walter Rauschenbush, a brilliant Baptist clergyman and America's foremost Social Gospel theologian, spoke approvingly of socialism, and many less illustrious Christian reform leaders followed suit; if most did not become out-and-out socialists, they were at least sympathetic. But the Christian Socialism with which the reformers either identified or sympathized was vague, and it took so many individual forms that one historian of the Social Gospel movement remarks that when a reform leader called his position "Christian Socialism" he only meant by this phrase, "essentially a social gospel."[2]

Even though reformers could not always agree about the exact meaning of Christian Socialism, almost all of them were certain that it did not mean Marxism. To be sure there were exceptions—Henry Demerest Lloyd and George Herron, for example—but, on the whole, Donald Meyer's generalization is correct. "Marxist socialism had always seemed alien, at least in their understanding of it, to the social gospel pastors. They had objected to the Marxist sanction for violence, to Marxist animus against religion, to Marxist materialism, and to Marxist assignment of an executive role in social redemption to the proletariat."[3]

Like Henry Demerest Lloyd and George Herron, Vida Dutton Scudder was an exception; as the result of a personal crisis that occurred at the turn of the century, she moved beyond the Social Gospel movement, developed her own synthesis of Christianity and Marxism, and became an active member of the Socialist Party. Accepting Marxism, though, is only one way she moved beyond the Social Gospel. In order to accept Marx and political socialism she had to abandon the optimistic worldview of liberal Social Gospel reform. At a time when more and more Americans came to believe that social abuses would be remedied by a gradual but inevitable progress directed by the reform movement, Vida Scudder grappled with the realization that the reform movement had failed to effect any fundamental improvements in the social order. All the enthusiasm for change had not and would not alter one jot the horrendous fact that in a capitalist society—even if it paid more than lip service to Christianity—the poor would always be with us. Before she could accept a new social theory that offered hope for the future, Vida Scudder had to develop a theology that recognized and transcended catastrophe and defeat.

Because she was able to formulate a theological perspective that encompassed catastrophe and defeat, Vida Scudder was able to continue her work as a social reformer when after World War I the country as a whole returned to normalcy and the Social Gospel movement came to an end. Unlike so many former progressives, muckrakers, and social reformers who succumbed to regret and cynicism during the jazz era (and their number was legion), Vida Scudder went on fighting the good fight and became a vital link connecting the reform movements of the Social Gospel era and those of the Red Decade.

### Breakdown and Recovery

In March 1901, Vida Scudder suddenly collapsed.

While returning [to Boston] one evening by train from Wellesley . . . where I had been hostess to some distinguished guest, something crashed in my head. I was used to severe headaches; this was different. I staggered home and for many weeks lay sleepless in a darkened room, with explosions of such pain as I didn't know possible going on inside my brain.[4]

Medical authorities were consulted, but even the specialists could find no specific organic cause for this mysterious illness that lingered on with diminishing severity until 1904. The doctors diagnosed a deep exhaustion brought on by overwork. There can be no doubt that Scudder was seriously overworked—the years since 1887 had been filled with an astonishing amount of productive activity—but the medical diagnosis did not disclose the real reason for her sudden collapse and continuing illness. Overwork was merely a symptom of deeper problems.

In the second year of the new century Vida Scudder celebrated her fortieth birthday; now she was middle aged, and she felt seriously dissatisfied with her life. Fifteen years earlier, motivated by her "best impulses, compounded of shame and of adventurous urge toward trail making,"[5] she had broken out of the "prison of class" and tried to make herself useful. She began teaching and writing and she plunged headlong into the exciting but exacting task of helping the poor and improving society. With the passing of the years, however, she discovered that the demands of her diverse commitments pulled her in different directions. Believing that, "Worthwhile people never scattered their energies [I] coveted the single track mind. . . . But my own energies were scattered far and wide. While I so eagerly played my part in the developing social movement, delight in my profession had grown stronger every year."[6]

While racked by diverse commitments, each of which "demands the whole of you," she found herself deeply troubled by aspects of her involvement in the very activities that pulled her apart. If her delight in the academic profession grew every year, her doubts about it likewise began to increase. She thoroughly enjoyed teaching—keeping "my students as well as myself in the presence of significant racial experience embedded in forms of undying beauty"—but was impatient with Ph.D. research, " . . . rummaging about in literary byways in pursuit of unimportant information."[7] More significant, she "hated her salary"; the contrast between her own modest Back Bay comfort and the squalor and misery of the slums was "excruciating." Her sense of personal guilt was intensified when Wellesley College was offered "tainted money" by Standard Oil. A "disagreeable conflict" erupted when she and other faculty members signed a "vehement protest." Quite naturally, the college considered its own financial need and readily accepted the gift, questioning not the business ethics of Standard Oil, but the loyalty of those faculty who protested against the gift's acceptance. As a result, her relations with the college she deeply loved became acutely strained, and for a time she and her fellow dissidents even considered resigning.[8]

She could not turn from academic problems to find release or solace in her social involvements because she was even more dissatisfied with the specific duties of her role in the developing social movement. "As time went on, I realized that I was only on the fringe of that great world of social endeavor. . . . By degrees relations with working people, alas, grew fewer; the old prison wall of class again closed round me." She found to her disgust that she was putting more time on uptown committees and administrative planning than on actual human fellowship. "This I never ceased to mourn."[9]

Interestingly enough, Vida Scudder did not mention in her autobiography what must have been the most significant and heart-rending discouragement that she experienced at the turn of the century. It was revealed only in the opening chapter of *Socialism and Character*, a chapter devoted to reviewing her personal experience during the last quarter-century. The passage communicates the emotional intensity that accompanied her disillusion; a decade had not erased its impact.

> The new crusade whose call we had answered gathered its hosts to fight the serried forces of industrial and social wrong. . . . It was splendid; it was inspiring; it was by all odds the best thing that the modern world had to show. But what did it achieve? What had they *done*—all the laborious committees? . . . The answer was plain. *The great mass of misery, corruption and injustice remained practically unaffected by our efforts.* . . . From the time that this conviction first struck inward, a disillusion graver far than the discouragements of youth settled on men's spirits. . . . It is not too strong to sum up the situation by saying that when the twentieth century opened . . . a considerable proportion of the more thoughtful and liberal minds of the day confronted the failure of reform. . . . It was a depressing moment. . . . The dark modern spectacle of poverty and waste rose before us unaltered in the main by all those compassionate activities which not only in our generation but throughout the Christian ages had shed upon it a faint phosphorescent shining. . . . Where was comfort to be found? *Not in personal sacrifice: this last resort of self-deception was only a final indulgence. Not in philanthropy or reform. . . . The whole heart was sick, the whole man faint, and the whole situation seemed a device to rouse the derisive laughter of the fiends who jeer at human endeavors from their aeriel theatre.* [emphasis mine][10]

This sensitive and acutely self-conscious individual was deeply troubled by her inescapable involvement in what is now called the "system." Her attitude toward it was certainly complex. Today, in the admittedly admirable interest of descriptive clarity, we have come to distinguish too sharply between the terms *reformer* and *revolutionary*. Differentiating nuances of meaning must not be forgotten, but the terms are not mutually exclusive. Vida Scudder was inspired by the vision of a Christian commonwealth, a vision that was profoundly revolutionary. It proclaimed as Lord the one who made all things new. More radical than any mundane utopia, it promised a new heaven and a new earth. The power of this vision made Vida Scudder a social reformer; it called her to things of this world. She did not repudiate the here and now to escape into chiliastic fantasy or abstract speculation; rather, she set about to right wrongs and improve her own present evil age. The vision was revolutionary; the method was reformist. The vision rejected the imperfect here and now, but the method implied living with the status quo, at least as the starting ground for improvement. But, as Scudder wholeheartedly devoted her time and energy to reform, the vision began to dim. She could still see it with the eye of conscience, but she found it increasingly difficult to believe that she could fashion even her own life in its image. The here and now world proved far more powerful than her worst expectations. She was not improving it; subtly and insidiously it was corrupting her. Under these circumstances her furious activity was both an attempt to keep faith with the vision that inspired her and a means of blotting out her own growing sense of frustration, failure, and guilt. Finally, she drove herself too hard; she had ignored her severe headaches too long; her system could no longer stand the strain. She collapsed.

Vida Scudder suffered a physical breakdown; the causes were mental and spiritual. The very nature of her personality—so full of enthusiasm for knowledge and compassion for others, so exacting in its demands on the self—had led to her collapse. Yet her personality was not diseased; at root she was psychologically sound. She revealed a remarkable insight into her own problems when she had Hilda confess to Father Phillips that she needed something to lean on, some "answer to the eternal problem of the races" I have pointed out that her Oxford conversion was primarily a matter of discovering religious tastes. These Anglo-Catholic tastes were superimposed on a stern Calvinist sense of duty inherited from her New England background. Her religious outlook made enormous demands, but it offered little personal solace. She had accepted neither the comforting ecclesiology of the Anglo-Catholics nor the Evangelical assurance of personal salvation. During the frantically busy years since 1887 she had been far too concerned with social problems to take the time to develop a personal theology. Maurice had saved her from disbelief in college and his incarnational theology provided a firm foundation for her Social Gospel, but now in this moment of crisis there were

197

different problems. She did not need to be saved from unacceptable theological oversimplifications; she did not need a framework for relating Christianity and social reform; she needed something to lean on, a sustaining weltanschauung that would enable her to confront "the failure of reform."

Vida Scudder's writings during the last decade of the nineteenth century reveal that she shared the prevailing optimistic spirit characteristic of the Social Gospel movement during that period.[11] Always she points to signs that a better day will come, and she offers concrete suggestions for hastening its arrival. Then with the dawn of a new century her optimism vanished "reform had failed . . . the whole heart was sick. . . . Where was comfort to be found?"

Three months after her breakdown, the Scudders and their friend, Florence Converse, sailed for England. Scudder's health had improved—"I could stand the light now several hours a day"[12]—and in London she found a specialist whose advice opened the way to her spiritual and physical recovery. Fortunately, he understood his patient's restless and energetic temperament, and he did not prescribe rest and inactivity. "You are to do something you never did before, and completely to forget your old interests," he advised.[13]

Following his advice, the Scudder party spent the next year on the continent, where she occupied her mind by writing poetry. There, an ocean away from Boston's academic and social problems, she continued to grow stronger. A journey to Italy brought still greater benefits: she discovered the saints. "In this year I put myself under the direction of two spiritual guides who have controlled my life." In Assisi, M. Paul Sebatier introduced her to St. Francis. "I met St. Catherine first in Florence, though I was to know her better by and by in her beloved native Siena."[14]

Discovering the saints was extremely important for Vida Scudder; probably it was the critical turning point in her life, occupying the same place in her history that the Aldersgate meeting did for Wesley and the "experience in the tower" did for Luther.[15] As she explains, "My life took a new turn; it is not too much to say that it acquired a new center of interest."[16] She remained devoted to this center of interest for the rest of her life. Four of her subsequent books deal directly with St. Catherine and St. Francis, and everything else that she wrote reflects their influence. But she was not merely a hagiographer, and these saints were not only scholarly interests. She accepted them, their lives and their words, as spiritual guides. Their guidance was something to lean on, and through them she discovered a personal faith that enabled her to develop a sustaining worldview that supported her during the crises and disillusionments of the next fifty years. What she learned from studying Francis and Catherine she carried over into her active life, and under their influence she became both "more religious and more radical."

## The Influence of St. Catherine

In Florence Scudder purchased an Italian translation of Fra Raimondo of Capua's biography of St. Catherine, together with four volumes of her letters. In these books, especially the letters, she found "such companionship and guidance as I had never known."[17] Other reading brought her back again and again to Catherine and her Famiglia, "that varied group so like us, who gathered round her in loving discipleship."[18] Plans for a novel immediately began to take shape in her mind, but J. M. Dent, the British publisher,[19] convinced her that the public needed an English translation of Catherine's letters. As soon as she returned to the United States, Scudder set to work and in 1905 the *Letters of St. Catherine of Siena* appeared on the market.[20] Then, primed with a thorough scholarly knowledge of the material, she turned again to the novel that Dent published in 1907 under the title, *The Disciple of a Saint*.

In her first novel, religion was only one of many voices, albeit an important voice. In *Disciple* the religious focus is sharp and clear, and religion and social reform are closely integrated. This close integration reflects the author's intellectual development, but also is a natural result of a change of milieu. The novel is set in Italy and France during the last quarter of the fourteenth century, a time when religious and social issues were more tightly intertwined by the nature of the contemporary culture.

I have mentioned that all of her novels are semiautobiographical. How can an imaginary biography of a man of the fourteenth century say anything about the life of a modern woman? Certainly this book depicts nothing of the author's day-to-day existence. It does, however, say a great deal about her inner life, and it reveals in greater detail than the autobiography the nature of the companionship and guidance that Vida Scudder found in St. Catherine's letters, especially those addressed to Raniero de Landoccio dei Pagliaresi, the subject of this imaginary biography. Despite their difference in sex and the long years that separated them, Vida and Raniero shared common religious and personal problems. Catherine's letters to Ranieno were equally helpful to Vida, and like him, she became a disciple of this saint.[21]

199

Of course, Raniero was more than the author in disguise; he was a real person, one of the earliest members of the Famiglia of St. Catherine and her first secretary. History has not left a great deal of information about him, but something of the outline of his life can be traced in the literature about the saint, and his biographer found this information "full of suggestions."[22]

The Raniero suggested to the author by historical documents was an engaging and sympathetic person; a generous, sensitive, idealistic man, much given to reflection, often melancholy and appearing distant and preoccupied. As befits the descendant of Sienese scholars and teachers, he had a vigorous intellect and many interests. Poetry, the visual arts, humane studies, and religion all excited his imagination and aroused his enthusiasm. Like his biographer in this stage of her life, Raniero suffered from "confusion of mind," an agonizing state of perpetual spiritual restlessness and lack of certainty. He found it easy to question and doubt, but difficult to believe. He was torn between the different ideas and attitudes toward life current in his time.

These different approaches to life are represented by three secondary characters, Lariella, Louis de Frontaigne, and St. Catherine. Lariella, Raniero's cousin, was also a troubled soul. Although the name obviously derives from Petrarch, her personality seems drawn from the *Decameron*. Less bawdy than a Boccacio character, more subdued certainly, but equally caught up in reviving paganism, Lariella devoted herself to sensual enjoyment. But behind her glittering impetuousness, behind her frenzied devotion to the joys of the flesh for their own sake, the nihilistic terror of the abyss nagged at her soul. Raniero loved the beautiful, doomed creature, and she became both a moral and a physical temptation.

Louis de Frontaigne was an urbane, cultivated, secular ecclesiastic, a type who reached an apogee during the Renaissance in men like Cardinal Bernardo Dovizi da Bibbiena, Leo X's teacher and intimate friend. An intellectual, Louis regarded the first stages of the revival of learning with enthusiasm; a connoisseur of rare and wide sensitivity, he was equally attracted by the poems of Petrarch and by the flowering of the fine arts at the papal court in Avignon. Even at its best, however, Louis's type remains a man of this world, bound by the limitations of its sensibility. Truly devoted, in his own way, to the church, he advanced through its hierarchical ranks to the Avignonese Sacred College during the Great Schism, but the church he served was only a supremely civilized secular institution—what Bernard Berenson styled the greatest work of art created by Western man. Raniero was strongly attracted by his friend's sophisticated humane ideas, but, good as they were, he found them lacking. Raniero's passionate, tormented idealism demanded something more than civilization.

He discovered this something more through his association with a dyer's daughter, that remarkable "child of the people," Catherine of Siena. The Catherine who emerges from the pages of this book is no creation of the charmingly naive piety of medieval *laggenda*; we are confronted here by a complex, flesh-and-blood person. The author called her "the prototype of all modern women idealists, reminiscent of Jane Addams, but with a difference. For if Catherine was a great statesman, she was also a great contemplative."[23] Her uniqueness and her charismatic power derive from a union of the active and the contemplative spirits in her personality. Modern social reformers, the author included, began with a focus on the world's problems and a sense of their individual guilt: a negative spirit seeking positive ends. Raniero's approach was like theirs. But from an early age Catherine had been nourished by mystical visions, and her mystical life endowed her with great personal assurance and stability, a positive force that enabled her to act vigorously. Without being simpleminded, she was able to be single-minded in the pursuit of her goals.

Her single-minded, active personality had a steadying effect on the ever wavering intellectual Raniero, whose irresolution was born out of too much thought. Even Catherine, though, could not free him from his native mental confusion; she could only help him to live with it, to accept his own nature, and thus free him to act despite it. From her he learned that the God of infinite love demands not finished works but only "infinite desire";[24] he discovered that "Faith is activity, not vision."[25]

Raniero first met Catherine quite by chance while he was hurrying on business through the unhealthy streets of Siena during the great plague. The saint, tending a man struck down in the street by the terrible disease, asked Raniero to bring the victim a cup of water. Mastering fear and revulsion, Raniero obliged. At once he was struck with the realization that the woman possessed a unique power, and before long he became deeply involved in her mission.

One now is immediately impressed by the similarity between Catherine's mission as it unfolds in Vida Scudder's narrative and the development of the turn-of-the-century Christian radicalism. Both began with specific charitable acts designed to alleviate human suffering, in Catherine's case caring for victims of the plague. Both attempted to eliminate abuses by persuasive propaganda; Catherine wrote no reformist articles, but she deluged popes and princes with reproving letters that urged reformation. Each was called on to settle disputes; Catherine mediated no strikes, but she often reconciled feuds in Siena and she tried to negotiate a peace between Florence and the papacy. And, like the radical wing of the Social Gospel movement, Catherine envisioned a reform of existing society and the establishment of a renewed social order. In its final phase, Catherine's mission became a grandiose plan for a new world based on the pope's return to Rome, a reconciliation between European states and estates, and a final crusade undertaken by a united Christendom.[26]

We know from history that Catherine's mission ended in catastrophe. The papacy returned to Rome, but the return produced the Great Schism. Europe was ravaged by civil and international wars, and Christendom became little more than an antiquated verbal expression. But Catherine was not destroyed by her failure; she died weighed down by the world, greatly agonized by it, but she never lost her vision of faith and hope. Raniero had always been too clearheaded to be convinced of the plan's ultimate success, but his contact with the saint and his involvement in her mission proved beneficial. He had forgotten himself in the service of others, and self-forgetfulness had steadied his spirit.

Activity had led to expanded, if not perfect vision. Associating with Catherine had meant participating in the life of the church, and its liturgical, ascetic, and sacramental devotions had buttressed Raniero's spirit by ordering and refreshing his life. If his objections to the church—all the venality, corruption, and selfishness that proclaimed worldliness at its worst—remained, Catherine had opened his eyes to positive possibilities by showing him what the church could be, what it could do for men. Also, Catherine's very existence testified to deeper sources of strength and inspiration hidden by the corruptions of the institutional surface. She was the child of the church; it had formed her; she would have been impossible without it. An institution that produces saints cannot be dismissed lightly.

It cannot be dismissed lightly, but it was not the something more that the young idealist sought. Raniero never achieved the full vision of faith that is at the center of the Christian experience, but in Catherine he saw its effects and felt its power. He knew that it was there, and this knowledge became a sufficient substitute. "I who have not seen, yet have believed."[27] After Catherine died, Raniero's allegiance to her kept him loyal to the institution she loved, and he found in it solace and strength.

When Catherine died, her mission was finished. Without her the Famiglia did not have the vision and assurance to continue. The group scattered, and

Raniero became a hermit. The passing years brought him increasing tranquility and peace of mind, but the great days were over. Only memory kept them alive. The great mission had failed.

On the surface the cause of social reform appeared to be blooming during the years when *The Disciple of a Saint* was written. Progressive politics, the Social Gospel, even socialism were recognized public forces growing in popularity, and many reformers felt increasingly optimistic about the future. Vida Scudder did not share this optimism; it had vanished, never to return in its assured and innocent state, when she realized that the reform movement could not and would not fundamentally alter the basic structure of an unjust society. In *The Disciple of a Saint* she recounts the story of another reform movement that came to naught, and following the historical sources she does not minimize the failure. Her picture of St. Catherine of Siena does not inspire easy optimism; one learns that failure and defeat are part of the reformer's experience—knowledge that Vida Scudder learned firsthand from her own life.

Where then was comfort to be found? What guidance did St. Catherine offer to Vida Scudder? What sustaining worldview would Vida Scudder pass on to us?

On a purely personal level, St. Catherine gave Raniero and Vida some excellent psychological advice. Vida Scudder collapsed because she drove herself too hard. Her conscience, which had been trained in the stern and unyielding rigors of New England Calvinism, pursued her like the Furies and would allow her no rest. Popular Protestantism in the United States tended to equate salvation with success and failure with sin. In a land of golden opportunity, it was assumed, a righteous, hardworking, God-fearing man could not but succeed. If a man failed, if he were poor, it must be because he had become addicted to some besetting sin.[28] Vida Scudder, who knew the poor, never applied such strictures to them, but she could not evade a personal sense of guilt. The first generation of college-educated women, she felt, had a responsibility to improve society through social change. When society refused to change Scudder felt personally culpable, interpreting her failure as somehow sinful. St. Catherine brought solace to the New England reformer by pointing out that the God of infinite love was less demanding than her own conscience. God did not require that Vida Scudder create a new earth; her desire for it was sufficient. Vida Scudder could accept this advice from St. Catherine because it reflected the wisdom of a woman who herself gave her life to the cause of Christian reform. Once she accepted the guidance of St. Catherine, Vida Scudder could regain her health in good conscience.

Such was the crucial kind of personal assistance that St. Catherine of Siena offered Vida Scudder. But *The Disciple of a Saint* also proclaims a wider and deeper message that goes beyond the merely personal to suggest a comprehensive vision, a sustaining weltanschauung. In the book's final scene, Louis, Cardinal de Frontaigne questions the hermit Raniero about the progress of history and the general welfare of mankind. The disciple answers his worldly-wise friend with a defense of "The Church of God, the Body of Christ," and in his answer we discover the first statement of Vida Scudder's theology of the cross, that personal faith that she created out of the ruins of liberal Social Gospel optimism.

As it is presented here, it has a decidedly religious, even ecclesiastical focus; but because it was a comprehensive worldview the theology of the cross is also applicable to social issues. Vida Scudder never lost the Mauricean passion for unity—ultimately religious and social problems were one to her—and as she became more religious she also became more radical.

The primary element in the theology of the cross involved a radical reinterpretation of the meaning of failure and defeat. St. Catherine's advice to Raniero had taught Vida Scudder that failure was not sinful, only the result of natural human limitations. The example of St. Catherine, the utter failure of her mission in history, led Vida Scudder to the paradoxical proposition that failure may be connected with blessedness. In order to understand her position on this point it is helpful to recall the complex symbolism of the cross in the Christian tradition. The cross represents a union of opposites that will not admit to a conventional rational interpretation; at once the cross is the instrument of the most ignominious death and the means by which the world is redeemed. The cross marks the apparent end of Christ's earthly career, and yet, as Raniero, speaking for Vida Scudder, explains to his friend:

> Christ [is] forever lifted up upon the Cross, that He may draw all men unto Him. Nails would not have held Him there had not love held Him; *and they who love are nailed there by His side.* Still His sacrifice endures, and still His faithful feed on it, that they may be one with it. *Where is the sacrifice, there is the Church.* . . . I say that they who are one with Christ through the Sacrament of Unity, who with him lay down their lives for the healing of the peoples, shall never perish from off the face of the earth. *Their sacrifice is their Eucharist, their failure is victory, their dying is the life of the world.* [emphasis mine]

For support Raniero cites the last vision of St. Catherine:

"Fear not for I am He who is. Open the eye of thy mind and look upon my hands." And I looked, and in His hands I saw held all the universal world. Then He said: "For My Bride, the Church, I hung upon the Cross, nor shall she ever perish. For none can behold My beauty in the Abyss of the Trinity but by means of that Sweet Bride."[29]

When failure is interpreted as sacrifice, it becomes a necessary element of Christian experience, and more important, becomes part of the *opera Dei* for the ultimate redemption of the world. This primary emphasis on the theology of the cross, or the "Secret of Naughting," as she was later to describe it, is developed much farther in Vida Scudder's Franciscan writings, but it is important to note the genesis of the idea here. It was one of the great gifts of Catherine of Siena.

A second element in the theology of the cross relates more directly to mundane history and human hope.

Sacrifice and not vision, is the strength of the Church; but the vision that leads to sacrifice can never lead astray. Let the desire of men be one with God's desire; their action, though it move by ways abhorrent to our blindness, can but aid His Holy will. . . . The witnessing saints are the power of the Church. . . . I walk all my days in the light of the countenance of those whose faces see God. They are like the stars of the heaven for number, and new stars are forever rising to lighten the ages as they pass.[30]

The novel ends with a sign, faithful to history, that Raniero's vision is justified. A young Franciscan friar appeared at the mountain hermitage to sing the evening office with the hermit and the cardinal. It was Bernardo Albizzeschi, a youthful friend and disciple of Raniero—a disciple of a disciple. Those who recognize him will remember that he became the social reformer and the saint known to the future as Bernardino of Siena.

## A Christian Marxist

I have mentioned that the influence of Saint Catherine and Saint Francis led Vida Scudder to become both more religious and more radical. In the past, settlement house work had been at the center of her social activity, but after she recovered from her breakdown her horizons began to expand. ". . . my little social activities have two phases, the first leading gradually into the second: work in the College Settlements movement, in the foreground until well into the twentieth century; and later widening vision, developing into revolutionary connections, which continue to this day."[31]

In 1908, a year after the publication of *The Disciple of a Saint*, *The Hibbert Journal* carried "The Social Conscience of the Future"; it was the first of many articles that later were collected and organized into *Socialism and Character*, the work that marked her progress from Fabian to Marxist socialism. From 1908 to 1921 Vida Scudder was extremely active as an apologist and propagandist for international socialism and the Socialist Party. She maintained her scholarly and educational interests—both her highschool textbook, *A History of English Literature* and *La Morte d'Arthur, An Introduction to Sir Thomas Malory* were published during these years—but the bulk of her literary production dealt with socialism and issues related to it. In the last decade of the nineteenth century, Vida Scudder had produced a trilogy of interrelated books dealing with religion, literature, and social reform; in the second decade of the twentieth century she produced a second trilogy of interrelated books dealing with religion and socialism.[32]

The first trilogy, *The Witness of Denial*, *The Life of the Spirit in the Modern English Poets*, and *Social Ideals in English Letters*, grew out of her classroom experience and was related to academic as well as social and religious issues. In the second trilogy, *Socialism and Character*, *The Church and the Hour*, *Reflections of a Socialist Churchwoman*, and *The Social Teachings of the Christian Year*, the academic element is for the most part missing. Literature and intellectual history play a secondary, even tertiary, part in *Socialism and Character*, but most of the second trilogy is a gathering into book form of articles and addresses that had a definitely propagandistic intention. Like "Socialism and Spiritual Progress," they were designed to convince, to win over an audience to a particular political position. One must be careful not to draw too drastic a distinction; after all, *The Witness of Denial* was a Christian apologia, but, as Vida Scudder would have been the first to recognize, there is a great difference between the classroom and the political stump. During this period her scholarly and social-religious interests tended to draw apart, and they were not fully reunited until she turned her attention to Franciscan studies during the 1920s.

Virginia Huntington, a longtime intimate friend of Vida Scudder's older years, remarks that she was "essentially an intellectual and an aristocrat," never quite at ease with the poor. "She had a loving heart, but mind dominated. When she held classes for the poor Italians of Boston they laughed at her with affection; she talked in Classical Italian!"[33] *On Journey* and other autobiographical writings reveal that Vida Scudder was aware that her personality limited her ability to communicate fully with those less fortunate than herself. She believed that she learned more from them than they from her. Probably the recognition of her own limitations was one reason Vida Scudder did not devote herself to the awakening and mobilization of the proletarian masses. Her socialist propaganda was directed at people like herself; she continued to speak primarily to the audience she addressed in "Socialism and Spiritual Progress," the educated, liberal, religious middle-class elite. Like Ludlow and many Christian reformers before and after her time, she was preaching socialism in an attempt to "socialize Christianity."

In the dedication addressed to Florence Converse, which is a type of prologue to *Socialism and Character*, she admits that this book is designed to ease the puzzlement that the religious "gently nurtured and college bred" feel about socialism.[34] The journals that published the articles later included in *Socialism and Character* could hardly have achieved popularity among the proletariat: *The Hibbert Journal* brought out the already mentioned "Social Conscience of the Future," "The New Righteousness," and "Christianity in the Socialist State"; *The Harvard Theological Review*, "Religion and Socialism"; and *The Atlantic Monthly*, "Socialism and Sacrifice," "Class Consciousness," and "The Forerunners." All seven articles appeared between 1908 and 1911.

Although her pen was active, she did not rely on it alone to communicate the socialist message. In February 1909 she and her close friend and colleague, Emily Green Balch, the Wellesley economics instructor who was later awarded the Nobel Prize for Peace, organized a three-day Boston conference, "Socialism as a World Movement." No doubt out of deference to the opinions of Balch, who described herself as a "half-way ally" of the Socialist Party, the organizers' statement read that

> . . . membership in the committee does not imply acceptance of socialism or responsibility for the views of any of the speakers. The Committee simply undertakes to provide a calm and considerate hearing for a type of social unrest which is beginning to make itself felt significantly in nearly all civilized countries.[35]

The meeting sounds like an intellectual gathering, but Morris Hillquit and Victor Berger gave addresses and perhaps these Socialist Party stalwarts attracted some workers. Certainly their participation would have been welcomed by the professional organizers.

Ever since the dissolution of William Dwight Porter Bliss's Church of the Carpenter in 1896, American Anglicans who were also socialists had no organization to call their own. The Church Association for the Advancement of the interests of Labor and the Church Social Union performed nobly in the cause of social reform, but neither was specifically a socialist organization. In 1911, when the Episcopal Church appointed a full-time secretary for the newly established Commission on Social Service, the Social Union, considering that the Episcopal Church had finally taken over the work for which the Social Union had been striving since its organization in 1891, formally disbanded and gave over its legacy to the Social Service Commission. The Christian Social Union had never been as radical as The Society of Christian Socialists, nor as active as The Church Association for the Advancement of the Interests of Labor, but it had broken new theoretical ground in the area of social problems and it had been an excellent source of reform propaganda. Since Vida Scudder's devotion to the church became progressively more pronounced as her political opinions became more radical, it is not surprising that she joined with other Anglican reformers to create a new organization to fill the void left by the disbanding of the Christian Social Union.

In 1911 Canon Bernard Iddings Bell, then rector of Grace Church, Chicago, "gathered a nucleus [of a new organization] that was to include Bishop Franklin S. Spalding of Utah and his successor the Right Reverend Paul Jones, the Right Reverend Benjamin Brewster, Bishop of Maine, and Professor Vida D. Scudder."[36] The new organization, moving vocally to the left of the Social Union, called itself The Church Socialist League; Joseph Fletcher and Spencer Miller assert that the English organization of the same name inspired the creation of its American counterpart.[37] The American League, however, was much less radical than its English namesake, which rose up in the north of England after the strong showing of the Labour Party in the election of 1906 and was, in fact, an association of clergy and laymen who supported that party.[38] The English league went into the churches and the streets, adopting many of the direct action techniques of the rabble-rousing Guild of St. Matthew, to spread a definite political message, while the American league for the first five years of its existence contented itself with publishing a quarterly, *The Social Preparation for the Kingdom of God*. The English league set out to convert the whole country to socialism; the American league never even mounted a vigorous membership campaign, and in 1916 it had fewer than one hundred members.[39]

The constitution of the Church Socialist League meant that after a hiatus of fifteen years there was once again an organization of Anglican socialists in the United States. If it was smaller, it was also considerably more radical than the Christian Social Union and in *The Social Preparation for the Kingdom of God* Anglican social reform propaganda had a voice on the left. During the First World War and the red scare that followed it, the league and its members exhibited great courage and in the best tradition of radical dissent stood firm against the overwhelming popular passions of the day, defending causes they believed to be just.

Although modesty and a sense of her own limitations prevented Vida Scudder from attempting to instruct and organize the working class, she did not hesitate to commit herself personally on their behalf. Probably the clearest sign of how far she had moved to the left since the "tainted money controversy" is indicated by her involvement in the Lawrence textile strike of 1912. The leadership of the strikers had been captured from the moderate American Federation of Labor by the picturesque, openly revolutionary Industrial Workers of the World, and the social activist was well aware that she was part of "the storm center of class struggle."[40] She met Big Bill Haywood, visited workers' homes, attended strike meetings, and addressed a mass rally. Her speech expressed the moral indignation that prompted her involvement: "I speak for thousands beside myself when I say that I would rather never again wear a thread of woolen than know my garments had been woven at the cost of such misery as I have seen and known past the shadow of a doubt to have existed in this town."[41]

Even in the midst of the class struggle, she advocated nonviolent resistance, quoting for support the Vulgate version of the beatitude, "Blessed are they who suffer for justice's sake."[42] *The Boston Transcript* denounced those activities, demanding her resignation from Wellesley; another exhausting and disheartening academic controversy broke out, but this time Vida Scudder had no thoughts of resigning. Aided by her uncle, the conservative E. P. Dutton who sat on the Board of Trustees, she stayed to fight and win. She had to abandon her course on Social Ideals in English Letters for a few years, but by successfully resisting a popular newspaper's hysterical, antiradical campaign, she strengthened the cause of academic freedom.

A few months before the academic controversy engendered by her participation in the Lawrence textile strike, Houghton Mifflin had brought out "my favorite but forgotten book, *Socialism and Character*."[43] Although it is certainly her most venturesome work, it never achieved wide popularity—probably because the reading public in 1912 was not ready to accept a synthesis of Catholic Christianity and Marxism. While it will never lay claim to the hearts of readers like *On Journey*, *The Franciscan Adventure*, and her religious novels, it might well be her most important critical work. In her oeuvre only *Social Ideals in English Letters* rivals its broad scope, its argumentative skill, and its sustained thematic development. The fabric of this book is so well knit that one is astonished to discover that nearly half of the material in *Socialism and Character* had been published before in magazines.

*Socialism and Character* is Vida Scudder's summa. It recapitulates her past work—indeed, it is the logical extension and culmination of the social-religious trilogy of the 1890s—and it introduces new insights that prefigure the work yet to come. From the past we can note the continuing influence of Frederick Denison Maurice. Once again she reaffirms the basis of his controversial method, recapitulating the argument for tolerance she first expounded in *The Witness of Denial*.[44] More significant, she advances for the first time the Mauricean interpretation of eternal life:

> . . . only be it noted that eternity is construed today in a new light, and is no longer mainly concerned with a heavenly future; rewards and punishments to compensate for present injustice in a world to come are rarely suggested by modern religion. Eternity is here and now, and endless duration is merely a corollary from the perception of a quality in mortal deeds that lifts them out of the category of time.[45]

His views on eternal life had cost Maurice his teaching position at King's College, and Anglo-Catholics had joined with Evangelicals at the time to repudiate his position.

As the culmination and logical extension of the works of the 1890s, *Socialism and Character* was the heir both of "Socialism and Spiritual Progress" and *Social Ideals in English Letters*. From the latter it inherited a comprehensive scope and the conviction that literature spoke with a prophetic voice on social issues. The early chapters of *Socialism and Character* retrace the ground already covered in *Social Ideals in English Letters*, and the contributions of Carlyle, Arnold, Ruskin, et al. to the development of social thought are considered once again. This time, however, three new prophetic voices are recorded—Friedriech Nietzsche, Henrik Ibsen, and Count Leo Tolstoy. The apostle of international socialism was becoming increasingly cosmopolitan in her choice of literary sources.[46]

210

I have alluded to the common propagandistic intention linking *Socialism and Character* to "Socialism and Spiritual Progress," but there are yet more specific and more significant similarities between the two works. As the title *Socialism and Character* reveals, Vida Scudder's progress from Christian Fabianism to Christian Marxism did not alter her primary concern for the condition of the individual soul and the development of personal character. She states her position with absolute frankness in the introductory chapter.

> The point of view of the book is that of a socialist—a class-conscious, revolutionary socialist if you will—to whom nonetheless the spiritual harvest, the fruits of character are the only result worth noting in the economic order. . . . For what happens to the individual soul is the only matter of real consequence in the world.[47]

Also, she retains substantially unchanged her personal interpretation of Social Darwinism, her concern for the Protestant work ethic, and her conviction that in the past persons drawn from the middle class have made the most substantial contributions to the cause of social improvement.[48] Finally, she continues to distinguish between socialism and utopia. Unlike some secular Marxists, she did not confuse a socialist society with the millennium. Her Christian faith recoiled from any consummation of history other than the Kingdom of God, and "the consummation of that Kingdom is in eternity and not in time."[49]

It is important to recognize the continuity between the works of the 1890s and *Socialism and Character*, but we must also remember that as a result of the personal crisis that occurred in the first years of the twentieth century, the author had outgrown many of her earlier positions and had developed a new center of interest and a different outlook on life. When she accepted Marxism she abandoned that curious hybrid known as Christian Socialism, a phenomenon she dismissed as having little "numerical or intellectual importance. 'Christian Socialism' draws to itself sentimentalists, cranks, and an occasional stray saint or philosopher; but organized socialism and organized religion agree in ignoring it."[50] Such uncharacteristic, brutal frankness reveals her growing political realism and also testifies to her dissatisfaction with "the vague socialist sympathy [that was] the order of the day." Disillusioned with the slow progress of reform, Vida Scudder hoped to hasten the new order by converting fellow travelers into party stalwarts and militant activists.

After Vida Scudder had recovered from her breakdown, she chose a direct, personal medium—the semiautobiographical novel—in order to communicate her experience and express her new outlook on life. Within the context of *The Disciple of a Saint* the personal and more strictly religious dimensions of her theology of the cross had been emphasized; its social relevance appeared mainly by implication. In *Socialism and Character*, however, the secular dimensions of the theology of the cross become fully manifest, and it takes its place at the very center of her social vision. The optimistic worldview of Social Gospel liberalism with its tacit assumption of inevitable progress through peaceful, gradual evolution has vanished; the harsher realities portrayed in the novels have replaced it. *Socialism and Character* repeats their stern wisdom: the history of social reform is a history of failure.

I have previously cited the lengthy, moving account of her recognition that the American movement had failed; here I should note the pessimistic tone that pervades her interpretation of the reform impulse at other places and in other times. Most significantly, two new idealistic figures, Count Leo Tolstoy and St. Francis of Assisi, are introduced as failures. The Russian nobleman, whose impassioned effort to escape communal guilt through renunciation and a life of apostolic poverty attracted her deepest sympathy and respect, is reluctantly dismissed with the descriptive phrase "the most significant, most appealing, most futile figure of this strange modern world."[51] A similar gloom colors the first detailed picture of the Franciscan movement to appear in her work.

> Even in Umbria, even during the life of Francis, we see the brave experiment fail. . . . Within less than two centuries, the bravest adventure to follow the social ethics of Jesus which history has ever known had made total shipwreck; the Church was richer by a new monastic order, destined in its turn to be a parasite on society, and the world was poorer by the loss of an ideal.[52]

Oddly enough, St. Catherine of Siena plays no role in *Socialism and Character*. That no allusion is made to her strongly suggests that St. Francis, whose movement had greater historical impact, had already become Vida Scudder's paramount spiritual guide. But if Catherine herself is absent, her influence is pervasive. The encounter with the saint had altered Scudder's mental outlook: she is no longer internally driven to present "finished works to God"; the desire for the good is recognized as personally sufficient. Catherine's great lesson was so thoroughly absorbed that it comes to the surface even in a justification for socialism. *"Socialism is adventure, not achievement*; but it is surely the noblest adventure, and undertaken in the surest   expectation of attaining a righteous goal, of any quest that has

212

summoned the human spirit since history began" [emphasis mine].[53] Also, as we have mentioned, the central proposition of the theology of the cross, another fruit of the encounter with Catherine, is reiterated here: "When the socialists fling the bitter taunt of failure at us, Religion retorts with the mystic exaltation that by failure the world is saved. For through failure and defeat alone can we know ourselves and all our transient race to be the heirs of eternity."[54]

Paradoxically, once Vida Scudder abandoned Social Gospel optimism for the tragic realism of the theology of the cross, she discovered new grounds for hope in the future. Although "the great mass of misery, corruption, and injustice remained practically unaffected by [the reformer's] efforts," one could remedy these abuses by abolishing the system that produced them. Socialism could succeed where reform had failed, and *Socialism and Character* was written in the assurance that some kind of socialism would triumph in the not too distant future even in the United States. "Socialism is now making itself felt in every Anglo-Saxon country, not merely as an academic theory, but as a political force."[55]

The political realist had no need to base her renewed optimism about the future on theoretical doctrines of inevitable progress; the growing power of the Socialist Party was obvious to anyone who looked at election statistics. In 1903, there were 15,975 dues-paying members of the Socialist Party; nine years later there were 118,045. By 1908, 1,039 of them held elective office, and more and more people demonstrated their willingness to entrust the highest public office of all, the presidency, to the socialist standard-bearer, Eugene Debs. In 1904 he polled 402,400 votes; in 1908, 420,820; and in 1912, 897,011.[56] During the years when *Socialism and Character* was written the party's presidential vote had more than doubled, and its membership had increased more than seven-fold. Abroad, in the other Anglo-Saxon countries, socialism was even more successful. In England a Liberal-Labour coalition had challenged the authority of the Tory-dominated House of Lords and, with a successful appeal to the electorate, had altered the unwritten British constitution by removing the veto power of the upper house. The German Social Democrats captured one-third of the votes cast in the 1912 election, thereby electing 110 members of their own party and 35 Progressive Party allies to the Reichstag. This victory was at the expense of the conservative-centrist coalition, known as the Blue-Black Block, and brought about a change in the government.[57]

Written in the assurance that socialism was the movement of the future, *Socialism and Character* attempted to hasten the dawn of the new day by enlisting the allegiance of liberal Social Gospel reformers. Socialists and Christians, the author affirmed, had fewer differences than each believed; far from being antithetical, the movements were at root complementary. To demonstrate her thesis, Vida Scudder employed essentially the same approach she had used in "Socialism and Spiritual Progress": first she offered a rebuttal to the major Social Gospel criticisms of Marxist socialism, and then she advanced her own positive synthesis of Marxism and Catholic Christianity.

Social Gospel liberalism had four basic objections to Marxism: they objected to its animus against religion, to its assignment of an exclusive role in social redemption to the proletariat, to its materialism, and to the sanction it gave to violence in the concept of "class struggle." To counter the first objection we are asked to examine history; "history is excellent at explanations."

> At once we face the significant fact that socialism was born of revolt from religion as religion was presented by the contemporary ecclesiastical system. . . . When socialism arose [the church] was at her worst. . . . The Church had long abandoned the democratic passion of her youth, and ensconced herself comfortably under the wings of property and privilege; now at the crisis she put herself in position, honestly and instinctively, as champion of the existing order. . . . Inspired by intense distaste for Christianity as encountered in politics, stung to scorn by the laissez faire attitude of a Church which was allowing the appalling phenomenon of modern wage-slavery to reach its lusty prime without scarcely a whispered word of protest, the social radicals expressed their reaction in terms uncompromising and violent. . . . So the alienation of the Church from socialism was completed . . . we find the blame difficult to fix; but if we look back to origins we can hardly evade fastening it on the Church, for she was first in the field. Did she wish to undo the effect of her past, she would have to express radical sympathies with uncompromising and conspicuous clearness. This she has never yet been ready to do. . . . Until she does so, the historic situation in the main must persist.[58]

History, she claims, vindicates the socialist revolt against the church. As the guilty party the church has no right to denounce socialism's antireligious bias. It is the church and not socialism that must alter its conduct.

Responding to the first objection, Vida Scudder clearly espouses the claims of socialism against the objections of the church, but on the second point at issue she is not so clear. Obviously she could not be; the very existence of *Socialism and Character*, a book written to win over middle-class Christian liberals to socialism, reveals that she did not assign the proletariat an exclusive role in social redemption. Such an idea ran counter to her long-standing belief that individuals drawn from all classes must participate in the creation of the better world to come. "Conscious of the mystical union with the proletarian and the outcast, assured *that they and we united can shape the world as we will*, we rise to the splendid summons" (emphasis mine).[59]

As a Marxist, however, this middle-class Christian willingly accorded a primacy in social redemption to the working class. Their primacy derived from two sources. First, their numbers—the working class constitute the majority of mankind, and in a democracy the will of the majority must be paramount. Second, their superior insight—"The working classes must show the way to social advance. They alone, free from sentimentality, the curse of the privileged, and from abstract theorizing, the curse of the scholastic, have that grim experience of economic conditions on the majority from which right judgment can be born."[60]

Vida Scudder's respect for the working class did not grow out of Marxist speculation; rather Marx's theories confirmed what she had learned from firsthand experience. Fellowship with the poor, cultivated in settlement houses, union organization, and strikes, long ago had disabused her of any notions of aristocratic noblesse oblige. Nor could she forget that it was an illiterate "child of the people," Catherine of Siena, who had provided the spiritual guidance that rescued her from the most significant personal crisis of her life. One might even say that it was the proletarian saint, Catherine, who made it possible for Vida Scudder to accept the doctrines of the middle-class revolutionary, Marx.

The same sense of political realism that led Vida Scudder to assert the primacy of the working class in the task of social redemption also caused her to recognize the limitations of its role. The working class alone could not determine the better world to come because they lacked the expertise.

But if their function be to furnish momentum, and corporate wisdom, the power of individual initiative and dictatorship will often in the nature of things be generated among those governing classes in whom these gifts have been fostered. If education and administrative experience are valuable enough to share, it is obvious that the dumb proletariat must to a certain extent look to the classes that possess them for the revelation of its own sealed wisdom and the guidance of its own confused powers. The enlightened energy of those who come to serve it from other groups should not be slighted. Their high impulses, their rich devotions, are also to ultimate vision, within, not without the evolutionary process,—a process broader, deeper than current Marxianism admits.[61]

By justifying the socialist animus against religion, she risked alienating the unsocial Christians; her views on the respective roles of the proletariat and the governing classes in the society of the future aroused the ire of an anti-Christian socialist, W. Q. Inkpin, who criticized her article "The New Righteousness" in the letters to the editor column of *The Hibbert Journal*. He accused her of not taking the class war seriously enough and objected to her emphasis on morality as equal to economic and political motives in bringing about socialism.[62] Replying in a subsequent issue Scudder clarified her position on these points.

> I think that moral forces, although largely engendered and conditioned by economic systems do, when once they appear, react on those systems and play their active part in social advance. . . . One can read his history either with the economic determinist or with the idealist. I want to read *mine with both*. . . . Heaven forbid that I should "think little" of the self assertion of the poor! I believe that self assertion to be essentially a right and potentially a holy thing, but I want to see it supplemented and enriched by the accession to the socialist ranks of all who are poor in spirit.[63]

Obviously, however, she felt that Inkpin had touched on important points for when she published *Socialism and Character* in book form she explained her views on economic determinism and class-consciousness at great length. The length of her treatment is merited by the importance of the subjects, for the doctrines of economic determinism and class-consciousness were central to the Marxist analysis. By comparison, the preceding points of objection were peripheral.

One need not look for an elaborate theoretical justification of economic determinism replete with charts, graphs, and weighty analysis in *Socialism and Character*; such a task was as far beyond the competence of the author as it was far outside her range of interests. She spoke to Christians concerned about social improvement. Middle-class reformers objected to economic determinism because it seemed crude and vulgar, emphasizing what was base in man to the exclusion of his higher nature. If man's action was determined by his economic needs, where was there scope for moral virtue? Gentle souls recoiled from a worldview based on such crass materialism.

Vida Scudder was a social reformer and a Christian, and her defense of economic determinism—vague, complex, and confusing as it sometimes becomes in the course of a lengthy exposition—was based on two points: practical reality and Christian theology. First, she examines practical reality, using as an example the working girl, an example she knew well from her own efforts on their behalf.

> . . . gather up in imagination the total effect of all the benevolent agencies that exist to help her. . . . Measure the force of their reactions on her personality in comparison with that of two crude economic facts,—the wage she receives and the duration of her working day. The worth of our eager efforts dwindles both comically and tragically in our eyes, and the broad economic condition hulks out of all proportion as the real master of that woman's life. On the surface, our sympathies may tinker away pleasantly and our charities may afford relief: in the depths her life will never be affected till the economic factor be altered. Widen the vision, look through history; where can we point to social sacrifice or service on a scale sufficiently large radically to alter the course of events? The answer may be painful; let it at least be honest. The deep, the basal, the creative forces, have in nine times out of ten been rooted in economic principles of self-interest or class expediency. Through the indomitable pressure of life itself, craving for satisfaction and expansion, and in no other wise, effective advance has been achieved. Thus we are forced to . . . face the truth. Economic necessity is the determining base of permanent social change.[64]

The moral effect of her example in this instance is far more telling than volumes of abstract economic speculation. "Economic determinism," she assures her readers, is simply "the eager appeal to social realities for guidance."[65] It need not imply a Godless universe.

> These "determined," these automatic forces, which mechanically generate our passions and powers,—may they not themselves be messengers, fulfilling a central Will? It were impertinent to assert the contrary. . . . For the great economic order, with its steady trend toward a goal that we perhaps begin to discern, is no dead thing because its movements are not in our keeping. The material universe, forever evolving into new likeness through forces in which our conscious efforts have so limited a share, is neither an evil to fight or ignore, nor an ultimate end to rest in. *It is a sacrament ordained to convey spiritual life to us.* [emphasis mine][66]

Here she asserts a Catholic truth all too often forgotten by high-minded reformers disgusted with mere materialism, but clearly stated in the creed. "We believe in One God, the Father Almighty, maker of heaven and earth, and of all things visible and invisible." A frank recognition of material reality need not exclude divine providence; the lord of history can and does work through material reality. Her sacramental view of the universe, like Stewart Headlam's, denied a distinction between sacred and secular, between spiritual and material.

As we might well expect, her discussion of the doctrine of the Incarnation exposes her position most completely.

> The Christian who is also a socialist can say that, despite superficial appearances to the contrary, it has really been the belief in the Incarnation working in the depths, misunderstood by its most ardent adherents, that has led the western nations on to their present strong and clear demand for the rehabilitation of the natural order . . . the Christian who reproaches the socialist with materialism because he wants to begin the process of social redemption with the establishment of right physical conditions is disloyal. *Belief that the spirit must and can be revealed only through the instrument of the flesh is natural to one who has knelt at Bethlehem. In the doctrine of the Incarnation is the warrant to all thinking Christian men for the socialist hope, so scouted by many followers of a false idealism,* that the effective protection of bodily health and material decencies will emancipate the higher life of mind and spirit. And we may surely picture to ourselves this doctrine, so closely associated with the most effective Teacher of the ethics that must underlie the very foundations of the socialist state, commending itself more completely in that state than ever before.[67]

Because the "Word became flesh," Christians, like Marxists, were not committed to philosophical idealism. To reject economic determinism because it is materialistic is not good theology; indeed, it smacks of that false idealism which the Catholic faith repudiated when it anathematized the Manicheans and Gnostics who shrank "affrighted and disgusted from a real Incarnation."[68] Vida Scudder's incarnational theology derives, of course, from the tradition of F. D. Maurice, Stewart Headlam, and Charles Gore, but she pushed its social implications to more radical conclusions than any of her mentors had dared.

Emily Green Balch expressed the opinion of most turn-of-the-century reformers when she wrote, "I never accepted the theory or practice of the class struggle which I rejected both on scientific and ethical grounds."[69] Vida Scudder chose to defend a less explosive term, class-consciousness, but she accepted the violent and divisive implications of the concept that had caused her friends, like Balch, to reject it. Surely class-consciousness, or class struggle, or class war was the aspect of Marxist thought most repugnant to humane, well-intentioned reformers.

> For the stubborn moral sense still recoils from many implications of the doctrine. . . . The class struggle spells obstinate hate. . . . The good people who would fain see all social progress proceed from the growing generosities of realized brotherhood, find a mere travesty of their desires in gains won through

self-assertion. Shall the lovers of peace sympathize with a movement for quickening discontent and making hatred effective?[70]

Clearly Vida Scudder understood why class-consciousness repelled the reformers. Given her own ethical and religious values how could she champion such a doctrine? Her stance is thoroughly Marxist: class-consciousness is not some new theory socialists are trying to introduce; class-consciousness is a fact of life in the present order.

> For the class-war is a fact, and a stern one. It lurks in every factory, it flares out in every instance of extortion and oppression. . . . By common consent, the term class-consciousness is usually applied to the working people. But in accurate speech, it should not be so limited, for it describes quite as truly the stubborn struggle of the employing class to maintain supremacy. The persistence of this class in defending its prerogative is as natural a product of the industrial situation as the pressure of the proletariate.[71]

Since class-consciousness is a fact of life in capitalist society, the choice is not between class war and cooperation. Given class struggle the real question is that put in the old union song: "Which side are you on, boys, which side are you on?" Three primary reasons incline the author to espouse the cause of proletarian class-consciousness. First, it has ennobling effect on those who are drawn toward its practice.

> From tribal days, group consciousness has always . . . been one of the chief forms of moral education. The larger the group toward which loyalty is evoked, the greater the emancipation from pettiness; and if class-consciousness is the most impressive form of group-consciousness up to date, it because the working people include a majority of the human race.[72]

Specific examples, more moralistic than Marxist, are cited to substantiate the generalization. Today one may be amused by the story of the Italian immigrant, Luigi, who abandoned loose living when he discovered proletarian solidarity, but we should not sneer at any idea that teaches the holiness of life and the necessity for responsible human conduct.

Second, one affirms proletarian class-consciousness because it has for its goal the end of all class-consciousness:

> . . . the leaders who labor most earnestly to strengthen working class solidarity do so because they hate class with a deadly hatred, and see in it the only means of putting an end to it altogether. If we agree with them to the point of holding

that class, like war, is provisional, it would seem that these are the people to whom our sympathy is due.[73]

Class-consciousness is a weapon in the struggle to put an end to the undeclared class war now being waged against the poor. It need not necessarily portend violence; "even extremists ardently hope that we may spell our Revolution without the R."[74] A peaceful, democratic revolution could enact reforms eliminating the abuses that breed violence today. Vida Scudder accepted militant means to achieve peaceful ends.

The final defense of class-consciousness is religious; the implications of class-consciousness are in harmony with a sacramental view of life.

> The real basis of our faith in class-consciousness must be religious. . . . It does more than carry with it a faith in the plain people: It relates this faith to the new reverence for that natural order to which it is their function to minister. When nature and the flesh were conceived as the seat of hostility to the spirit those whose energy is absorbed in physical toil and in supplying physical needs were inevitably relegated to an inferior position in the scheme of things, as happened from the time of Plato on. Rising to the modern conception, however, granting that the very basis of life has its sacramental sanctity, we should ascribe new dignity to those who maintain this basis for us, and should be ready as never before to hail them as masters of the future.[75]

In my description of Vida Scudder's defense of Marxism I have allowed her to speak for herself as much as possible. It is as important to understand the way she communicated, as it is to know the substance of her communication. Emily Green Balch's pacifism was too strong ever to be won over by a theory that sanctioned violence, but at least when she and others like her encountered *Socialism and Character* they found Marxism explained in their own language. They could evaluate the issues in a context they understood.

If the high-minded tone characteristic of the era tends to date *Socialism and Character*, making it something of a period piece, its theological-social message seems to prefigure the grimmer, more realistic worldview of our own angry age. Unlike most liberal, reform-conscious Protestants in the optimistic days before World War I, Vida Scudder did not shy away from violence and catastrophe; both her own personal experience and the Catholic tradition to which she adhered required that she face these problems squarely and attempt to comprehend them within the wider context of God's world-historical plan for the redemption of His people.

For the orthodox Christian the process of human redemption is founded on Jesus Christ; He is the redeemer whose teachings reveal God's purpose to man and whose life perfectly embodies that purpose. Of course, Christians have not always agreed about what His life and teachings mean. Like most reform-minded Christian intellectuals of her period, Vida Scudder's interpretation of Jesus was strongly colored by the results of contemporary higher criticism, which she believed made her generation "better equipped to comprehend what manner of man he was, and to what end he lived, than any generation since his contemporaries." The Jesus revealed by "devoted labor spent on sources and documents" was at the very least "one of the chief social idealists of the world."

> The old conception of a compassionate Saviour, wandering gentle and aimless . . . healing the sick . . . uttering almost at random parable and sermon . . . centered interest . . . in that death by which He was to redeem the world must yield to another image; that of a man of power, inspired by one permanent and relentless purpose which shapes all of his activities in word and deed. In the Gospels we confront . . . a protagonist, fighting even unto the death a desperate battle to insure the continuity of such a purpose in the world. The purpose of Jesus is the establishment of the Kingdom of God on earth.[76]

What is the Kingdom of God? Rejecting the two predominant interpretations—pietistic Protestantism's inward, personal, and spiritual state, and ecclesiastical Romanism's grace-dispensing church—on the grounds that these views are ahistorical, partial disclosures of Christ's full meaning, Vida Scudder advanced the proposition that the kingdom idea expressed the social teachings of Jesus. "However he modifies crude contemporary ideas, he ratifies the faith of his people that a visible society, holy unto the Lord, is the ideal for which they work and pray."[77] The constitution of that visible society was exposed for all men to see in the Sermon on the Mount, the first great event of Jesus' public ministry. "The ideal [of the Sermon on the Mount] is a fellowship and only in fellowship can [its] counsels be obeyed. Without the social assumption, the counsels to the individual are not only paradoxical, but . . . exasperating."[78]

It is for this visible society, holy unto the Lord, that Christians pray when they repeat the petition, "Thy Kingdom come on earth as it is in heaven."[79] Wearied by the present evil age and anxious for the consummation of his prayer, the believer may wonder how will the kingdom come? In the Gospels we discover that Jesus' teachings contain two complementary answers to this question: one was advanced early in his ministry; the other appeared near its end.

> We need dwell on only one point in the early parables concerning the Kingdom. . . . The sown field, the mustard tree . . . the seed growing secretly . . . the leaven—also a living organism—these are the homely, vital parallels used to suggest the advance of the Kingdom of God. This constant reversal to figures and metaphors of growth shows the ever present sense of process—the evolutionary nature to use the modern phrase—of Jesus' conception.[80]

> To this coming of the Son of Man, however, catastrophe is now seen as a necessary introduction. . . . The Kingdom is to be ushered in by convulsion and crisis. The destruction of nations, the upheaval of nature, the strange invasion of time by eternity, are its precursors. . . . These later teachings contain solemn recognition of an essential and permanent principle in all social progress. It is the correlate to the principle stressed in the earlier teaching. Evolutionary ideas control the Sermon on the Mount: later, the great mind of Jesus faced the necessity of revolution. . . . Christ gives us the clear and fearless statement that in a dislocated and imperfect world not only must growth be fostered, but catastrophe must be watched for and welcomed. Judgment as well as progress is essential to the furtherance of the Kingdom of God.[81]

Scudder's statement on judgment recalls the proclamations of Oxford's Bishop Gore, and it anticipates the searching comments of Reinhold Niebuhr, for whom also, according to Donald Meyer, Marxism was able to make sense of catastrophe.[82] So too, her rejection of absolute pacifism during this stage in her career reminds us of the arguments of the Neo-Orthodox American theologian.

> The Apocalypse which ends with Jerusalem, Vision of Peace, is chiefly occupied with chronicling in succession of awesome symbols the eternal Wars of the Lord. In the teachings of Christ there are three bitter sayings against smooth conventionality for one against violence, since the context shows that the saying about non-resistance is personal, not social in application. We may not dismiss class-consciousness as evil on the mere score that it arouses the passions of war. To determine its values, its ends must be questioned, and the qualities evoked by the conflict must be scanned.[83]

For both Scudder and Niebuhr, peace without justice was no true peace. Neither could accept absolute pacifism because neither believed violence to be in and of itself an absolute evil. Violence had to be evaluated in context, and its meaning was determined by the end it served.

Thus far I have emphasized how the social thought of *Socialism and Character* anticipates the work of the social realists of subsequent postwar decades; now I look at the theology. I cannot argue that Vida Scudder's theology was characteristically neo-Orthodox, but neither can I assert that she gave uncritical acceptance to turn-of-the-century liberal theology's emphasis on the immanence of God and the natural goodness of man. Her Catholic understanding of the doctrines of the Incarnation and atonement was at once liberal and orthodox; each balanced the other. While recognizing that Christian dogma developed within the process of history, she affirmed the suprahistorical truth of its message. "Christianity is not a relative theory, but a revelation of absolute though unfolding truth."[84]

> . . . in the faith in the Incarnation and the indwelling of the Holy Spirit—apprehended as they have always been within western Christendom— . . . may lie the corrective for those exclusively immanential ideas which already threaten to become current. For this faith presents the point of union for transcendental and immanential thought. To the Christian that power which expresses God through man is no mere product of an evolving nature; it must descend from above. That Spirit who is the Lord and Giver of Life . . . flows in upon us from a region beyond the universe we know or surmise.[85]

Ever since the hungry forties when England's original band of Christian Socialists gathered around F. D. Maurice, J. M. Ludlow, and Charles Kingsley, the theology of the Anglican left had emphasized the primary importance of the Incarnation. That doctrine, sometimes it seems almost to the exclusion of all others, had formed the basis of its religious and social teaching. Maurice, very much against his own will, had founded a school whose influence on religious thought and practice had been salutary. Much evangelical teaching had been excessively subjective and individualistic; in its revivalist phase, especially in the United States, it nearly became fixated on accepting Christ as personal savior. If one believed that Jesus' death ransomed man from the wages of sin—paying, as it were, man's debt to God—and lived in a generally godly, sober, and righteous manner, one received the "blessed assurance" of a heavenly reward. Incarnational theology brought religious aspiration back down to earth and restored a genuinely social gospel to the Anglican Communion. By emphasizing our Lord's humanity, it corrected an unwitting Evangelical tendency toward Gnostic dualism, recovering for the church the fullness of Catholic Christology. But because evangelical teaching had been so preoccupied with the atonement, those who reacted against the excesses of that movement were inclined to underestimate that doctrine's importance. Major thinkers of the caliber of Maurice and Gore were not guilty of such oversimplification, of course, but many of liberal theology's popular champions lacked their theological subtlety and sophistication.

Although Vida Scudder was not a profoundly original theologian, her thought was sound, balanced, and Catholic. Her deep respect for the spiritual heritage of the past gave her a perspective that kept her free from the tyranny of the merely contemporary. Her theology was grounded on the Incarnation, but the atonement was its keystone, for in that doctrine she recognized the church's historic formulation of her own "Secret of Naughting," the principle of sacrifice.

> Among all ideas potent in historic Christianity, that of the Atonement is today the most unpopular. . . . Still, though all thought of propitiating an angry God or buying off a malignant devil has faded, the faith in redemption as essential, as accomplished, works secretly at the heart of all which lives in religion. . . . The ideal of sacrifice, deeply implanted in all great religions has been transfigured by Christianity with strange new glory.[86]

Just as her incarnational understanding had comprehended both the immanent and transcendental aspects of the divine nature, so her atonement theology recognized both good and evil as operative in man.

> We cannot, even casually, contemplate sacrifice without encountering the . . . consciousness of sin. Sin! The modern world evades the word. . . . Yet conviction of sin is the first conviction of growth. The thought of sacrifice implies not only a giving but a receiving, and the race that produces saviors must need to be saved. . . . One shrinks from imagining a society devoid of the life giving stings of remorse. . . .[87]

The human limitations of man's fallen state, however, did not drive her to despair; for all of her theological and social realism, she found reason to hope in the future. But she was convinced that the better world of the future could be created only at the cost of great sacrifice.

> Under the growing perception of the divine fulfilled in the human, we come to know that redemption is achieved, not by God working apart from His creation and performing isolated miracles, but by the union in sacrificial passion of all who would spend themselves for the world's need and rescue it from its sins by the very anguish of their penitence. . . . That such sacrifice is eternally necessary to progress has always been clear to the Christian vision. . . . For Calvary is ever

near to the metropolis. We labor to build Jerusalem, and hope to succeed in part. . . . Beside our New Jerusalem, as beside the Old, will rise the Hill of Golgotha. So it will be till we attain that Jerusalem which is above and free, the mother of us all: through all imaginable social transformations, Christ in the person of his followers, will still be despised and rejected of men, and still the despised and rejected may be the saviors of the race.[88]

In 1914, two years after the publication of *Socialism and Character*, the Great War broke out in Europe. Working-class solidarity was washed away in a flood of nationalism and militarism and Vida Scudder's socialist new day never dawned. Men and treasure, on a scale unprecedented in Western history, were sacrificed by martial nation-states, but that sacrifice brought the kingdom no nearer. Golgotha's hill of pain loomed over Jerusalem and for a time almost obscured it from view.

Then came the war, with its appeal for devotion to the uttermost; and the peoples of Europe responded with a sort of sacred joy. They obey the call of governments to destroy fellow-men at any personal cost in the name of patriotism, and their readiness puts to shame the failure of the Church to enlist them for the protection of manhood in the holier name of Christ.[89]

The church's glaring failure was the subject of an address delivered to the Anglican Church Congress held in Norfolk, Virginia, in May 1916; in printed form it appeared first in the *Yale Review* and then was reprinted as the central article in *The Church and the Hour, Reflections of a Socialist Churchwoman*, published in 1917. The social and theological perspective of this little book is almost identical to that of *Socialism and Character*. Several points, however, should be mentioned. Two reprinted letters to the editors of *The Masses* fraternally berate the New York know-it-alls for their "provincial" attitude toward Christ and His church. Although the content is serious, the style is light and ironic, demonstrating that when she chose, Vida Scudder could communicate in the language of the educated secular radicals, a point that a reader of *Socialism and Character* might easily forget. A deeper, far more serious form of communication is briefly explored in "A Plea for Social Intercession," an article written by one obviously committed to the principles of the Society of the Companions of the Holy Cross. Its place at the end of the book testifies to the author's evaluation of its importance. For Vida Scudder intercessory prayer was a primary duty of every Christian interested in social reform and she saw no incongruity in including a plea for its practice in a volume otherwise devoted to more mundane matters.

No new significant motifs appear in *The Church and the Hour*, but the warnings of judgment, first sounded clearly in *Socialism and Character*, are stronger now. Her tone verges on the apocalyptic:

> This is sure; after the war old evils will be fiercer than ever, while aspirations toward righteousness also will be fired with a new intensity. . . . Many masks have fallen now, many conventions are destroyed. The social order is seen stark naked: it is not a lovely sight. In passing, one may notice that the convulsion which stripped humanity was not caused by the radical forces once so dreaded, but one is almost tempted to say, by the Devil himself, masquerading as gentleman, patriot, and diplomatist. In the hideous glare of the firing, it is possible to see Mars and Mammon twin supporters of the old Capitalistic order, rushing on their destruction. . . . When His Church loses thought of catastrophe, and devotes herself comfortably—and half-heartedly—to furthering growth, omens of future judgment are likely to gather, as they are gathering now. We shall do well, if, obeying Christ's indubitable teachings, we join to our steadfast efforts to promote the cause of the Kingdom on earth, the awestruck readiness for sudden judgment. Of that day and that hour knoweth no man; but it is sure to come.[90]

When the war came, Vida Scudder did not oppose it. Unlike many of her reforming friends and like most militant Marxists and orthodox Christians, she was not yet an absolute pacifist. While she rejected aggressive warfare and even renounced personal self-defense, she "did believe in the duty to defend the weak, and to fight in a righteous cause, and I looked on both outward and inward conflict as the necessary source of valor and sacrifice."[91]

Although she did not personally oppose the war she sympathized with persons whose opposition brought them persecution and personal distress. A. J. Muste, then a young clergyman, resigned his pastorate at the fashionable Central Congregational Church in Newton Center, Massachusetts, when his pacifist position became increasingly embarrassing to him and his congregation. After resigning, he began the active career that made him one of America's foremost advocates of nonviolence, by joining the Fellowship of Reconciliation and becoming chairman of Boston's League for Democratic Control, an organization devoted to securing the rights of conscientious objectors.[92] "During two difficult years, he said later, he had been sustained by the sympathetic support and intellectual prestige of 'three brilliant women at neighboring Wellesley,' Mary Calkings, Vida Scudder and Emily Balch."[93]

The best contemporaneous expression of her complicated position on the war is in "A Doubting Pacifist" published by the *Yale Review* in 1917; her thoughts were occasioned by rereading the *Bhagavad Gita*, the Hindu spiritual classic she had discovered as a young girl in her father's library. At first one may be disconcerted by her affirmative attitude; her attacks on a pacifist materialism that recoils from destroying life and property is all too reminiscent of the argumentative premises of Barrès and other mystical nationalists of the French far right. To imply as she does, that aversion to killing may spring from a denial of the resurrection of the body, is unworthy of an author who not long before had advanced a Mauricean interpretation of eternal life in her own works.[94] Even Vida Scudder, it seems, was not immune to the corrupting influence of war.

Withal, "A Doubting Pacifist" is no vulgar tract; it contains none of the simplistic enthusiasm that led other Social Gospel reformers to embrace the colors with the bright-eyed ardor of nationalistic zeal.[95] Her qualified support of the war rests on two long and deeply held convictions encountered before in her work. It is not too strong to characterize the first as her disgust with the old order of things:

> The last years have demonstrated that John Henry Newman was right when he insisted to an annoyed Victorian England, intoxicated with "progress" that civilization is not good in itself. . . . It is quite conceivable that the frank barbarism . . . into which Europe has been driven, may be a more wholesome condition just because more shocking, than the rotten civilization, riddled with cruelties, egotisms, and greeds of five years ago. . . . Now these radicals [and she speaks for herself] in pain night and day over the real implications of our civilization, felt a certain horrified relief when the war broke out. . . . And if peace, or even the permanent abolition of war, meant return to the old status quo, many feel today with deep gravity that they would not take it.[96]

The second is the belief, which had been developing over the years, that improvement can be purchased only at the cost of great sacrifice and redemptive suffering.

> The pain from which Christianity seeks to release the world, is that of the victim: the pain which it cherishes is that of the savior. . . . The sufferings of the victim are involuntary; those of the savior are voluntary. . . . A large proportion of the sufferings of war are voluntarily assumed, and this is of course the secret of the religious ecstacy which war has always inspired and inspires still. *The eager sacrifice of its youth purifies contemporary Europe by pity and terror, and the longing to share that sacrifice is a distinct factor in the satisfaction with which many Americans see our country enter the war.* [emphasis mine][97]

Like many American idealists, including President Wilson, Vida Scudder hoped that the sacrifices entailed by the war would purge the corruptions of the old regime and prepare the way for a just future and a lasting peace. But her just future was a revolutionary new order.

> The only true pacifist is he who sees that no campaign against war can be effective which views war in isolation. He is forced . . . into a constructive social radicalism; his vision travels past the battlefield, past the political relationship of the nations. These are to him part of the universal struggle, result of a system which drives peoples, classes, and individuals alike, into a defensive and potentially hostile attitude towards one another. . . . So long as conflicting interests are the ruling principle of the economic order, it is hopeless to expect the political order to escape the curse of war. To point this out, to link war into the whole causal circle where it belongs—here is the great opportunity of the pacifist. He will deserve the nobler name peace-maker if he can press this truth home to the world.[98]

Would the better future come? She was not sure; the more she thought of the moral aspects of the struggle, the darker the future grew. She felt an unspeakable dread when she contemplated war's aftermath: "the loss of liberties, temporarily waived at the country's call, not easy to regain; the inrush in a mighty backwater of ancient bad political and social ideas; the undermining of painfully acquired habits of productive peace."[99] Worst of all, she reflected, the young whose sacrifice had been offered and accepted, "will not be here to help."

Bitter experience confirmed her worst expectations. Attorney General Palmer inaugurated a savage, often illegal, persecution of pacifist and radical dissenters; the Senate refused to permit the United States to enter the League of Nations; and the nation turned away from reform to embrace Warren G. Harding and normalcy. Bitterest pill of all, the two institutions she loved above all others, Wellesley College and the Protestant Episcopal Church, succumbed to the antipacifist frenzy and purged her old friends and comrades, Emily Green Balch and the Right Reverend Paul Jones, bishop of Utah. Balch's teaching contract at Wellesley was not renewed, and Bishop Jones resigned his diocese. Vida joined with other faculty to protest the trustees' decision, but there was little that a laywoman from Massachusetts could do to prevent Utah from deposing its bishop.[100]

The Church Socialist League, divided as it had been over America's entry into the war, closed ranks behind Bishop Jones, who was its president. A protest document signed by church people from every state was presented in his behalf to a special session of the House of Bishops. At the General Convention in Detroit in 1919 the League and the Society of the Companions of the Holy Cross secured the passage of a resolution urging the government to exercise clemency in the cases of political prisoners still jailed for expressing their wartime opinions. It was the league's last important act. "The time and the hour were inhospitable, the *Social Preparation for the Kingdom of God* ceased appearing and in 1924 the League disbanded."[101] Scudder herself was so distressed by antipacifist sentiment within the church that had the 1919 clemency resolution not passed, she seriously considered leaving it to join the Society of Friends. Disgust with postwar hysteria and repression moved her farther along the road to absolute pacifism. The process was completed when Helena Dudley, the old head-worker at Denison House who was an active member of the Women's International League for Peace and Freedom, made her home with Scudder in Wellesley in 1922. Looking back on her old qualified prowar stance, Vida Scudder observed that war continues to hold the suffrages of many high-minded people on the score of protecting the weak. "Mars dearly likes to dress in the accoutrements of chivalry."[102]

The war's aftermath erased her optimism, but it did not dampen her radical fire. It burned even more brightly in *The Social Teachings of the Christian Year*, a volume explicating the social message of the Collects, Epistle, and Gospel passages fixed by *The Book of Common Prayer* for each Sunday and major feast in the church calendar. "People who are indifferent to organized religion are strongly advised by the author to keep away from this book," warns the first line of the preface.[103] *The Social Teachings* is enlightening, but it is a specialized work that speaks most forcefully to a select audience. What distinguishes this book from her earlier works, *Socialism and Character* in particular, is not so much a basic change of opinion, but rather a change of tone; it is a question of emphasis. The apocalyptic speculations in *Socialism and Character* had been secondary; in *The Social Teachings of the Christian Year* they attract immediate attention. Of course, the Christian year begins with Advent, a time when Christ's majestic second coming is proclaimed, but usually, in practice, the *tuba mirum* is drowned out by nativity carols. The Babe of Bethlehem obscures the vision of Him who shall come to judge the quick and the dead. *The Social Teachings* restores the millennial expectation; we see again the image that so rightfully terrified Martin Luther: Christ on the rainbow; the righteous Lord with a crown on His head, a sword in His teeth, and great staring eyes, burning for justice.

Advent is only the first season of the Christian year, but it was the season of her heart when she wrote this book. One is not surprised then, to notice that Vida Scudder greets the Russian Revolution with sympathy and approval.[104] This book, which might be considered one of her most narrowly religious, is also one of her most radical. It marks the end of a period of her life. In 1921 the Social Gospel era in the United States was over; when six years later she wrote another book, it was a novel about a follower of St. Francis of Assisi.

## *The Franciscan Adventure*

The end of the Social Gospel era filled Vida Scudder with a deep and lasting sense of disappointment.

> . . . we all found it hard to maintain steady faith in those post-war years. There is a worse type of Depression than the economic; such was shared by most people who in the pre-war period had joyfully hailed what seemed the rising forces of social redemption. . . . It was not easy to watch the surging flood of disillusion which threatened to submerge the idealism and drown the hopes of the world, for to see the reforms on which hope and effort had centered, hardly without exception halted or destroyed. Those ten exhausted years were the most discouraged I have known, and I say this in 1936.[105]

Disappointment and discouragement, however, did not drive her into retirement. Her theological perspective enabled her to face despair and defeat without succumbing to the cynicism and regret that plagued so many former progressives, muckrakers, and social reformers during the jazz era. In 1921 Vida Scudder turned sixty, but she redoubled her efforts on behalf of reform. As before, much of her energy went into writing articles for intellectual, popular, or liberal religious journals. A selection from a Thanksgiving Day proclamation that appeared in *The Christian Century* is representative of her propagandistic writing in the postwar period.

> May the dangers we face invigorate our purpose and clarify our minds: may they summon us to the purification of our national life and to re-examination of the principles on which it rests. Let us gratefully remember the high adventure and stern disciplines in the pioneer days of our dear country, and resolve that, trusting in the guidance in which our fathers trusted, and following their example, we may leave behind at whatever cost an outworn civilization, and

advance fearlessly toward that new world where the kindly earth shall be our common heritage and where privilege unshared shall be unknown.[106]

Of course, her service to the cause of reform was not limited to writing. She was an activist who participated in many radical organizations. *On Journey* does not mention all of them, but Elizabeth Dilling, a former radical turned zealous conservative, has left a fairly comprehensive report on Scudder's organizational allegiances in the "Who's Who in Radicalism" section of her exposé, *The Red Network*. Of most interest, we discover that Scudder, along with Norman Thomas, Scott Nearing, John Nevin Sayre, the Reverend Harry Ward, and later Communist Party stalwart, Elizabeth Gurly Flynn, was on a list distributed by the Department of Justice in 1921 describing America's most important and dangerous radicals.[107] It is difficult to imagine how even the Department of Justice could so describe an upper-class, Anglican, English professor at Wellesley College, unless their judgment was based on the organizations to which she lent her support. *The Red Network* lists the following: Conference for Progressive Political Action, The Church Socialist League, Peace Patriots, The American Civil Liberties Union, *Il Nuovo Mondo*, The League for Industrial Democracy, and The Church League for Industrial Democracy.[108] To this list should be added the Fellowship of Reconciliation and The Women's International League for Peace and Freedom. In many of these organizations Scudder held executive office. Finally, she was active in the movement to secure freedom for Sacco and Vanzetti.

Of all these organizations, the Church League for Industrial Democracy was probably closest to her heart. In 1919 when it was organized she served as its first chairman and she remained active in it as long as she lived. In many ways the league was the true successor to the Church Socialist League, although it was larger and more active than that body and not limited to persons espousing a socialist viewpoint. During the twenties, thirties, and forties it became the most militant organization of church people to espouse the cause of social justice, playing an active role in support of workers during the textile strikes in Paterson and Passaic, New Jersey. Its magazine, *The Clipsheet*, kept the members in touch with the work of its officers and supplied a current analysis of affairs and trends in industry.[109] "The group's dominating figure was the courageous and controversial executive secretary, the Reverend William B. Spoffard." During the thirties and forties, Spoffard became convinced that fascism posed a grave danger to the United States and urged a pragmatic alliance with the Communist Party in united front activities to combat that danger. "Other leaders of the C.L.I.D., Vida Scudder, for instance, agreed with Spoffard that it was both possible and wise for Christians to cooperate with Communists in united front movements."[110] In 1938 *The Living Church* attacked the C.L.I.D. for being soft on communism and the same charges were raised in the General Convention of their church that year.[111] During the forties and fifties, Spofford's positions on national and international issues continued to raise the criticism that he was a fellow traveler, but his old friend Vida Scudder remained loyal to him.[112] Her support for Spofford gained her the reputation of naivete toward communism. While she admired the dedications of the communists and sympathized with aspects of the "Soviet experiment," violence and authoritarianism were at root alien to her outlook.[113] Her new earth could best be established by a Christian revolution that followed in the footsteps of Francis, the patron saint of the poor.

Over the years, Vida Scudder had become increasingly devoted to St. Francis, and during the postwar years of disillusionment and disappointment she found in him a source of inspiration and strength. During her sabbatical year 1921-22, she made a pilgrimage to the Franciscan Shrines in Umbria and the March of Ancona; in Assisi she renewed her friendship with the noted Protestant Franciscan scholar, Paul Sabatier. Her devotion to Francis was shared with many friends and associates who in turn stimulated her own interests. Probably the single most important source of stimulation was the Society of the Companions of the Holy Cross, that organization of Anglican women to which she became increasingly devoted as she grew older. She wrote *The Social Teachings of the Christian Year* at their retreat, Adelynrood, during the summer of 1920, and she dedicated her Franciscan novel, *Brother John*, to the companions, "who would fain learn what Saint Francis has to teach the modern world."

Francis's teachings and the movement he inspired became her paramount interest during her later years; scholarship, social reform, and religion once again became fully integrated in her work. In 1923 she published "Franciscan Parallels"; both title and content suggest that her Franciscan studies grew out of her concern with contemporary social and religious issues.[114] Subsequently she also wrote "The Larks of St. Francis" and "Joachim of Flora and the Friars." After she retired from Wellesley in 1927, the professor emeritus was able to devote herself full-time to a study of the saint and his order. The result of this study was *The Franciscan Adventure*, a book ten years in the making, published in 1931. While writing this work she was able to utilize Paul

Sabatier's vast collection of Franciscan memorabilia, which thanks to her influence had been donated in Sabatier's will to the Boston Public Library. Further reflections on Francis and his movement fill two chapters of her autobiography published in 1937; one of these chapters bears the significant title, "The Christian Revolution." Francis's influence pervades her writing even when the topic at hand is not strictly Franciscan; it shines through most strongly in "The Cross in Utopia," an article written for *The Hibbert Journal*, containing her further reflections on motifs dominant in her later work, nonviolence and sacrifice.[115]

During the thirties the depression brought about a renewed interest in social reform and Vida's spirits revived. Although she remained active in reform organizations, a woman in her seventies could hardly fill her old combat role on the front line. Freed from the immediately pressing duties of a teacher and reformer, she turned increasingly to speculating about the finest possible type of reforming spirit. This spirit was bound up in what she called "The Christian Revolution": it was based on full adherence to Catholic truth, revealed in the creeds of the church, and it combined a radical commitment to social justice, exemplified by the communists, with Gandhi's deep devotion to the principle of nonviolence as the ultimate method of inducing social change.

All of this spirit she saw prefigured in the Franciscan adventure, a term that recalls the youthful enthusiasms that propelled her into the cause of social reform. In recounting this final period in the development of her life and thought I focus on *Brother John*, her last novel. As before, she was able to express her thoughts most directly in fictional form. Unencumbered by the demands of scholarship, she was able to speak from the heart, and it was her heartspoken message that drew readers and gave the work its modest popularity. It is not a totally successful novel, but it is a powerful book.

*Brother John*, her first book on the Franciscans, was written during the author's final years at Wellesley and bears the mark of the "exhausted and discouraged" twenties. Once again she returned to the problems raised in the epilogue of *The Disciple of a Saint*. This time, however, defeat and failure appear at the very beginning: Brother John is in prison on the day of his death, and his story unfolds in a series of flashbacks. From a purely literary point of view the flashback technique is the least satisfactory aspect of the novel; the application is self-conscious and stands out as an obvious device. But this device enables the author to reiterate her point: Brother John is defeated. We cannot lose ourselves in the progress of the narrative; the scene frequently reverts to the prison, and we are reminded that John's cause has come to naught.

Lord John of Sanforth, the hero of the last novel, is cut from the same cloth as Hilda and Raniero. Like them he is born into the upper classes, and motivated by compassion for the poor, a high sense of adventure, and a deeper sense of guilt, he forsakes his advantages and begins a new life. But, reflecting his creator's personal growth, the friar is stronger and more assured than either of his predecessors. Unlike Raniero, he is not troubled by "confusion of mind," and he is less of a passive listener than Hilda. He is not so much searching for a way, as following an appointed path. Significantly, this book, like *A Listener in Babel* and *The Disciple of a Saint*, is not the story of someone who renounces the world and finds peace and fulfillment in a noble cause. John's difficulties really begin when he becomes a Franciscan.

The rule of Francis, unlike all previous monastic and canonical rules, was neither an external code nor a propaedeutic to perfection; it was an enunciation of an imitation of Christ in certain aspects of His life. The Friars Minor did not constitute an elect body shut off from the world by the walls of the cloister; it was their duty to move in the world, to call it to repentance and reform, both by the example of a life of service to "all sorts and conditions of men," and by direct formal evangelization. Reacting against some of the most notorious abuses of thirteenth-century religious practice, Francis included in his rule three significant commands: the friars were to practice absolute poverty, neither touching money as a possession nor owning things in common; they were not permitted to solicit or to accept ecclesiastical privilege; and they were to renounce all human learning. John's path, as a follower of Francis, was determined by the rule. His life was an attempt to be faithful to it, both spirit and letter, and his faithfulness brought him victory and led to his defeat.

John's victories were won over himself. Following the rule of Francis was no easy task; an imitation of Christ required enormous self-discipline because it demanded great self-sacrifice. The essence of the rule was the way of renunciation, "the secret of naughting."

Material possessions and social position did not tempt John. He abandoned them readily and found that life without them was filled with joyous freedom. The intellectual life could not, however, be cast aside with such ease. John was by nature bookish, and he fell under the spell of Roger Bacon, the Franciscan master of medieval science. Here John encountered humane learning at its best, free from any desire for material reward, seeking knowledge for its own sake and for the benefit of mankind. Bacon, recognizing his young countryman's intellectual gifts, asked John to join him in his work. After considerable reflection John rejected Bacon's offer as a lesser good. The savant, he realized, remained a member of the privileged classes; only the labor of the poor brought him the leisure to pursue knowledge. John elected to follow the rule and serve the poor, devoting himself to building a new social order where knowledge would not be so dearly bought.

In Paris John met a young Franciscan, Pierre Taine. They had much in common and became fast friends. The friendship ripened as they journeyed together toward Italy in a company of Franciscans. Suddenly, and for no apparent reason, Pierre withdrew into himself and rudely rejected his friend; then, at a critical moment, he disappeared. John felt deeply wounded by the Frenchman's attitude, but he could not abandon him. He realized that Pierre was disturbed, and he was worried by this eccentric behavior. It was a bitter experience and a severe test of John's ideals because he had been forced to renounce his only possession: the knowledge that his affection was appreciated and returned. Aided by the examples of Christ and Francis, who were also forsaken by their friends, John purged himself of all desire for reciprocated friendship. When the two finally were reunited John learned that Pierre had not rejected him; more important, John's purified affection proved crucial to Pierre's well-being. Victorious over himself John realized, "we lose to find."[116]

No amount of self-discipline, however, enables a man to change the course of history. John tried to reform the world; he wanted to direct men toward the new earth proclaimed by the example of Francis and embodied in the Rule. John held back nothing of himself, but despite his best efforts the world would not change. Even the Franciscans, whom John saw as the first children of a new age, could not live up to the ideals proclaimed by Francis. The organization found it impossible to carry out literally the rule of absolute poverty; it simply was not practical.

Once again John was forced to choose, and he chose the rule rather than the order. Personal experience, loyalty to Francis, and a conviction that the ideal was more important than practical necessity dictated his choice. He joined the revolt against the luxury-loving, tyrannical minister general, Brother Elias, and when Elias's deposition failed to resolve the controversy over the rule, he sided with the Zealots, the extreme wing of the Franciscan spirituals. This faction possessed great vision, devotion and zeal, but they were poor politicians, as was John himself. Sent to Pope Gregory IX with documents proving that Elias had been conspiring with Gregory's arch-enemy the

Emperor Frederick II, John was so overcome by the experience that he forgot the documents and the conspiracy, and lectured the pope about Joachim of Flora's "age of the Spirit."[117] Immediately after Elias's fall, Brother Lymon summoned John and pleaded with him to assume a position of leadership in the order. "Come down from that mountain! Return to the present. After all you live in it. . . . Our order is destined to rise in importance. . . . Our touch shall be the life of nations, and if we compromise with the world, it will be that the world may be saved."[118] But John had "heard another voice": "I can do no other. I know my life may be cast away useless, but I do believe that those who follow the Gospel literally, as Francis did, though it lead them to prison and to judgment, are the soul of the Church to be."[119] Again faithful to Francis's rule, John refused to accept ecclesiastical privilege and renounced all power in the order. He scored another victory over temptation, the selfless temptation to seek power to do good.

A better politician—if an equally dedicated man—accepted the role John had refused and rose to be minister general of the Franciscans. Political necessity forced this man, known to us as St. Bonaventura, to send the Zealots to prison. Prison was John's severest test; there like Shelley's Prometheus he "suffered woes which hope thinks infinite" and experienced the depth of despair. Four dank walls forever separated him from the world he had been so anxious to save; he could no longer do anything to spread the redemptive message of sacrificial love. He realized that he had failed, and failure gave rise to doubt. "He had kept the faith. But was it the true faith? Alas, Brother John had never been sure."[120] Even his own life seemed to lose all meaning. Had he sacrificed his life for nothing? After all, the Zealots were dreamers, and confused and bewildered dreamers at that.

> Drawn some of them by the strong undertow of heresies, practising often, even when orthodox, an extreme asceticism which denied Francis' lauds of creatures and his sane knowledge that the loss of life is not the end, only the beginning of life in its fullness. Fanatics and foolish, none of them was sure of the way.[121]

John was an enthusiast, even an extremist, but he was too clearheaded, ultimately too sane, to become a thoroughgoing fanatic. Now, in prison, even his clearheaded sanity served only to drive him to castigate himself. "Was not Brother Bonaventura the wisest of them all, and not with mere earthly wisdom. . . . Bonaventura had followed the genuine way of poverty, with just enough compromise to secure freedom and peace. . . .[He was] a true and holy man."[122] Only a true and holy man, and a thoroughly disillusioned one, would be so generous with the man who had imprisoned him. In his despair, self-doubt, and generosity John overlooked the fact that Bonaventura's accomplishments were based on his willingness to imprison innocent men. Francis would never have sanctioned such means to achieve his ends. Bonaventura was a brilliant minister general, a wise and learned man; the church has proclaimed him a saint and honored him with the title seraphic doctor, but Vida Scudder suggests, he was not a true son of Francis. The true sons of Francis died in jail.

This last novel reveals just how tired and discouraged the author had become during the twenties as she approached retirement and the end of her teaching career. Obviously, she was not directly comparing the programs of the spiritual Franciscans with those of the social reformers of the early twentieth century; they were quite different. But for all their differences, both movements suffered a common defeat at the hands of a world that was not interested in its own reformation. Social reformers during the twenties might well have applied to themselves the remarks of the jailer who discovered the corpse of Brother John: "They are a queer lot. . . . Why do they throw their lives away?"[123]

How can one justify an effort as futile, a failure as total as Brother John's? No single passage in the book attempts to answer that question; in a very real sense the entire book is an attempt to justify his position by presenting his life and letting it speak for itself.

Three points rise out of the despair to transcend disillusion. The first might be called a justification of the purist. John was defeated because he was an extremist, a moral purist. These purists seldom win because their ideals are too lofty for the world. Men of the middle way—like Bonaventura—the compromisers, get results; probably they are of greater use to their own generation. But when their compromises become stale, worn, and outdated, it is the example of the purists that speaks to the future, that stirs new life, that inspires men to dream, hope, and build anew.

The second justification rises out of a philosophy of history. This interpretation of history is related to the remarks of St. Catherine quoted by Raniero at the end of *The Disciple of a Saint*, but here it is stated more specifically and in a more fully developed form. Pierre's parting gift to John had been a parchment containing the writings of Abbot Joachim of Flora, and John, like many of his Zealot brothers, was inspired by the doctrines of the Calabrian Cistercian, whom they saw as a forerunner of St. Francis. Joachim prophesied the development of the Age of the Spirit out of the womb of time.

237

Ernst Becker explains that "this vision was a great and radical one" for it meant that the destiny of Christianity would be played out here on earth, would be realized here, and not in some Heavenly City."[124] Joachim gave specific meaning to the creed's assertion that "He shall come again in Glory. . . . Whose kingdom shall have no end." By bringing Christian eschatology down to earth, the Cistercian abbot raised social reform to a plane of eternal reality. The new earth became a theological fact. Believing that the Age of the Spirit was at hand, John's actions were directed to hastening the hour of its coming. Hilda Lathrope had been advised to "live the life of the future in the present": John put that advice into practice. He cannot be judged solely on the grounds of his immediate success or failure; one must also take into consideration the ultimate outcome of history. Seen from a worldly perspective, John's behavior may appear foolish, but the eye of faith perceives a higher foolishness wiser than the wisdom of man.

Both of the preceding arguments involve an appeal to the future; the third does not. It is a justification from the present, but the present is only indirectly considered as part of the temporal process; the experiences of the present are treated as part of an eternal reality that defies the dimension of time. We are dealing here with an almost mystical intuition and the author does not present it as a logical argument. She describes, instead, the visionary perception of a symbolic icon. Like the burning bush, the descent of the dove, this image seeks to represent the nature of ultimate reality.

All his life, John had tried to follow Francis, obey his rule, and imitate Christ. In this attempt John had sacrificed everything, even belief in his own cause. At the moment of despair, he possessed nothing; he was completely helpless. Was he not then most truly the follower of the saint whose body bore the stigmata of the Lord who had suffered the total defeat of the cross? At La Verna, the holiest shrine of the Franciscans, John had seen a vision:

A vision of the Crucified, encircled by those mighty wings which burned with celestial fire. Vision baffling to the mind. Suddenly now the meaning came home to him. . . . That nailed Figure! Hands that could not be reached out in healing; feet that could not tread earth's ways. The helplessness of the Cross. Weakness, shame, defeat to the uttermost—they were the center of the symbols of Power! The Seraph Crucified! Wings that transcended earth, that bore the weight of the most holy Cross and of Him who hung thereon, Love's sacrifice, up into the eternal light, and down, on fire with that light to earth's extremest need. *The Naughting of the Cross was life, not death. It was the source of all creative life.* [emphasis mine][125]

Here is Vida Scudder's "Theology of the Cross" stated in its most extreme form. With an irony characteristic of Romantic thought at its most profound, it finds in failure the grounds for highest optimism. Is it a convincing world-historical vision? Each reader must decide for himself the answer to that question, but one point must be made in its favor: it enabled her to face the deepest sense of defeat without succumbing to despair. She continued to work on through the twenties and that work formed a bridge between the Social Gospel era and the renewed social consciousness that characterized the church in the Red Decade.

*The Franciscan Adventure* adds little to the basic message proclaimed in *Brother John.* Everyone interested in the Franciscan movement could read it with profit, but the essence of her scholarly research had been distilled in the preceding novel. The history recounts the full story of the first hundred-odd years of the Franciscan movement; there are not many differences in interpretation. One, though, does stand out; *The Franciscan Adventure* is far more sympathetic to St. Bonaventura. As the passion for social justice began to revive during the Great Depression, the author began to mellow and she developed a deeper respect for the honest compromiser. Looking at history, she thought, intensified one's sympathy for both sides in the conflict. "Our affection goes out more readily to the Spirituals; yet it is evident that men like Aymon of Faversham and Bonaventura, who opposed them, had often a wider and saner vision.[126] Her appreciation for the complexity of historical problems and her desire to give each man his just due make this a valuable study. One is tempted to regret that literature and not history was the subject of most of her scholarly work.

Joseph F. Fletcher of the Episcopal Theological School in Cambridge, Massachusetts, a noted Anglican social reformer himself, has described her influence in the dedication to *Christianity and Property*, a volume of essays on Christianity and social reform to which she herself contributed at the age of eighty-six.

> There is no other person in the American scene to whom a book on Christianity and property could so rightly be dedicated. She and her work, for all these years . . . have enormously influenced us all. Hosts of her former students brighten when her name is mentioned. To know her now is to have a lively foretaste of the communion of saints. Her wisdom, her faith in social redemption, her vast learning and mature sense of humor have been towers of strength in . . . fellowships that look forward to a new day.[127]

The towers of strength described by Fletcher we know were painfully constructed out of the debris of her own fears and failures. Here lies her true greatness. Although she was in the vanguard of many noble movements, others—Jane Addams, James Huntington, William Dwight Porter Bliss—may be more justly acclaimed as innovators and founders. Vida Scudder was a sustainer. She persevered; her efforts brought life and leadership to many organizations devoted to noble ends. Her perseverance inspired others and thanks in part to her perseverance the American church today has voices that speak out for social justice. Her works remain and those who read them cannot fail to find a vitality and enthusiasm that is truly infectious. Her faith sustains, her life inspires us to look forward to a new day, to work toward a new earth.

# EIGHT

# Conclusion

Vida Scudder died on 9 October, 1954, almost two months to the day before her ninety-fourth birthday. She long had outlived her radical contemporaries in the post Civil War generation of Anglican social reformers, and her death marked the end of their era. A chapter in the history of the Anglican left was closed.

When Vida Scudder died only 108 years had passed since John Ludlow called on Frederick Denison Maurice at Lincoln's Inn and inadvertently inaugurated the first modern movement for social reform in the Anglican Communion. Little more than a century—and yet it was a period of profound change. What had the movement accomplished during those first 108 years?

There were many achievements, contributions to the church and to the history of reform in general. The movement's influence was broader within the expanded horizons of secular society, but the church felt its impact more deeply and directly.

First among the movement's contributions to social reform are two innovative institutions—producers' cooperatives and settlement houses. The Council of Promoters of Working Class Associations introduced the producers' cooperative idea to England. The council failed; producers' cooperatives have not replaced finance capitalism or state socialism as basic means of production. They have never been as successful as consumers' cooperatives, which occupy a modest place in our economy. But the strength of the idea lives on. We can note a similar inspiration in plans for profit sharing and stock options for workers, and in the increasing participation of labor representatives in industrial planning and decision making.

The settlement house movement was more immediately and obviously successful. The Working Men's College pointed the way, and Toynbee Hall was created by Anglican undergraduates deeply influenced by Maurice, Kingsley, and the other first-generation Christian Socialists. Toynbee Hall inspired the Women's College Settlement Association in the United States, and I have recounted the important role played by Vida Scudder both in its foundation and during its early years. Of course, I do not mean to suggest that the settlement house movement was exclusively an Anglican or even Christian venture; but the idea was introduced and spread by the Anglican reformers.

The ritualist slum priests and their followers made another important contribution by developing the institutional church as a community center. They introduced no fundamental structural innovations; but rather adapted the long established parish system to meet the demands of urban industrialized society. For centuries parish churches had been deeply involved in primary education and charitable relief work. Expanding on these traditional services, the slum ritualists, ably assisted by women's religious orders, added libraries, gymnasiums, summer camps, and meeting rooms where the people of the neighborhood could meet for study, relaxation, and recreation. Many of these services also were offered by settlement houses, but no settlement house had the strong ecclesiastical devotional focus of a ritualist parish. Ritualist parishes tended to be highly organized, and perhaps their greatest contribution to the reform movement came about through their grass roots organization of slum neighborhoods for social improvement. When men like Dolling, Stanton, and Huntington led the agitation for new parks, better sewers, and the regulation of public houses, they were asserting the basic right of the people to improve the quality of their lives by controlling their immediate environment. Today we call similar organizing at the grass roots level participatory democracy, and slum churches of many denominations are still centers of agitation for neighborhood improvement.

I should also reiterate John Ludlow's modest but significant contribution to the formulation of the modern idea of the welfare state. Aimé Huber and Lujo Brentano communicated Ludlow's concern for the poor to the "Socialists of the Chair" who developed an institutionalist school of economics and helped draw up the German Public Insurance Acts of the 1880s. Certainly Prince Bismarck's concern for the social welfare of the German workers owed more to his desire to undercut the influence of the socialists than to any Christian Socialist principle, but Ludlow's ideas influenced the men who drew up the legislation. A modest contribution, but it is real.

Important as the innovative contribution of the Anglican left has been, however, the movement's role as popularizer and educator has proven even more significant. Only a few of the Anglican reformers were truly original thinkers, but almost all of them were prolific writers. They supported many ideas and causes. John Ludlow introduced many of the precepts of French utopian socialism to the English; Canon Scott Holland helped popularize T. H. Green's notion of the positive state; and Richard T. Ely brought German institutionalist economics to the United States. Stewart Headlam and James O. S. Huntington were dedicated and persuasive proponents of Henry George's single tax. W. D. P. Bliss, Headlam, and Vida Scudder spread the precepts of Fabian socialism; Bliss's wider role as an educator was truly encyclopedic. Vida Scudder championed Ruskin, Marx, and Gandhi as well as St. Catherine of Siena and St. Francis of Assisi. In addition to the specific contributions of these individuals we must remember the incredible amount of information on social reform spread by the Guild of St. Matthew, the Christian Social Union, the Church Social Union, the Society of Christian Socialists, the Church Socialist League, C.A.I.L., and other like-minded organizations. The volume of Anglican reform propaganda rose to a crescendo during the high noon of the Social Gospel era, and it was only muted, never silenced, in the dark discouraging years that followed.

As a group the Anglican reformers were devout and dedicated church people, but they were not narrowly sectarian in outlook. Beginning with the early Christian Socialist band of brothers, the movement demonstrated a willingness to learn from and work with a wide variety of people who were not Anglican, who were not necessarily Christian, and who were not respectable middle class. The movement's catholic vision, its openness to new ideas, and its cooperative spirit are the qualities that have insured its impact on the development of British and American society as a whole. Ultimately the Anglican left has been most influential as a vital part of the general movement for political democracy and social reform, which has played such a substantial role in the history of Great Britain and the United States during the last century and a half.

Maurice had hoped to Christianize socialism. This dream proved impossible; neither enough Christians nor enough socialists were interested. If the movement did not succeed in Christianizing socialism, however, it did insure that Christian principles and Christian people were deeply and continuously involved in the social reform process.

The Anglican reformers were predominantly middle class and it is as responsible Christian members of a privileged class that they made their two greatest contributions to the Anglo-American reform movement. First, they allied themselves with the lower classes in the struggle to change society and they worked on their behalf to improve living conditions. Second, and even more important, they preached social responsibility, social concern, and social reform to the privileged classes who for the most part were strongly identified with the formal practice of the Christian religion. By presenting social issues in terms their audience understood they were able to awaken the conscience of the morally sensitive, to inspire the idealism of younger generations, and to enroll them along with the politically active members of the lower classes and the various groupings of secular radicals in the long, hard struggle for social change and improvement.

The Anglican left did not dominate the movement for political democracy and social reform in either England or America, but it played a constant, vital role in that process, and it is here that its influence has been broadest. Its impact on the church—while it reached fewer people—has been far more profound. Modern society might be much the same without the contribution of the Anglican left; one cannot make the same statement about the church.

Before 1846 Anglicanism in England and the United States by and large was identified with the political right and the social status quo. During the War of Independence many Anglicans—especially members of the clergy—had sided with the Tories, and for most of the first half of the nineteenth century the church retained the "quality of upper-classishness" to which Manross referred. In England the church was part of the Erastian establishment and none of the major church parties of the time—the old High Churchmen, the Evangelicals, and the Tractarians—advocated social or political change. As individuals many Anglicans—particularly Evangelicals and Tractarians—were distressed by the social problems produced by the agricultural revolution and rapid industrialization, but they responded in the traditional manner by giving charity to individuals in need. They lacked the social vision that would enable them to attack the problem at its roots.

The great contribution of the Anglican left was just such a social vision; they offered a theology and practice that enabled the church to come to terms with the problems of urbanization and industrialization in the modern world. The work done by the original Christian Socialists and the ritualist slum priests was of critical importance in defining this new theology and practice.

No single individual did more to shape the new theology than Frederick Denison Maurice. His emphasis on the significance of the Incarnation restored the here and now to its proper place in the Christian view of redemption. Also, his insight that salvation was a social process involving ultimately the entire human race provided the intellectual basis for Christian participation in reshaping society.

The Christian Socialists, especially John Ludlow, and the ritualist slum priests defined the practice. Taking their clue from Edward Bouvarie Pusey, the second-generation ritualist priests moved into the slums and ministered to the poor. Gradually, under the pressure of circumstances, they moved beyond traditional charity and relief and began agitating for the reform of society through social change.

During the Social Gospel era the two streams converged and together they became a powerful force in change within the church. The Anglican left did not take over the church in the sense that their views became normative dogma. From the time of the Elizabethan settlement in the sixteenth century the Anglican Church has been a comprehensive institution which, on the whole, has tolerated a wide diversity of faith and practice among its communicants. Throughout the period I have been studying and even today there are many Anglicans who have maintained a strong conservative social and political position.

The change has come with the church as an institution; it is no longer identified with the political right and the social status quo. During the Social Gospel era Anglican reformers first attained positions of considerable importance within the ecclesiastical hierarchy. Scott Holland became a canon of St. Paul's and Charles Gore occupied several episcopal sees. Both men had been associated with university education before their preferment, and the Anglican left traditionally has been strong among the religious intelligentsia, the teachers, writers, and spokesmen of the church. Through these people the Anglican left has entered the mainstream of the church. One might say that their position was fully established when William Temple became archbishop of Canterbury in 1942. A man long identified with Christian social reform became primate of all England and head of the Anglican communion.

These then were the four greatest achievements of the Anglican left in the 108 years between the first meeting of John Ludlow and Frederick Denison Maurice in 1846 and the death of Vida Dutton Scudder in 1954: they actively participated in the establishment of full political democracy in England and the United States; they contributed to the creation of the modern welfare state; they led the Protestant Church into the social reform movement, and they changed the political complexion of the Anglican establishment. Their achievement was substantial, and their impact has been lasting.

# Notes

## INTRODUCTION

1. Arthur Mann, *Yankee Reformers in an Urban Age* (Cambridge: Belknap Press, 1954), p. 90. Mann succinctly states an opinion expressed in all the major studies of the early period of American social Christianity. See also Henry May, *Protestant Churches and Industrial America* (New York: Harper & Brothers, 1949), pp. 182-87; Charles Howard Hopkins, *The Rise of the Social Gospel in American Protestantism* (New Haven: Yale University Press, 1940), pp. 38-39; and Aaron Ignatius Abell, *The Urban Impact on American Protestantism* (Cambridge: Harvard University Press, 1943), pp. 10, 17-18.
2. *The Christian Union*, November 28, 1891, pp. 1024-25. The editors were commenting on a symposium on socialism held at the Church Congress of 1891, where various socialists and single taxers addressed the assembled church leaders.
3. Walter Rauschenbush, *Christianizing the Social Order* (New York: Macmillan Company, 1914), p. 22. Although Rauschenbush's generalization is technically correct, it deserves some explanation and qualification. The Episcopal Church did not take an official stand on the slavery issue because it feared a denominational split into regional sects. Such splits had already divided the Methodists and Presbyterians, and Episcopalians, whose high doctrine of the church equated schism with sin, were particularly determined to remain united. While the Episcopal Church remained neutral, individual Episcopalians were active in the abolitionist cause. The aristocratic Jay family, for example, was prominent both in the Episcopal Church and in the antislavery movement in New York. For a complete discussion of this issue written by an Episcopal historian, see William W. Manross, "The Episcopal Church and Social Reform," *The Historical Magazine of the Protestant Episcopal Church* (December 1943): 339-66. Likewise, the church remained neutral on the alcoholic beverage issue, but individual Episcopalians were concerned about the social problems caused by alcohol. The Church Congress discussed "The Prevention and Cure of Drunkenness" in 1876, and the Reverend R. Heber Newton, a pioneering Anglican social reformer, proposed the formation of a Church Temperance Society based on the English model to deal with the problem. In 1881 the society was formally organized by several clergymen under the leadership of the

Reverend B. F. DeCosta, another active social reformer. Interestingly, the Church Temperance Society antedated the Methodist national committee on temperance by over twenty years. Branches of the Church Temperance Society engaged in "aggressive rescue work" and opened "coffee houses which resembled saloons in everything but the liquor." Abell, *Urban Impact*, p. 143; see also pp. 48-49, 142. On the whole, though the Episcopalians advocated temperance rather than abstinence. They did not urge communicants to "take the pledge" and they continued the use of wine at eucharistic celebrations.

4. William Wilson Manross, *A History of the American Episcopal Church* (New York: Morehouse-Gorhan Co., 1959), p. 73.

5. M. A. DeWolfe Howe, *Memoirs of the Life and Services of the Rt. Rev. Alonzo Potter* (Philadelphia: J. B. Lippincott and Co., 1871), p, 64.

6. May, *Protestant Churches*, pp. 15-16. My discussion of Potter's book is based on May and on Howe, *Memoirs of Potter*, pp. 62-66. When not expounding the iron laws of Manchester economics the bishop struggled against social injustice. He opposed alcohol and defended blacks. During the General Convention of 1862 he circulated a petition to President Lincoln on Indian rights. It was signed by nineteen bishops, ten priests, and ten laymen. See Manross, *American Episcopal Church*, p. 318.

7. Manross, *American Episcopal Church*, pp. 104-45.

8. Rauschenbush, *Christianizing*, p. 22.

9. See May, *Protestant Churches*, pp. 148-50; Hopkins, *Rise of Social Gospel*, p. 7; James Dombrowski, *The Early Days of Christian Socialism in America* (New York: Columbia University Press, 1936), p. 102; Manross, *American Episcopal Church*, pp. 318-19; and Raymond W. Albright, *A History of the Protestant Episcopal Church* (New York: Macmillan Company, 1964), p. 313.

10. Joseph Fletcher and Spencer Miller, *The Church and Industry* (New York: Longmans, Green, and Company, 1930), p. 52. Their description of the English movement is sketchy and has been outdated by recent research.

11. Carlyle introduced the word into written English when he published *The French Revolution* in 1837.

# CHAPTER ONE

1. The phrase is Ludlow's. "My idea was to form what, in Nelson's life, he sought to make his captains before Trafalgar, a band of brothers." From an unpublished autobiography by N. C. Masterman in *John Malcom Ludlow, The Builder of Christian Socialism* (Cambridge: Cambridge University Press, 1963), p. 101. The "band of brothers" idea was popular at the time; one thinks immediately of the Pre-Raphaelite brotherhood. Shakespeare, of course, coined the term in "Henry V."

2. Today these ideas may appear vague and impractical, but they created a stir when they were presented to the public in Disraeli's Young England trilogy,

*Conningsby*, *Sybil*, and *Tancred*. It is impossible to estimate the extent of their influence, but, especially in novel-reading Victorian England, Disraeli's romances reached a far wider public than parliamentary blue books and political platforms.

3. Shaftesbury's life and career are sympathetically depicted in J. Wesley Bready's *Lord Shaftesbury and Socio-Industrial Programs* (London: George Unwin, 1926). Bready's work is enthusiastic and uncritical, but the description of Shaftesbury's various works is detailed. For a more balanced interpretation of the man's significance see J. L. and B. Hammond, *Lord Shaftesbury* (London: Constable and Company, Ltd., 1973).

4. Fletcher and Miller, *Church and Industry*, p. 5. Although I find this statement essentially true, it is a bit too sweeping to be accepted without some qualification. The Evangelical movement had engendered countless reform organizations that were organized expressions of a social conscience. Nowadays we tend to neglect the Evangelical social conscience because it was often very unlike our own. The English Christian Socialists were the first *modern* expression of an organized social conscience in the church. The Evangelicals had an almost exclusive concern with the souls of the poor. Their charity did not help the poor *out* of their misery, but only helped them *in* it. They emphasized personal reformation; the Christian Socialists stressed social reform. One further point must be noted in favor of Miller and Fletcher's generalization: the Evangelical Society Movement gained supporters in, but it was not necessarily *of*, the Church of England. Its impulse owed as much to chapel as to church. The same can be said of the movement to abolish slavery, even though its hero and leader, Wilberforce, was a strong churchman.

5. Peter d'A. Jones, *The Christian Socialist Revival* (Princeton: Princeton University Press, 1968), p. 10. See also Maurice Reckitt, *Maurice to Temple* (London: Faber and Faber Limited, 1947).

6. The phrase is Ludlow's cited by Frederick Maurice in *The Life of Frederick Denison Maurice*, 2 vols. (New York: Charles Scribner's Sons, 1884), 1: 430. This book, which is primarily a collection of Maurice's letters, is still the best primary source for his life.

7. Ibid.

8. The description is his own and appears in many letters.

9. Masterman, *Ludlow*, p. 46.

10. Maurice Reckitt's Scott Holland Memorial Lectures, which were published under the title *Maurice to Temple*, were delivered to celebrate the centennial anniversary of the first meeting between Maurice and Ludlow. Reckitt also considers this meeting the birthdate of the movement: "the centenary of their first meeting is one which could not be passed over without impiety" (p. 14).

11. The same attitude prevailed on this side of the Atlantic. To cite only one example: Vida Dutton Scudder, who was a scholar and knew a good deal about the history of Christian Socialism, refers in her autobiography to "the Christian Socialist adventure led by him [Maurice] and Charles Kingsley." *On Journey* (New York: E. P. Dutton and Co., Inc., 1937), p. 162.

12. Owen Chadwick, *The Victorian Church*, Part I (New York: Oxford University Press, 1966), p. 351. Chadwick's discussion (pp. 346-63) is the most sensitive and perceptive brief statement of the subject that I have found.

13. Jones, *Christian Socialist Revival*, p. 14. See also Masterman, *Ludlow*, pp. 51-73, especially p. 61. The first historical study to recognize Ludlow's importance was C. E. Raven's *Christian Socialism, 1848-1854* (London: Macmillan and Co., Ltd., 1920).

14. The incident was recalled by Ludlow in his autobiography and is cited by Masterman, *Ludlow*, p. 10.

15. For the letters and issues involved see Maurice, *Life of Maurice*, 1: 432-56.

16. Alex R. Vidler, *F. D. Maurice and Company* (London: S. C. M. Press Ltd., 1966), p. 8. See also W. R. Inge, *The Platonic Tradition in English Religious Thought* (London: Longmans, Green, and Co., 1926), p. 96.

17. Since then, however, there has been a real renaissance. Among the most significant recent studies are H. G. Wood, *Frederick Denison Maurice* (Cambridge: Cambridge University Press, 1950); A. M. Ramsey, *F. D. Maurice and the Conflicts of Modern Theology* (Cambridge: Cambridge University Press, 1951); and W. Merlin David, *An Introduction to the Theology of F. D. Maurice* (London: S.P.C.K., 1964). Even when forgotten elsewhere, Maurice's theology was remembered by the Society of the Sacred Mission, an Anglican religious order at Kelham. In an article written in 1910 but not published until 1959 in the *Society of the Sacred Mission Quarterly*, Herbert Kelly called him the "greatest of all teachers since Augustine." Maurice's work as a theologian appears to have been better known in the United States, where it was championed by Phillips Brooks, a leading American churchman. Albright, *History of the Protestant Episcopal Church*, p. 303. Now scholarship has come full circle. Three major studies of Maurice have recently appeared, which emphasize his work as a theologian and play down his role as a social reformer. See Olive J. Brose, *Frederick Denison Maurice, Rebellious Conformist* (Athens: Ohio University Press, 1971); Torben Christensen, *The Divine Order, A Study in F. D. Maurice's Theology* (Leiden: E. J. Brill, 1973); and Frank Mauldin McClain, *Maurice, Man and Moralist* (London: S.P.C.K., 1972).

18. Maurice, *Life of Maurice*, 2: 137.

19. F. D. Maurice, *Moral and Metaphysical Philosophy*, in Vidler, *Maurice and Company*, p. 18.

20. C. F. G. Masterman, *F. D. Maurice* (London: A. R. Mobray and Co., 1907), p. 219.

21. Maurice, *Life of Maurice*, 2: 286.

22. Alex R. Vidler, *Witness to the Light* (New York: Charles Scribner's Sons, 1948), p. 9. The full title of Maurice's work is *Lectures on the Ecclesiastical History of the First and Second Centuries*.

23. Vidler, *Witness to the Light*, p. 16.

24. H. Richard Niebuhr, *Christ and Culture* (New York: Harper & Brothers, 1951), p. 229.

25. Torben Christensen, *The Origin and History of Christian Socialism* (Copenhagen: Universitelsforlaget I Arbus, 1962), p. 67. A careful perusal of Maurice's letter, especially to Ludlow, substantiates Christensen's assertion. See Maurice, *Life of Maurice*, 2: 103-38.

26. Maurice, *Life of Maurice*, 2: 131.

27. F. D. Maurice, *The Kingdom of Christ* cited in Davis, *Spearheads for Reform*, p. 124.

28. Maurice, *Life of Maurice*, 2: 128.

29. F. D. Maurice, *The Commandments Considered as Instruments of National Reformation*, cited in Melvin Richter, *The Politics of Conscience, T. H. Green and His Age* (Cambridge: Harvard University Press, 1964), pp. 316-17.

30. Masterman, *Ludlow*, p. 5.

31. Ibid., p. 61.

32. Maurice, *Life of Maurice*, 1: 458.

33. Ibid., p. 459.

34. The complete text is in Una Pope-Hennessy, *Canon Charles Kingsley* (London: Chatto and Windus, 1948), pp. 76-77.

35. Christensen, *Origin of Christian Socialism*, p. 89.

36. Peter d'A. Jones implies that Ludlow followed the theories of P. J. P. Buchez, and Jones explains these theories in some detail in *Christian Socialist Revival*, pp. 14-19. Masterman, however, asserts that Beatrice Webb, "who wished to minimize the role of the Christian Socialists in working class history," highly overemphasized Buchez's influence on Ludlow. Masterman claims that Ludlow never read a line of Buchez at the time and that his influence can have been only partial and indirect. Jones cites Masterman's work frequently, but never attempts to explain what new evidence, if any, led him to disagree on this point. I cannot resolve the conflict, but in the absence of either evidence or argument from Jones, I tend to trust Masterman who is the Ludlow specialist. For his position see *Ludlow*, pp. 99-100.

37. Christensen, *Origin of Christian Socialism*, p. 105.

38. Chadwick, *Victorian Church*, p. 355.

39. Maurice, *Life of Maurice*, 1: 93.

40. Ibid., 2: 35.

41. Chadwick, *Victorian Church*, p. 358.

42. Masterman, *Ludlow*, pp. 106-7.

43. Ibid., p. 101.

44. Chadwick, *Victorian Church*, p. 358.

45. Christensen, *Origin of Christian Socialism*, p. 226. My interpretation on this point follows Chadwick, Masterman, and Christensen. Jones, I think, expects too much from the Christian Socialists, considering the great differences between the classes in England during the 1850s.

46. Masterman, *Ludlow*, p. 124.

47. Ibid., p. 130. In his *Life* Maurice's son omitted that passage (see 2: 105).

48. These letters to Ludlow, in Maurice, *Life of Maurice*, 2: 105-32, would have convinced a far more cynical and hostile man. They demonstrate why Maurice's friends unanimously hailed him as a fine man, even when they found him most difficult.

49. Lockhart, the editor at the time, was disgusted by the article, out Crocker's influence with Tory magnates was so great that he had the right to publish articles even if the editor disapproved. Also, the editor had to publish them without comment. Ibid., p. 71.

50. Crocker's attack goes on for pages and pages. My frequent omissions do not alter the sense of the text, but I felt it necessary to remove superfluous denunciation for the sake of reasonable brevity. The attack is cited at greater length in ibid., pp. 72-73.

51. Ibid., p. 71.

52. Ibid., pp. 100-101.

53. Ibid., p. 172.

54. The passage that inspired Maurice's interpretation is St. John 17: 2-3. "For thou hast made him sovereign over all mankind, to give eternal life to all whom thou hast given him. This is eternal life: to know thee who alone art truly God, and Jesus Christ whom thou has sent."

55. Chadwick, *Victorian Church*, p. 547.

56. Maurice, *Life of Maurice*, 2: 176.

57. Christensen, *Origin of Christian Socialism*, p. 351.

58. The College's history is described by J. F. C. Harrison, *A History of the Working Men's College, 1854-1954* (London: Routledge, 1954).

59. Christensen, *Origin of Christian Socialism*, p. 362.

60. Masterman, *Ludlow*, p. 149.

61. Ibid., pp. 197-213.

62. Richard T. Ely, *Ground Under Our Feet* (New York: Macmillan Company, 1938), pp. 41-47.

63. J. A. Hobson, *John Ruskin, Social Reformer* (Boston: Dana Estes and Company, 1898), p. vi.

64. Toynbee Hall grew cut of a meeting held in the rooms of a Balliol undergraduate named Cosmo Gordon Lang, who was afterward archbishop both of York and Canterbury. Reckitt, *Maurice to Temple*, pp. 117-18. In his youth Lang was very moved by a life of Kingsley and "the Kingsley ideal of Christianity." "I should wish," he wrote, "to take my stand with those who have incorporated many of the best elements in the High Church ideal with the teaching of men like Maurice and Kingsley." J. G. Lockhart, *Cosmo Gordon Lang* (London: Hodder and Stoughton, Ltd., 1949), p. 74.

65. For the influence of Toynbee Hall on the founders of the American settlement house movement see Alan F. Davis, *Spearheads for Reform* (New York: Oxford University Press, 1967), pp. 8-14.

66. Maurice, *Life of Maurice*, 1: 519.

# CHAPTER TWO

1. John Henry Newman, *Apologia Pro Vita Sua* (New York: D. Appleton and Company, 1865), p. 83.
2. William George Peck, *The Social Implications of the Oxford Movement* (New York: Charles Scribner's Sons, 1933), p. 44.
3. Richard Hurrell Froude, *Remains* (London: J. S. and F. Rivington, 1839), 2: 258-73.
4. R. W. Church, *The Oxford Movement, Twelve Years 1833-45* (London: Macmillan and Co., 1892), p. 50.
5. John Henry Newman, *Parochial and Plain Sermons* (London: Rivington's, 1868), 4: 175-78.
6. Ibid., 3: 246-47.
7. John Henry Newman, *The Arians of the Fourth Century* (London: Basil Montagu Pickering, 1876), p. 258.
8. Desmond Bowen, *The Idea of the Victorian Church* (Montreal: McGill University Press, 1968), p. 286.
9. Owen Chadwick in *The Mind of the Oxford Movement* (London: Adam and Charles Black, 1960), p. 227.
10. Ibid., p. 228.
11. Ibid.
12. George W. E. Russell, *Dr. Pusey* (London: A. R. Mowbray, n.d.), p. 174.
13. Bowen, *Idea of Victorian Church*, p. 63.
14. Ibid., p. 81.
15. Ibid., p. 297. See also Russell, *Dr. Pusey*, pp. 121-22. In addition to rescuing sick children, Pusey served on the special hospitals committee, visited the sick and dying as an unpaid assistant-curate to Septimus Hansard of Bethnal Green, and used his extensive knowledge of Hebrew to explain sanitary precautions to neighboring Jewish immigrants who did not understand English.
16. Edward Bouverie Pusey, *The Councils of the Church from the Council of Jerusalem to the Council of Constantinople* (Oxford: Rivingtons, 1857), pp. 4-5.
17. See Bowen, *Idea of Victorian Church*, pp. 112-14 for a brief description of the work done at St. Saviour during the forties and fifties.
18. According to A. M. Alchin, *The Silent Rebellion* (London: S. C. M. Press Ltd., 1958), p. 47, the words *monastic* and *religious* were used interchangeably in England after the reformation. Froude's plan was not strictly "monastic."
19. Froude, *Remains*, 1: 332; Peck, *Social Implications*, p. 64 says that Froude's letter was addressed to Newman, but Newman and Keble deleted all of Froude's greetings when they published letters in his *Remains*. Newman himself, though, certainly was interested in reviving the "religious" life as his "monastic" community at Littlemore and subsequent career in the Roman Church demonstrate.
20. H. P. Liddon, *Life of Edward Bouverie Pusey* (London: Longmans, Green, and Company, 1894), 2: 40.

21. Alchin, *Silent Rebellion*, p. 59.
22. In 1849 she moved to the parish of St. Thomas the Martyr, Oxford, where she assisted the rector, her cousin Mr. Chamberlain, with his work among the poor. Two years later she took a house on St. John Street in the parish of St. Giles, Oxford, where she continued her parochial work and, with Pusey's assistance, established the Society of the Holy and Undivided Trinity. For a more detailed description of her call to the religious life and the history of the order she founded see Peter F. Anson and A. W. Campbell, *The Call of the Cloister* (London: S. P. C. K., 1964), pp. 288-97.
23. Pusey was the most important cleric to support the sisterhood, but much of the impetus for the project came from a group of laymen, among whom were William E. Gladstone and Lord John Manners. Alchin, *Silent Rebellion*, pp. 61-65 and Anson and Campbell, *Call of the Cloister*, pp. 220-39 describe in detail the complex problems that beset the founders.
24. The number eighteen excludes women's orders founded in 1865 and is limited to orders established in Great Britain. My total is based on Anson and Campbell's descriptions, *Call of the Cloister*, pp. 220-397.
25. For this assertion I cite the authority of Dom Gregory Dix. In his dedication to *The Shape of the Liturgy* (London: Dacre Press, Adam and Charles Black, 1945), p. ix, he calls the Cowley fathers, "the oldest, the most respected, and in more ways than one the greatest of our Anglican communities of priests." I have discounted Newman's group at Littlemore because it was informal and because most of the members went to Rome. There were numerous attempts during the middle of the nineteenth century to establish an Anglican religious order for men, but they were unsuccessful. Some lasted months; some struggled along for a few years. Anson and Campbell's discussion of the problems, *Call of the Cloister*, pp. 29-72 and for the United States pp. 531-40, is sympathetic and detailed. Probably the most fascinating failure was a community of Benedictines founded by Brother Ignatius (Joseph Leycester Lyne). Like most of the attempted men's orders, these Benedictines were too quixotic and bizarre to survive long; and yet, Anson and Campbell are right to conclude, "There is something inexpressibly tragic about Llanthony." The Baroness de Bertouch's *The Life of Father Ignatius*, OSB. (London: Methuen and Co., 1904) is a sympathetic account of his life and work. For another sympathetic, but more realistic, assessment of Brother Ignatius, see B. G. A. Cannell, *From Monk to Busman* (London: Skeffington and Son, Ltd., 1935), pp. 29-56. Cannell was a novice at Llanthony who left when Brother Ignatius's behavior became high-handed and eccentric.
26. Alchin, *Silent Rebellion*, p. 120.
27. Ibid., p. 207. The Sisters of the Church, *A Valiant Victorian* (London: A. R. Mowbray and Co., Ltd., 1964) offers a full account of her life and the work of the order she founded.
28. Anson and Campbell, *Call of the Cloister*, p. 270.
29. Ibid., p. 269.

30. This figure is based on descriptions in ibid., pp. 377-476. Not all of these orders survived intact. A few joined with more successful orders and the Benedictine nuns of Milford Haven went over to Rome en masse.
31. Ibid., p. 438.
32. Cecil Blanche Woodham-Smith, *Florence Nightingale* (New York: McGraw Hill, 1951), p. 49.
33. There is no definitive critical modern biography of Neale. The most useful general introduction to his work is A. G. Lough, *The Influence of John Mason Neale* (London: S. P. C. K., 1962). For Neale and the Society of St. Margaret see pp. 52-70. Also useful, but much less sympathetic, is James F. White, *The Cambridge Movement* (Cambridge: Cambridge University Press, 1962).
34. Mandell Creighton, bishop of London from 1897-1901, was a moderate High Churchman whose relations with the sisterhoods were generally cordial. Nevertheless, he wrote with some exasperation: "This is the bad point about sisterhoods. They want to be absolutely independent, obedient only to their own will." Mrs. Mandell Creighton, *Life and Letters of Mandell Creighton* (London: Longmans, Green and Co., 1905), 2: 271.
35. Anson and Campbell, *Call of the Cloister*, p. 436.
36. For specific information about these unsuccessful attempts see ibid., pp. 29-72.
37. Alchin, *Silent Rebellion*, pp. 183-205 has an excellent discussion of the Cowley fathers and their work.
38. Pusey, *Councils of the Church*.
39. Deiter Voll, *Catholic Evangelicalism* (London: The Faith Press, 1963), p. 89.
40. For example, S. C. Carpenter, *Church and People, 1789-1889* (London: S. P. C. K., 1933) devotes a chapter to "Ritualism and Prosecution," but has only one paragraph on slum ritualists in his chapter on "The Social Conscience." Owen Chadwick's recent study on the Victorian church mentions the ritualists in connection with "The Troubles of Eucharistic Worship" and not with "Religion in the Slum."
41. Bowen, *Idea of Victorian Church*, p. 285.
42. Ludlow wrote that the notorious riots that disrupted services at the famous slum church, St. George's-in-the-East during the late fifties and early sixties were "largely stimulated by the Jewish sweaters of the East End whose proceedings Mr. Bryan King's curates, Messers. Macknonochie and Lowder, had the unheard impertinence to denounce and interfere with." In a rare ecumenical gesture, "Anglican vestrymen" joined the "Jewish sweaters" to support—some say financially—antiritualist disruptions. These vestrymen who were publicans and probably brothel-keepers also had their "proceedings denounced and interfered with." Michael Reynolds, *Martyr to Ritualism* (London: Faber and Faber, 1965), pp. 50-71, has an excellent account of the St. George's riots, which cites many firsthand reports of the disruptions.
43. Bowen, *Idea of Victorian Church*, p. 291.
44. Reynolds, *Martyr to Ritualism*, pp. 190-91.
45. Voll, *Catholic Evangelicism*, p. 97.

46. Reynolds, *Martyr to Ritualism*, p. 232.
47. Stanton felt a great sense of kinship with the Methodists, although they, naturally, had their differences. "The Wesleyans love Jesus," he wrote, "and if only they loved His Mother for His Sake," Voll, *Catholic Evangelicism*. It is of course often forgotten that the author of "Amazing Grace" was an Anglican clergyman.
48. For an illuminating discussion of the ritualists' reasons for restoring the practice of private confession and the problems raised by the resumption see Reynolds, *Martyr to Ritualism*, pp. 211-28 and *passim*.
49. Voll, *Catholic Evangelicism*, p. 107, attributes the words to Dolling; Reynolds, *Martyr to Ritualism*, p. 235, believes that the attribution is apocryphal, although he admits that the quotation reflects Dolling's sentiments. For a brief but informative and appreciative account of Dolling's life and work at Landport see B. C. Boulter, *The Anglican Reformers* (London: Philip Allan, 1933), pp. 63-73.
50. Voll, *Catholic Evangelicism*.

# CHAPTER THREE

1. Carpenter, *Church and People*, p. 328.
2. Even at the height of its popularity in the early nineties, the Guild never numbered more than four hundred members of whom about one-third were clergy. Jones, *Christian Socialist Revival*, p. 129.
3. Ibid., p. 223.
4. Maurice B. Reckitt, *Faith and Society* (London: Longmans, Green, and Company, 1932), p. 92.
5. F. S. Bettany, *Stewart Headlam* (London: John Murray, 1926), p. 7. This book is still the only full length study of Headlam and I have used it as a source for all biographical data.
6. Ibid., p. 12.
7. Ibid., p. 20.
8. Ibid., p. 24.
9. From an unpublished description of the Church and Stage Guild by Headlam, ibid., pp. 100-102. A detailed account of the guild's work can be found on pp. 97-108.
10. G. C. Binyon, *The Christian Socialist Movement in England* (London: S.P.C.K., 1931), p. 119.
11. Kenneth Leech, "Stewart Headlam, 1847-1924, and the Guild of St. Matthew," in *For Christ and the People*, ed. Maurice B. Reckitt (London: S.P.C.K., 1968), p. 63. Leech's article is the best short work on Headlam, but it is more concerned with Headlam the man and thinker than with the history of the guild.
12. Jones, *Christian Socialist Revival*, p. 160.

13. Bettany, *Headlam*, p. 21.
14. " . . . if the label Ritualist as applied to me has justification, the justification dates from my curacy at Bethnal Green and my visits to Father Nihill's Church [St. Michael's, Shoreditch]." In 1875 Headlam wrote of the clergy at St. Albans, Holborn, "Really these ritualists, they are the boys and second to none." Soon after arriving at St. Matthew's he secured Hansard's permission for an early celebration on all Sundays and holy days. Ibid., pp. 37-38.
15. Maurice, *Life of Maurice*, 2: 624. This opinion was expressed in a private letter to Mr. Read on December 12, 1870, and, of course, Headlam would have no way of knowing what Maurice had said in his private correspondence at the time. When the letter was published fifteen years later Headlam's position had already been formed.
16. Horton Davies, *Worship and Theology in England from Newman to Martineau, 1850-1900* (Princeton: Princeton University Press, 1962), p. 116. Denison's position was contested and the disagreement grew into one of the causes célèbres of mid-nineteenth-century party warfare. For accounts of the famous Denison Case (1853-58) see Carpenter, *Church and People*, p. 248 and Chadwick, *Victorian Church*, pp. 491-95. In 1869 Sir Robert Phillimore, a judge in the Court of Arches, ruled that this Anglo-Catholic doctrine of the sacrament was permissable.
17. Horton Davies, *Worship and Theology in England from Watts and Wesley to Maurice, 1690-1850* (Princeton: Princeton University Press, 1961), p. 312. In my discussion of Maurice's position I have relied heavily on Davies, pp. 306-12 and Vidler, *Maurice and Company*, pp. 121-26. Maurice's most comprehensive statement on this issue can be found in *The Kingdom of Christ* (London: James Clarke and Co., 1959), 2: 43-80. He criticizes the partial nature of the doctrines that various denominations held on the nature of the divine presence in the sacrament and, often by implication, reveals his own viewpoint.
18. Maurice, *Kingdom of Christ*, 2: 56.
19. For a clear and complete explanation of Calvin's doctrine of the Eucharist see Killian McDonnell, OSB, *John Calvin, the Church and the Eucharist* (Princeton: Princeton University Press, 1967), especially pp. 221-27. Another excellent but less extensive study is B. A. Gerrish, "The Lord's Supper in the Reformed Confessions," *Theology Today*, Vol. 23, no. 2 (July 1966): 224-43. Maurice, of course, did not consider himself a Calvinist and in *The Kingdom of Christ* he was expressly critical of what he called Calvin's "receptionist" doctrines. See especially 2: 58-64. Maurice wasn't a Calvin specialist, and he confused the opinions of many of his "Calvinistic" contemporaries with those of Calvin himself. It is likely that Calvin's doctrines were transmitted to Maurice through the Thirty-Nine Articles and the Catechism, which Gerrish says are respectively "cautiously Calvinistic" and faithfully Calvinistic" (pp. 236-37).
20. Vidler, *Maurice and Company*, p. 123.
21. Jones, *Christian Socialist Revival*, p. 160.
22. This is not to say that he was simpleminded or that he lacked subtlety. Headlam's aesthetic sensibility was refined, subtle, and broad. I have already

mentioned his affection for ballet, theater, and opera. He also had a deep interest in the visual arts and was a discriminating patron. He commissioned A. H. Mackmurdo, the avant-garde architect, to "do up" his rooms when he moved to Upper Bedford Place and he filled these rooms with "Burne-Jones and Rossetti pictures and Morris wallpaper and curtains." Ada Leverson, *Letters of the Sphinx to Oscar Wilde* (London: Duckworth, 1930), p. 27. Pearcy Dearmer, a man of no mean taste himself, said that Headlam was one of the "first clergymen of his time to take to live interest in art in its modern manifestations." Bettany, p. 128.

23. Ibid., p. 211.
24. Ibid., p. 216.
25. See Davies, *From Watts and Wesley*, pp. 283-92.
26. From *The Commonwealth*, in Reckitt, *Maurice to Temple*, p. 135.
27. Jones, *Christian Socialist Revival*.
28. Niebuhr, *Christ and Culture*, p. 228. Niebuhr's discussion of Maurice's thought, pp. 220-29, is probably the best brief treatment of the subject.
29. Hancock, while favoring a free church, rejected the idea of disestablishment. For an appreciative discussion of his life and work see Stephen Yeo, "Thomas Hancock," in Reckitt, *For Christ and the People*.
30. Bettany, *Headlam*, p. 38.
31. Jones, *Christian Socialist Revival*, p. 112.
32. Bettany, *Headlam*, pp. 85-86.
33. Ibid., p. 84.
34. Webb's recollections of Headlam, which give a good picture of the man, appear in ibid., pp. 85-86.
35. Binyon, *Christian Socialist Movement*, p. 143.
36. Jones, *Christian Socialist Revival*, p. 117. For a summary of the economic speculations that led George to the formulation of his single tax program consult pp. 48-57.
37. Ibid., p. 116.
38. Ibid. Jones incorrectly cites Bettany, *Headlam*, pp. 143-44 as his source. This confidence in the community as expressed through the state characterized all varieties of Anglican social Christianity until Guild Socialism appeared shortly before World War I. Unlike the Fabian Socialists, though, most Anglicans, including Headlam, strongly disapproved of bureaucracy.
39. Binyon, *Christian Socialist Movement*.
40. Jones, *Christian Socialist Revival*, p. 129.
41. For Headlam's arguments with other Fabians on this matter, see H. G. Wells's reminiscences of Headlam in Bettany, *Headlam*, pp. 142-44.
42. Jones, *Christian Socialist Revival*, p. 120.
43. Bettany, *Headlam*, pp. 87, 109, 120.
44. For the Guild's demonstrations see Jones, *Christian Socialist Revival*, pp. 126-31.

45. For examples of snubs, affronts, abuse, etc., see Bettany, *Headlam*, pp. 118-19 and *passim*.
46. The figures come from Jones, *Christian Socialist Revival*, p. 129, table 5.
47. He added that if an inspector came he would "lock the door of the school and tell the boys to put you in the pond." Chadwick, *Victorian Church*, p. 344.
48. Jones, *Christian Socialist Revival*, p. 133, says almost half of the clerical members and a quarter of the lay members signed.
49. For the complete transcripts of the trials and an excellent discussion of the case see H. Montgomery Hyde, ed., *The Three Trials of Oscar Wilde* (New York: University Books, 1956).
50. Frances Winwar, *Oscar Wilde and the Yellow Nineties* (New York: Harper & Brothers, 1958), p. 304, quotes Headlam as saying Wilde's work "had shown him beauty on a high hill." No source is cited.
51. Jones, *Christian Socialist Revival*, pp. 146-47.
52. Bettany, *Headlam*, p. 130.
53. Sir Compton Mackenzie, *Certain Aspects of Moral Courage* (Garden City: Doubleday and Co., Inc., 1962), p. 61.
54. Ibid., pp. 61-66; Jones, *Christian Socialist Revival*, pp. 145-48; and Bettany, *Headlam*, pp. 129-31.
55. Rupert Hart-Davis, ed., *The Letters of Oscar Wilde* (New York: Harcourt, Brace and World, Inc., 1962), pp. 536-64. There is no record that Wilde ever wrote Headlam a word of thanks for his great generosity. He did, though, send him one of the twenty-four presentation copies of *The Ballad of Reading Gaol*. See the list in Hart-Davis, p. 700.
56. Mackenzie, *Moral Courage*, p. 62.
57. When the hysteria had passed, Adderly and Headlam were reconciled and Adderly made amends for his behavior by visiting Wilde in prison. Bettany, *Headlam*, p. 131.
58. Mackenzie, *Moral Courage*.
59. Bettany, *Headlam*.
60. Jones, *Christian Socialist Revival*, p. 154.
61. For a sympathetic but judicious study of Marson see Maurice B. Reckitt, "Charles Marson and the Real Disorders of the Church," in *For Christ and the People*, pp. 89-135.
62. From the *Church Reformer* in Jones, *Christian Socialist Revival*.
63. Bettany, *Headlam*, p. 91.
64. Jones, *Christian Socialist Revival*, p. 155.
65. Conrad Noel, *Autobiography* (London: J. M. Dent and Sons, 1945), p. 60.
66. Reckitt, *Maurice to Temple*, p. 138.
67. Wilfred S. Knox and Alex R. Vidler, *The Development of Modern Catholicism* (Milwaukee: Morehouse Publishing Company, 1933), p. 94.
68. Branches were opened in both London and Oxford; at Oxford the Guild of St. Matthew was dissolved and reconstituted as the Christian Social Union. Each branch claimed historical precedence. The provisional committee for the union

was set up at a meeting in St. Paul's Chapterhouse in London on June 14, 1889. The Oxford branch was formally constituted on November 16, 1889. For information about this minor squabble see Jones, *Christian Socialist Revival*, pp. 177, 179, 180. At most, it must have been a question of a few days.

69. Binyon, *Christian Socialist Movement*, p. 158.

70. Stephen Paget, *Henry Scott Holland: Memoir and Letters* (New York: E. P. Dutton and Company, 1921), pp. 170-71.

71. Charles Gore, "Holland and the Christian Social Union," in ibid., p. 242.

72. Reckitt, *Faith and Society*, p. 93.

73. Carpenter, *Church and People*, p. 536. Carpenter's discussion of *Lux Mundi*, pp. 536-68, is one of the best I have read.

74. Jones, *Christian Socialist Revival*, p. 164. He is of course talking about the early days of the union.

75. Gore, "Holland and the Union."

76. G. L. Prestige, *The Life of Charles Gore, A Great Englishman* (London: William Heinemann, 1935), p. 25.

77. K. S. Inglis, *Churches and the Working Classes Victorian England* (London: Routledge and Kegan Paul, 1963), p. 276.

78. Albert Mansbridge, *Edward Stuart Talbot and Charles Gore* (London: J. M. Dent and Sons Limited, 1935), p. 29.

79. James Carpenter, *Gore, A Study in Liberal Catholic Thought* (London: The Faith Press, 1960), p. 25.

80. For Westcott see the classic multivolume Victorian biography by Arthur Westcott, *Life and Letters of Brooke Foss Westcott* (London: Macmillan and Co., 1903) or the excellent shorter study by Joseph Clayton, *Bishop Westcott* (London: A. R. Mowbray and Company, 1906). Westcott was painfully shy and felt out of place amid the "muscular Christianity" of a Victorian public school. Gore must have been one of the very few students he influenced; most of the boys held him in a mixture of amusement and awe. See Clayton, pp. 26-46.

81. Prestige, *Life of Gore*, p. 9.

82. Clayton, *Bishop Westcott*, p. 171.

83. Carpenter, *Gore*, pp. 24-25. Despite his desire for ceremonial enrichment, Gore always remained a prayer book Catholic. Prayer book Catholics restored the use of late medieval vestments, gestures, and other appurtenances, but they celebrated mass strictly according to the rite of the Book of Common Prayer. No deletions were permitted, and there were no interpolations from the Roman missal. Prayer book Catholics tried to be English as well as Catholic and they were not Romanizers. The Community of the Resurrection, an Anglican religious community for men founded by Gore, adhered to prayer book Catholic precepts in the conduct of its services. See Anson and Campbell, *Call of the Cloister*, pp. 122-39, esp. 132. Gore's ideas about what was permissible Anglican usage could be quite as rigid as those held by the mid-century Episcopal persecutors of ritualism. His insistence that the Anglican Benedictines

of Caldey Island abandon the use of the *Missale Monasticum* for the Book of Common Prayer and his prohibition of the extraliturgical services of Exposition and Benediction of the Blessed Sacrament sent them on the road to Rome. See Prestige, *Life of Gore*, pp. 339-41, and Peter Anson, *The Benedictines of Caldey* (London: The Catholic Book Club, 1940), pp. 166-69 and the same author's "corrections" in *Abbot Extraordinary* (London: The Faith Press, 1958), pp. 169-74, for details. If Gore was rigid, the Benedictines were excessive; they seem to have been openly Roman in everything except submission to the authority of the Holy See.

84. Ragnar Ekstrom, *The Theology of Charles Gore* (London: C. W. K. Gleerup, 1944), p. 2.
85. From J. Carpenter's introduction to *Lombard Street in Lent*, p. 28.
86. Ibid.
87. Arthur M. Ramsey, *Charles Gore and Anglican Theology* (London: S.P.C.K., 1955), p. 4.
88. Carpenter, *Gore*, p. 267.
89. Paget, *Holland*, p. 3. Mr. Holland was an old-fashioned Tractarian high Tory who never appreciated his son's social and political views. See Spencer L. Holland, "Home Life," in Paget, p. 120.
90. Holland used to refer to the two most famous members of the guild as "Headlong and Shuttlecock." Bettany, *Headlam*, p. 90. It is unlikely, however, that Holland meant any serious disrespect. Part of his boyish fun was a passion for amusing nicknames. See Spencer Holland in Paget, *Holland*, p. 115. His brother believes the passion was inherited from his mother's family!
91. Paget, *Holland*, p. 9-15.
92. Ibid., p. 19.
93. From an account of Holland at Balliol by Lord Kilbrachen, in ibid., p. 24.
94. Ibid., p. 95.
95. Ibid., p. 24.
96. Ibid., p. 41.
97. Bishop Gore, in ibid., p. 248.
98. Jones, *Christian Socialist Revival*, p. 195.
99. All quotations are from a letter from Green, Paget, *Holland*, p. 40.
100. Ibid., p. 21.
101. Ibid., p. 52.
102. Ibid., p. 64. For an excellent statement of Green's opinions about Christianity see his letter to Holland, ibid., pp. 65-68.
103. Ibid., p. 68.
104. Ibid., p. 97.
105. Ibid., p. 100.
106. For Gore's "turning point" see the Catholic sociologist, P. E. T. Widdrington in *Prospects for Christendom*, ed. Maurice B. Reckitt (London: Faber and Faber, 1945), pp. 250-51. Gore wrote Widdrington that it was the Oxfordshire tour and not Maurice's theology that made him a social critic and reformer. For a

discussion of how the "turning point" related to Gore's mature social thought see Carpenter, *Gore*, pp. 244-68.

107. Paget, *Holland*, p. 105.
108. Carpenter, *Gore*, p. 34.
109. Prestige, *Life of Gore*, p. 79.
110. Paget, *Holland*, p. 113.
111. Ibid., p. 169.
112. All quotations from *Christian Economics* in Jones, *Christian Socialist Revival*, pp. 176-77.
113. Ibid.
114. W. J. H. Champion, "Christianity and Politics," in *Lux Mundi, A Series of Studies in the Religion of the Incarnation*, ed. Charles Gore (New York: Lovell, Coryell, and Company, n.d.), pp. 376-77. It is interesting to note that Champion never officially mentions the Incarnation in his discussion of Christianity and property.
115. Charles Gore, "The Holy Spirit and Inspiration," in ibid., p. 301. My discussion is particularly indebted to S. C. Carpenter, *Church and People*, pp. 549-53 and J. Carpenter, *Gore*, pp. 95-105.
116. Prestige, *Life of Gore*, p. 105.
117. Gore, "Holy Spirit and Inspiration," p. 269. Jones, *Christian Socialist Revival*, p. 173 goes much too far when he asserts that Gore's position "directly echoed the idealist principles of T. H. Green and the 'positive state.' " Gore is discussing the church as a social body and salvation as a social process; he does not even mention the state, let alone the "positive state."
118. From the guild's aims, cited in Paget, *Holland*, p. 170.
119. Ibid., p. 243.
120. Ibid., p. 169.
121. Inglis, *Churches and the Working Classes*, p. 277.
122. Holland to Dr. Copleston, cited in Paget, *Holland*, p. 170.
123. Clayton, *Bishop Westcott*, pp. 97-102. The workers returned to work after they accepted a 10 percent reduction in wages, so the settlement was by no means a trade union victory. Management, however, had been holding out for a reduction of 13.5 percent, and Westcott convinced them to moderate their demands. The radicalism of Bishop Westcott's Christian Socialism is questioned by Vidler in *Maurice and Company*, pp. 259-78. Vidler concludes that it was "basically conservative, not radical or egalitarian, adverse to identification with concrete economic remedies."
124. From *The Church Reformer* in Jones, *Christian Socialist Revival*, p. 196.
125. Ibid., pp. 183-84. Also see Inglis, *Churches and the Working Classes*, p. 277.

# CHAPTER FOUR

1. The phrase is quoted in a perceptive analysis of the 1886 election by Howard H. Quint, *The Forging of American Socialism* (Indianapolis: Bobbs-Merrill Company, Inc., 1953) p. 41.

2. Louis F. Post, "The Prophet of San Francisco, Personal Memories and Interpretations of Henry George," in Dombrowski, *Early Days of Christian Socialism*, p. 46.

3. Huntington was not the only Anglican priest in New York City to support Henry George's mayoral candidacy. R. Herber Newton, the rector of All Souls, also backed George. Newton's record as a social reformer was most distinguished, but he was never a radical in the sense that he wanted to replace the status quo with a new order. Newton supported George because he was the reform candidate; Huntington supported George because he believed in the single tax. Also, Newton never adopted the radical propagandistic technique of taking to the streets and haranguing the crowds to drum up votes.

4. Recent issues of *The Holy Cross* magazine show pictures of a young and growing community. The same cannot be said for the Cowley Fathers in Cambridge or the Anglican Benedictines at Two Rivers, Michigan.

5. No confusion exists here. The term *congregational* describes only the church's polity; its theology was Unitarian.

6. Arria G. Huntington, *Memoir and Letters of Frederick Dan Huntington* (Boston: Houghton Mifflin Company, 1906), p. 153. This biography of the bishop of central New York has provided most of my information about F. D. Huntington.

7. For family background, see James Huntington, *Sixth Reunion of the Huntington Family* (Norwich Town, Conn.: Privately printed, 1917). Huntington is very proud of his family and many of his assertions should be taken *cum grano salis*.

8. The descriptive phrase is cited from an article by Frederick Dan Huntington written in 1845 in Vida Dutton Scudder, *Father Huntington* (New York: E. P. Dutton and Co., Inc., 1940), p. 32.

9. Huntington, *Memoir of Huntington*, p. 141.

10. Scudder, *Father Huntington*, p. 37.

11. Ibid., p. 39. For a detailed examination of this issue, see Douglas C. Strange, "The Conversation of F. D. Huntington," *The Historical Magazine of the Protestant Episcopal Church*, Vol. 39 (September 1968): 287-98.

12. Scudder, *Father Huntington*, p. 50.

13. Huntington, *Sixth Reunion*, p. 5.

14. Harvard class book for 1875 cited by Scudder, *Father Huntington*, pp. 60-61.

15. Ibid., pp. 66-67.

16. Ibid., pp. 63-64.

17. Ibid., p. 67.

18. Ibid., p. 77.

19. Ibid., p. 71, from an unpublished manuscript of Mrs. Ruth Huntington Sessions. The two worked closely together at Calvary, and Ruth shared her older brother's enthusiasm.
20. James O. S. Huntington, "Philanthropy: Its Success and Failures," in *Philanthropy and Social Reform* (New York: Thomas Y. Crowell and Company, 1893), p. 138.
21. Ibid., p. 204.
22. Ibid., see pp. 111, 136.
23. Scudder, *Father Huntington*, pp. 40-41.
24. Robert Cheney Smith, S.S.J.E., *The Cowley Fathers in America* (Boston: Privately printed for the Society of Saint John the Evangelist, n.d.), pp. 8-26.
25. Anson and Campbell, *Call of the Cloister*, p. 77.
26. J. O. S. Huntington, "Beginnings of the Religious Life for Man in the American Church," *Historical Magazine of the Protestant Episcopal Church* 2 (March 1933): 40.
27. Anson and Campbell, *Call of the Cloister*, p. 540.
28. Scudder, *Father Huntington*, p. 73.
29. Huntington, "Beginnings of the Religious Life," p. 39.
30. Ibid., p. 40, For Carter, see Anson and Campbell, *Call of the Cloister*, pp. 304-17.
31. Huntington, "Beginnings of the Religious Life".
32. Scudder, *Father Huntington*, pp. 79-80.
33. Huntington, "Beginnings of the Religious Life," p. 40.
34. Smith, *Cowley Fathers*, p. 26.
35. Robert Cheney Smith, S.S.J.E., *The Shrine on Bowdoin Street* (Boston: Privately printed for the Society of St. John the Evangelist, 1958), p. 56.
36. Smith, *Cowley Fathers*, p. 27.
37. The rule is discussed by Alan Whietemore, superior of the Order of the Holy Cross, in his preface to Scudder's *Father Huntington*, p. 11.
38. Ibid., p. 87.
39. See ibid., pp. 91-107 for numerous responses to the profession. Fr. Huntington's brother, George, himself a priest, advised his brother "to consider the requirements of custom in masculine apparel, which forbids the concealment of the feet or ankles. And to give a visible assurance of neat shoes and pantaloons is in itself, desirable."
40. Huntington, "Beginnings of the Religious Life," pp. 41-42.
41. Huntington, "Philanthropy," p. 119.
42. Ibid., p. 120.
43. Scudder, *Father Huntington*, p. 130.
44. Ibid., p. 132.
45. Ibid., p. 131.
46. The guild of the Iron Cross was founded in 1883 by Charles Neal Feild, S.S.J.E., a cleric attached to St. Clement's, Philadelphia. The purpose of the guild was "to attempt to elevate the condition and increase the good qualities of all working men." For further details see Smith, *Cowley Fathers*, pp. 32-37.

NOTES TO PAGES 101-112

47. Scudder, *Father Huntington*, p. 116.
48. Ibid., p. 134. He also spoke out against the nationalistic doctrine that Edward Bellamy proposed in *Looking Backward*.
49. Ibid., p. 135. Huntington wrote relatively little and published even less about the rationale behind his social programs. The biography by his old friend Vida Scudder is therefore the single most important source for this period of his life. My interpretation of Huntington is heavily indebted to her work, although I have often made explicit what is only implicit in her work.
50. May, *Protestant Churches* p. 155.
51. Scudder, *Father Huntington*, p. 141.
52. See ibid., pp. 287-94.
53. Ibid., p. 132.
54. May, *Protestant Churches*, p. 103.
55. Scudder, *Father Huntington*, pp. 164-65.
56. May, *Protestant Churches*, p. 106.
57. Ibid., p. 221.
58. Scudder, *Father Huntington*, p. 123.
59. Ibid., p. 151, from a sermon, "The Haves and the Have Nots," preached in Nebraska.
60. For details see ibid., pp. 122-25.
61. Ibid., p. 161.
62. Abell, *Urban Impact*, p. 112.
63. Ibid.
64. Scudder, *Father Huntington*, p. 162.
65. Quint, *Forging of American Socialism*, p. 111.
66. Huntington, "Beginnings of the Religious Life," p. 42.
67. Ibid., p. 43.
68. Scudder, *Father Huntington*, p. 170.
69. Huntington, "Beginnings of the Religious Life."

# CHAPTER FIVE

1. Quint, *Forging of American Socialism*, p. 109.
2. Christopher L. Webber, "William Dwight Porter Bliss: Priest and Socialist," *Historical Magazine of the Protestant Episcopal Church* 28 (March 1959): 21.
3. May, *Protestant Churches*, p. 246.
4. Webber, "Bliss," p. 13.
5. John Clark Archer, "Edwin Elisha Bliss," in *The Dictionary of American Biography*, ed. Allen Johnsen (New York: Charles Scribner's Sons, 1928), 2: 371. This article is the source for all of my discussion of the elder Bliss.
6. When Edwin Elisha Bliss died in 1892 his son published a moving eulogy in *The Dawn*.

7. Quint writes, "on entering the congregationalist ministry, he [Bliss] knew that his calling was not to convert the heathen of foreign lands."

8. William J. Ghent, "William Dwight Porter Bliss," in *The Dictionary of American Biography*, 2: 377.

9. Mann, *Yankee Reformers*, p. 97.

10. Quint, *Forging of American Socialism*, p. 109.

11. Webber, "Bliss," p. 14.

12. Ghent, "Bliss."

13. Quint, *Forging of American Socialism*, p. 110.

14. Webber, "Bliss," p. 16.

15. See William Dwight Porter Bliss, "Socialism in the Church of England," *The Andover Review* 10 (July-December 1887): 488-503.

16. Ibid., p. 496.

17. Ibid., p. 493. Stewart Headlam would have affirmed that he was a socialist because he was a Catholic priest; Bliss, by contrast, converted to Anglicanism because he had first become a social reformer.

18. Fletcher and Miller, *Church and Industry*, p. 76.

19. *The Dawn* 3 (February 1891): 4.

20. Ibid., 1 (January 1890): 4.

21. Ibid., 3 (February 1891): 4.

22. Quint, *Forging of American Socialism*, pp. 79-82, describes the composition of the first Nationalist Club with wit and thoroughness.

23. Ibid., p. 112. Quint's dating of events is the most precise of all the Bliss commentators and I have relied heavily on it throughout my discussion.

24. William Dwight Porter Bliss, ed., *The New Encyclopedia of Social Reform* (New York: Funk and Wagnalls Co., 1908), p. 263. Horace Dutton, a Congregationalist social reformer and uncle of Vida Dutton Scudder, was the organization's secretary.

25. Hopkins, *Rise of the Social Gospel*, p. 175.

26. Dombrowski, *Early Days of Christian Socialism*, p. 99.

27. *The Dawn* 1 (May 1889): 3. The declaration is also quoted in Dombrowski, *Early Days of Christian Socialism*, pp. 99-100.

28. Ibid.

29. *The Dawn* 1 (May 1889): 5.

30. Hopkins, *Rise of the Social Gospel*, p. 179.

31. *The Dawn* 1 (May 1889): 5.

32. Ibid., 1 (February 1890): 5.

33. Ibid., 2 (June 1890): 92.

34. Quint, *Forging of American Socialism*, p. 117.

35. Ibid.

36. May, *Protestant Churches*, p. 244.

37. *The Dawn* 4 (May 1892): 12.

38. Ibid., 2 (June 1890): 85.

39. Ibid., 3 (December 1890): 8.

40. Ibid.
41. W. D. P. Bliss, *What is Christian Socialism?* (Boston: Office of *The Dawn*, 1894), pp. 7-8.
42. *The Dawn* 4 (May 1892): 7.
43. Ibid., 2 (May 1890): 41.
44. *The Churchman* 61 (April 19, 1890): 485.
45. Quint, *Forging of American Socialism*, p. 118.
46. *The Dawn* 3 (April 1892): 485.
47. Ibid., 2 (May 1890): 42.
48. From the 1893 Massachusetts Convention Journal, in Webber, "Bliss," p. 22.
49. *The Dawn* 3 (August 1891): 13.
50. Ibid., 3 (November 1891): 7.
51. Dombrowski, *Early Days of Christian Socialism*, p. 102.
52. *The Dawn* 3 (November 1891): 8.
53. Dombrowski, *Early Days of Christian Socialism*, p. 97.
54. *The Dawn* 4 (May 1892): 16.
55. Ibid. (October 1892): 4.
56. Quint, *Forging of American Socialism*, p. 119.
57. See above, p. 71.
58. From the *Churchman*, in Abell, *Urban Impact*, p. 107.
59. Quint erroneously described the union as a "Christian Socialist body," a generalization his sources do not support.
60. From an Executive Committee report in Abell, *Urban Impact*, p. 108.
61. Hopkins, *Rise of the Social Gospel*, p. 259.
62. Ibid., p. 262.
63. Ghent, "Bliss," p. 378.
64. Mann, *Yankee Reformers*, p. 98.
65. Abell, *Urban Impact*, p. 108.
66. Fletcher and Miller, *Church and Industry*, p. 83.
67. Abell, *Urban Impact*.
68. See *The Dawn* 6 (May 1894): 67, and 6 (February 1895): 5.
69. Abell, *Urban Impact*, p. 109.
70. Webber, "Bliss," p. 26. Also see *The Dawn* 3 (April 1892): 6-8.
71. *The Dawn* 3 (April 1892): 9.
72. Quint, *Forging of American Socialism*, p. 120.
73. There is some question concerning Vida Scudder's membership in the Church of the Carpenter. For a discussion of the problem, see Chapter Four.
74. For a comprehensive and illuminating discussion of the involvement of Howells and other intellectual reformers, see Clara and Rudolf Kirk, "Howells and the Church of the Carpenter," *New England Quarterly* 32 (1959): 188-206.
75. *The Dawn* 2 (July-August 1890): 10.
76. Hopkins, *Rise of the Social Gospel*, p. 183.
77. From *Socialism and the American Spirit* in Mann, *Yankee Reformers*, p. 93; for Gilman, see pp. 83-86.

78. Dombrowski, *Early Days of Christian Socialism*, p. 104.
79. Hopkins, *Rise of the Social Gospel*, p. 180.
80. May, *Protestant Churches*, p. 243.
81. Webber, "Bliss," p. 24.
82. Webber's article was published in 1959, when the horrors of Stalinism were still very much a living reality.
83. Bliss's prolific oeuvre and the vagueness and obscurity of much of his thought and expression make determining his position a complex task requiring a somewhat lengthy exposition. For reasons of clarity and economy I postpone a comparative discussion of Christian Socialism, socialism and progressive Protestant middle-class reform until Chapter Six when I will use Vida D. Scudder's "Socialism and Spiritual Progress" as a point of focus. Hers is a representative Christian Socialist statement. As mentioned, she attended the Church of the Carpenter and was a member of the Society of Christian Socialists. The work was read to the society, was subsequently reprinted in *The Dawn*, and Bliss praised it highly.
84. *The Christian Union* published a series of articles by Richard T. Ely, "Christian Socialism in England," May 28, June 4, and June 11, 1884, pp. 7-8, in each issue. May, *Protestant Churches*, p. 149. No commentator has directly linked Ely's articles to Bliss's decision to become a reformer, although Hopkins, *Rise of the Social Gospel*, p. 173 and Webber, "Bliss," p. 13, mention a series of articles on social problems featured in *The Christian Union* in 1885 as having influenced Bliss's decision. Neither Hopkins nor Webber cites primary sources to support his contention, but if it is correct, then it is more than likely that Ely's articles were among those Bliss read. Bliss could have read articles published in 1884 and 1885 or Hopkins's dating might be slightly off. It could also be the case that Bliss read the articles in 1884 when they appeared and that they influenced his conversion to Anglicanism and reform the next year. Be that as it may, it is tempting to believe that Bliss read Ely's articles, for if he did, we can then understand how a Congregationalist clergyman became acquainted with the Maurice-Ludlow-Kingsley band of Anglican Christian Socialists.
85. "Seven years ago the writer dreamed of a church different from any church he knew." The year 1885 was seven years before 1892.
86. Ghent, "Bliss."
87. As Arthur Mann points out in "British Social Thought and American Reformers of the Progressive Era," *Mississippi Valley Historical Review* 112 (1956): 672-92, American social reformers in the last decades of the nineteenth century were enormously influenced by British critics. The English influence on Bliss was probably even more significant than that of Bellamy because it was so diverse. For Mann's discussion of Bliss, see pp. 687-88.
88. He, of course, did not neglect them in *The Dawn*, where he had an audience interested in Christian Socialism.
89. Quint, *Forging of American Socialism*, p. 77. Quint's description of Bellamy and nationalism, pp. 72-102, is the finest brief discussion of the topic that I have seen.

90. Edward Bellamy, "First Steps toward Nationalism," *The Forum* 1 (1890): 183.
91. Dombrowski, *Early Days of Christian Socialism*, p. 102.
92. *The Dawn* 1 (September 1889): 4-5.
93. Ibid., 2 (June 1891): 27.
94. Ibid., 2 (September 1890): 197.
95. Dombrowski, *Early Days of Christian Socialism*, p. 109.
96. *The Dawn* 7 (February 1895): 2.
97. Bliss, *New Encyclopedia of Social Reform*, p. 1129.
98. Quint, *Forging of American Socialism*, p. 90, observes that for "the Yankee puritan, Bellamy, equality of wages was an ethical rather than an economic question."
99. *The Dawn* 2 (November 1890): 315.
100. For Bliss's support for specific reforms see Webber, "Bliss," p. 29, Hopkins, *Rise of the Social Gospel*, p. 177, and May, *Protestant Churches*, p. 245. My list of reforms he supported does not purport to be all-inclusive.
101. *The Dawn* 2 (July-August 1890): 110.
102. Ibid., p. 111.
103. Ibid., pp. 110-11.
104. For details of Bliss's activities subsequent to his resignation from the Church of the Carpenter, see Quint, *Forging of American Socialism*, pp. 254-73.
105. Webber, "Bliss," pp. 29-30.
106. Quint, *Forging of American Socialism*, pp. 243-44 discusses Bliss's reaction to the election of 1896.
107. Ibid., p. 261.
108. For De Leon and the Socialist Labor Party, see ibid., pp. 142-74.
109. Ibid., p. 124. Quint's analysis of the S.L.P. supports Bliss's objections to them.
110. For Social Democratic factionalism, see ibid., pp. 319-88.
111. Bliss's criticism is from an article in another of his short-lived magazines, *Social Unity*, ibid., p. 273.
112. Ghent, "Bliss," p. 328.

# CHAPTER SIX

1. Horace Scudder's moving record of his brother David's life, *The Life and Letters of David Coit Scudder, a Missionary in Southern India* (New York: Hurd and Houghton, 1864), is the source of my biographical data. For David's influence on his daughter, see her autobiography, *On Journey*, especially pp. 15-17, 38-40, and 433-34. The work concluded with a quotation from the *Bhagavad Gita*, a book Vida found in her father's library.
2. Mann, *Yankee Reformers*, p. 219.
3. Scudder, *On Journey*, p. 19.
4. Ibid., p. 39. The family took denominational differences very seriously. When she was fourteen, Vida confided to her "dearest friend," Grandmother Scudder,

that Phillips Brooks was preparing her for Episcopal confirmation. "Very stern, straight and grave, she said: 'I am glad your father did not live to see this day.'" Ibid., p. 37.

5. Ibid., p. 49. Her last book, published when she was ninety-one, bears the significant title, *My Quest for Reality.*

6. Scudder, *On Journey*, p. 44.

7. Ibid., p. 41.

8. Ibid., p. 73.

9. For a discussion of the important role played by the new social sciences in the development of social reform, see T. B. Bottomore, *Critics of Society* (New York: Random House, 1968), pp. 22-26.

10. Brooks avidly championed Maurice's incarnational theology, but not his Christian Socialism. Social issues did not concern Brooks until late in his life, and, even then, he never became a major reform leader. The most useful modern study of this great preacher and significant religious leader is Raymond W. Albright, *Focus on Infinity: a Life of Phillips Brooks* (New York: The Macmillan Company, 1961). For his ideas on social reform, see pp. 158, 358, 379. In her later years Vida Scudder valued Brooks as a "great spiritual leader" but she recognized that he failed "to draw out the social significance of the Gospels." See Vida D. Scudder, *The Church and the Hour* (New York: E. P. Dutton and Company, 1917), p. 4.

11. Scudder, *On Journey*, p. 37.

12. Ibid., p. 72.

13. As always, popular religious practice lagged behind contemporary theology. Vida was fortunate to have been raised in the Broad Church tradition of Trinity Church. If she had attended an Evangelical or Anglo-Catholic parish she probably would have found a similar emphasis on the atonement, if not on the techniques of revivalism. The Evangelicals' interpretation of the atonement was one of the greatest stumbling blocks for the new generation. Jane Addams also had problems with the traditional Evangelical orthodoxy. See Christopher Lasch, *The New Radicalism in America* (New York: Alfred Knopf, 1965), pp. 3-38.

14. Scudder, *On Journey*, "Crudities" suggests that personal religious taste played an important part in the younger generation's revolt against Evangelical revivalism. Techniques that had been successful on the frontier during the great awakening had a negative effect on the younger members of the educated urban upper middle class. Sharing an animus common to most Anglo-Catholics, Vida Scudder suggests that "the stern terrors of Calvinism" were the *fons et origo mali*, but it is very probable that Calvin would have been as critical of revivalism as any Broad Church or High Church Anglican, perhaps even more so.

15. Ibid., p. 92.

16. Ibid., p. 78.

17. A strange choice for a well-bred young Anglo-Catholic, but her action is not unique. Beatrice Webb, a quasi-agnostic theist, did the same thing. Something about the crude raw vigor of the army must have been attractive to these

refined young ladies. To both, I think, it represented an avenue of escape from the hothouse gentility that surrounded upper-middle-class females. The army suggested the "real life" that they both believed they needed. But whatever it may have symbolized, the army's concern for the poor was real; it was doing something definite to help them. Also, we must remember, the army welcomed women into its ranks.

18. Scudder, *On Journey*, p. 92. Vida Scudder was, of course, only one of many young people in her generation who became social reformers after returning home from a European journey. For an illuminating discussion of the wider context, see Mann, "British Social Thought."

19. Scudder, *On Journey*.

20. Ibid., p. 89.

21. Ibid., p. 94.

22. The problem is discussed in some detail and with some retrospective ironic humor in "Influence and Independence. A Discussion of Individualism," by Miss S. K. and Miss V. D. S. *The Andover Review* 13 (1890): 167-81. *The Andover Review*, which published several of Vida Scudder's early works was a liberal Congregational journal printed by Houghton Mifflin.

23. Scudder, *On Journey*, p. 92.

24. The thesis was published in two issues by *The Andover Review* 8 (1887): 225-46; 351-66, and was later incorporated in her first important book of literary criticism, *The Life of the Spirit in the Modern English Poets*.

25. Vida Scudder, "The Moral Dangers of Musical Devotees," *The Andover Review*, 8 (1887): 49.

26. Ibid., pp. 52, 51, 50.

27. Ibid., pp. 49-53. In later life the author regarded her early broadside against music with some amusement. "My position was slightly impertinent," she confesses, "in view of the fact that I could never tell one tune from another." Scudder, *On Journey*, p. 93. She soon outgrew the excesses of of her ideological position, but her aversion to *fin de siècle* aestheticism reappears in her first autobiographical novel, *A Listener in Babel*, written at least fifteen years later.

28. For the complete text see F. M. B[rooks] and V. D. S[cudder]. *Mitsu-Yu-Nissi, or the Japanese Wedding* (Chicago: T. S. Denison, 1887). The central question seems to be summed up on page 15, "Has knowledge taught you to value your own happiness above the good of your own people?"

29. The quotations from "The Educated Woman as a Social Factor" are in ibid. My interpretation of Vida Scudder at this stage in her career draws heavily on Mann's work. *On Journey* is inadequate as a source for this period of her life. Mann relates that when he talked to Vida Scudder in the 1950s she had forgotten her old hostility to the feminists.

30. Scudder, *On Journey*, pp. 124, 114.

31. Mary Barnett Gilson, *What's Past is Prologue* (New York: Harper & Brothers, 1940), pp. 12-13. Another vivid impression of Vida Scudder as a teacher was recorded by the Jewish essayist and short story writer Ruth Sapin Hurowitz in

her "Coming of Age at Wellesley," *The Menorah Journal*, vol. 38, no. 2 (Autumn 1950): 231-42. Inspired by Scudder and Emily Green Balch, another Wellesley teacher whom I describe in more detail later, Ruth Hurowitz played an active role in Denison House during her college years. After graduating she devoted the next four years to settlement house work. Of Vida Scudder she writes: "She was best known on campus for her course on 'Social Ideals in English Letters.' To my keen regret I was unable to take it because of conflict with other courses. . . . She was one of the few socialists I ever knew who was at the same time a person of fervid religious faith. A small squat figure dressed nearly always in unrelieved black, there was about her a firm craggy quality. It was unthinkable that, like many another religious and humanitarian leaders of that day and this, she would ever be dismayed by the battering difficulties assailing every sincere reformer, that she would ever detour along some sunnier, pleasanter highway. No smug 'peace of mind'—or 'peace of soul'—for such as she. Whether conversing at Scribbler's Club [a small student-faculty group devoted to discussing practical writing problems] meetings with less that a score of girls, or talking in her rapid, vivid style to several hundred in lecture hall or at vesper services, her electric fervor and unquenchable religious faith were projected upon listeners. Here indeed was not just a profession of faith, but faith itself." It is interesting to note the positive image that Vida Scudder projected to her students. This woman who exuded faith and inspired it in others was often troubled in her inner life by profound doubts. Frequently she had to combat despair.

32. For example, see Max J. Herzberg et al., *The Readers' Encyclopedia of American Literature* (New York: Thomas Crowell Company, 1962), p. 1009.

33. Mann, *Yankee Reformers*, p. 227.

34. Vida D. Scudder, *The Witness of Denial* (New York: E. P. Dutton and Company, 1895), pp. 5-6.

35. For Maurice's formal controversial style at its best, see *The Kingdom of Christ* of the *Theological Essays*.

36. Scudder, *Witness*, p. 42.

37. Ibid., p. 40.

38. Ibid., pp. 43-44.

39. Ibid., p. 68.

40. Ibid., pp. 80, 87.

41. Ibid., pp. 91-92.

42. An excellent summary statement of Maurice's Christology can be found in Vidler, *Maurice and Company*, pp. 38-62. Maurice is not directly cited in *Witness* because, as the author explains in the preface, "the critical accompaniment has been disgarded." Maurice is, though, specifically mentioned as one of the writers considered in the lectures from which the book was taken. Maurice's Christology and the Catholic faith were not as antithetical as Vida Scudder believed; certainly Maurice did not contradict the teachings of many of the fathers. But the important point here is that Vida Scudder accepted Maurice instead of what she understood to be Catholic faith.

43. Scudder, *Witness*, p. 92.
44. Ibid., pp. 103, 113.
45. Ibid., p. 111.
46. Ibid., pp. 115-17.
47. Ibid.
48. Ibid., p. 129.
49. Ibid., pp. 139, 141.
50. Ibid., p. 149. It is worth noting that no mention of the evangelical revival is made here. Only the High and Broad Church traditions are accorded the recognition they deserve.
51. Ibid., p. 152. How amused Stewart Headlam would have been by her description of the church purged of power and privilege. Certainly her assertions were far too sanguine on this point.
52. It might be argued that Coleridge was more important as a critic, philosopher, and theologian than as a poet. If his influence as a poet was wide, the size of his work was small. Scudder revered Coleridge as a sage and religious leader and her infrequent comments on his poetic works are favorable. See Vida D. Scudder, *The Life of the Spirit in the Modern English Poets* (Boston: Houghton Mifflin Company, 1895), pp. 61, 63, 146-47, 175, 312. She strongly disapproved of Byron on moral grounds; probably this was her reason for excluding him. The most emphatically negative comment in the book concerns Byron: "the vicious brilliancy of *Don Juan* signals his spiritual end" (p. 231).
53. There is much trenchant social commentary in this book, particularly in "Wordsworth and the New Democracy" and "Ideals of Redemption Medieval and Modern," and it is the intention of the author to relate poetry to its social context. Nonetheless, this is not a social history. Vida Scudder examines the development of the idea of social reform, not its practice. The French Revolution is considered, for example, because it changed the mental outlook of Wordsworth and Shelley.
54. Compare Scudder, *The Life of the Spirit*, pp. 5-55 and *The Andover Review* 18 (1887): 225-46; 351-66.
55. Her approach to literary studies had already been formulated when she wrote her introduction to *Prometheus Unbound*. In a preface she announces her intention to write a "study of the drama as a work of art and as an historic product." Percy Bysshe Shelley, *Prometheus Unbound*, edited with an introduction by Vida D. Scudder (Boston: D. C. Heath and Company, 1892), p. iv. Her introduction to *Prometheus Unbound* also appeared that year in a three-part series in *The Atlantic Monthly* 70 (July-December 1892): 106-15, 261-72, and 391-401. The texts are virtually identical.
56. See Vida D. Scudder, "The Poetry of Mathew Arnold," *The Andover Review* 13 (1890): 232-49. Over the years her ideas about Arnold did not alter radically but her expression of these ideas improved considerably.
57. Scudder, *Life of the Spirit*, p. 4.
58. Ibid., p. 3.
59. Ibid., p. 245.

60. Ibid., p. 342. For the full statement of the theme, see also p. 341.
61. Ibid., pp. 9-10.
62. She did not say that they anticipated the full scientific principle of natural selection, only that these works spoke of evolution as distinct from the current idea of successive special creations. See ibid., pp. 10-12.
63. Ibid., pp. 57-96, especially pp. 73-73, 90-92.
64. The flaws in Vida Scudder's interpretation have been noted. For example, Jerome H. Buckley in a brief history of the criticism of Victorian poetry writes, "By an odd arrangement of materials that permits Browning to come last, Vida Scudder's *The Life of the Spirit in the Modern English Poets*, though published in the skeptical nineties, concludes that Victorian poetry has moved joyously from Romantic pantheism toward Christianity." See Jerome H. Buckley, "The Content of Victorian Poetry," in *The Victorian Poets*, ed. Frederic E. Faverty (Cambridge: Harvard University Press, 1968), p. 22.
65. Scudder, *Life of the Spirit*, p. 333.
66. Mann, *Yankee Reformers*, p. 220.
67. Vida Dutton Scudder, *Social Ideas in English Letters*, edited with a new introduction by Martin Tucker (New York: Johnson Reprint Corporation, 1969), pp. vi-vii.
68. Vida D. Scudder, *Social Ideals in English Letters* (Boston: Houghton Mifflin Company, 1898), pp. 3, 5.
69. Ibid., p. 20.
70. Ibid., pp. 16, 76-77.
71. Ibid., p. 113.
72. Ibid., p. 117.
73. Ibid., p. 119.
74. Barely a page is devoted to this stage of development in the text. Perhaps the author did not wish to retrace ground already covered in *The Life of the Spirit*, although—strangely enough—she never directs her reader to that earlier work.
75. Scudder, *Social Ideals*, p. 161.
76. Ibid., p. 127.
77. Ibid., p. 214.
78. Ibid., p. 193.
79. Ibid., pp. 190, 187.
80. Ibid., p. 179.
81. Ibid., p. 258.
82. Ibid., p. 265.
83. Ibid., p. 277.
84. Ibid., p. 280.
85. Ibid., p. 288. This disclaimer is the only time Marx's name is mentioned in the argument.
86. Ibid., pp. 300-301.
87. Ibid., p. 318.
88. Scudder, *On Journey*, pp. 109-10. See also Mann, *Yankee Reformers*, p. 223, and Davis, *Spearheads for Reform*, pp. 10-11.

89. V. D. S. [Vida Dutton Scudder], "A Propitious Outlook," n.d., p. 1, a short, printed brochure, privately circulated among the friends of the settlement house project to keep them abreast of events. From internal evidence, it was written between May and October 1889.
90. Davis, *Spearheads for Reform*, p. 261.
91. Not quite entirely; "A Propitious Outlook" mentions that there is room for a man in the basement.
92. Mann, *Yankee Reformers*, p. 223.
93. "A Propitious Outlook," p. 2.
94. From "A Protest," June 16, 1887, in Mann, "British Social Thought," p. 683.
95. "A Propitious Outlook," p. 2.
96. Ibid., p. 1; *On Journey*, p. 141. Ninety-five Rivington Street was never the "bleak tenement building" described by Davis, *Spearheads for Reform*, p. 11. Nor should it have been one. No concerned parents could allow their daughter to subject herself to the living conditions of a tenement. The settlement was, beyond doubt, a genteel establishment, but one should not for that reason adopt a condescending attitude toward the inhabitants. Silver hinges may have been excessive, but a house of "mansion" size was required to house seven women and give them room to work. In 1889 two servants were hardly too many; someone had to keep the house in order while the volunteers were doing their work. "No one," Vida Scudder wrote, "can accuse Andover House or the Rivington Street settlement of luxury." "The Place of College Settlements;" *Andover Review* 18 (October 1892): 341.
97. Scudder, *On Journey*, pp. 139-40.
98. Scudder, "The Place of College Settlements," p. 345.
99. Davis, *Spearheads for Reform*, pp. 141-42.
100. Scudder, *Social Ideals*, pp. 296-97.
101. Davis, *Spearheads for Reform*, p. 15.
102. *The Dawn*, vol. 3, no. 8 (March 18, 1891): 4, and vol. 3, no. 13 (August 1891): 1.
103. Ibid., vol. 4, no. 12 (December 1894): 179.
104. Scudder, *On Journey*. p. 165.
105. Alexander C. Zabriskie, *Bishop Brent* (Philadelphia: The Westminster Press, 1948), pp. 32-43.
106. The evidence concerning Vida Scudder's association with the two churches is confusing. In *On Journey*, p. 165, she recounts that Bliss founded his Church of the Carpenter and that "Robert Woods, Harry Lloyd, Mr. McNeil *and I were of his congregation*" (emphasis mine). Yet when *The Dawn*, vol. 5, no. 5 (February 4, 1893): 1, published a list of the church's charter members Vida Scudder's name was not on the list. It is possible that she joined later, but further references to her in *The Dawn* seem to belie the fact. On February 18, 1894, "the Church of the Carpenter passed an especial vote of thanks to Miss Vida L. [*sic*] Scudder, for her efforts on its behalf, at the time of its darkest hour . . . now when the church seems to be in the way of prosperity, *it*

*remembers its friends*" (emphasis mine). Ibid., vol. 6, no. 4 (April, 1894): 58. Surely had she been a member she would have been called "devoted parishoner" or some such name, not simply a friend. On one occasion, of course, such a minor slip-up could have been made easily, but in *The Dawn*'s next issue we read, "The work of the parish has the cordial endorsement of the Bishop . . . Miss Vida D. Scudder, . . . and others." Vol. 6, no. 5 (May 1894): 79. It is odd that "the cordial endorsement" of a member of the parish would have to be pointed out; one would assume that it would be taken for granted. No one piece of evidence here is conclusive, but taken together they very strongly suggest that *On Journey* to the contrary, Vida Scudder was not a member of the Church of the Carpenter. *On Journey* was written forty-five years after the formation of the Church of the Carpenter and the author's memory could have been hazy at this point. Also, the activities that she describes attending are more reminiscent of the Brotherhood of the Carpenter that met in the afternoon for evensong, supper and discussion. Since most of the members of the church also belonged to the brotherhood it is easy to understand how forty-five years later one could become confused. Finally, "were of his congregation" suggest but does not explicitly state that she was a member of the parish. Perhaps she was not confused, but unintentionally used words easily open to misinterpretation. In any event, even if she was not formally a member she was closely associated with the Church of the Carpenter.

But that is only part of the confusion. Nowhere in *On Journey* does she directly state that she was a member of St. Stephen's. She mentions that she became acquainted with Charles Brent, rector of a newly organized parish noted for "queer Anglo-Catholic ways . . . unconventional social thinking and vital Christian practice" soon after Denison House was established (p. 159). Later she refers to him as her rector. Since Brent was elevated to the episcopacy after having served as rector only of St. Stephen's, it is obvious that she was a member of that parish. This she reveals in a letter to Marion Talbot, "You know that I belong to St. Stephen's parish." The contents of the letter suggest that she has been a member of the parish "for a long time," but I can definitely state only that she became a member of St. Stephen's sometime between 1892, when Denision House opened, and December 1899, when the letter was written.

107. Emily Malbone Morgan, *A Little White Shadow* (Chicago: G. P. Brown, 1889).
108. Scudder, *On Journey*, pp. 113-14, 379.
109. Ibid., p. 377. Biographical information about Emily Morgan appears on pp. 377-82. The most comprehensive source for Emily Morgan is Vida Dutton Scudder, ed., *Letters to Her Companions by Emily Malbone Morgan*, with a biographical sketch by Emily Sophie Brown (South Byfield, Mass.: Privately printed for The Society of the Companions of the Holy Cross, 1944). Equally important is Emily Malbone Morgan, *Prior Rahere's Rose* (Hartford: Belknap and Warfield, 1893), a sentimental but moving tale of redemption. This brief piece of fiction exposes the character of the woman who wrote the letters and who established the vacation houses. It is a period piece, and a casual reader unacquainted with the author's life might be tempted to dismiss it as merely

quaint; but it is more illuminating than factual biography. One can see how a mystical Anglo-Catholic piety enamored with the Age of Faith led to an abiding concern for the spiritual and economic deprivations of the poor, and one can understand why Morgan lived a life of self-denying social service. Amid the incense-scented prose there is her important message: visions often give birth to noble acts and a man's "good works" can live after him and benefit others. I am indebted to William George Kibitz, formerly rector of Christ Church, New Haven, and Richard Brumbaugh, sometime member of that parish, for sharing with me some of their personal knowledge about Morgan.

110. For a fuller discussion of Scudder's conception of stewardship see, Vida Dutton Scudder, *The Christian Attitude Toward Private Property* (Milwaukee: Morehouse Publishing Company, 1934).

111. Scudder, *On Journey*, pp. 384-86. See also "A Plea for Social Intercession," in *The Church and the Hour*, pp. 119-31.

112. Lasch, p. 271.

113. Walter Fuller Taylor, *The Economic Novel in America* (New York: Octagon Books, Inc., 1964), p. 97. Taylor's generalization is faulty because it fails to realize how sex can alter a point of view. Upper-class women had not all been, in Archbishop Laud's vivid phrase, "grinding the faces of the poor"; many of them were devoted to acts of self-sacrifice and charity. The guilt was all the more profound because it could not be traced to specific activities that could be abandoned for the pursuit of nobler goals: education, art, social reform, etc. The women had the leisure to pursue noble goals, but their inherited advantages and their very style of life, as noble, elevated, and cultivated as it might be, made them unwilling accessories before and after the fact to the crimes of society. Theirs was a tragic predicament for the morally sensitive, and they had the leisure to brood over moral problems. Only Arthur Mann recognizes the importance of sexual distinction. See *Yankee Reformers*, pp. 217-28. See also Lasch's description of Jane Addams in *The New Radicalism*. Lasch does not explicitly raise the issue, but his information is useful.

114. Walter B. Rideout, *The Radical Novel in the United States* (New York: Hill and Wang, 1966), p. 27.

115. Scudder, *On Journey*, p. 181.

116. Compare Vida Dutton Scudder, *A Listener in Babel* (Boston: Houghton Mifflin Company, 1903), p. 43, and *On Journey*, p. 176.

117. Scudder, *Listener*, p. 11.

118. There is no evidence to suggest that Walter Ferguson was drawn directly from life. I think he is an abandoned "imaginary possibility." In *On Journey*, p. 212, the author confesses, "Until I was thirty, I wanted terribly to fall in love. I didn't care so much about being loved; almost any woman can manage that if she cares to try. But I was so eager for the experience without which, all literature assured me, life misses its consummation. Once or twice I tried to compass it, but I couldn't." The romantic anguish, though, is not less real for being imaginary. The closest prototype for Dorothy, Walter Ferguson's beloved, is Clara French, Vida Scudder's dearest girlhood friend, who died in 1888.

Commenting on French's death in *On Journey*, p. 113, Scudder writes, "I told myself that my whole life was changed. And so it was. From the day that the friend of my youth died, the door to what people call passion swung to in my heart. That door had previously been open, and open to a stormy land. My years have been passed in a calmer air." It is more than likely that Vida Scudder transformed her own anguish over the death of Clara French into Hilda's painful experience of unrequited love. Certainly both Hilda and Vida used the experience of deep personal loss as an occasion for perceiving a wider "brotherhood of pain" that bound mankind together, and both Hilda and Vida attempted to assuage pain by losing themselves in service to the less fortunate. The intensity that most people put into sexual relationships Vida Scudder directed toward social reform and friendship. This is made especially clear in the novels. The relationship between Raniero and Lariella in *The Disciple of a Saint* is half love, half friendship. The best example of an intense friendship is Brother John's affection for Pierre. Inadvertently, Vida Scudder was living proof of the feminist assertion that a woman did not have to marry to lead a full and useful life. See *On Journey*, pp. 210-12, 217-28, and Vida Dutton Scudder, "Plato as Novelist," *The Yale Review* 4 (1914-1915): 791-95.

119. Vida Scudder believed that one of the most important contributions made by the settlement house movement was the change they effected in the minds of the volunteers. In the long run she felt that this change was more significant than the settlement's ability to improve the living conditions of the poor. Alan Davies, historian of the settlement house movement, agrees.

120. In the early 1900s the gifts of the robber barons raised many of the same moral problems posed today by United States government grants. Vida Scudder became personally involved when Wellesley College accepted money from Standard Oil.

121. Scudder, *Listener*, pp. 153-54.

122. Ibid., p. 213.

123. Ibid., p. 214.

124. Ibid., p. 217.

125. Scudder had previously, of course, extolled the social value of intimate personal communication between the classes in *Social Ideals in English Letters*, p. 296. Hilda's experience is an expression of the same idea on the individual level. The important point is that the poor can contribute as much to the wealthy as the wealthy can to the poor.

126. Scudder, *Listener*, p. 243. That Huntington is made much of while Bliss is ignored would suggest that the former played a more significant role in the author's personal development. I find this especially significant because Bliss was in Boston (Brenton) at the time the novel takes place and Huntington was not.

127. Ibid., p. 263.

128. Ibid., pp. 285, 288.

129. Mildred Ellis's work and personality bring Emily Malbone Morgan to mind. Like Hilda, though, Mildred represents what her prototype would have liked to have done, rather than what she was able to do.

130. Scudder, *Listener*, p. 319.
131. In 1901 Vida Scudder suffered a breakdown far more serious than Hilda's. The autobiography says little about *A Listener in Babel*; the author did not think that her first novel was an unqualified success. Biographical sources give no clues to establish when it was written, but internal evidence suggests a postbreakdown dating. It was published two years after her initial breakdown, before her illness was cured. The author mentions that she wrote sonnets while recovering in Europe; she does not mention working on a novel. Two sonnets written at this time, however, are included in the novel, on pages 24 and 212-13. They are well integrated into the text and do not appear to be an afterthought. The author's decision to place Hilda's dedication to social reform in Assisi suggests a postbreakdown dating. Also Hilda's return to her old profession may mirror Scudder's decision to return to teaching. But *A Listener in Babel* says nothing about the causes of the author's recovery. She developed a new center of interest, which gave her a reason to continue. That Hilda does not share this new interest may suggest that the author herself had not yet become fully aware of its importance when she wrote this book. *A Listener in Babel* looks back to the nineties and sums up that period. Like her heroine, Vida Scudder was preparing for new departures, but these are not fully manifested in this book.
132. Scudder, *On Journey*, p. 168.
133. "Socialism and Spiritual Progress" is the only Anglican exposition of the Christian Socialist position not by William Dwight Porter Bliss discussed by Quint in *Forging of American Socialism*. See pp. 198-99.
134. The Reverend Jesse H. Jones, a Congregationalist minister from North Abington, Massachusetts, had championed Christian Socialism during the early 1870s, but his was a lone voice. As Ralph Henry Gabriel remarked, "When Jones advocated socialism he put himself beyond the pale of respectability." Christian Socialism as a movement began to develop late in the 1880s only after Henry George and Edward Bellamy had helped make socialism respectable among the more progressive elements of the educated middle class. For more detailed treatments of Jones see Gabriel, *The Course of American Democratic Thought* (New York: Ronald Press Company, 1940), pp. 308-9; Dombrowski, *Early Days of Christian Socialism*, pp. 77-83; Hopkins, *Rise of the Social Gospel*, pp. 42-49; May, *Protestant Churches*, pp. 75-79; and Mann, *Yankee Reformers*, pp. 86-90.
135. Quint, *Forging of American Socialism*, p. 35.
136. Lyman Abbott, "Christianity versus Socialism," *North American Review* 148 (1889): 453. More than once in the course of this article Abbott's position reminds one of Dr. Wilkinson in *A Listener in Babel*. His Christ-based concern for individualism led him to take positions that even then must have aroused either fury or hilarity. For example, "It is not the business of ministers and churches to make clean streets or improved tenements. . . . It is their business, if they preach to the poor, to preach such a gospel of cleanliness and order and

decency that no man in his poverty will consent to live without these three things—fresh air, fresh water, God's sunlight" p. 452.

137. Edward S. Parsons, "A Christian Critique of Socialism," *The Andover Review* 11 (1889): 604.

138. For descriptions of the profound impression made by Darwin and his popularizing disciple, Herbert Spencer—whose conclusions often went beyond those of his cautious mentor—on American religion, see the classic account by Richard Hofstadter, *Social Darwinism in American Thought* (Philadelphia: University of Pennsylvania Press, 1944), pp. 11-17, 86-91. Also useful, though heavily indebted to Hofstadter's treatment, is Merle Curti, *The Growth of American Thought* (New York: Harper & Row, 1964), pp. 533-39, 560-63.

139. Gabriel, *American Democratic Thought*, p. 173.

140. Vida D. Scudder, "Socialism and Spiritual Progress—a Speculation," *The Andover Review* 16 (1891): 49.

141. Ibid., p. 50. This passage suggests that she was not only familiar with Edward Parsons's "Christian Critique of Socialism," but also that her own speculation was an attempt to refute his argument.

142. Ibid., pp. 50-51.

143. Hofstadter, *Social Darwinism*, p. 19. Three years later Vida Scudder took on Herbert Spencer again in *The Witness of Denial*, where she attacked his religious position.

144. Scudder, "Socialism and Spiritual Progress," p. 45. This statement reveals just how high-minded the moral idealists of that era could be.

145. Ibid., p. 55. The English agnostic philosopher and reformer Bertrand Russell made a similar observation nearly thirty years later in his *Proposed Roads to Freedom* (New York: Henry Holt and Company, 1919). Indeed, much of his defense of socialism is not unlike Scudder's.

146. Scudder, "Socialism and Spiritual Progress,"p. 49.

147. Ibid., p. 57.

148. Ibid., pp. 58-59.

149. Ibid., p. 61.

150. Ibid., p. 62.

151. Ibid., p. 65.

152. Ibid., p. 66.

153. Ibid., p. 67.

154. David F. Bowers, "The Socialist Philosophy of History," in Donald D. Egbert and Stow Persons, eds., *Socialism and American Life* (Princeton: Princeton University Press, 1952), 1: 422.

155. Scudder, *On Journey*, p. 163.

# CHAPTER SEVEN

1. The "Social Creed of the Churches" issued in 1908 by the Federal Council of Churches is only the most obvious indication that mainline Protestantism had appropriated the Social Gospel. The Federal Council spoke for institutional elite of the Protestant denominations; certainly there were many within each denomination who either rejected or ignored the message of the Social Gospel.
2. Hopkins, *Rise of the Social Gospel*, p. 70.
3. Donald B. Meyer, *The Protestant Search for Political Realism* (Berkeley: University of California Press, 1960), p. 232.
4. Scudder, *On Journey*, p. 231.
5. Ibid., p. 179.
6. Ibid., p. 175.
7. Ibid., pp. 179-80.
8. Two years earlier, Vida Scudder had rehearsed the arguments against accepting such funds in "Ill Gotten Gifts to Colleges," *Atlantic Monthly* 86 (July-December 1900): 675-79. The issue is considered in the abstract and no names are mentioned, but the administrators and trustees of Wellesley College hardly could have remained oblivious to the fact that their decision was under fire.
9. Scudder, *On Journey*, p. 180. She had singled out "the surprising spread of practical fellowship between members of the alienated classes" in *Social Ideals in English Letters* as the single most important movement toward social regeneration to become apparent in the previous decade. Feeling cut off from the most vital aspect of the reform movement must have been an incredibly frustrating experience. Her sense of pessimism and frustration is evident in two articles written at this time, "Democracy and Society" and "Democracy and the Churches," *Atlantic Monthly* 90 (July-December 1902): 348-51, 521-27. Both articles address themselves to the question of communication and fellowship between the separated classes and the conclusion reached is that not enough is being done either in the church or in secular society. Neither article is openly pessimistic—Vida Scudder almost never voiced her fears and discouragements in her propagandistic work—but the optimism that had characterized her work in the nineties is missing. Her tone now is sober and touched with melancholy; the prophetic note of judgment is heard more frequently.
10. Vida D. Scudder, *Socialism and Character* (Boston: Houghton Mifflin Company, 1912), pp. 18-22. The whole of Chapter I is an extremely important source for her thoughts at the period of her breakdown. Her breakdown is never mentioned here, just as her autobiography never mentions her conviction that reform had failed. Only by combining these sources can we arrive at a deeper appreciation of the causes of her breakdown. Note also the repetition of the demonic image first introduced in conjunction with Hilda's crisis in *A Listener in Babel*.
11. For a stimulating discussion and critique of social gospel optimism, see Dombrowski, *Early Days of Christian Socialism*, pp. 22-29. His position reflects

strong neo-orthodox and Marxist influences, but if his biases are recognized and taken into account, his analysis remains enlightening.

12. Scudder, *On Journey*, p. 238.
13. Ibid., p. 239.
14. Ibid., pp. 239, 241.
15. It is the significance of the experience and its results, not the specific character of the experience that I am comparing. Reacting against the excesses of Evangelicalism, as so many of her generation did, Vida Scudder does not record a classic conversion experience. Her account in *On Journey* is more low-keyed and breezy than either Luther's or Wesley's.
16. Scudder, *On Journey*, p. 241.
17. Ibid., p. 252.
18. Ibid., p. 254.
19. E. P. Dutton and Company was the American agent for Dent's publishing house and Dent was a personal friend.
20. The book is more than an edition of St. Catherine's letters. Scudder not only selected and translated the letters she considered the most significant from the four volume Italian edition, but also interspersed the letters with a narrative commentary. She refers to the book as an attempt at "informal biography."
21. One letter from St. Catherine to Raniero di Landoccio dei Pagliaresi appears in Vida D. Scudder, *The Letters of St. Catherine of Siena* (London: J. M. Dent and Company, 1905), p. 93. Whenever St. Catherine speaks in the novel her words are taken from the letters or other historical records. Since St. Catherine never learned how to write, we cannot be sure that these are her exact words, but Scudder was as faithful to the saint as the evidence would allow.
22. The historical data appear in the introduction to Vida Scudder, *The Disciple of a Saint* (London: Dent, 1907), pp. vii-xiv.
23. Scudder, *On Journey*, p. 243.
24. The quotation from St. Catherine's letters, "Care not to present a finished work to God, who is infinite love, and demands from thee only infinite desire," stands as an epigraph to *The Disciple of a Saint*. After her "conversion" this phrase became one of Vida Scudder's favorite quotations. Her bookplate, copied from Durer's etching of St. Jerome in his study, bears a complementary message taken from Robert Browning's "Grammarian's Funeral": "Man has Forever."
25. Scudder, *Disciple*, p. 239.
26. The new order envisioned by Catherine was based on traditional contemporary social ideas, but if these ideals had been put into practice the result would have been radically new.
27. Scudder, *Disciple*, p. 381.
28. The association of success and salvation, failure and sin has been incorrectly ascribed to John Calvin. It was in fact a corruption of and commercialization of English Puritan ideas about predestination. See M. M. Knappen, *Tudor Puritanism* (Chicago: University of Chicago Press, 1965), pp. 412-23.
29. Scudder, *Disciple*, pp. 378-79.
30. Ibid., pp. 379, 381.

31. Scudder, *On Journey*, p. 110.
32. *The Social Teaching of the Christian Year* was not published until 1921, but the Cambridge Conference lectures on which she expanded in this book were delivered in 1918.
33. Huntington said that Scudder "had one of the most brilliant minds I have ever known." Her brilliance, however, according to Huntington, made her something of an "intellectual snob" who "did not suffer fools gladly." Scudder was aware of this aspect of her personality and tried to balance it with humility and a self-deprecating wit.
34. Scudder, *Socialism and Character*, pp. vi-viii. She also affirms, though, "that all blood circulates perforce to the same rhythm, and that only when the contribution of the races [read also, classes] shall blend in one can this country attain her destiny."
35. From the committee's statement of purpose, in Mercedes M. Randall, *Improper Bostonian* (New York: Twayne Publishers, 1964), p. 108.
36. Hopkins, *Rise of the Social Gospel*, pp. 243-44.
37. Fletcher and Miller, *Church and Industry*, p. 93.
38. For a firsthand account of the English Church Socialist League's foundation, see Conrad Noel's *Autobiography*, pp. 57-60. W. E. Moll, Percy Widdrington, Canon Adderly, George Landsbury, and Lady Warwick were prominent league supporters.
39. Fletcher and Miller, *Church and Industry*, p. 94.
40. Scudder, *On Journey*, p. 184.
41. Ibid., p. 187.
42. Ibid. This idea and the text reappear in *Socialism and Character*, p. 406.
43. Scudder, *On Journey*, p. 168.
44. Compare *The Witness of Denial*, p. 42, and *Socialism and Character*, p. 125.
45. Scudder, *Socialism and Character*, p. 107. By accepting a Mauricean interpretation of eternal life, Vida Scudder appears to be repudiating the position advanced by Father Phillips (Huntington) in *A Listener in Babel*. Evidently, her conversion to Marxism convinced her at this time that a doctrine of personal immortality was no longer necessary as a "strong consolation for the race."
46. Observations that echo *Social Ideals in English Letters* appear throughout *Socialism and Character*, but for a discussion of literary figures see especially pp. 23-70, 102-3, 187, 196-97, 298, 301-2.
47. Ibid., pp. 3, 5-6.
48. For the social implications of Darwin's theory of evolution, see ibid., pp. 57-60; for the Protestant work ethic, see pp. 244-45; and for the role of the middle class in social reform, see pp. 10-13, 16-18, 263. She no longer contends, however, that Christ and His apostles were middle class.
49. Ibid., p. 400. See also p. 258.
50. Ibid., p. 73.
51. Ibid., p. 49.

52. Ibid., pp. 224-27. The Franciscan failure haunted Vida Scudder for years; this is her first treatment of a subject to which she later devoted two books and numerous articles. As time passed, her ideas changed, as her perspective deepened, but she never lost sight of the fact that in worldly terms Francis and his closest followers were failures.
53. Ibid., p. 276.
54. Ibid., p. 107.
55. Ibid., p. v.
56. Harry W. Laidler, *History of Socialism* (New York: Thomas Y. Crowell Co., 1968), p. 588.
57. See Carl E. Schorske, *German Social Democracy, 1905-1917* (Cambridge: Harvard University Press, 1955), pp. 228-35.
58. Scudder, *Socialism and Character*, pp. 74-78. This is an example of her Marxist rhetoric at its most militant.
59. Ibid., p. 14.
60. Ibid., p. 175.
61. Ibid., pp. 175-76.
62. *The Hibbert Journal* 7 (1908-09): 912-14.
63. Ibid., Vol. 8, pp. 191-92.
64. Scudder, *Socialism and Character*, p. 132.
65. Ibid., p. 133.
66. Ibid., pp. 146-47.
67. Ibid., pp. 354-55.
68. Ibid., p. 354. See also pp. 235-56.
69. Randall, *Improper Bostonian*, p. 124.
70. Scudder, *Socialism and Character*, pp. 149-53.
71. Ibid., pp. 149, 169.
72. Ibid., p. 163.
73. Ibid., p. 170.
74. Ibid., p. 153.
75. Ibid., p. 173.
76. Ibid., p. 374.
77. Ibid., pp. 379-80.
78. Ibid., p. 381. I have reversed the sentence order in this quotation.
79. Obviously, this interpretation of kingdom theology is heavily indebted to the thought of Walter Rauschenbush, whose *Christianity and the Social Crisis* is cited several times. But the Mauricean position as developed by Headlam, Holland, and Gore likewise emphasized the this worldly significance of Jesus' kingdom proclamation. Hopkins, *Rise of the Social Gospel*, p. 235, perhaps inadvertently gives the impression that the social teachings of *Socialism and Character* derive from Rauschenbush, which is not the case. Vida Scudder was not a disciple of the great Baptist theologian and although she admired his work, she found it necessary to distinguish her own socialist position from his. She understood him to be opposed to the doctrines of economic determinism and class conflict. See *Socialism and Character*, pp. 279-80.

80. Scudder, *Socialism and Character*, pp. 385-86.
81. Ibid., p. 390.
82. Meyer, *Protestant Search*, p. 234.
83. Scudder, *Socialism and Character*, p. 156. Compare "Intellectual Autobiography of Reinhold Niebuhr," in *Reinhold Niebuhr, His Religious, Social and Political Thought*, ed. Charles Kegley and Robert Bretall (New York: Macmillan Company, 1955), pp. 7-10. In this essay Niebuhr discusses the development of his ideas, relating pacifism to Marxism, liberalism, etc. Neibuhr the antipacifist Marxist appears at his best in Reinhold Niebuhr, *Moral Man and Immoral Society* (New York: Charles Scribner's Sons, 1932).
84. Scudder, *Socialism and Character*, p. 370.
85. Ibid., p. 355.
86. Ibid., p. 356.
87. Ibid., pp. 362-63.
88. Ibid., pp. 365-66.
89. Scudder, *The Church and the Hour*, p. 61.
90. Ibid., pp. 61-62, 72.
91. Scudder, *On Journey*, p. 282.
92. Muste's congregation, which was far more sympathetic than most having a pacifist clergyman, did not demand his resignation; they defended him from outside attacks and accusations that he was pro-German, but requested that he take a leave of absence. See Ray H. Abrams, *Preachers Present Arms* (Philadelphia: Round Table Press, Inc., 1933), pp. 182, 185, 205.
93. Randall, *Improper Bostonian*, p. 237.
94. "A Doubting Pacifist" was republished in Vida Dutton Scudder, *The Privilege of Age, Essays Secular and Spiritual* (New York: E. P. Dutton and Company, Inc., 1939).
95. Abrams, *Preachers Present Arms*, cites an embarrassing number of examples.
96. Scudder, *Privilege of Age*, pp, 153-55.
97. Ibid., pp. 161-62.
98. Ibid., pp. 166-67.
99. Ibid., p. 164.
100. For details of her role during Emily Balch's dismissal, see Randall, *Improper Bostonian*, pp. 245-50. For details of the Jones case, see Abrams, *Preachers Present Arms*, p. 201. He was not forced to resign; one cannot force resignation on an Episcopal bishop. A commission appointed by the House of Bishops concluded that his usefulness in Utah had come to an end and recommended his resignation. The House of Bishops *rejected* the commission's recommendation, but *accepted* Bishop Jones's resignation.
101. Fletcher and Miller, *Church and Industry*, p. 96.
102. Vida Dutton Scudder, *The Franciscan Adventure* (New York: E. P. Dutton and Company, 1931), p. 357. When she reprinted "A Doubting Pacifist" in 1939, she remarked that the Spanish Civil War and Japan's invasion of China tempted

her to abandon the absolute pacifist position. See Scudder, *The Privilege of Age*, p. 152.

103. Vida D. Scudder, *The Social Teachings of the Christian Year* (New York: E. P. Dutton and Co., 1921), p. v.

104. Scudder, *The Social Teachings*, p. 214.

105. Scudder, *On Journey*, pp. 299-300.

106. Vida D. Scudder, untitled contribution to a Thanksgiving Symposium, *The Christian Century* 48 (July-December 1931): 1457.

107. From *Congressional Record*, 69th Congress, in Elizabeth Dilling, *The Red Network* (Chicago: Published by the author, 1934), p. 144.

108. Ibid., p. 320.

109. See Fletcher and Miller, *Church and Industry*, pp. 97-110.

110. Robert Moats Miller, *American Protestantism and Social Issues* (Chapel Hill: University of North Carolina Press, 1958), p. 83.

111. Ibid., p. 124.

112. See Ralph Lord Roy, *Communism and the Churches* (New York: Harcourt, Brace and Company, 1960). The author's position is strongly anticommunist, but he is not ill-disposed toward social reformers in general.

113. Her article, "A Little Tour in the Mind of Lenin," *The Christian Century* 53 (January-June 1937): 379-92, is an excellent source for her position on communism, and it should put to rest any allegations that she was directed by the party line. She was "soft" on communists only in the sense that she believed Christians could learn from them, a basic Maurician position.

114. See Vida D. Scudder, "Franciscan Parallels," *The Anglican Theological Review*, vol. 5, no. 4 (1923): 282-98.

115. "The Cross in Utopia" was reprinted in Scudder, *The Privilege of Age*, pp. 301-19. Its importance is attested to by the fact that it concludes the work.

116. Vida Dutton Scudder, *Brother John, A Tale of the First Franciscans* (New York: E. P. Dutton and Company, 1927), p. 218.

117. Ibid., pp. 241-53. Vida Scudder was as vividly aware of her hero's impracticality as any neo-orthodox or political realist critic of idealistic dreamers. It is an amusing, touching, and sad scene.

118. Ibid., p. 294.

119. Ibid., p. 295.

120. Ibid., p. 328.

121. Ibid., p. 307.

122. Ibid., p. 332.

123. Ibid., p. 336.

124. Ernst Becker, *Beyond Alienation* (New York: George Braziller, 1967), p. 292.

125. Scudder, *Brother John*, p. 309.

126. Scudder, *The Franciscan Adventure*, p. 390.

127. Joseph F. Fletcher, ed., *Christianity and Property* (Philadelphia: Westminister Press, 1947). Her essay "Anglican Thought on Property" appears on pp. 124-51.

# Bibliography

Abell, Aaron Ignatius. *The Urban Impact on American Protestantism*. Cambridge: Harvard University Press, 1943.

Abrams, Ray H. *Preachers Present Arms*. Philadelphia: Round Table Press, 1933.

Adam, Ruth and Kitty Muggeridge. *Beatrice Webb*. New York: Alfred Knopf, 1968.

Albright, Raymond W. *A History of the Protestant Episcopal Church*. New York: Macmillan Co., 1964.

_____. *Focus on Infinity: a Life of Phillips Brooks*. New York: Macmillan Co., 1961.

Alchin, A. M. *The Silent Rebellion*. London: S. C. M. Press, 1958.

Allen, Alexander. *Life and Letters of Phillips Brooks*. 4 vols. New York: E. P. Dutton, 1901.

Anson, Peter F. *Abbot Extraordinary*. London: Faith Press, 1958.

_____. *The Benedictines of Caldey*. London: Catholic Book Club, 1940.

Anson, Peter F., and A. W. Campbell. *The Call of the Cloister*. London: S.P.C.K., 1964.

Becker, Ernst. *Beyond Alienation*. New York: George Braziller, 1967.

Bellemy, Edward. "First Steps toward Nationalism." *Forum* 1 (1890): 174-84.

Bertouch, The Baroness de. *The Life of Father Ignatius, OSB*. London: Methuen and Co., 1904.

Bettany, F. S. *Stewart Headlam*. London: John Murray, 1926.

Billing, Elizabeth. *The Red Network*. Chicago: By the author, 1934.

Binyon, G. C. *The Christian Socialist Movement in England*. London: S.P.C.K., 1931.

Bliss, William Dwight Porter. "Socialism in the Church of England." *The Andover Review* 10 (July-December 1887): 488-503.

_____. *What is Christian Socialism?* Boston: Office of *The Dawn*, 1894.

_____, ed. *Dawn, A Journal of Christian Socialism*. 8 vols. (May 15, 1889-March 1896).

_____, ed. *The New Encyclopedia of Social Reform*. New York: Funk and Wagnalls Co., 1908.

Bottomore, T. B. *Critics of Society*. New York: Random House, 1968.

Boulter, B. C. *The Anglican Reformers*. London: Phillip Allan, 1933.

Bowen, Desmond. *The Idea of the Victorian Church*. Montreal: McGill University Press, 1968.

Bready, J. Wesley. *Lord Shaftesbury and Socio-Industrial Programs*. London: George Unwin, 1926.

B[rooks], F. M., and V. D. S[cudder]. *Mitsu-Yu-Nissi, or the Japanese Wedding*. Chicago: T. S. Denison, 1887.

Brooks, Van Wyck. *New England: Indian Summer*. New York: E. P. Dutton and Co., 1940.

Brose, Olive J. *Frederick Denison Maurice, Rebellious Conformist*. Athens: Ohio University Press, 1971.

Carpenter, James. *Gore, A Study in Liberal Catholic Thought*. London: Faith Press, 1960.

Carpenter, S. C. *Church and People, 1789-1889*. London: S. P. C. K., 1933.

Chadwick, Owen. *The Mind of the Oxford Movement*. London: Adam and Charles Black, 1960.

_____. *The Victorian Church*. Part I. New York: Oxford University Press, 1966.

_____. *The Victorian Church*. Part II. New York: Oxford University Press, 1970.

Christensen, Torben. *The Divine Order, A Study in F. D. Maurice's Theology*. Leiden: E. J. Brill, 1973.

_____. *The Origin and History of Christian Socialism*. Copenhagen: Universitelsforlaget I Arbus, 1962.

Church, R. W. *The Oxford Movement, Twelve Years 1833-45*. London: Macmillan and Co., 1892.

Clayton, Joseph. *Bishop Westcott*. London: A. R. Mowbray and Co., 1906.

Creighton, Mrs. Mandell. *Life and Letters of Mandell Creighton*. London: Longmans, Green, and Co., 1905.

Curti, Merle. *The Growth of American Thought*. New York: Harper & Row, 1964.

David, W. Merlin. *An Introduction to the Theology of F. D. Maurice*. London: S. P. C. K., 1964.

Davies, Horton. *Worship and Theology in England from Watts and Wesley to Maurice, 1690-1850*. Princeton: Princeton University Press, 1961.

_____. *Worship and Theology in England from Newman to Martineau, 1850-1900*. Princeton: Princeton University Press, 1962.

Davis, Alan F. *Spearheads for Reform*. New York: Oxford University Press 1967.

Dix, Dom Gregory. *The Shape of the Liturgy*. London: Dacre Press, Adam and Charles Black, 1945.

Dombrowski, James. *The Early Days of Christian Socialism in America*. New York: Columbia University Press, 1936.

Egbert, Donald D., and Stow Persons, eds. *Socialism and American Life*. Princeton: Princeton University Press, 1952.

Ekstrom, Ragnar. *The Theology of Charles Gore*. London: C. W. K. Gleerup, 1944.

Ely, Richard T. *Ground Under Our Feet*. New York: Macmillan Co., 1938.

Fletcher, Joseph F., ed. *Christianity and Property*. Philadelphia: Westminster Press, 1947.

Fletcher, Joseph, and Spencer Miller. *The Church and Industry*. New York: Longmans, Green, and Co., 1930.

Froude, Richard Hurrell. *Remains*. 6 vols. London: J. S. and F. Rivington, 1839.

Gabriel, Ralph Henry. *The Course of American Democratic Thought*. New York: Ronald Press Co., 1940.

Gerrish, B. A. "The Lord's Supper in the Reformed Confessions." *Theology Today* 23 (July 1966): 224-43.

Gilson, Mary Barnett. *What's Past is Prologue*. New York: Harper & Brothers, 1940.

Gore, Charles, ed. *Lux Mundi, A Series of Studies in the Religion of the Incarnation*. New York: Lovell, Coryell, and Co., n.d.

Hammond, B., and J. L. Hammond, *Lord Shaftesbury*. London: Constable and Co., 1973.

Harrison, J. F. C. *A History of the Workingmen's College, 1854-1954*. London: Routeledge and Kegan Paul, 1954.

Hobson, J. A. *John Ruskin, Social Reformer*. Boston: Dana Estes and Co., 1898.

Hofstadter, Richard. *Social Darwinism in American Thought*. Philadelphia: University of Pennsylvania Press, 1944.

Hopkins, Charles Howard. *The Rise of the Social Gospel in American Protestantism*. New Haven: Yale University Press, 1940.

Howe, M. A. DeWolfe. *Memoirs of the Life and Services of the Rt. Rev. Alonzo Potter*. Philadelphia: J. B. Lippincott and Co., 1871.

Huntington, Arria G. *Memoir and Letters of Frederick Dan Huntington*. Boston: Houghton Mifflin Co., 1906.

Huntington, J. O. S. "Beginnings of the Religious Life for Men in the American Church." *Historical Magazine of the Protestant Episcopal Church* 2 (March 1933): 35-43.

————. "Philanthropy: Its Success and Failures." In *Philanthropy and Social Reform*, pp. 117-42. New York: Thomas Y. Crowell and Co., 1893.

Huntington, James. *Sixth Reunion of the Huntington Family*. Norwich Town, Conn.: By the author, 1917.

Hurowitz, Ruth S. "Coming of Age at Wellesley." *Menorah Journal* 38 (Autumn 1950): 231-42.

Inge, W. R. *The Platonic Tradition in English Religious Thought*. London: Longmans, Green, and Co., 1926.

Inglis, K. S. *Churches and the Working Classes in Victorian England*. London: Routledge and Kegan Paul, 1963.

Jones, Peter d'A. *The Christian Socialist Revival*. Princeton: Princeton University Press, 1968.

Killian, McDonnall, OSB. *John Calvin, the Church and the Eucharist*. Princeton: Princeton University Press, 1967.

Kirk, Clara and Rudolf. "Howells and the Church of the Carpenter." *New England Quarterly* 32 (1959): 188-206.

Knox, Wilfred S., and Alex R. Vidler. *The Development of Modern Catholicism*. Milwaukee: Morehouse Publishing Co., 1933.

Laidler, Harry W. *History of Socialism*. New York: Thomas Y. Crowell Co., 1968.

Lasch, Christopher. *The New Radicalism in America*. New York: Alfred Knopf, 1965.

Liddon, H. P. *Life of Edward Bouverie Pusey*. 4 vols. London: Longmans, Green, and Co., 1894.

Lockhart, J. G. *Cosmo Gordon Lang*. London: Hodder and Stoughton, 1949.

Lough, A. G. *The Influence of John Mason Neale*. London: S. P. C. K., 1962.

Mann, Arthur. "British Social Thought and American Reformers of the Progressive Era." *Mississippi Valley Historical Review* 112 (1956): 672-92.

————. *Yankee Reformers in an Urban Age*. Cambridge: Belknap Press, 1954.

Manross, William W. "The Episcopal Church and Social Reform." *Historical Magazine of the Protestant Episcopal Church* 12 (December 1943): 339-66.

————. *A History of the American Episcopal Church*. New York: Morehouse-Gorham Co., 1959.

Mansbridge, Albert. *Edward Stuart Talbot and Charles Gore*. London: J. M. Dent and Sons, 1935.

Masterman, C. F. G. *F. D. Maurice*. London: A. R. Mowbray and Co., 1907.

Maurice, Frederick. *The Life of Frederick Denison Maurice*. 2 vols. New York: Charles Scribner's Sons, 1884.

Maurice, Federick Denison. *The Kingdom of Christ*. London: James Clarke and Co., 1959.

May, Henry. *Protestant Churches and Industrial America*. New York: Harper & Brothers, 1949.

Meyer, Donald B. *The Protestant Search for Political Realism*. Berkeley: University of California Press, 1960.

Miller, Robert Moats. *American Protestantism and Social Issues*. Chapel Hill: University of North Carolina Press, 1958.

Morgan, Emily Malbone. *A Little White Shadow*. Chicago: G. P. Brown, 1889.

————. *Prior Rahere's Rose*. Hartford: Belknap and Warfield, 1893.

Newman, John Henry. *Apologia Pro Vita Sua*. New York: D. Appleton and Co., 1865.

————. *The Arians of the Fourth Century*. London: Basil Montagu Pickering, 1876.

————. *Parochial and Plain Sermons*. London: Rivington's, 1868.

Niebuhr, H. Richard. *Christ and Culture*. New York: Harper & Brothers, 1951.

Niebuhr, Reinhold. *Moral Man and Immoral Society*. New York: Charles Scribner's Sons, 1932.

Noel, Conrad. *Autobiography*. London: J. M. Dent and Sons, 1945.

Paget, Stephen. *Henry Scott Holland: Memoir and Letters*. New York: E. P. Dutton and Co., 1921.

Parsons, Edward S. "A Christian Critique of Socialism." *Andover Review* 11 (1889): 597-611.

Peck, William George. *The Social Implications of the Oxford Movement*. New York: Charles Scribner's Sons, 1933.

Pope-Hennessy, Una. *Canon Charles Kingsley*. London: Chatto and Windus, 1948.

Prestige, G. L. *The Life of Charles Gore, A Great Englishman*. London: William Heinemann, 1935.

Pusey, Edward Bouverie. *The Councils of the Church from the Council of Jerusalem to the Council of Constantinople*. Oxford: Rivington's, 1857.

Quint, Howard H. *The Forging of American Socialism*. Indianapolis: Bobbs-Merrill Co., 1953.

Ramsey, Arthur M. *Charles Gore and Anglican Theology*. London: S.P.C.K., 1955.

_____. *F. D. Maurice and the Conflicts of Modern Theology*. Cambridge: Cambridge University Press, 1951.

Randall, Mercedes M. *Improper Bostonian*. New York: Twayne Publishers, 1964.

Rauschenbush, Walter. *Christianizing the Social Order*. New York: Macmillan Co., 1914.

Raven, C. E. *Christian Socialism, 1848-1854*. London: Macmillan and Co., 1920.

Reckitt, Maurice B. *Faith and Society*. London: Longmans, Green, and Co., 1932.

_____. *Maurice to Temple*. London: Faber and Faber, 1947.

Reynolds, Michael. *Martyr to Ritualism*. London: Faber and Faber, 1965.

Richter, Melvin. *The Politics of Conscience, T. H. Green and His Age*. Cambridge: Harvard University Press, 1964.

Rideout, Walter B. *The Radical Novel in the United States*. New York: Hill and Wang, 1966.

Russell, George W. E. *Dr. Pusey*. London: A. R. Mowbray, n.d.

Scudder, Horace. *The Life and Letters of David Coit Scudder, a Missionary in Southern India*. New York: Hurd and Houghton, 1864.

Scudder, Vida D. *Brother John, A Tale of the First Franciscans*. New York: E. P. Dutton and Co., 1927.

_____. *The Christian Attitude Toward Private Property*. Milwaukee; Morehouse Publishing Co., 1934.

_____. "Christianity in the Socialist State." *Hibbert Journal* 8 (1909-1910): 561-81.

_____. *The Church and the Hour*. New York: E. P. Dutton and Co., 1917.

_____. "Democracy and the Churches." *Atlantic Monthly* 90 (July-December 1902): 521-27.

_____. "Democracy and Society." *Atlantic Monthly* 90 (July-December, 1902): 348-51.

_____. *The Disciple of a Saint*. London: J. M. Dent and Co., 1907.

_____. *Father Huntington*. New York: E. P. Dutton and Co., 1940.

_____. *The Franciscan Adventure*. New York: E. P. Dutton and Co., 1931.

_____. "Franciscan Parallels." *Anglican Theological Review* 5 (1923): 282-98.

_____. "Ill Gotten Gifts to Colleges." *Atlantic Monthly* 86 (July-December 1900): 675-79.

_____. "Is the Church Christian?" *Christian Century* 38 (January-July 1921): 11.

_____. *The Letters of Saint Catherine of Siena*. London: J. M. Dent and Co., 1905.

_____. *The Life of the Spirit in Modern English Poets*. Boston: Houghton Mifflin Co., 1895.

_____. *A Listener in Babel*. Boston: Houghton Mifflin Co., 1903.

_____. "A Little Tour in the Mind of Lenin." *Christian Century* 53 (January-June 1937): 379-92.

_____. "The Moral Dangers of Musical Devotees." *The Andover Review* 8 (1887): 46-53.

_____. "The New Righteousness." *Hibbert Journal* 7 (1908-09): 578-95.

_____. *On Journey*. New York: E. P. Dutton and Co., 1937.

_____. "The Poetry of Matthew Arnold." *The Andover Review* 13 (1890): 232-49.

_____. *The Privilege of Age, Essays Secular and Spiritual*. New York: E. P. Dutton and Co., 1939.

_____. "Religion and Socialism." *Harvard Theological Review* 3 (1910): 230-47.

_____. "The Social Conscience of the Future." *Hibbert Journal* 7 (1908-09): 314-32.

_____. *Social Ideas in English Letters*. Boston: Houghton Mifflin Co., 1898.

_____. *The Social Teachings of the Christian Year*. New York: E. P. Dutton and Co., 1921.

_____. *Socialism and Character*. Boston: Houghton Mifflin Co., 1912.

_____. "Socialism and Sacrifice." *Atlantic Monthly* 105 (January-June 1910): 836-49.

_____. "Socialism and Spiritual Progress—a Speculation." *The Andover Review* 16 (1891): 49-67.

_____. *The Witness of Denial*. New York: E. P. Dutton and Co., 1895.

The Sisters of the Church. *A Valliant Victorian*. London: A. R. Mowbray and Co., 1964.

Smith, Robert Cheney, S.S.J.E. *The Cowley Fathers in America*. Boston: By the Society of Saint John the Evangelist, n.d.

_____. *The Shrine on Bowdoin Street*. Boston: By the Society of St. John the Evangelist, 1958.

Stein, Roger B. *John Ruskin and Aesthetic Thought in America*. Cambridge: Harvard University Press, 1967.

Strange, Douglas C. "The Conversion of F. D. Huntington." *Historical Magazine of the Protestant Episcopal Church* 37 (September 1968): 287-98.

Tager, Jack. *The Intellectual as Urban Reformer: Brand Whitlock and the Progressive Movement*. Cleveland: The Press of Case Western Reserve University, 1968.

Taylor, Walter Fuller. *The Economic Novel in America*. New York: Octagon Books, 1964.

Vidler, Alex R. *F. D. Maurice and Company*. London: S. C. M. Press, 1966.

_____. *Witness to the Light*. New York: Charles Scribner's Sons, 1948.

Voll, Deiter. *Catholic Evangelicalism*. London: Faith Press, 1963.

Webber, Christopher L. "William Dwight Porter Bliss: Priest and Socialist." *Historical Magazine of the Protestant Episcopal Church* 28 (March 1959): 11-39.

Westcott, Arthur. *Life and Letters of Brooke Foss Westcott*. London: Macmillan and Co., 1903.

White, James F. *The Cambridge Movement*. Cambridge: Cambridge University Press, 1962.

Wood, H. G. *Frederick Denison Maurice*. Cambridge: Cambridge University Press, 1950.

Woodham-Smith, Cecil Blanche. *Florence Nightingale*. New York: McGraw-Hill, 1951.

Zabriskie, Alexander C. *Bishop Brent*. Philadelphia: Westminster Press, 1948.

# Index

(continued, over)